The Edinburgh Companion to the Gaelic Language

The Edinburgh Companion to the Gaelic Language

Edited by

Moray Watson and Michelle Macleod

Edinburgh University Press

© editorial matter and organisation Moray Watson and Michelle Macleod, 2010
© the chapters and their several authors, 2010

Edinburgh University Press Ltd
22 George Square, Edinburgh

www.euppublishing.com

Reprinted 2010, 2011

Typeset in 11/13 Cambria and Times New Roman
by Moray Watson,
and printed and bound in Great Britain by
CPI Antony Rowe, Chippenham and Eastbourne

A CIP record for this book is available from the British Library

ISBN 978 0 7486 3708 9 (hardback)
ISBN 978 0 7486 3709 6 (paperback)

Dedicated to James and Andrew

Contents

Notes on Contributors

David Adger is Professor of Linguistics at Queen Mary, University of London. He is the editor of the journal *Syntax* and the book series *Oxford Studies in Linguistic Theory*. He is author of *Core Syntax* and co-author of *Mirrors and Microparameters*. He has published articles in *Language, Linguistic Inquiry, Natural Language and Linguistic Theory*, and many other major journals on syntactic theory, how syntax interfaces with semantics, morphology and prosody, syntactic variation and Celtic syntax. He held a Leverhulme Major Research Fellowship (2006–2009) on the connection between grammar and meaning in Scottish Gaelic. He is a Trustee of the Board of Sabhal Mòr Ostaig, Skye, and is a board member of the Centre for Advanced Study in Theoretical Linguistics, Tromso, Norway.

Ronald Black is Gaelic Editor of *The Scotsman* and a former Senior Lecturer in Celtic in Edinburgh University.

Anna R. K. Bosch is an associate professor of Linguistics and English at the University of Kentucky, where she has taught since receiving her PhD in linguistics from the University of Chicago. She has twice been a fellow of the Institute for Advanced Studies in the Humanities at Edinburgh University and a visiting scholar in Celtic and Scottish Studies, and received a   sabbatical fellowship from the American Philosophical Society to support her research in Edinburgh in the archives of the Linguistic Survey of Scotland. She has written on various aspects of the phonology of Gaelic.

Andrew Breeze, FRS, FRHistS, was educated at Sir Roger Manwood's G. S., Sandwich, and the Universities of Oxford and Cambridge. Since 1987 he has taught at the University of Navarre, Pamplona. Married with six children, he is the author of the controversial study *Medieval Welsh Literature* and *The Mary of the Celts*, and co-author with Richard Coates of *Celtic Voices, English Places*.

Richard A. V. Cox's interests include Gaelic language and literature, including modern poetry and prose writing, publishing, lexicography, linguistics, onomastics and Norse–Gaelic contact. Formerly at the Departments of Celtic at Glasgow and then Aberdeen, he is currently Professor at Sabhal Mòr Ostaig, Isle of Skye.

Robert Dunbar is Reader in Law and Celtic at the University of Aberdeen. His degrees include a PhD from the University of Edinburgh. He works on the poetry of John MacLean and other emigrant bards. He has published many papers on language planning and minority language rights.

Emily McEwan-Fujita received her PhD from the University of Chicago in 2003. She is a lingustic anthropologist, who studies minority language revitalisation efforts, with a particular emphasis on Gaelic. She currently teaches in the Department of Anthropology at the University of Pittsburgh.

Kenneth MacKinnon is a board member of the Scottish Government's Gaelic language authority Bòrd na Gàidhlig, and of OFCOM's Gaelic media authority, MG Alba, which is responsible for the Gaelic television channel BBC Alba. He is an Honorary Professor at the University of Aberdeen in Celtic language planning and development, and is also Visiting Professor and Reader Emeritus in the Sociology of Language at the University of Hertfordshire, where he worked fulltime between 1974–1992. He has undertaken numerous surveys and research studies in Gaelic communities since 1972, has undertaken extensive demographic analysis of Gaelic and other lesser–used language-groups, and has published extensively. He has been an associate lecturer of the Open University since its commencement in 1969, in Social Sciences, Education and Language Studies.

Michelle Macleod is Gaelic Lecturer at the University of Aberdeen, having previously been Language Planning Manager at Bòrd na Gàidhlig and Director/Head of Studies at Ionad Chaluim Chille Ìle. She works on sociolinguistics, language planning, modern Gaelic literature and society. Her edition of the plays of Tormod Calum Dòmhnallach will appear in 2011 and she is a co-editor of the forthcoming *Edinburgh Biography of Scottish Writers*.

Kenneth E. Nilsen holds the Chair in Celtic at St Francis Xavier University. He has a Master's degree and PhD in Celtic from Harvard

University. His research interests include the Celtic languages in North America. He has published extensively on both Gaelic and Irish.

Colm Ó Baoill was born in the city of Armagh in 1938, and educated there and in the Department of Celtic at Queen's University, Belfast, whose Head was Heinrich Wagner. He graduated there in 1960 with a BA in Celtic Studies. He taught in that Department for a few years before coming to Aberdeen University as a lecturer in 1966. He was made Professor of Celtic at Aberdeen in 1996 and retired in 2003.

Moray Watson lectures in Celtic and Gaelic at the University of Aberdeen, where he also did his PhD. He works on literary stylistics, translation studies and literary criticism. His edited collection of the Gaelic poems of Iain Crichton Smith is due for publication in 2010, and Edinburgh University Press will publish his monograph on Gaelic fiction in 2010. He is joint editor, with Lindsay Milligan, of *Vestiges to the Very Day: New Voices in Celtic Studies*.

Seosamh Watson held the Foundation Chair of Modern Irish at University College Dublin from 1998 to 2008, and has published extensively on Gaelic linguistics, literature and tradition. He serves on the editorial board of *Atlas Linguarum Europae,* and is co-founder of *Oideas Gael* and the International Society for Dialectology and Geolinguistics.

Acknowledgements

The editors would like to acknowledge the financial support of the University of Aberdeen's College of Arts and Social Sciences. We are grateful to the staff at Edinburgh University Press, including, but not limited to Sarah Edwards, James Dale, Eliza Wright, Bridget Maidment, and Rebecca Mackenzie. A special word of thanks is due to Esmé Watson, for her exceptional patience and unstinting support. We wish to record our indebtedness to all of the generous contributors to this volume and, in particular, to Colm Ó Baoill for his advice and encouragement at the early stages of the project.

Abbreviations

ACC	Augmented Copular Construction
BnaG or BNAG	Bòrd na Gàidhlig
CCG	Comataidh Craolaidh Gàidhlig
CnaG or CNAG	Comunn na Gàidhlig
CTG	Comataidh Telebhisean Gàidhlig
dat.	dative
EG	Early Gaelic
EI or EIr	Early Irish
Eng.	English
EP	East Perthshire (Gaelic)
ER	Easter Ross (Gaelic)
ES or ESG	East Sutherlandshire (Gaelic)
gen.	genitive
GIDS	Graded Intergenerational Disruption Scale
GM and GME	Gaelic-Medium and Gaelic-Medium Education
GROS	General Register Office for Scotland
HIDB	Highlands and Islands Development Board
HIE	Highlands and Islands Enterprise
ICC	Inverted Copular Construction
LASID	Linguistic Atlas and Survey of Irish Dialects
nom.	nominative
NT	New Testament
OG	Old Gaelic
OI	Old Irish
ON	Old Norse
OT	Old Testament
RLS	Reversing Language Shift
SAC	Substantive Auxiliary Construction

ScG	Scottish Gaelic
SGDS	Survey of the Gaelic Dialects of Scotland
SMO	Sabhal Mòr Ostaig
SSPCK	The Society in Scotland for the Propagation of Christian Knowledge (sometimes the word 'Promotion' is used)
WR	Wester Ross (Gaelic)

Preface

This book is aimed at the student, teacher, academic and general reader with an interest in the Gaelic language. It brings together in one volume original chapters on the history and development of the language, both social and linguistic, in Scotland and in North America. Its publication is particularly timely in the context of the heightened public and governmental interest in Gaelic in Scotland, reflected in the Gaelic (Scotland) Act 2005. The chapters point towards the burgeoning of Gaelic Studies as a distinct branch of Celtic Studies, a development which mirrors the way the other modern Celtic languages have developed in universities in their home countries. The volume thus also seeks to reaffirm the links between the more traditional Celtic Studies approach to the Gaelic language and the recent innovations in the use of social scientific, political scientific and stylistic/discourse analyses of the language.

The chapters are set out in an order that tries to group areas of interest, for the reader's convenience. The first two chapters place the language within a historical and social context. The next two, on place-names and literature, focus on two areas where the language may most easily be found and studied. There follows a chapter on the position of Gaelic in Canada, which is itself followed by a chapter which gives a sample study of some representative dialects. The next three chapters may broadly be categorised as sociolinguistic, although each takes rather different approaches. The final five chapters turn again to areas traditionally studied by linguists: vocabulary, writing systems, phonology, morphology and syntax.

The discrete nature of the chapters means that the reader might easily dip in and read topics in any order, although there is a small element of progression. For instance, we would recommend that most readers begin with Colm Ó Baoill's introduction to the history of the language, which provides an invaluable background for understanding most of the other chapters. David Adger's two chapters might best be read in the order in which they appear in the book, since this makes best sense of the ways in which they refer to each other. In most other cases, however, the reader may navigate through the topics in whatever way the current of interest flows.

We are very grateful to all of the expert contributors who have so kindly given their hard-won knowledge to this book, believing, as we editors also do, that it goes some way towards filling a gap that has hindered the study of Gaelic. There were other chapters we would like to have seen, but which proved impossible to arrange, and other authors we would have liked to have write chapters. The exigencies of real life have unfortunately curtailed our ambitions, but we believe the book is of great value nevertheless. Any shortcomings in terms of scope or vision are, of course, the responsibility of the editors and not the individual authors.

Moray Watson and Michelle Macleod
Aberdeen 2010

CHAPTER 1

A History of Gaelic to 1800

Colm Ó Baoill

INTRODUCTION: CELTIC AND GAELIC LANGUAGES

For the purpose of this collection the word 'Gaelic' means 'Scottish Gaelic': this is a convenient short-hand which will be understood in most contexts, but strictly it is inaccurate. In Ireland the word 'Gaelic' would be primarily understood as meaning 'Irish (Gaelic)'. We also have the third form of modern Gaelic, known in English generally as 'Manx'. It is, of course, confusing to discuss the various forms of Gaelic through the terminology of English, but in this case it is probably unavoidable.

Our three modern forms of Gaelic descend from a single parent which we properly call *Gaelic* (though scholars use the term *Goidelic*, or *Goedelic*, to cover the strictly linguistic aspects of Gaelic) and from which they diverged only in relatively recent centuries. This Goidelic, or *Common Gaelic*, parent is a branch of the *Celtic* languages and is primarily associated with Ireland, just as the other branch, the *Brythonic* branch, is associated primarily with Britain. Goidelic can also be conveniently distinguished as *Q-Celtic*, while the Brythonic languages (Welsh, Breton and Cornish and their earlier relatives) are *P-Celtic*. This means that wherever the old (theoretical) Indo-European language, from which Celtic branched off, had the *q*-sound /k^u/, Gaelic retained that sound until, it is thought, around 500 AD, when it was replaced by the /k/ sound, always written as *c* in Gaelic. The P-Celtic languages, on the other hand, had at an early stage replaced the Indo-European /k^u/ with a *p*, and thus we get, for instance, the opposition in the words for 'head', *cenn* in early Gaelic (*ceann* in modern Gaelic) but *pen* in Welsh.

This distinction between P-Celtic and Q-Celtic also existed on the continent, even before groups of Celtic-speakers came to these islands. These are called '*insular* Celts' by scholars; no offence intended: this merely distinguishes them from their *continental* kinsfolk. The very sparse evidence, literary/historical, linguistic and archaeological, suggests that their coming to the islands may have happened somewhere around 500 BC, though not necessarily by means of any large-scale invasions of Celts, for archaeology gives no support for such invasions. New languages can be introduced or imposed by relatively small numbers of newcomers, especially if they are military or cultural elites. In the absence of any more detailed evidence, the simple picture which has come to be widely accepted is that somewhere in the wide period around 500 BC P-Celts brought their language from the European continent to Britain and over time expanded to cover most of that island; and Q-Celts, from whom descended the Gaels, came to Ireland and expanded there, perhaps around the same time. In reality it is quite likely that some P-Celtic speakers reached Ireland too, and possible that Gaelic developed as a Q-Celtic language in these islands rather than being a descendant of a Q-Celtic language imported from the continent: there is no real evidence.

GAELIC GROWS IN SCOTLAND

The history of Gaelic which became widely accepted in modern times is that these Gaels in Ireland were attacking and raiding Britain between the first century AD and the fifth, their aggression becoming more successful as Roman power waned there after 400 AD. In what is now Wales two significant Gaelic-speaking communities were (quite undoubtedly and historically) established during that period of intrusion from Ireland. Cornwall had Gaelic settlements at that time too, and it was then that the Isle of Man was conquered for Gaeldom. Similarly, we are told, the small Gaelic kingdom of Dál Riada in the north-east of Ireland expanded, around 500 AD, to cover a large part of Argyllshire: on the very arbitrary nature of that date, however, see Dumville (2002: 185–94). Because the Gaels, in Ireland at first, were known to Latin writers as *Scotti* (a name which remains without a reliable explanation), their continued expansion from that Argyllshire powerbase for another 500 years led directly to the establishment of *Scotland*.

This suggests that the Scottish and Manx forms of Gaelic are likely to have developed from forms introduced from Ireland, which may indeed be historically the case. But recent archaeological work by Ewan Campbell (see Campbell 2001) argues strongly against any alleged Dàl Riada invasion: archaeological evidence offers no support for such an invasion, whereas it could easily be interpreted as part of a political myth constructed (at almost any subsequent date) in support of Irish claims to rule the Scottish part of Dàl Riada. We can then ask other questions: if the Q-Celtic Gaels, or their ancestors, came to Ireland from the continent what was their route? They may well have travelled via Britain (there is no direct evidence, of course) and if they did are they not likely to have crossed into Ireland at the shortest crossing point, that between south-west Scotland and north-east Ulster, which archaeology has shown to be a favoured crossing point for numerous cultural imports to Ireland (cf. Mac Eoin 1988: 593)? And might some of these Celts (Q-Celts or otherwise) not simply have remained and expanded and developed their language in the south-west, while others brought their language and their culture across to Ireland? This might help to explain the broad archaeological similarity Campbell sees between Ireland and Argyllshire at that time, and therefore the old Dàl Riada invasion story must at least be held open to question. But whatever Dàl Riada's earlier history, it is still accepted that Gaelic was spoken throughout what is now Argyllshire, and a little beyond, by the seventh century (see Bannerman 1971: 70): we find in Adomnán's *Vita Columbae* (written *c.*700) that the saint, who died in 597, needed an interpreter when he went to Skye, though the implications of that fact are open to question (see Sharpe 1995: 136, 293–4).

Detailed study of the origins of the Gaels and their language are obviously continuing and we are far from final answers. There have been numerous theories, some well-argued and some barely defensible: a recent work claimed to have established the existence of Etruscan Gaelic, and some medieval Gaelic scholars argued, on the basis of the similarity of the names, that the Scots came from Scythia. Other theories have included the suggestion that Scottish Gaelic grew directly from its Celtic ancestor in Britain, independent of the Gaelic of Ireland and Man. But this has received little support among modern scholars and it is now generally accepted that in those earliest historical times Gaelic (though doubtless with minor variations from place to place) was essentially the same language in Scotland, Ireland and Man.

OGHAM: THE EARLIEST WRITTEN GAELIC

The earliest written form of Gaelic is found inscribed on stones in the alphabet known in Gaelic as *Ogham* (early Gaelic *Ogam*). These early Ogham stones date from between about the fourth century and about the seventh and are found in Ireland, Wales and Man, with only a few questionable examples in southern Scotland: accounts of these Scottish stones, in south-west Argyll, may be found in Forsyth (1996:

lxvii). Ogham inscriptions consist almost entirely of names, carved with letters formed by groups (one to five) of simple short lines: full details can be found in McManus (1991). There are no verbs, adjectives or prepositions in the inscriptions (see McManus 1991: 84), and therefore no sentences and no literature. The language reflected in the inscriptions (sometimes called *primitive Old Irish*, but this is inaccurate: for 'Irish', as in numerous instances, read 'Gaelic') is on the whole 'primitive' in comparison with later forms of Gaelic (though different age-strata within Ogham itself are detectable, see McManus 1991: 96–9): as we have seen, the language retains the old *q* in many cases, it retains many final and medial syllables lost in later Gaelic (so we find INIGENA for later *ingen*, Scottish Gaelic *nighean*, 'daughter'; and IVAGENI for later *Éogain*, modern *Eòghainn*; McManus 1991: 50, 103), and it shows no sign of the systematic initial mutation which came to be a feature of all the later insular Celtic languages. Much has been made of the importance of this alphabet as evidence for the unusual interest in language which the early Gaels had, and indeed we only know the meaning of the Ogham characters by virtue of the fact that later Gaelic writers, right down till the seventeenth century, continued to write and speculate about this early alphabet.

The majority of Scotland's Ogham stones are located in the east and their language is (arguably) not Gaelic. They belong to a later period, perhaps the eighth–ninth centuries, though the alphabet has clearly been adopted from the earlier Gaelic stones. There has long been considerable disagreement among scholars about the language or languages used on these eastern Ogham stones (Jackson 1955: 140–2; Forsyth 1997; Cox 1999). We still await an agreed answer.

THE CHURCH AND GAELIC WRITING

Christianity was famously brought from Britain to the Gaels in Ireland by Saint Patrick in the fifth century, and thence to Scotland by Colum Cille in the sixth. We should remember that at that time Gaelic was still being inscribed on stones in the Ogham alphabet, the only form of Gaelic writing yet known, and it was from the Latin of the church that the Gaels learned again to write – first in Latin, of course, but then also in their own language. As is well known also, the church among the Gaels developed many distinctive features, some of which have led to modern romanticised notions of the 'Celtic Church' as a kind of earthly paradise (for a healthy antidote to such notions read Meek 2000). But among the real contributions the Gaelic church made was the development of the Latin alphabet to form a new elegant script, especially acclaimed in such religious works of art, written in Latin, as *The Book of Kells* (written mainly in Iona in the late eighth century) and the *Lindisfarne Gospels* (*c.*700; the monastery of Lindisfarne in Northumbria was a daughter house of Iona). Again, details are hard to come by, but the Latin script was also adapted in that early Christian period to fit the Gaelic language and regularly adjusted again and again over the centuries as Gaelic evolved. Some examples of this script from a variety of periods will be found in Ó Murchú (1985a: 37–51).

Already by around 500 AD dialectal differences must surely have existed within the Gaelic language, perhaps a thousand years after the putative coming of the first Gaels. An interesting point on the adaptation of the Latin alphabet to fit the Gaelic language has been made on the basis of a dialect difference which exists today, where two different syntactical practices are noted in the formation of a relative clause with a preposition: *a' bhean dan tug mi gaol*, 'the woman to whom I gave love', deemed to be typically Scottish, and *an bhean a dtug mé grá di*, 'the woman I gave love to', Irish. It has been suggested that Gaelic may have been first given its written standard in the northern part of the Gaelic world, because the first of these types of relative, now the norm in 'a northern locale', was clearly the standard in written Gaelic before 900 AD (McCone 1985: 96–7). The reality with regard to these relatives in modern Scottish Gaelic dialects is not quite so simple (see Adger and Ramchand 2006), but with further study along the lines of dialect geography Iona may yet emerge as a viable candidate for the location of this first adaptation of the Latin alphabet to the Gaelic language. In any case, from the introduction of this Latin-based writing, wherever it occurred, it is clear that among those Gaels who could write (always a small minority) a single standard form of grammar and spelling was imposed and used, probably due to the power of both the church and the secular learned classes. As a result we really know very little about the various dialects (the real spoken Gaelic language) during the early centuries, though comparative reconstruction, supported in some cases by earlier forms, suggests that some of the differences between the modern Gaelic dialects can reasonably be traced back to the pre-1200 period (see Ó Maolalaigh 2008: 190–5).

Scholars designate the early period of the language, from the adaptation of the Latin alphabet till about 900 AD, as *Seann Ghàidhlig* or *Old Gaelic* (though outside Scotland, and even inside Scotland, respectable scholars often mistranslate this as 'Old Irish'). The main body of material, crucial for our knowledge of the language, consists of Gaelic glosses written in Latin manuscript texts preserved on the

European continent. The Gaelic church, as is well known, spread its message, its monks and some of its distinctive practices to much of mainland Europe from the early seventh century, so that Gaelic-speaking scholars there may have felt obliged or inspired to insert in their Latin books, as 'glosses', their own interpretations of the Latin; and so we rely heavily on the Würzburg Glosses (from about 750 AD), the Milan Glosses and the St Gall Glosses, among others, for our knowledge of early Gaelic. Alternatively, of course, many of the manuscripts containing these might have had the glosses inserted in Gaelic Scotland, Ireland or Man and then brought to the continent by the monks.

The principal phonological and morphological developments which distinguish Old Gaelic from its 'primitive' predecessor, the Gaelic of the older stratum of Ogham inscriptions, are *lenition, apocope* and *syncope*; apocope denotes the loss of final vowels from words, syncope the loss of medial vowels, and lenition is the 'softening' which essentially and systematically affects consonants in intervocalic position. Thus the word spelt on an Ogham stone as INIGENA has its G lenited (changing its sound from a stop to a fricative in Gaelic, but the early Gaelic writing system cannot mark this sound change), then loses its final vowel (by apocope) and its second –i– (by syncope); this results in early Gaelic *ingen*, Classical Gaelic *inghean*, modern Scottish Gaelic *nighean*, 'daughter'. These processes of change are detailed in McCone (1996: 89–91, 121–30); McManus (1991: 85–93); Ó Murchú (1985a: 39).

Lenition in Gaelic is probably inherited from the Celtic ancestors on the continent, for a very similar process exists among the P-Celtic languages, and it seems clear that even on the continent initial consonants could be affected, probably because (in Celtic languages) an initial consonant which follows a word ending in a vowel may in effect be intervocalic, and therefore subject to the same sound-rules as an intervocalic consonant within a word. The writers of Old Gaelic therefore needed to come up with a system for writing this systematic lenition, and in this they were remarkably slow and conservative. They adopted from Latin the digraphs *ph, th* and *ch* (which occur there in borrowings from Greek) to denote the lenited forms of *p, t* and *c* (thus *athair* from the same origin as Latin *pater*; and *a Phàdraig*, the modern vocative use of the name *Pàdraig*). But the lenition of *b, d, g* and *m* had to remain unmarked at this early stage, and what now seems the obvious solution, the introduction of *bh, dh, gh* and *mh* (as in the modern *mo mhàthair*, 'my mother'), was not systematically adopted until the end of the Middle Gaelic period around 1200 AD; so in the early Gaelic word *ingen* (above) the –g– was certainly lenited but there was no way to mark the lenition in writing.

In the Old Gaelic period a great number of Latin borrowings were made into Gaelic, especially terms of religion (whence the modern words *sagart*, 'priest', *feasgar*, 'vesper; evening', *beannachd*, 'blessing') and literacy (*leabhar*, 'book', *litir*, 'letter', *sgrìobh*, 'write'). It is also worth noting that a small number of words were borrowed into Gaelic from Old English (Anglo-Saxon) before 900 AD, but exactly where these borrowings were made we cannot know: best known are perhaps *seòl*, 'a sail', probably from Old English *segel*, and *seabhag*, 'a hawk' (Old Gaelic *sebac*), from Old English *heafoc*. It is usual (at least in Ireland) to assume that these words entered the language in Ireland, but it is perfectly possible that the borrowing was made from the speech of the Angles in south-east Scotland.

THE VIKINGS

It was late in the Old Gaelic period that the Vikings came, their assaults being first recorded in Iona and in an Irish monastery in 795 AD: their impact on the language has long been the subject of study and was clearly important, but the extent to which they can be said to have brought to an end the Old Gaelic period is still open for discussion. Clearly, in any case, the strict certainties, rules and conventions established (to a large extent in the monasteries) in the Old Gaelic period began to weaken, and we date the *Middle Gaelic* period from around 900 AD till around 1200 AD, a period of great expansion in the bulk of Gaelic literature but also of considerable change and innovation. It was doubtless in that period that numerous Norse borrowings came into the language, including especially seafaring terms (modern *acair*, 'anchor', *stiùir*, 'rudder', and *bìrlinn* for a kind of ship), as well as numerous Norse place-names, especially in the Hebrides – though the number of word-borrowings from Norse has sometimes been overstated (see Oftedal 1962). Because Norse, like English, was a Germanic language, there are some cases where a well-known Gaelic word may, for all we know, be a borrowing from either Norse or English: *bròg*, 'a shoe', and *sgilling*, 'a penny', are examples.

The phonological feature known as *preaspiration*, occurring in many Scottish Gaelic dialects and absent in Irish and Manx, is usually thought of as due to Norse influence, for a similar feature occurs in some Scandinavian dialects today. The term denotes the practice of inserting a breathing before *p*, *t* or *c* following a stressed short vowel (often a long vowel also): the breathing can vary from a light aspiration /ʰ/ to a full velar fricative /x/ or /xʲ/, the former (/ʰ/) being typical of the north-west, and the latter of some eastern dialects (especially in Perthshire) where *cat* can be pronounced as /kaxt/. It may be that the Vikings introduced the light preaspiration, which Scottish dialects of the east then developed towards the fricative (Clement 1983), but an alternative (non-Norse) explanation of the feature in Gaelic has also been put forward (Ó Murchú 1985b). Preaspiration is largely absent in the dialects of Kintyre and Arran, closest to Ireland, and in those of Sutherland in the north (for detailed evidence on some examples see Ó Dochartaigh 1994–7, items 158–60, 211, 213–15).

Norwegian control of the Hebrides (and the Isle of Man) ended with the Treaty of Perth in 1266, but even then the Norse language was not suddenly driven out. The evidence is so scanty, in fact, that we cannot really be sure that Gaelic was the language of the Outer Hebrides before the coming of the Norse: perhaps it was, perhaps Gaelic had spread that far from Dàl Riada before *c.*795, and replaced some older language(s). For some discussion of the placename evidence on this point see Nicolaisen (1976: 142–4); Cox (2002: 114–18); Cox (2007).

What effect, if any, the coming of the Norsemen to the western seaboard had on the power of the Gaels of Argyllshire and their expansion eastwards and southwards we may never know. By 843 (still in the Old Gaelic period) the Gaels had imposed their rule on the Pictish lands of the east, and it has been argued that there must have been Gaelic settlements in the Pictish kingdoms long before that: *Ath-Fhódla*, 'new Ireland', is the original Gaelic form of *Atholl* and is on record (as *Athfoitle*, genitive) in the *Annals of Ulster* for 739; *Dunottar*, near Stonehaven, is likewise a Gaelic name, *Dùn Fhoithear*, attested in the *Annals of Ulster* as early as 681. Whatever this place-name evidence really proves, the fact that the Picts have virtually disappeared from history by the end of the ninth century would suggest that the Gaelic linguistic conquest of Pictland had begun long before 843. After that the Scotticisation (= Gaelicisation) of northern Britain continued with southward expansion, until by 1034 the Gaels had more or less established the modern southern border of their kingdom, Scotland. The distribution of Gaelic place-names over much of the south illustrates the linguistic success of the kingdom, while the dearth of such place-names in the Anglian-speaking south-east (Berwickshire, Roxburghshire and Selkirkshire), as in Orkney, Shetland and eastern Caithness, marks some of its early limitations (see Nicolaisen 1976: 124).

SCOTTISH FEATURES EMERGING

The first significant body of Gaelic writing we have which was certainly done in Scotland appears in the *Book of Deer*, a small copy of part of the Gospels in Latin in which blank portions of pages are taken up by Gaelic text, written in the Gaelic monastery of Deer, Aberdeenshire, between *c.*1138 and *c.*1150 (the manuscript has been in Cambridge University since the early 1700s). The text, in both languages, is written in attractive Gaelic hands, and the inserted Gaelic sections (plus one section in Latin) consist of accounts of how the monks of Deer obtained their rights to the various lands they owned in the area. Professor Kenneth Jackson, who published an important and reliable edition of these Gaelic sections ('Notitiae' or 'Notes'), held that the language of the *Book of Deer* was simply Middle Gaelic, indistinguishable from the language of texts being produced in Ireland at the same time (Jackson 1972: 149–50), but scholars have seriously disputed this: the most recent study of the Gaelic in the *Book of Deer* is Ó Maolalaigh (2008).

One relevant feature is the marking of the Gaelic phonological feature known as *eclipsis* or as *nasalisation*. Certain small words (prepositions, articles etc.) which must previously have ended with –*n* have in the Old and Middle periods come to end with a vowel, but cause a systematic nasal mutation to affect the initial of the next word: thus the preposition *i*, meaning 'in' (also often written *a*), can appear in Old and Middle Gaelic writings in *i mbaile*, 'in a place', where the initial *b*- of *baile* has been *nasalised* by the preceding nasal. Some scholars believe, on the evidence of modern Irish, that in the early language the –*b*- in this *mb*- would have been *eclipsed*, and *mb*- pronounced simply as *m*-. Similarly 'of the cows' in the early language was written *inna mbó*, and this way of writing systematic initial nasal mutation became normal in Classical (*post*-1200) Gaelic and in modern Irish. Linguists often write these nasalising words as i^n and *inna*^{n}, to indicate that they end in the vowel but nasalise the initial of the next word (if that word begins with *p, c, t* or *f* the effect is voicing rather than nasalisation). In modern spoken Scottish Gaelic, however, the effect of this nasalisation varies widely across the dialects (see Ó Maolalaigh 1995/6): in writing, these short words retain their full nasal endings and show no mutation of the following initial, thus *an toiseach*, 'in [the] beginning'; *nam bò*.

One of the 'rules' of the written early (and Irish) language was/is that an initial *s*- cannot be subject to eclipsis (or at least cannot show it): thus modern Irish *i saoire*, 'in freedom', Scottish Gaelic *an saoire*. This phrase occurs four times in the *Book of Deer* (texts I–VII in Jackson 1972: 30–2), in saere I.4, i ssaere II.21, in sore V.2, i ssaeri V.9: the first and third of these may point to the existence of 'Scottish practice', along with the 'normal' Middle Gaelic practice (for *i saíre* or *i ssaíre*). Clearly both practices are present in the *Book of Deer*, and the 'Scottish' usage is also present there in *d'an síl*, 'to their descendants' II.23 (do + an + síl, with the Scottish possessive pronoun *an*, rather than a^n); (see further Ó Maolalaigh 2008: 241–55). It may be that the pressure on writers in this period, especially in monasteries, to conform to a standard system of writing, as mentioned above, has meant that only a few instances of a Scottish feature have found their way into a book written in an area where the feature was common in the spoken language.

Much work on eclipsis/nasalisation remains to be done, but it is already clear that the study of its history has been seriously impaired by the fact that, since serious Celtic scholarship began in the nineteenth century, only the evidence of eclipsis to be found in written Gaelic and in Irish dialects has been considered: a better historical picture may well emerge when the Scottish dialectal evidence is taken seriously.

The distinctively Scottish system of nasal initial mutation, and the range of dialectal variants within the system, may well be specifically British features of the Gaelic of Scotland, for the system has many points in common with mutations in Welsh. Scottish Gaelic also appears to have a tendency (significantly greater than that of Irish Gaelic) to simplify the use of cases in nouns, and of conjugations and tenses in verbs: these have been similarly simplified in Welsh (see Greene 1983). Some nouns have been borrowed into Scottish Gaelic from P-Celtic languages (including Pictish) and do not appear in the Irish Gaelic of any period: these include *monadh*, 'a hill' (cf. Welsh *mynydd*), and *preas*, 'a bush, thicket' (cf. Welsh *prys*). A Pictish term for 'a piece of land' (or 'township') was borrowed into the Gaelic of Scotland at an early stage and is first attested in the *Book of Deer* as *pett* (cf. Welsh *peth*, 'a thing'): it forms the basis for numerous place-names (like *Pitfichie, Pitcairn, Pitmedden*), mainly in the east, but has not survived as a common noun in the later spoken or written language (see Watson 1926: 407–14).

CLASSICAL GAELIC AND THE NORMANS

The changeover from Gaelic ways to Norman ways can be placed between *c.*1070, when the king of Scots, Malcolm (Maol Colaim) III, married his Saxon queen Margaret, and 1153, when David I, the third of their sons to succeed them, died. Malcolm belonged to the Gaelic royal family which traced its ancestry back to Dàl Riada but, perhaps largely due to his wife's influence, his Gaelic kingdom came to be centred in the south-eastern Lowlands, and in the end its capital came to be Edinburgh in Lothian, an area which was probably never fully Gaelicised. Their sons led Scotland towards a Norman-French-speaking monarchy, Gaelic ceased to be the language of the court and English (or 'Inglis') began to spread northwards along the east coast, supported by the foundation, by the kings and by others, of commercial burghs over the next few centuries: the pressure on Gaelic and its recession towards the north-west have continued ever since. Which kings, if any, following Malcolm III could speak Gaelic we may never know for certain, but the prestige of Gaelic was maintained in the west in the partly independent Lordship of the Isles, until it was forfeited to the crown in 1493.

We can see the end of the Middle Gaelic period in the late twelfth century, when the learned classes were somehow able to reform, not only the grammatical rules of the written language, but also the social status and clout of the poets. This was at least partly caused by the upheaval in Ireland following the Norman invasion there in and after 1169: the Irish learned classes, taking due account, it seems, of linguistic realities in Scotland and Man as well as Ireland, developed the new *(Early) Modern Gaelic* standard written language, most strictly enforced in the form of *Classical Gaelic* in the work of the professional poets. Brian Ó Cuív (1980) aptly referred to this development as 'a medieval exercise in language planning'. As with earlier written standards, Classical Gaelic was imposed throughout the learned Gaelic world, and we have a solid body of poems in the strict Classical form from Scotland in the thirteenth century, notably (but not only) in the work of Muireadhach Albanach, who came from Ireland and from whom descended the illustrious learned family of MacMhuirich (see Simms 2007). This learned language remained the rigid and unchanging standard for professional poets in Scotland and Ireland down to the seventeenth century, becoming further and further removed from any spoken dialect as the centuries went on.

The new Classical rules for the writing of Gaelic point to revolutionary change around 1200: the variability and 'disorder' of Middle Gaelic were drastically simplified and new rules put in place. The marking of lenition was regularised by bringing *bh*, *dh*, *gh* and *mh* into the system, and the familiar 'broad to broad/slender to slender' rule was established to mark consonant quality. It may be that the most drastic modernisation was what happened to the morphology of the verb: in the Old and Middle periods verbal forms were extremely complicated (the bane of all students of early Gaelic), but much of the complexity was now swept away, and we are presented around 1200 with what is essentially the much simpler modern Gaelic verb. As we have seen, Scottish Gaelic has in general gone even further than Classical and Irish Gaelic in simplifying its grammar. On the other hand Classical Gaelic (doubtless following Irish dialects) to a large extent abandoned the old *hiatus* between vowels which is a feature of the early language and remains strong in modern Scottish Gaelic. It was already being lost in written Gaelic as early as the tenth century, the two adjacent vowels in a word being reduced to a single diphthong (thus Old Gaelic *fiäch*, 'a raven', has two syllables, like Scottish Gaelic *fitheach*, whereas Classical and Irish Gaelic *fiach* has only one syllable) (see also Ó Maolalaigh 2008: 190–2). But still this new Classical Gaelic, despite its imposition only among the learned classes, did ultimately originate in the spoken language of the people, and its method of writing, established around 1200, is still used effectively today to write the Gaelic of Scotland and Ireland.

We must also remember that there were important contributions to Gaelic prose in this Early Modern period, where the poets' strict rules did not always apply and where the language, with much freer grammar, was consequently probably closer to common speech; the differences between the language used in prose and that used in the poetry are studied (in Irish) in McManus (1994). This prose includes new versions of tales from the old Gaelic cycles, saints' lives and learned treatises in medical manuscripts, of which Scotland has a considerable body. We also have a small number of Scottish legal documents and contracts in Gaelic from that Classical period, and it may be that many more of these once existed, especially among the papers of the Lordship of the Isles, but have been lost over the centuries. Similarly, the amount of extant Scottish Classical verse is small in comparison with that of Ireland, and it could be that much has simply been lost.

Spoken Gaelic continued to develop, of course, independent of systems of writing, which are not necessarily affected by phonetic change in the spoken language. As an example of this, the evidence, mainly from external written sources, as examined in O'Rahilly (1930), suggests that in Gaelic generally it was somewhere around the mid-thirteenth century that the letters *th* and *dh*, till then pronounced with the dental fricatives /θ/ and /ð/, began to be pronounced respectively as /h/ and as /ɣ/ or /j/: yet modern (including Classical) Gaelic continues to write *th* and *dh* (see further Ó Maolalaigh 2008: 225–8). While O'Rahilly's work was essentially concerned with Ireland, he did indicate his belief that very much the same development occurred in Scotland: but the Scottish evidence on this remains to be examined in detail.

From external sources we learn a good deal also about Lowland attitudes to the Gaels (or Highlanders). From the later fourteenth century onwards Lowland writers and historians distinguish Gaels from Lowlanders mainly by telling us how much less civilised the Gaels are. It is in 1494 that the term 'Scots' first appears in an extant source as a name for what had been called 'Inglis': an important political development, for now Gaelic was no longer to be *the* language of the Scots. Gaelic comes to be called 'Irish' or *Erse*, with the obvious implication of foreignness in the 'Scots'-speaking state. It has been pointed out that the pioneering Scottish Education Act of 1494–6 decreed that lairds and chiefs must send their children to be educated in the Lowlands, and that 'this meant that the formative years of the children of the leading citizens of Gaeldom were to be spent in an alien environment – a feature of Highland education which recurs throughout the educational history of Gaelic Scotland and remains alive to our own day' (MacKinnon 1991: 42). In general, Gaelic seems to have had no official place at all in the late medieval Scots-speaking state. There are some notable exceptions, like the well-known case of the school in Aberdeen whose rule-book in 1553 allowed the speaking of Greek, Latin, Hebrew and Gaelic but forbade the use of the vernacular, Scots (see Forte 2007: 24–5). Nevertheless, Scots/English sources from the fourteenth century till the eighteenth and beyond display little regard for the Gaels and their language – which in the sixteenth century, according to some authorities, was still the language of half the population of Scotland.

During that same post-Norman period borrowings into Gaelic from French and English grew quickly in number, the borrowing from English, of course, continuing apace ever since. Some of the French borrowings in Scottish Gaelic seem to have entered by way of Scots, as in the case of words like *seòmar*, 'a room' (Manx *shamyr*), Scots *chaumer* < French *chambre*; *cùpall* (Manx *cubbyl*), Scots/northern English *couple* < French *couple*; Classical Gaelic and Irish borrowed these directly from French, or via southern dialects of English (which preserved the final vowel in such borrowings long after Scots had lost it), as *seomra* and *cúpla*. But on the whole we have few sources of information on the detailed development of spoken Gaelic in Scotland during the Classical period, the very time during which Scottish Gaelic must have been developing the main features which today distinguish it from Irish and Manx Gaelic (for some discussion of the nature and growth of such features see Ó Buachalla 2002: 7–8).

WRITING SYSTEMS FOR SCOTTISH GAELIC

The most important Scottish collection of verse from the Classical period is *The Book of the Dean of Lismore*, a manuscript (Adv. 72.1.37 in the National Library) written in Perthshire between 1512 and 1542 and containing poems from several of the preceding centuries. But the scribes, James MacGregor, Dean of Lismore, and his brother Donnchadh, used neither the old Gaelic script nor the established Classical spelling of Gaelic: instead they used a spelling based on Scots and written in the 'secretary hand' of Scots, to convey an approximation of the Gaelic sounds. While this has made it very difficult sometimes to understand fully the text of a poem, it does also give us useful information on the pronunciation of Gaelic at that time, the first significant source we have for such information, which allows us to see clearly some features distinctive of the spoken Scottish Gaelic we know today. For a detailed discussion of what the Dean's Book can tell us about the vernacular see Watson 1923.

The Dean's Book is not unique in using Scots-based spelling to write Gaelic literature (see Meek 1989), and indeed such a spelling system might well have become the norm for the written language in Scotland (as it did for Manx) towards the end of the Classical period. But when the first Gaelic book ever printed appeared from Robert Lekprevik's press in Edinburgh in 1567 its spelling was essentially the Classical spelling of the poets, and this has underlain Gaelic writing and printing ever since. The book was John Carswell's *Foirm na n-Urrnuidheadh*, his adaptation of John Knox's *Book of Common Prayer*, the product of Carswell's devotion and that of his patron Gilleasbaig Donn, fifth Earl of Argyll, to the cause of the Reformation, which was officially adopted in Scotland in 1560. The new ecclesiastical system had great difficulty for three centuries thereafter in reconciling the reformers' zeal for spreading education among the masses with the establishment's need to 'extirpate' the Gaelic language: nevertheless religious literature quickly became the principal product of Gaelic publishing, and remained so for two centuries or more. Carswell's 1567 work was a product of the relatively Gaelic-friendly Synod of Argyll, and the new church's majority was a good deal less friendly, supporting in many cases the anti-Gaelic culture headed at first by King James VI (1567–1625) and his governments.

Perhaps the most famous measure taken by James and his Privy Council to bring Gaeldom under control was the signing of the *Statutes of Iona* by a number of Gaelic chiefs in 1609. They had been abducted at the Council's command during the previous year, and were only released when they agreed to sign the document. This consisted of nine points, including commitments to have the chiefs' heirs educated in the Lowlands so as to learn to speak, read and write English, and to have the patronising of 'bairds' outlawed. Harsh as these impositions must have seemed to the Gaelic chiefs who signed them, the Act of the Privy Council of 1616 which ratified the statutes is a much more ferociously anti-Gaelic document, concerned, among other things, 'that the vulgar Inglishe toung be universallie plantit, and the Irishe language, whilk is one of the cheif and principall causis of the continewance of barbaritie and incivilitie amongis the inhabitantis of the Iles and Heylandis, may be abolisheit and removit' (Donaldson 1970: 174–5, 178; MacKinnon 1991: 46–8). A detailed and readable account of the fits and starts which led in the succeeding centuries both to a serious weakening of the language and to the publication of religious material in it will be found in Durkacz (1983, chapter 1).

In Ireland the first printed Gaelic book appeared in 1571, again in a prose form of Classical Gaelic; Irish scholars rarely note the primacy of Carswell in this matter. But the Gaelic presses used by the Irish from the start had their characters modelled on the old Gaelic script, as used in manuscript by the early church and by the scribes of the Classical period. Lekprevik's Edinburgh press, on the other hand, had only the normal Roman letters used for Scots and English, and as a result the old script has only very occasionally been used since 1700 to write Gaelic in Scotland.

Before the nineteenth century, it is clear, we have very little direct evidence on the nature of the Gaelic spoken by the majority who did not use writing. For written evidence, apart from the Book of the Dean of Lismore (1512–42), we have the Fernaig Manuscript of 1688–93, a remarkable collection of verse written in Wester Ross with a spelling system based (like that used in the Dean's Book) on the pronunciation of Scots/English: the manuscript is in the library of the University of Glasgow, and a good transcription may be found in Mac Phàrlain (1923). But we also have a valuable source for the seventeenth-century (or even earlier) language in the sizeable body of Gaelic song which survives today in oral tradition from that period, or was written down from oral tradition in the eighteenth century or later: this is part of the unwritten literature of the people, kept for us in the oral tradition for up to 400 years. Many such songs, including most waulking songs for instance, are of anonymous composition, and many are the work of well-known named poets like Màiri nighean Alasdair Ruaidh (c.1615–c.1705) and Iain Lom (c.1624–c.1695). Study of these songs, their rhythms and rhymes as well as the historical events and persons dealt with in their texts, confirms that many of them were composed, in the seventeenth century or before, quite certainly in very much the same Gaelic of the common people as is still fully understood today: this is the first time we can get a really clear view of Scottish Gaelic, distinct from Classical Gaelic and also from Manx and Irish.

At the end of the seventeenth century it is still (very broadly) fair to think of the Highlands as Gaelic-speaking and the Lowlands as Scots-speaking, but even then Scots and English were spreading within Gaeldom. While most of the Highlands (as well as some other places, including part of Galloway) can be represented on a map as a Gaelic-speaking unit in the eighteenth century, the work of Charles Withers (1984, especially chapters 4 and 5) has shown that the various social contexts in which Gaelic was the norm might change as new influences (such as formal education or commerce) from the Lowlands brought the English language or Scots to certain social domains, even in mainly Gaelic-speaking parishes. And so the decline of Gaelic is to some extent measurable in the eighteenth century. It is generally accepted that as Gaelic weakened in the Highlands and Islands it was usually replaced not by Scots but by English (in a Scottish form), though Scots still had its part to play (see Mather and Speitel 1975: 9). For one thing, most Gaelic dialects today have a considerable number of words borrowed from Scots rather than from standard English (such as *saplas* and *great*, both meaning 'soapy water', from Scots *sapples* and *graith*; see Quick 1990); for another, it has been shown that Gaelic in Deeside, Aberdeenshire, has been replaced by Scots rather than English (Watson and Clement 1983: 384; Watson and Allan 1984: xiv).

After 1600 written Gaelic and printed Gaelic remained heavily influenced by the Classical language. The New Testament was printed in this Classical-based prose in Ireland in 1602, produced by the (Episcopalian) Church of Ireland using a font based on the old Gaelic script. The Church of Scotland's Synod of Argyll set out in 1649 to encourage the translation of the Bible, as they rather confusingly put it, 'into the Irish language' (MacTavish 1943: 127) and, although that aim was not then achieved, the works they succeeded in publishing, especially their *Shorter Catechism* of 1659, show clear examples of usages much closer to the Scottish Gaelic of the people, and further from Classical (and Irish) Gaelic, the first serious move we know of in that direction. As R. L. Thomson (1962: xxxix) put it, the language of the *Shorter Catechism* 'represents the spoken language of Scotland with some rather half-hearted attempt at keeping up the fiction of a standard literary language different from the spoken one'. Perhaps this overstates the case a little, for many features of the literary language remain clear in the *Shorter Catechism*; for instance, the marking of initial nasalisation remains 'overwhelmingly normal' (Thomson 1971: 46), that is, in accordance with the practice of Classical Gaelic. In the Scottish Gaelic poems published in the Preface to Edward Lhuyd's *Archaeologia Britannica* of 1707 the writers (probably the poets themselves) still struggle towards a Scottish and non-Classical way of marking initial nasalisation, as in *na nttír úd*, 'of those countries' (Robert Campbell; *tìr*, 'a country'); *a nglo*, 'into print' (Seumas MacMhuirich; *clò*, 'print').

In 1685 Bishop William Bedell's complete Bible, in Classical-based Gaelic, was published in Ireland, and when it reached Scotland the unfamiliar print was a difficulty to many, so Robert Kirk (?1644–92), Episcopal minister of Aberfoyle, transcribed Bedell's entire Bible into Roman print and had it published in London in 1690 for the Scottish faithful. But 1690 was not a happy year for Episcopalians, and 'Kirk's Bible', though welcomed by some, was much criticised by others, especially for being 'Irish' (and perhaps to some extent because of its Episcopalian origins); its language is not, of course, any colloquial Irish Gaelic, but Classical Gaelic in a prose form. The progress towards a vernacular Scottish Bible was maintained, however, dominating educated debate in the eighteenth century, and when the New Testament appeared in 1767, to be followed by the completion of the Old Testament in 1801, an acceptable way of writing an acceptable form of Scottish Gaelic had at last been established (Durkacz 1983: 52–67, 96–108).

BIBLIOGRAPHY

Adger, D. and Ramchand, G. (2006), 'Dialect Variation in Gaelic Relative Clauses', in Wilson McLeod, James E. Fraser and Anja Gunderloch (eds), *Cànan & Cultar: Language & Culture: Rannsachadh na Gàidhlig 3*, Edinburgh: Dunedin Academic Press, pp. 179–92.

Bannerman, J. (1971), 'The Scots of Dalriada', in Gordon Menzies (ed.), *Who are the Scots?*, London: BBC, pp. 66–79.

Barrow, G.W.S. (1989), 'The Lost Gàidhealtachd of Medieval Scotland', in Gillies 1989, pp. 67–88.

Campbell, E. (2001), 'Were the Scots Irish?', in *Antiquity* 75, pp. 285–92.

Clement, R. D. C. (1983), 'Gaelic: Preaspiration', in Thomson 1983, pp. 104–5.

Cox, Richard A. V. (1999), *The Language of the Ogam Inscriptions of Scotland*, Aberdeen: Department of Celtic, University of Aberdeen.

Cox, Richard A. V. (2002), *The Gaelic Place-names of Carloway, Isle of Lewis*, Dublin: Dublin Institute for Advanced Studies.

Cox, Richard A. V. (2007), 'Notes on the Norse Impact on Hebridean Place-names', in *The Journal of Scottish Name Studies* I, pp. 139–44.

Donaldson, G. (1970), *Scottish Historical Documents*, New York: Barnes & Noble.

Dumville, D. N. (2002), 'Ireland and North Britain in the Earlier Middle Ages: Contexts for *Míniugud Senchasa Fher nAlban*', in C. Ó Baoill agus Nancy R. McGuire (eds), *Rannsachadh na Gàidhlig 2000*, Aberdeen: An Clò Gaidhealach, pp. 185–212.

Durkacz, V. E. (1983), *The Decline of the Celtic Languages*, Edinburgh: John Donald.

Forsyth, K. (1996), *The Ogham Inscriptions of Scotland: An Edited Corpus*, Ann Arbor: University Microfilms.

Forsyth, K. (1997), *The Language of Pictland: The Case Against 'non-Indo-European Pictish'*, Utrecht: de Keltische Draak.

Forte, A. D. M. (2007), '"Ane Horss Turd"? Sir John Skene of Curriehill – a Gaelic-speaking Lawyer in the Courts of James VI?', in *Scottish Gaelic Studies* XXIII, pp. 21–51.

Gillies, W. (ed.) (1989), *Gaelic and Scotland: Alba agus a' Ghàidhlig*, Edinburgh: Edinburgh University Press.

Greene, D. (1983), 'Gaelic: Syntax, Similarities with British Syntax', in Thomson 1983, pp. 107–8.

Jackson, K. (1955), 'The Pictish Language', in F. T. Wainwright (ed.), *The Problem of the Picts*, Edinburgh: Nelson, pp. 129–60.

Jackson, K. (1972), *The Gaelic Notes in the Book of Deer*, Cambridge: Cambridge University Press.

James, S. (1999), *The Atlantic Celts: Ancient People or Modern Invention?*, London: British Museum Press.

MacAulay, D. (ed.) (1992), *The Celtic Languages*, Cambridge: Cambridge University Press.

McCone, K. (1985), 'The Würzburg and Milan Glosses: Our Earliest Sources of "Middle Irish"', in *Ériu* 36, pp. 85–106.

McCone, K. (1996), *Towards a Relative Chronology of Ancient and Medieval Celtic Sound Change*, Maynooth: St Patrick's College.

Mac Eoin, G. (1988), 'The Decline of the Celtic Languages', in Gordon Maclennan (ed.), *Proceedings of the First North American Congress of Celtic Studies*, University of Ottawa, pp. 589–602.

MacKinnon, K. (1991), *Gaelic: A Past and Future Prospect*, Edinburgh: Saltire Society.

McManus, D. (1991), *A Guide to Ogam*, Maynooth: An Sagart.

McManus, D. (1994), 'Teanga an Dána agus Teanga an Phróis', in Pádraig Ó Fiannachta (ed.), *Léachtaí Cholm Cille* 24, Maynooth: An Sagart, pp. 114–35.

Mac Phàrlain, C. (1923), *Lamh-Sgrìobhainn Mhic Rath: Dorlach Laoidhean*, Dun-de: Malcolm C. MacLeod.

MacTavish, D. (1943), *Minutes of the Synod of Argyll 1639–1651*, Vol. 37, Edinburgh: Scottish History Society.

Mather, J. Y. and Speitel, H. H. (1975), *The Linguistic Atlas of Scotland: Scots Section*, Vol. 1, London: Croom Helm.

Meek, D. E. (1989), 'Gàidhlig is Gaylick anns na Meadhon Aoisean', in Gillies 1989, pp. 131–45, 233–5.

Meek, D. E. (2000), *The Quest for Celtic Christianity*, Edinburgh: Handsel Press.

Nicolaisen, W. F. H. (1976), *Scottish Place-names: Their Study and Significance*, London: Batsford.

Ó Buachalla, B. (2002), '"Common Gaelic" Revisited', in C. Ó Baoill agus Nancy R. McGuire (eds), *Rannsachadh na Gàidhlig 2000*, Aberdeen: An Clò Gaidhealach, pp. 1–12.

Ó Cuív, B. (1980), 'A Medieval Exercise in Language Planning: Classical Early Modern Irish', in Konrad Koerner (ed.), *Progress on Linguistic Historiography* (Studies in the History of Linguistics, Vol. 20), Amsterdam: Benjamins, pp. 23–34.

Ó Dochartaigh, C. (1994–7), *Survey of Scottish Gaelic Dialects*, 5 vols, Dublin: Dublin Institute for Advanced Studies.

Oftedal, M. (1962), 'On the Frequency of Norse Loanwords in Scottish Gaelic', in *Scottish Gaelic Studies* IX.2, pp. 116–27.

Ó Maolalaigh, R. (1995/6), 'The Development of Eclipsis in Gaelic', in *Scottish Language* 14/15, pp. 158–73.

Ó Maolalaigh, R. (2008), 'The Scotticisation of Gaelic: A Reassessment of the Language and Orthography of the Gaelic Notes in the Book of Deer', in Katherine Forsyth (ed.), *Studies on the Book of Deer*, Dublin: Four Courts, pp. 179–274.

Ó Murchú, M. (1985a), *The Irish Language*, Dublin: Department of Foreign Affairs and Bord na Gaeilge.

Ó Murchú, M. (1985b), 'Varia VIII: Devoicing and Pre-aspiration in Varieties of Scots Gaelic', in *Ériu* 39, pp. 195–8.

O'Rahilly, T. F. (1930), 'Notes on Middle Irish pronunciation', in *Hermathena* 20, pp. 152–95.

Quick, I. (1990), 'The Scots Element in the Gaelic Vocabulary of Domestic Furnishings and Utensils', in Derick S. Thomson (ed.), *Gaelic and Scots in Harmony*, Glasgow: Department of Celtic, University of Glasgow, pp. 36–42.

Sharpe, R. (1995), *Adomnán of Iona: Life of St Columba*, Harmondsworth: Penguin.

Simms, K. (2007), 'Muireadhach Albanach Ó Dálaigh and the Classical Revolution', in Thomas Owen Clancy and Murray Pittock (eds), *The Edinburgh History of Scottish Literature*, Vol. I, Edinburgh: Edinburgh University Press, pp. 83–90.

Thomson, D. S. (1983), *The Companion to Gaelic Scotland*, Oxford: Blackwell.

Thomson, R. L. (1962), *Adtimchiol an Chreidimh*, Edinburgh: Scottish Gaelic Texts Society, Vol. VII.

Thomson, R. L. (1971), 'The Language of the Shorter Catechism (1659)', in *Scottish Gaelic Studies* XII, pp. 34–51.

Watson, A. and Allan, E. (1984), *The Place Names of Upper Deeside*, Aberdeen: Aberdeen University Press.

Watson, A. and Clement, R. D. (1983), 'Aberdeenshire Gaelic', in *Transactions of the Gaelic Society of Inverness* LII, pp. 373–404.

Watson, W. J. (1923), 'Vernacular Gaelic in the Book of the Dean of Lismore', in *Transactions of the Gaelic Society of Inverness* XXXI, pp. 260–89.

Watson, W. J. (1926), *The History of the Celtic Placenames of Scotland*, Edinburgh: Blackwood.

Withers, C. W. J. (1984), *Gaelic in Scotland 1698–1981: The Geographical History of a Language*, Edinburgh: John Donald.

CHAPTER 2

Language in Society: 1800 to the Modern Day

Michelle Macleod

INTRODUCTION

This chapter offers a glimpse at many aspects of Gaelic in society since 1800: it is not a linguistic analysis of how the language has changed in this period; rather it highlights some of the key areas of linguistic and social interaction. The nineteenth century was a period of immense change for Gaelic speakers. Highland and rural society, in which Gaelic was mainly based, changed dramatically over the course of the century and the process of change that began in the nineteenth century is still felt today. Issues relating to the nineteenth-century Gaelic community have been well documented (Withers 1984, 1988, 1998; Hunter 1976, 2000; Meek 1996, 2007; Durkacz 1983; MacKinnon 1991) and this chapter attempts to summarise the key points made by these and other scholars. This information will be contextualised alongside an analysis of Gaelic society in the twentieth and twenty-first century: here, scholars from a variety of disciplines including anthropology, economics, linguistics (language planning), education, etc., as well as traditional Celtic and Gaelic scholars, have enhanced our appreciation of society in this era. Although the chapter is split into two main sections, this split is somewhat artificial and does not represent a significant change in society at the turn of the nineteenth and twentieth century.

THE NINETEENTH CENTURY

We do not have access to the same sort of statistical analysis of the Gaelic communities for the beginning of the nineteenth century that we have even for the end of the century or for the following centuries.

However, MacKinnon estimates that at the beginning of the nineteenth century there were around 300,000 monoglot Gaelic speakers living in the Highlands, an area which would have had a population of approximately 335,000 (Mackinnon 1991: 63). As Mackinnon shows elsewhere in this book, this number has been continuously eroded for the subsequent 200 years.

The process of mass migration and forced emigration which began in the eighteenth century continued well into the nineteenth century; this mass movement away from the Highlands had a huge impact on the language, weakening its traditional homeland; as Donald Meek maintains: this movement is 'generally summarised in the convenient (but misleading) catch-all phrase "the Highland Clearances"' (Meek 2007: 254). Hunter (1976, 2000) and Withers (1998) have written extensively on this period. The eighteenth and nineteenth centuries witnessed a change in the economic organisation of Highland leadership. After a period of successful anglicisation by the 'government' of the traditional leaders of the Highland clans, a monetary system became more valued than kinship. In his seminal work on Highland history, James Hunter has called the eighteenth century 'the end of an old order' (Hunter 1976: 6). As the Highlands lost their old sense of leadership with chiefs becoming more like landlords, the common folk became open to abuse. The economic situation in the eighteenth century changed favouring the large-scale production of wool and kelp; landlords changed the organisation of their land and often these pieces of land were not sufficient to support the tenant and his family and thus the tenants were forced into seeking additional income and moved from the central highlands and islands to the coastal areas: this, claims Hunter, is how crofting, as we know it, came into existence (Hunter 1976: 12).

In the early nineteenth century, not all Highland tenants were prepared to accept the wishes of their landlords, and so began the mass migration from the Highlands: Hunter notes that in 1803 alone it was estimated that 20,000 people were likely to have left their homes for America; they took with them their language and culture (see Nilsen in this collection for discussion on Highland migrants in Canada). Various successes and failures in highland industries in the nineteenth century affected migration patterns to both the New World and lowland Scotland. Withers (1998) estimates that according to the 1851 census there were approximately 29,548 Highlanders living in urban settlements.

When discussing the Highland Clearances, some commentators refer to the passivity of the Gaels, at least initially, in the face of severe hardship. Hunter explains this in terms of the traditional relationship of the common clan member (or crofter as he became) with the clan chief. Although a clear class system existed in the clans, there was always loyalty to the chief and the clan. The commoner also had a clear sense of loyalty to one clan and one location, rather than any unified sense of Gaelic or Highland identity. Thus, when the old structures began to fall apart and the chiefs turned into landlords, the old sense of identity and traditions hindered the Highlanders (Hunter 1976: 90–1). It was not until the 1880s that the crofters began to demonstrate and agitate for better conditions: thus started the period of the Highland Land Wars, surely one of the key factors in contributing to the Highlanders beginning to view themselves as a cohesive unit.

Different communities organised protest, through the media, parliamentary campaigns, refusal to pay rent and militant action. There are many reports of military or police intervention against the crofters throughout the Highlands. As a result of their agitation and growing political support, the government ordered an enquiry into the condition of the crofters: Hunter states that the Napier Commission enquiry is the 'single most important source of information about the social and economic situation in the Highlands in the later nineteenth century' (Hunter 1976: 109). Although the passing of the Crofting Acts in 1886 and 1892 led to some stability and ended evictions in the Highlands, migration from the traditional Gaelic communities has continued to occur since this period with a very destabilising effect on the existence of a solid language base.

Gaelic scholars such as Meek and Kidd promote the use of literary texts as first-hand source material showing how the social and economic changes were impacting on the lives of everyday Gaelic speakers. Meek, the leading scholar in this area, has rejected the criticism of earlier Celticists that the literature of this era is 'sad, soft, sentimental' verse; he contends that this does not do justice to the variety of materials from this period which did reflect on the social circumstances of the Gaels, but was not at all restricted to this type of verse (Meek 2007: 261–2). Meek's work on *Màiri Mhòr nan Òran* (1997) and his recent collections *Tuath is Tighearna* (1995) and *Caran an t-Saoghail* both dispel the earlier dismissal of the nineteenth century as an era of poor literature and provide personal accounts of that time. Likewise, Kidd commends the prose literature (such as the works of the Rev. Dr Norman MacLeod [Caraid nan Gaidheal] and the Rev. Alexander MacGregor) of this era as a further source for contemporary discussion on social issues (Kidd 2000, 2003, 2007).

During the nineteenth century another national event had great significance and impact in the Highlands and on Gaelic culture. The secession away from the established church to form a new church, the Free Church, is known as the Disruption. One of the contributing factors to the Disruption was the unease that many ministers felt with the state handling of the land problems; they also objected to the Established Church's practice of allowing a landlord to veto the appointment of a minister to his parish; there are of course many other reasons for the Disruption, but these are key to an understanding of the relationship between the Free Church and Highlands and particularly the land issue (for a detailed study see, for example, MacColl 2006). The Free Church supported the crofters in their claims for better land rights; this naturally did not endear them to the landed class, who often made it difficult for them to gain land on which to build churches or worship. MacColl discusses how various Free Churches supported the Highland Land Law Reform Association (MacColl 2006: 105) and was the most vociferous group of clergy to give evidence to the Napier Commission (109).

Although the Free Church dominated in many areas of the Highlands and islands, it was not the only church in these places. The Established Church remained strong in Argyll, west-Inverness-shire had remained strongly Roman Catholic after the Reformation and the Baptist Church was strong in some of the Inner Hebridean Islands, such as Tiree (MaColl 2006: 21). Although there was diversity in religious practice, MacColl maintains that 'the religious tradition that was followed by most Highlanders in the nineteenth century, Evangelical presbyterianism, had also become intrinsically identified with the cultural identity of the region' (74). MacColl identifies Gaelic-language preaching, the dissemination of the Gaelic Bible, catechising and formal education as key factors in transforming nineteenth-century Highland society. Withers goes further in his discussion of education in the nineteenth century; he maintains that because Highland schools often taught the reading of Gaelic scriptures this 'not only helped to reinforce Gaelic's place as a church language but further influenced Highland consciousness in making a distinction between Gaelic as the language of spiritual affairs, English of worldly advance' (Withers 1988: 151).

During the nineteenth century, before the establishment of state education, the churches (predominantly the Church of Scotland and the Free Church) and various religious and educational societies played an important part in developing education in the Highlands and also increasing Gaelic literacy in the area. Durkacz (1983), MacKinnon (1991) and Withers (1984, 1988) have written extensively on the role of education in both maintaining and damaging the Gaelic language in the Highlands in the eighteenth and nineteenth centuries. One of the main players in education in the Highlands was the Society in Scotland for the Propagation of Christian Knowledge (SSPCK), established in 1709; it seems the SSPCK and other schools societies attempted to fill a void left by, as Durkacz puts it, the Highlands' 'widespread evasion of the 1696 Act for Settling of Parochial Schools' (Durkacz 1983: 48). The SSPCK were largely suspicious of Gaelic, associating it with Jacobitism and Catholicism, and thus they initially attempted to ignore Gaelic in their efforts to teach the scriptures in English; Durkacz points out that the SSPCK appreciated even from an early stage that Gaelic-speaking teachers would need to be employed in the Highlands. Realising the limitations of relying too heavily on English to achieve their aims, they admitted Gaelic as the medium of instruction in their Highlands schools from as early as 1767 (MacKinnon 1991: 56). MacKinnon continues that the SSPCK proposed in 1824 that Gaelic-speaking children were to be taught Gaelic first and then English (MacKinnon 1991: 63). With this change in attitude new Gaelic textbooks and religious tracts were introduced and Gaelic literacy grew (this was one of the reasons, though not the only one, for the expansion of Gaelic publishing in the nineteenth century).

Other organisations involved in education in the Highlands in the nineteenth century include: the Edinburgh Gaelic School Society (established in 1811) whose only object was to teach people to read the Bible in Gaelic (Durkacz 1993: 112); they adopted the circulating school system (unlike the SSPCK) whereby a teacher would only stay in a location for as long as it took to teach a specific number of people to certain standards; Withers reports that there were a maximum of eighty-five schools in the Highlands in 1826 (Withers 1988: 146). The Glasgow Auxiliary Gaelic School Society (established in 1812), on the other hand, had as its main object the promotion of English (Durkacz 1993: 113). Similar societies in Inverness and Dundee and the Free Church and Church of Scotland Ladies' Auxiliaries also supported or provided education in the Highlands.

The Education Act (Scotland) 1872 resulted in the passing over of all SSPCK, Church and Gaelic Schools Societies schools to local school boards; the act has been criticised for its failure to consider Gaelic at all; consequently, the use of Gaelic was actively discouraged within schools. In spite of objections by the Gaelic Society of Inverness in 1876, the Educational Institute of Scotland in 1897, the Napier Commission Report in 1885, and An Comunn Gaidhealach in 1918 (Mackinnon 1991: 76–7), it was not until the 1918 Education (Scotland) Act that Gaelic was recognised in law (for more on this see the section on education in the twentieth and twenty-first centuries below). There was, however, some provision made for Gaelic prior to this: the Schools (Scotland) Codes 1873 and 1878 allowed teachers to use Gaelic in the classrooms, but funding often made this difficult (Thomson 1994: 260). It seems, however, that, in spite of all the efforts by different societies, most parents wanted their children to become literate in English as this was viewed as the key to success in life: Anderson perhaps rather crudely overstates the result of this education practice that 'once literacy in English became general, the speaking of Gaelic rarely lasted more than a generation or two' (Anderson 2002: 153); but there is no doubt that Gaelic was let down by various early education policies.

Gaelic education took a leap into the tertiary sector in the nineteenth century when various Gaelic societies became involved in campaigning for the establishment of a Chair of Celtic in the University of Edinburgh; the campaign was championed by Professor John Stuart Blackie, Professor of Greek at Edinburgh University. The first Chair of Celtic was Donald MacKinnon from Colonsay (1839–1914); his inaugural address gives some indication of the effort expended from various quarters and in particular John Blackie (MacKinnon 1883).

As a natural result of mass migration from the Gaelic Highland heartlands, new settlements of Gaels sprung up in the urban areas of Scotland: particularly Glasgow and Inverness. Finding themselves in urban situations for the first time, the Gaels organised themselves differently to how they were accustomed to conducting themselves in their traditional homelands. During the nineteenth century Gaelic publishing blossomed: Mackinnon estimates that between 1830 and 1900, 905 Gaelic titles were published (MacKinnon 1991: 68); Gaelic societies were established and a new type of middle-class Gael purposefully created new literary vehicles of expression and other artistic outlets, presumably to replace the *taigh-cèilidh* tradition.

As noted earlier, some of the first 'Gaelic' societies were established primarily with one focus: either education or to support the land agitation movement. One of the earliest Gaelic societies is the Highland (initially Gaelic) Society of London, established in 1777, followed shortly afterwards by the Gaelic Society of Glasgow in 1780; both of these remained active during the nineteenth century. Two of the societies which have had an important impact on Gaelic society and maintaining Gaelic tradition are the Gaelic Society of Inverness, established in 1871 and An Comunn Gaidhealach, founded in 1891.

The Gaelic Society of Inverness was formed with 'the specific purpose of cultivating the language, poetry and music of the Scottish Highlands and generally furthering the interests of the Gaelic-speaking people'.[1] In the nineteenth century, amongst other activities, the Society appealed for an investigation into the conditions of the crofting districts (the Napier Commission), campaigned for the Chair of Celtic at Edinburgh University and involved itself with the movement to include a Gaelic question on the 1881 census. While no longer so politically active, it still responds to Gaelic development initiatives. Today, it is particularly valued for its volume of learned essays it publishes approximately every two years (and has done since 1871); these essays are based on lecture series organised by the society. To date sixty-three volumes have been published and they represent a wonderful contribution to Gaelic scholarship (see MacDonald, 1970).

Interestingly, the Gaelic Society of Inverness did not lend its support initially to the establishment of one of Gaelic culture's most enduring and recognised organisations: An Comunn Gaidhealach. An Comunn was established in 1891 with the aims of promoting Gaelic music and literature and 'home industries of the Highlands'; encouraging the teaching of Gaelic; holding an annual competitive arts gathering, based on the Welsh Eisteddfod; publishing and fundraising (Thompson 1992: 13–14). The initial composition of the Executive Council and Patrons consisted of Highland aristocracy and learned Gaels. The first Mòd took place in Oban, An Comunn's spiritual home, in 1892. Oban hosted the Mòd again in 1893 and 1894 and then it moved on to Glasgow in 1895 and Perth 1896; so began the tradition of the rotating venue, a practice which is upheld to this day. An Comunn has not restricted itself to organising the Mòd, however; other early activity included setting up a Branch structure which facilitated an extended membership and spreading of its aims to grassroot level and publishing periodicals. An Comunn's first periodical was *An Deo-Ghreine*; it was first published in 1905 and ran until 1923 when it was superseded by *An Gaidheal* which ran until 1965 when it in turn was superseded by the fortnightly bilingual newspaper *Sruth*; An Comunn's most recent publication, *An Gaidheal Ùr*, ran from 1996 to 2009 (latterly it was only available electronically).

In addition to the specific 'Gaelic' societies, there were, in Glasgow in the 1870s, eleven locality-specific societies; according to MacPhail these were: the Sutherlandshire Association, the Skye Association, the Tiree Association, the Lewis Association, the Mull and Iona Association, the Ross-shire Association, the Islay Society, the Lochaber Society, the Appin Society, the Coll Society and the Ardnamurchan, Morvern and Sunart Association (MacPhail 1977: 169). In addition to these societies in Glasgow, there were other Gaelic societies elsewhere in Scotland: Greenock, Aberdeen and Dundee (169).

As an offshoot of the proliferation of societies in Glasgow with a Highland or Gaelic interest, Gaelic publishing prospered during the nineteenth century (in addition to the An Comunn journals mentioned above). Kenneth MacDonald notes that in Glasgow alone between 1801 and 1850, 114 Gaelic titles were published by thirty-five different publishers and between 1851 and 1900 there were 138 Gaelic publications with twenty-one publishers (MacDonald 2007: 188–9). Gaelic publishing was not limited to Glasgow. Donald John MacLeod states that 'the most important publishers of Gaelic in the nineteenth century were MacLachlan & Stewart of Edinburgh, Norman MacLeod of Edinburgh, Alexander Gardner of Paisley, Eneas Mackay of Stirling, and Archibald Sinclair of Glasgow' (MacLeod 1977: 203).

Gaelic publishing and writing was supported by the urban Gaels in the late nineteenth century. MacLeod and MacDonald both discuss the impact of the urban 'cèilidh' on publishing. At such events organised by the various Gaelic societies audiences enjoyed listening to readings and it is from this background that titles such as Henry Whyte's (1852–1913) *The Celtic Garland* (Glasgow, 1881) originate (see Watson 2008).

Perhaps the most striking innovation in publishing in the nineteenth century is the birth of the Gaelic periodicals. MacLeod discusses the merits of the various periodicals (1977) and the following list is derived from his discussion: *An Rosroine* (1803, four numbers); *An Teachdaire Gaelach* (twenty-one numbers between 1829 and 1831); *Cuairtean nan Gleann* (forty numbers between 1840 and 1843); *An Teachdaire Ur Gaidhealach* (1835–6, nine numbers); *Teachdaire nan Gaidheal* (1844–8, 13 numbers); *Fear-Tathaich nam Beann* (1848–50, 24 numbers); *An Gaidheal* (monthly between 1871 and 1877); *Mac-Talla* (in Cape Breton, weekly between 1892 and 1901 and then fortnightly until 1904). As noted earlier, Sheila Kidd has done some interesting work on analysing the literary and social merits of these journals, but there is still a lot of work to be done in the area of Gaelic publishing.

THE TWENTIETH AND TWENTY-FIRST CENTURIES

Like in the nineteenth century, there was much change in society which affected the Gaelic language in the twentieth and early twenty-first century. The First World War had a huge impact on Gaelic as a vigorous community language. With Highland communities seemingly suffering a proportionately higher casualty rate than elsewhere in the United Kingdom (MacKinnon 1990: 166), the language attrition and Highland depopulation continued to have almost devastating consequences for the future of the language. Yet although the language has declined dramatically over the course of the period with which this section is concerned, many innovations have taken place.

Perhaps the greatest social factor to continue to impact on the Gaelic language is the continued population shift in the traditional Gaelic areas. MacKinnon discusses the demographics of this shift in his chapter in this book. With approximately half of all Gaelic speakers now domiciled outside of traditional areas and heartland areas weakened, Gaelic society continues to change: there is no longer such a clear divide between the urban and rural Gael with Gaelic speakers in both locations being able to access many of the same facilities and services (for example, education and broadcast media). There is even a new discourse used by some for discussing the growing numbers of Gaelic speakers in the urban areas: these are the 'new Gaels', as opposed to the traditional Gaels (MacCaluim 2007, McLeod 2007, Morgan 2000). The Church is no longer a bastion for Gaelic language and culture; Donald Meek has noted the decline in numbers of students for the Gaelic ministry, the end of the Gaelic-speaking scholar-minister/priest, and the lack of any pro-active Gaelic policies (Meek 1996). Education, on the other hand, has risen to the challenge of the changing face of society, as have the arts and broadcasting.

To date, we lack a complete social history of Gaelic in the twentieth century, but much work has been undertaken by scholars on different aspects of the language in society, for example: Gaelic demographics (MacKinnon – see his chapter in this book); anthropological studies (Dorian, McEwan-Fujita, MacDonald – see McEwan-Fujita in this collection); education (Nicolson and MacIver 2003, MacLeod 2003, McLeod 2007, Robertson 2006). This section concentrates on a few key areas of language in society but because of space restrictions is by no means a complete overview.

For a good general historical overview of Gaelic in Education see MacLeod (2003). Although as indicated above the 1872 Education Act did not mention Gaelic, in 1905 a Lower Grade examination was introduced and in 1916 a Higher paper was established. The 1918 Education Act did take some cognisance of Gaelic: education authorities in Gaelic-speaking areas were required to make some provision for Gaelic. It was not until the 1960s that any real attempt was made to introduce Gaelic as the language of the classroom. The old Inverness-shire Council introduced a voluntary scheme in the 1960s which would give the Gaelic-speaking pupil the opportunity to use more Gaelic in the classroom, but as MacLeod points out 'its success was restricted to schools which happened to have enthusiastic teachers' (MacLeod 2003: 2).

The next major development in Gaelic education happened in the new political area of the Western Isles. The newly formed Western Isles Island Council (Comhairle nan Eilean and later, with no English version, as Comhairle nan Eilean Siar) adopted a bilingual policy. As part of this it created the Bilingual Education Project – one of this project's five main tasks was to 'devise situations and activities which will stimulate children to use Gaelic as a natural language for the exploration and description of experience' (Murray and Morrison 1984: 5). The bilingual project, although interesting and commendable in spirit, did not, as demonstrated by the demographics, stop the attrition of Gaelic in the Western Isles and it did not provide a framework for the consistent use of Gaelic as the language of instruction.

The end of the twentieth century saw the development of Gaelic Medium Education (GME). To no small extent GME owes its existence to the establishment of the Gaelic pre-school system. Comhairle nan Sgoiltean Àraich (the Gaelic Playgroup Association) was established in 1982 and it brought to Scotland a system of immersion language learning for pre-school children; by 1994 it had 148 groups and 2,620 children attending (MacLeod 2003:14). In recent years the number of children attending CNSA groups has waned; this is to a great extent to do with the statutory provision now made by local authorities at pre-school level.

The establishment of a network of Gaelic playschools throughout the country began to create a demand for Gaelic to be available to children when they entered into formal, primary education. The local authorities were required to respond to the demand created by the children attending playgroups. The first Gaelic-medium units were established in 1985–6 in Glasgow, Inverness, Portree and Breasclete (Lewis). GME was assisted by special funding from the Scottish Office and continues to be supported by a Scheme of Specific Grants for Gaelic from the Scottish Government. Gaelic-medium education increased fairly rapidly for the first dozen years or so; subsequently the rate of increase started to slow down and even decline. Each year the number of entrants to GME is measured by Strathclyde University. In 2008, there were 2,206 pupils in GME, primary, throughout Scotland.[2] While early education acts made little specific provision for Gaelic, The Standards in Scotland's Schools, etc., Act 2000 states that there is a duty on all education authorities in Scotland to publish an annual statement of improvement objectives which must include an account of the ways in which they will provide GME or the circumstances in which it will be supported. Gaelic is also listed as a national priority in the Education (National Priorities)(Scotland) Order 2000.

To date Gaelic Medium Education at secondary level is limited to the delivery of certain subjects in some secondary schools with the exception of Sgoil Ghàidhlig Ghlaschu which opened in August 2006; this is a 3–18 Gaelic Medium school with Pre-5, Primary and Secondary provision. Sgoil Ghàidhlig Ghlaschu aims to develop new courses and deliver a full curriculum through the medium of Gaelic. In academic year 2008 throughout the whole of Scotland, there were 397 pupils receiving GME at secondary level. Generally the subjects offered through the medium of Gaelic are severely limited in most schools. Education provision is supported at primary and secondary levels by the National Gaelic Resource Centre: Stòrlann Nàiseanta na Gàidhlig which was established in 1999. In addition to GME, Gaelic continues to be offered as a second language in both primary and secondary schools.

Some research has been carried out on the attainments of pupils attending GME units and schools (Johnstone et al. 1999) and regular assessments are made of the schools and units as part of Her Majesty's Inspectorate system: the assessment is on the whole positive with Johnstone (et al.) showing that some pupils attending GME outperformed English-medium pupils. However, some Inspection Reports raise concern about the level of linguistic competencies amongst some pupils; recent doctoral work on Gaelic education has been completed by Martine Müller and Irene Pollock; both works consider aspects of GME relating to Gaelic literacy. For example, Müller shows that 'it is easier for pupils to write down their thoughts in English than in Gaelic' and that Gaelic essays show many interferences from English in terms of 'phonology, morphophonology, morphology, syntax, lexicon and idiom' (Müller 2006: 137). More work is needed in assessing how language competencies are being maintained in the GM schools.

As Gaelic education has grown in the primary and secondary sectors, likewise it has continued to grow in the tertiary sector. As discussed above, Edinburgh University established a Chair in Celtic in the nineteenth century; Glasgow University introduced lectures on Celtic literature in 1900, and Aberdeen University followed in 1916. The first holder of the Chair of Celtic at Glasgow was Angus Matheson (1912–62); having already been the Head of the Celtic Department from 1938, he was made Chair in 1956 (Thomson 1994: 197). The University of Aberdeen did not have a Chair in Celtic until 1993; to date Donald Meek has been the only holder of this Chair, having left post in 2001. Aberdeen and Strathclyde Universities offer teacher training in Gaelic, having subsumed the teacher training colleges the Northern College and Jordanhill respectively.

An interesting and significant development in tertiary level education in the twentieth century is the establishment of the Gaelic college Sabhal Mòr Ostaig (hereafter SMO) in Sleat on the Isle of Skye in 1973. Roger Hutchinson has recorded the remarkable history of the college, noting the key activists and employees at the early stages.[3] The college operates now as partner in the UHI Millennium Institute: a network of colleges and research centres across the Highlands and islands. Gaelic Higher and Further Education is also available at Lews Castle College and at the SMO and Lews satellite centres in Islay and Benbecula, respectively.

Outside Highland areas, Gaelic is also taught at Further Education level in Clydebank College and is sometimes available at Ayr College, Telford College, Kilmarnock College, Jewel and Esk, Perth College, Stow College, Orkney College, Langside College and Reid Kerr College. Its presence in many of these places is very much dependent on student demand which is not steady; it is with this in mind that the Scottish Funding Council established small cohort funding to support this kind of teaching in 2008.

Adult education, in the form of Gaelic night-classes, summer and weekend courses and intensive courses, are available at different levels in various locations throughout Scotland (and abroad). To date there has been little coordination of effort and the number of Gaelic learners achieving fluency through these methods has been limited; MacCaluim (2007) has produced an extensive study of the Gaelic learner. There is little doubt, however, that although there is evidence to show that relatively few who begin on the path to learn Gaelic become fluent, there are increasing numbers of fluent Gaelic speakers who have learnt the language in non-traditional environments (i.e. not through intergenerational transmission), either as adults or through the GME systems and these speakers do not necessarily relate to traditional Gaelic culture. MacCaluim (2006), McEwan-Fujita (2010) and McLeod (2007) have explored this phenomenon to some degree, but this is likely to be an area for future research and one which will challenge language policy-makers.

Gaelic periodical publishing continued in the same vein as in the late nineteenth century in the early twentieth century. MacLeod cites the Hon. Ruaraidh Erskine of Mar as one of the key figures of this era having been involved in five periodicals, the most significant of which was *Guth na Bliadhna* (1904–25) (MacLeod 1977: 210). Mar was keen to improve and develop Gaelic prose writing and his periodicals provided a vehicle for fiction and non-fiction alike. The birth of Gaelic fiction writing can be attributed to this era (see Watson 2008 and elsewhere in this book); one of the contributors to Mar's periodicals, John MacCormick, was a prolific writer of stories and published the first Gaelic novel *Dùn-Aluinn* (1912) (see Watson 2008 and Kidd 2006). MacCormick's novel was followed swiftly by two others by Angus Robertson (*An t-Ogha Mór* 1913) and James MacLeod (*Cailin Sgiathanach* 1923); critics of Gaelic literature have noted these works for their presence and their contribution to the development of prose writing, but have not been excited about their literary merits. As some writers continued to experiment with Gaelic in fiction, others continued to use it for dialogues and essays in the periodicals and some newspapers. The longest-running periodical of the nineteenth and early twentieth century is An Comunn Gaidhealach's *An Deo-Ghreine*, later *An Gaidheal* (1905–67); MacLeod does not rate highly these periodicals' contribution to the development of Gaelic literature; he dismisses them as 'rather pedestrian' (MacLeod 1977: 214).

Gaelic periodical publishing was never to be so active again and no new publication is seen until 1952 when *Gairm* was first published by Derick Thomson and Finlay J. MacDonald: it ran until 2002 with a total of 200 issues. Over the years *Gairm* has had articles on a vast diversity of topics, science, religion, traditions, travel, etc., and has also provided a platform for creative writing; it has been accredited with invigorating the Gaelic short story (Macleod and Watson 2007: 273). 'Gairm' was also the name of Thomson's publishing company, which was one of the most prolific Gaelic publishing houses of the twentieth century. The journal *Gairm* was succeeded by *Gath* (2003–7, eight issues).

Other types of non-fiction prose in the twentieth and twenty-first century include journalism, academic essays and official printed matter. To date there is no regular Gaelic newspaper. An Comunn launched *An Gàidheal Ùr* in 1996 in a newsletter-type format to members and then increasing distribution through insertion in the *West Highland Free Press* and latterly online; *An Gàidheal Ùr* ceased production in March 2009. Mike Cormack discusses the need for a weekly paper in Gaelic (Cormack 2003), but to date there are at best weekly columns and occasional news-reporting in a smattering of papers in Scotland; these include: *The Scotsman*, *The Scotland on Sunday*, *The Press and Journal*, *Inverness Courier*, *Ross-shire Journal*, *West Highland Free Press* (which probably contains the most Gaelic on a weekly basis), *The Oban Times*, and *The Stornoway Gazette*. Some community papers also feature Gaelic, and Clì Gàidhlig produce a bilingual magazine quarterly aimed specifically at supporting Gaelic learners. There are also Gaelic contributions in the *Church of Scotland's Life and Work* and in *The Scottish Catholic Observer*.

One of the biggest growth areas for Gaelic writing in the twenty-first century is in official documents with many public bodies being required via the Gaelic Language (Scotland) Act 2005 to produce printed matter in Gaelic as well as in English; other organisations produce documents but are not necessarily required to. Wilson McLeod has questioned the linguistic accuracy of some of these documents and presses for control in terminology, orthography and grammar in such documents (McLeod 2000).

In relation to the number of Gaelic speakers, Gaelic writing appears to be abundant; writers of course must be supported by publishers. MacLeod notes that the most important publishers in the early twentieth century were: Alexander MacLaren & Son, Gardner, MacKay and Sinclair (MacLeod 1977: 209). As noted above, Gairm was one of the most important Gaelic publishers from the middle to the end of the twentieth century; other significant publishers of this era include: Club Leabhar Inbhir Nis (late 1960s and early 1970s); Acair Earranta (established in Stornoway in 1977, initially Acair concentrated on publishing Gaelic school material, but has expanded this remit); and Aberdeen and Glasgow University Celtic departments which have both had imprints for fiction and scholarly books. Gaelic publishing is supported by the Gaelic Books Council, established in 1968; the Books Council subsidises the publication of Gaelic books and supports writers and publishers. One of its recent projects, Ùr-sgeul, has been particularly successful in promoting Gaelic prose for adults and through the publisher CLÀR has brought about seventeen novels and seven collections of short stories (June 2009), giving a great boost to fiction writing. Other mainstream Scottish publishers also publish Gaelic materials: including Birlinn, Canongate and Dunedin Academic Press.

A new vehicle for Gaelic in the twentieth century was, of course, broadcasting; BBC radio first broadcast Gaelic in 1923, but it was not until after the Second World War that radio broadcasting became more regular: at the time of writing the BBC broadcast around sixty-five hours of Gaelic language a week; they are the only regular broadcaster of Gaelic radio programmes. Broadcasting in Gaelic has been supported by various legislative initiatives (see Dunbar 2003, 2006): in 1991 a Gaelic television fund of £9.5 million per annum was established and a new organisation Comataidh Telebhisean Gàidhlig (Gaelic Television Committee), established in 1990, were charged with administering this fund. This enabled a major increase in Gaelic broadcasting – there was a target to create around 200 hours of new and original television per annum. Following the Broadcasting Act 1996, the Committee was required to broaden its remit to include supporting radio broadcasting and it thus changed its name to Comataidh Craolaidh Gàidhlig (Gaelic Broadcasting Committee). A further legislative action, the Communications Act 2003, required a new body, the Gaelic Media Service (Seirbheis nam Meadhanan Gàidhlig), to replace CCG; SMG had extended statutory powers (Dunbar 2003: 73). The biggest development in recent years in broadcasting is the creation in 2008 of a new Gaelic digital television channel, BBC Alba: a partnership venture between the BBC and MG Alba (the operating name of Seirbheis nam Meadhanan Gàidhlig or Gaelic Media Service); the channel broadcasts for around seven hours per day. Some Gaelic programming continues on the terrestrial channels, including the independent Scottish stations. The BBC have also developed their Gaelic web-services significantly and provide excellent Gaelic language pages. The legislative development of Gaelic broadcasting has been documented and contextualised by Dunbar (2003, 2006); he and others, such as Mike Cormack, have also used modern language planning theory to develop the argument for supporting Gaelic language broadcasting as a tool in reversing language shift (Cormack and Hourigan 2007). Some interesting research has been done on the impact of Gaelic broadcasting in the Gaelic language community (for example MacNeil 2003; MacNeil and MacDonald 1997), but there is certainly room for more research in this area. There has been little research done on the language used by broadcasters, other than a significant piece of work by William Lamb about the registers used in certain broadcasting situations (1999, 2008).

While the nineteenth century saw the burgeoning of Gaelic and Highland societies, the twentieth century witnessed the professionalisation of Gaelic. While many of the societies established in the nineteenth century continue to exist, a number of organisations and businesses have been set up since the Second World War to provide services and facilities to Gaelic speakers. Under Section 23 of the National Heritage (Scotland) Act 1985, the Scottish Office, as it then was, was required to give funding for Gaelic cultural organisations. Bòrd na Gàidhlig continue this responsibility and fund fifteen organisations they classify as 'principal partners' (for a discussion on Bòrd na Gàidhlig, see Dunbar in this collection); these organisations are involved in a range of development activities within the arts (An Comunn Gaidhealach, Fèisean nan Gàidheal, Pròiseact nan Ealan), education (Colaisde a' Chaisteil, Sabhal Mòr Ostaig, Comhairle nan Sgoiltean Àraich, Stòrlann Nàiseanta na Gàidhlig), community (An Lòchran, Glasgow's Gaelic Centre, Ionad Chaluim Chille Ìle, a Gaelic education and cultural centre in Islay) and publishing (Acair and the Gaelic Books Council); others are Clì Gàidhlig (formally Comann an Luchd-Ionnsachaidh), the Gaelic access and promotion organisation with a special remit amongst Gaelic learners and non-native speakers; Colmcille, a tripartite organisation which promotes Gaelic and Irish in Scotland, Northern Ireland and the Republic of Ireland; Tobar an Dualchais, a significant multi-partner project involved in the archiving of thousands of Gaelic and Scots recordings in digital format. One of the most important Gaelic organisations is Comunn na Gàidhlig which, before the establishment of Bòrd na Gàidhlig, was the main Gaelic development agency and is one of Bòrd na Gàidhlig's most important partners, especially in initiatives involving the community, education, younger people and strategies and promotion.

To date, little research has been carried out on the development sector or on any of the organisations – other than commissioned histories of An Comunn Gaidhealach and Sabhal Mòr Ostaig (a history was commissioned for Comunn na Gàidhlig, but this has never appeared). Types of research activity carried out in this sector have mostly been of a commercial nature and/or of a reflective nature (see for example 'The Participants' Story: Attitudinal research on the Fèis movement in Scotland', Stephen Broad and Jacqueline France RSAMD National Centre for Research in the Performing Arts). Emily McEwan-Fujita produced a critique ostensibly of part of the funding process of Gaelic development and based it primarily around Comunn na Gàidhlig's Gaelic in the Community Scheme (McEwan-Fujita 2005).

It is evident from the above list that there is a propensity of Gaelic organisations that have the arts and culture as their main activity and some research, like the aforementioned, has been carried out in this field. Key researchers in this area are Sproull and Chalmers (1998, 2006); they have mostly concentrated on the economic value of Gaelic arts; little has been done on considering why the arts scene flourishes so well in such a small community or the linguistic value of government-sponsored artistic activity (although this was touched upon by Alison Laing, 2006). An interesting piece of research that remains to be done is a consideration of the role of the various Gaelic arts in terms of shaping and strengthening a sense of Gaelic identity and is there any specific reason that the Gaelic community seems to produce a significant quantity of varied and quality artistic expressions. Is there something in the Gaelic psyche (if indeed there is such a thing) that makes Gaelic culture a performance-based culture that encourages creativity and expression? For example, although the twentieth century saw the demise of the traditional cèilidh-house, it witnessed the birth of Gaelic drama and choral and competition singing (at Mods), all of which have taken root and flourished within society. Drama was deliberately created at the turn of the twentieth century; the first Gaelic play, according to Donald John MacLeod, was performed in Edinburgh in 1902. At the time of writing, there must be around 350 Gaelic plays in existence: An Comunn Gaidhealach have a database of well over 300 Gaelic plays, and the BBC also have a large number of Gaelic plays; there are now a handful of volumes of plays by single authors and several pamphlets of single-act plays, but the vast majority of plays are unpublished. Currently there are Gaelic drama groups in Glasgow, Edinburgh, Inverness and the islands; in the 1930s John Bannerman reports on one particular festival held in North Uist which lasted for three days and attracted five drama teams from this island alone (Bannerman 1934: 166). There are approximately thirty adult Gaelic choirs in Scotland and several outwith. The Gaelic arts are not restricted to choirs and drama: an active steering group, Pròiseact nan Ealan (The National Gaelic Arts Agency), established in 1987 by the Scottish Arts Council, is at the forefront of many innovative projects, for example: establishing the *fèis* umbrella group Fèisean nan Gàidheal, national Gaelic youth theatre, Gaelic children's comics, theatre-in-education, etc.; for a discussion on the activities of PNE up until 2000, see MacLean (2000). More recent initiatives by PNE include *An Leabhar Mòr: The Great Book of Gaelic* (a project which brought together 150 poets, visual artists, calligraphers and typographers from Ireland and Scotland) and more recently *St Kilda*, a multi-media, music-theatre production based on the story of St Kilda which took place in six European locations in June 2007 and which cost in the region of £1.5 million to stage.

Of course with the growth of Gaelic education, broadcasting and development, etc., there has been an increase in Gaelic-speaking employment opportunities. Some research is coming out in this area, including some interesting doctoral work (Macleod 2009); this is also an area of interest to policy-makers and commercial research into this area has been commissioned.

CONCLUSION

As Gaelic enters more areas of public life in the twenty-first century, there is increasing need for research here: policies concerning Gaelic need to be supported by up-to-date research, for example in the domains of education, the media, publishing, the church, language planning (see

Dunbar in this volume), etc. Current research need not be restricted to these areas, however, and there is still scope for good academic research over and above the kind which might relate to policy-makers: language in society scholarship can be more eclectic than this and also has to look at how Gaelic is used and regarded in society (as discussed by both MacKinnon and McEwan-Fujita in this volume); it can include the interface between the arts (including literature) and society. But of course, this research must not be restricted to current matters; there are still many research issues untackled in the nineteenth and twentieth centuries. A reflective history of Gaelic in the twentieth century would be enormously interesting given how much society has changed within that period; similarly more focused studies on language within specific social or geographic situations would be most welcome.

BIBLIOGRAPHY

http://www.bbc.co.uk/alba/tasglann/timeline/
http://www.cnag.org.uk
http://www.scotland.gov.uk/Topics/ArtsCultureSport/arts/gaelic
http://www.smo.uhi.ac.uk

Anderson, Robert David (2002), *Education and the Scottish People,
1750–1918*, Oxford: Oxford University Press.
Bannerman, John R. (1934), 'Fèill nan Dealbh-chluichean ann an
Uidhist-a-Tuath', *An Gaidheal*, An Lùnasdal, pp. 166–8.
Broad, Stephen and France, Jacqueline, (n.d.), 'The Participants' Story:
Attitudinal Research on the Fèis movement in Scotland', RSAMD
National Centre for Research in the Performing Arts.
Cameron, A. D. (1986), *Go Listen to the Crofters*, Stornoway: Acair.
Chalmers, Douglas (2003), 'The Economic Impact of Gaelic Arts
and Culture', unpublished PhD dissertation, Glasgow Caledonian
University.
Chalmers, Douglas and Danson, Mike (2006), 'Language and Economic
Development – Complementary or Antagonistic' in McLeod (2006:
239–56).
Cormack, Mike (2003), 'The Case for a Weekly Gaelic Newspaper in
Scotland', in John Kirk & Dónall Ó Baoill (eds), *Towards our Goals
in Broadcasting, the Press, the Performing Arts and the Economy:
Minority Languages in Northern Ireland, the Republic of Ireland and
Scotland*, Belfast: Queen's University Belfast, pp. 95–9.
Cormack, Mike and Hourigan, Niamh (2007), *Minority Language
Media*, Clevedon: Multilingual Matters.
Dunbar, Robert (2003), 'Gaelic Medium Broadcasting: Reflections on
the Legal Framework from a Sociolinguistic Perspective', in John
Kirk & Dónall Ó Baoill (eds), *Towards our Goals in Broadcasting, the
Press, the Performing Arts and the Economy: Minority Languages
in Northern Ireland, the Republic of Ireland and Scotland*, Belfast:
Queen's University of Belfast, pp. 73–82.
Dunbar, Robert (2006), 'Gaelic in Scotland: The Legal and Institutional
Framework', in McLeod (2006: 1–24).
Durkacz, Victor Edward (1983), *The Decline of the Celtic Languages*,
Edinburgh: John Donald Publishers.

Hunter, James (1976), *The Making of the Crofting Community*, Edinburgh: John Donald Publishers Ltd.

Hunter, James (2000), *Last of the Free: A Millennial History of the Highlands and Islands of Scotland*, Edinburgh: Mainstream Publishing.

Hutchinson, Roger (2005), *A Waxing Moon: The Modern Gaelic Revival*, Edinburgh: Mainstream Publishing.

Johnstone, R., Harlen, W., MacNeil, M., Stradling, R. and Thorpe, G. (1999), *The Attainment of Pupils Receiving Gaelic Medium Education in Scotland*, Stirling: Scottish CILT.

Kidd, Sheila (2000), 'Social Control and Social Criticism: The Nineteenth-Century Còmhradh', *Scottish Gaelic Studies* XX, pp. 67–87.

Kidd, Sheila (2003), 'The Rev. Alexander MacGregor: The Writer Behind the Pen-names', *Transactions of the Gaelic Society of Inverness* LXI, 1998–2000, pp. 1–24.

Kidd, Sheila (2006), 'The Forgotten First: John MacCormick's Dùn Àluinn', *Scottish Gaelic Studies* XXII, pp. 197–219.

Kidd, Sheila (ed.) (2007), *Glasgow: Baile Mòr nan Gàidheal*, Glasgow: Dept. Of Celtic, University of Glasgow.

Laing, Alison (2006), 'Cruthachadh is Cleachdadh: Ceistean air Planadh Cànain agus na h-Ealain Ghàidhlig', in McLeod (2006: 199–210).

Lamb, William (1999), 'A Diachronic Account of Gaelic News-speak: The Development and Expansion of a Register', *Scottish Gaelic Studies* XIX, pp. 141–71.

Lamb, William (2008), *Scottish Gaelic Speech and Writing: Register Variation in an Endangered Language*, Belfast: Cló Ollscoil na Banríona.

MacCaluim, Alasdair (2006), 'Air Iomall an Iomaill? Luchd-ionnsachaidh na Gàidhlig ann an Ath-thilleadh Gluasad Cànain', in McLeod (2006: 185–98).

MacCaluim, Alasdair (2007), *Reversing Language Shift: The Social Identity of Scottish Gaelic Learners*, Belfast: Cló Ollscoil na Banríona.

MacColl, Allan W. (2006), *Land, Faith and the Crofting Community: Christianity and Social Criticism in the Highlands of Scotland 1846–1893*, Edinburgh: Edinburgh University Press.

MacDonald, Kenneth (2007), 'Glasgow and Gaelic Writing', in Sheila Kidd (ed.), *Glasgow: Baile Mòr nan Gàidheal*, Glasgow: Department of Celtic, University of Glasgow, pp. 186–215.

MacDonald, Mairi A. (1970), 'History of the Gaelic Society of Inverness from 1871–1971', *Transactions of the Gaelic Society of Inverness* 46, pp. 1–21.

Macdonald, Sharon (1997), *Reimagining Culture*, Oxford: Berg.

McEwan-Fujita, E. (2005), 'Neoliberalism and Minority Language Planning in the Highlands and Islands of Scotland', *International Journal for the Sociology of Language* 171, pp. 155–71.

McEwan-Fujita, E. (2010), 'Ideology, Affect and Socialization in Language Shift and Revitalization: The Experiences of Adults Learning Gaelic in the Western Isles of Scotland', *Language in Society* 39:1.

MacKinnon, Donald (1883), University of Edinburgh Celtic Chair Inaugural Address, Edinburgh: MacLachlan & Stewart.

MacKinnon, Kenneth (1990), 'A Century of the Census: Gaelic in Twentieth Centuy Focus', in Derick S. Thomson D. (ed.), *Gaelic and Scots in Harmony*, Glasgow: Department of Celtic, University of Glasgow, pp. 163–83.

MacKinnon, Kenneth (1991), *Gaelic: A Past and Future Prospect*, Edinburgh: Saltire Society.

MacLean, Malcolm (2000), 'Parallel Universes: Gaelic Arts Development in Scotland, 1985–2000', in Gordon McCoy and Maolcholaim Scott (eds), *Aithne na nGael: Gaelic Identities*, Belfast: Institute of Irish Studies, Queen's University Belfast.

MacLennan, Ishbel (2003), 'BBC Craoladh nan Gaidheal: Co Sinn' in John Kirk & Dónall Ó Baoill (eds), *Towards our Goals in Broadcasting, the Press, the Performing Arts and the Economy: Minority Languages in Northern Ireland, the Republic of Ireland and Scotland*, Belfast: Queen's University Belfast, pp. 67–72.

MacLeod, Donald John (1977), 'Gaelic Prose', *Transactions of the Gaelic Society of Inverness* 49, pp. 198–230.

MacLeod, Donald John (2003), 'An Historical Overview', in Nicolson and MacIver (2003: 1–14).

Macleod, M. and Watson, M. (2007), 'In the Shadow of the Bard: The Gaelic Short Story, Novel and Drama since the Early Twentieth Century', in Ian Brown (ed.), *The Edinburgh History of Scottish Literature*, Vol. 3, Edinburgh: Edinburgh University Press, pp. 273–82.

Macleod, Marsaili (2008), 'The Meaning of Work in the Gaelic Labour Market in the Highlands and Islands of Scotland', unpublished PhD dissertation, University of Aberdeen.

MacLeod, Marsaili (2009), 'Gaelic Language Skills in the Workplace', in John Kirk and Dónall Ó Baoill (eds), *Language and Economic Development: Northern Ireland, the Republic of Ireland, and Scotland*, Belfast: Belfast Studies in Language, Culture and Politics 19. Cló Ollscoil na Banríona.

McLeod, Wilson (2000), 'Official Gaelic: Problems in the Translation of Public Documents', *Scottish Language* 19, pp. 100–16.

McLeod, Wilson (2001), 'Gaelic in the New Scotland: Politics, Rhetoric and Public Discourse', *Journal of Ethnopolitics and Minority Issues in Europe*; http://www.ecmi.de/jemie/download/JEMIE02MacLeod28-11-01.pdf (accessed 28 August 2009).

McLeod, Wilson (2006), *Revitalising Gaelic in Scotland: Policy, Planning and Public Discourse*, Edinburgh: Dunedin Academic Press.

McLeod, Wilson (2007), *Gàidhealtachdan Ùra, Nua-Ghaeltachtaí*, Edinburgh: Ceiltis agus Eòlas na h-Alba, Oilthigh Dhùn Èideann.

MacNeil, Catherine Ann (2003), 'The State of Gaelic Broadcasting in Scotland', in John Kirk and Dónall Ó Baoill (eds), *Towards our Goals in Broadcasting, the Press, the Performing Arts and the Economy: Minority Languages in Northern Ireland, the Republic of Ireland and Scotland*, Belfast: Queen's University Belfast, pp. 60–6.

MacNeil, Morag and MacDonald, Brian K. (1997), *Gaelic Television Programmes as a Resource for Language Learning*, Sleat, Isle of Skye: Lèirsinn Research Centre.

MacPhail, I. M. M. (1977), 'Prelude to the Crofters' War, 1870–80', *Transactions of the Gaelic Society of Inverness* 49, pp. 159–88.

Meek, Donald E. (1996), *The Scottish Highlands, the Churches and Gaelic Culture*, Geneva: Gospel and Cultures Pamphlet 11, WCC Publications.

Meek, Donald (2000), 'God and Gaelic: The Highland Churches and Gaelic Cultural Identity', in Gordon McCoy and Maolcholaim Scott (eds), *Aithne na nGael Gaelic Identities*, Belfast: Institute of Irish Studies, Queen's University Belfast.

Meek, Donald (2007), 'Gaelic Literature in the Nineteenth Century', in Susan Manning, Ian Brown, Thomas Clancy and Murray Pittock (eds), *The Edinburgh History of Scottish Literature*, Vol. 2, Edinburgh: Edinburgh University Press, pp. 253–66.

Morgan, Peadar (2000), 'The Gael is Dead: Long Live the Gaelic: The Changing Relationship between Native and Learner Gaelic Users', in Gordon McCoy and Maolcholaim Scott (eds), *Aithne na nGael Gaelic Identities*, Belfast: Institute of Irish Studies, Queen's University Belfast.

Müller, Martina (2006), 'Language Use, Language Attitudes and Gaelic Writing Ability Among Secondary Pupils in the Isle of Skye', in McLeod (2006: 119–38).

Murray, John and Morrison, Catriona (1984), *Bilingual Primary Education in the Western Isles: Report of the Bilingual Education Project 1975–1981*, Stornoway: Acair, 1984.

Nicolson, Margaret and MacIver, Matthew (eds) (2003), *Gaelic Medium Education*, Edinburgh: Dunedin Academic Press.

Pollock, Irene (2007), 'The Acquisition of Literacy in Gaelic-medium Primary Classrooms in Scotland', unpublished PhD dissertation, University of Edinburgh.

Robertson, Boyd (2006), 'Foghlam Gàidhlig: bho linn gu linn', in McLeod (2006: 87–118).

Sproull, A. and Chalmers, D. (1998), *The Demand for Gaelic Artistic and Cultural Products and Services: Patterns and Impacts*, Report to Proiseact nan Ealan, Glasgow: Department of Economics, Glasgow Caledonian University.

Sproull, Alan and Chalmers, Douglas (2006), *The Demand for Gaelic Arts: Patterns and Impacts – a 10 Year Longitudinal Study*, Glasgow: Cultural Business Group, Caledonian Business School, Glasgow Caledonian University.

Thompson, Frank (1992), *History of An Comunn Gaidhealach – The First Hundred (1891–1991)*, Inverness: An Comunn Gaidhealach.

Thomson, Derick (1994), *The Companion to Gaelic Scotland*, revision of first edn, 1983, Glasgow: Gairm.

Watson, M. (2008), 'Argyll and the Gaelic Prose Fiction of the Early Twentieth Century', *Scottish Gaelic Studies* XXIV, pp. 573–88.

Withers, Charles W. J. (1984), *Gaelic in Scotland 1698–1981*, Edinburgh: John Donald Publishers Ltd.

Withers, Charles W. J. (1988), *Gaelic Scotland: The Transformation of a Culture Region*, London: Routledge.

Withers, Charles W. J. (1998), *Urban Highlanders: Highland-Lowland Migration and Urban Gaelic Culture 1700–1900*, East Linton: Tuckwell Press.

NOTES

1 For more information about the Gaelic Society of Inverness, see their website at http://gsi.org.uk/about/ (accessed 16 September 2009).

2 Comunn na Gàidhlig collate the statistics provided by Strathclyde University on an annual basis; see http://www.cnag.org.uk/munghaidhlig/stats/bunsgoiltean1.php (accessed 19 September 2009).

3   In its first year SMO offered a course in Business and Highland Studies through the medium of Gaelic: seven students attended. Currently SMO have in the region of 100 full-time students, 160 students participating in distance-learning courses and approximately 900 students who attend informal short courses in the summer, most of them relating to Gaelic language or culture (http://www.smo.uhi.ac.uk/gd/colaiste/index.php).

CHAPTER 3

Gaelic Place-names

Richard A. V. Cox

INTRODUCTION

Gaelic is just one of several languages that make up the topo-nymic tapestry of Scotland: principally Anglian, Cumbric, Old Norse, Pictish, Scots, Scottish Standard English and Scottish Gaelic.

Although Gaelic as a community language was restricted to the Highlands and Islands from the mid-sixteenth century – and since that time has receded more or less to the Hebrides and the western seaboard – the evidence of place-names reveals that at one time or another Gaelic-speaking communities thrived throughout most of Scotland: from Aberdeen to St Kilda and from the Borders to Caithness, with settlement of any significance only absent in the south-eastern area of the Borders, in the most northerly part of Caithness and in Orkney and Shetland (see under Chronology, below).

SYNTAX

The word order of names may be simple or complex. Simple names consist normally of a simple noun phrase or simplex, i.e. a noun with or without its article, with or without one or more accompanying adjec-tives: *An Cnoc* 'the hill' (Knock, Lewis), *Am Baile Mòr* 'the large village' (Baile Mor, Iona), *A' Chille* 'the church', *A' Chille Mhòr* 'the large church' (Kilmore, Skye). An adjective, or a noun acting adjectivally, preceding a noun forms a grammatical compound with its noun: *An Sean Bhaile* 'the old village' (Shanwell, Moray), *An Cùl Phort* 'the rear harbour' (Coulport, Dunbarton).

Complex names consist of two or more simplexes, each in genitival relationship (here denoted by ×) to the preceding one: *Baile × na Cille* 'the village of the church' (Balnakilly, Perth), *Allt × Baile × na Cille* 'the stream of the village of the church'. Prepositional names occur also: *Eadar Dhà Chaolas* 'between two straits' (Eddrachillis, Sutherland). (Further, see Oftedal 1980; Cox 2002a.)

ONOMASTIC STRUCTURE

Names may consist of a generic element (ᵍ), in which, for simplicity's sake, the article can be included: ᵍ*An Cnoc*, or a generic plus a qualifying or specific element (ˢ): ᵍ*Am Baile* ˢ*Mòr*. Where names have two qualifying elements, the second qualifying element (ᵐ) modifies the generic group (ᴳ) consisting of generic + specific: ᴳ(ᵍ*Cnoc* ˢ*Mòr*) ᵐ*na h-Aibhne* 'the large hill of the river' (Knock, Lewis). Some qualifying elements, especially modifying elements, have a contrastive function (ᶜ): ᵍ*A' Bheinn* ˢ*Mhaoil* ᶜ*Mhòr* ~ ᵍ*A' Bheinn* ˢ*Mhaoil* ᶜ*Bheag* 'the greater/lesser bare mountain' (Breasclete, Lewis), ᵍ*A' Bhuail'* ˢ*Fhalach* ᶜ*Àrd* ~ ᵍ*A' Bhuail'* ˢ*Fhalach* ᶜ*Ìosal* 'the upper/lower hidden enclosure' (Borrowston, Lewis). On occasion, the contrastive element may precede the specific element: ᵍ*Loch* ᶜ*Mòr* ˢ*Gil Speireig* ~ ᵍ*Loch* ᶜ*Beag* ˢ*Gil Speireig* 'the greater/lesser lake of the ravine of the hawk' (Achmore, Lewis). In prepositional names such as *Eadar Dhà Chaolas*, the generic element is understood – contrast **Beinn Eadar Dhà Loch* 'the mountain between two lochs' (Benderloch, Argyll; see under Stress), in which the generic is stated.

Existing names are frequently used in the formation of new names, so that, for example, a small cattle fold (*buaile bheag*) belonging to the township, *Geàrr' na h-Aibhne* (Garynahine, Lewis), came to be called *Buaile Bheag Geàrr' na h-Aibhne*. While the name literally means 'the little fold of the enclosure of the river', onomastically it means 'the little fold of *Geàrr' na h-Aibhne*', just as the English name, *Fort William Station*, means 'the station of *Fort William*' and not 'the station of William's fort'.

The term *ex nomine* unit is used in such contexts to refer to an element or group of elements that is a former name. Some names consist of more than one unit: *Ceann* (*Loch* [*Mhùideart*]) 'the head of *Loch Mhùideart* (the lake of *Mùideart* [a fiord name borrowed from Norse speakers])' (Kinlochmoidart). Syntactical rules are sometimes broken in names formed in this way, e.g. *Loch a' Bhaile na Dùine* – instead of **Loch Baile na Dùine* (literally, 'the hill of the village of the fort'), because only the last in a series of nouns in a noun phrase is expected to take the article – whose structure is ᵍ*Loch* ˢ*a' Bhaile* ᵐ(*na Dùine*) 'the loch of the village of *An Dùn'*, where the modifier is the genitive of the township name (Doune, Lewis). (Further, see Cox 1991; Cox 2002a.)

STRESS

Generally, in natural speech, only one element bears full stress (') in qualified names, the remainder weak stress or half-stress (ˌ). The Gaelic article carries no stress. Full stress falls upon the specific element or, where it occurs, the modifier or, where it occurs, the contrastive modifier: ᵍ*Am* ˌ*Baile* ˢ'*Mòr*, ᵍˌ*Baile* ˢ*na* '*Cille*, ᵍ*A*' ˌ*Bheinn* ˢˌ*Mhaoil* ᶜ'*Mhòr*.

Where the specific, modifier or contrastive modifier are units consisting of more than one element, stress falls upon their own internal qualifying constituent: ᵍˌ*Ceann* ˢˌ*Loch* '*Mhùideart*.

Two full stresses may occur where a generic group is followed by a modifying or contrastive unit: ᴳ(ᵍˌ*Buaile* ˢ'*Bheag*) ᵐˌ*Geàrr' na* '*h-Aibhne*; or where a contrastive modifier precedes another qualifier: ᵍˌ*Loch* ᶜ'*Mòr* ˢˌ*Gil* '*Speireig* ~ ᵍˌ*Loch* ᶜ'*Beag* ˢˌ*Gil* '*Speireig*.

In the case of '*Meadarloch* (Benderloch; see under Phonology), stress has gravitated to the first, generic element. In prepositional names such as ˌ*Eadar* ˌ*Dhà* '*Chaolas* ([ˌɛdər ˌaˑ 'xɯːʟəs]), full stress has been drawn to the final, nominal element. (Further, see Cox 2002a.)

MORPHOLOGY

Gaelic place-names normally preserve traditional morphological features, specifically suffix, case and plural formations.

Suffixes with the general sense 'place of' found more or less frequently in place-names include: *-an*: *Riabhachan* (*riabhach* 'tawny' – Glenshiel); *Dòbhran* (*dobhar* 'water' – *Beinn Dòbhrain* – Ben Doran, Tyndrum); *-ag*: *A' Chraobhag* (*craobh* 'tree' – Borrowston, Lewis); *-ach*: *Feàrnach* (*feàrn* 'alder' – Fearnach, Argyll); *Dùnaidh* (Early Gaelic [EG] *Dúnaigh*, dative of *Dúnach* < EG *dún*, Scottish Gaelic (ScG) *dùn* 'fort' – Dounie, Ross); *Ràthach* (*ràth* 'fort' – Ratho, Mid Lothian; Nicolaisen 1996; Ó Maolalaigh 1998); and *-aidh*: *Camasaidh* (*camas* 'bay' – Gairloch). (Further, see Watson [1904] 1976; Cox 2002a.)

There are several names in the east of Scotland, whose proposed constructions with *-an* (< *-ín* etc.) have not been satisfactorily explained, e.g. (from Fife) Knockdavie (?< *cnoc* 'hill' + *dubh* 'black' + suffix), Pitcorthie (?< *peit* 'holding' + EG *coirthe* 'standing-stone' + suffix). If these examples are the result of a Gaelic development, they either break syntactical rules – unusually and spectacularly – or they represent an innovation in naming structures in which a name such as X has been used in the creation of a new name by the addition of a suffix: X-*an* 'X place'; neither solution is readily acceptable, though we may yet have to accept one of them. Contrast expected usage in Logie (< EG *lag* 'hollow' or **log* 'special place, church' + suffix). (Further, see Ó Maolalaigh 1998, Taylor 2006.)

Gender anomaly, e.g. *Beinn na Dùine* ('the mountain of the fort' – Carloway, Lewis) – in which *dùn* is apparently feminine, whereas it is masculine in the modern language – may be precipitated by loss of the neuter gender. (Further, see Ó Maolalaigh 1998; Cox 2002a.)

Case markers are slowly being dispensed with in the spoken language, and this is occasionally reflected in more recent coinages – or sometimes re-coinages – of place-names, e.g. ᵍ*Allt* ˢ*an Loch Dhubh* (Carloway, Lewis) – as opposed to **Allt an Loch Dhuibh* 'the stream of *An Loch Dubh*' – which partially preserves the radical form of the *ex nomine* unit.

There is a tendency for names to be transmitted in oblique (normally dative) case forms, reflecting the context in which they are, or once were, commonly used: *An t-Sean Bhaile* (besides *An Sean Bhaile* – Shawbost, Lewis) – and this can be reflected in anglicised forms of names: *An Tulaich* (< *An Tulach* 'the hill' – Tullich, Ross). (Further, see Watson [1904] 1976; Cox 2002a.)

Nevertheless, the nomenclature is generally conservative in nature and contains ample examples of traditional or archaic inflexions, e.g. *Creagan Biorach na Cailliche Mòire* 'the pointed hillock of the large old woman or hag' (as opposed to a modern-day **Creagan Biorach na Caillich Mhòir*, or similar – South Shawbost, Lewis), *Cnoc an Arbh* (as opposed to modern **Cnoc an Arbhair* – Doune, Lewis) and *Beinn na Dùine*, above, in which the specific shows an *s*-stem inflexion, as opposed to a modern-day *o*-stem, viz **Beinn an Dùin*.

Similarly, with plural endings, for example the vocalic endings: *Na Toma Dubha* 'the dark hills' (with *tom* – Breasclete, Lewis), *Daile Beag* 'the little valleys' (gen. *D(h)aile Beaga*, with *dail* – Dalbeg, Lewis); and with consonantal stems: *Uisgeacha Geala* ('the white waters', with *uisge* – Mull) and *Meall Reamhar Achanna nan Taobhan* 'the broad hill of the meadows of the hillsides' (with *achadh* – Mull). Elements sometimes show a variety of plural morphs on account of analogy and local levelling, e.g. *àirigh* 'shieling': *àireachan, àirichean, àirighean; geàrraidh* 'enclosure, etc.': *geàrracha, geàrrachan, geàrraidhean; beinn* 'mountain': *beinneachan, beanntan*. (Further, see Cox 2002a.)

PHONOLOGY

As stated, place-names may retain older forms of language. On a phono-logical level, this frequently occurs in language contact situations, i.e. when a phonological feature is borrowed into another language, before being overtaken by a sound change in the donor language: Eng. *Pitmedden* (Aberdeen) was borrowed from EG *Peit Medóin* 'the middle holding' (i.e. between two others), while EG -*d*- was still pronounced [ð]; subsequently, this was rendered [d] in Scots, while modern ScG *Peit Meadhain* [ˌpʰɛʰtʲ ˈmĩ-aɴʲ] demonstrates how EG /ð/ has since been lost and replaced by hiatus in this word; contrast Eng. *Pitmain* (Badenoch), also from EG *Peit Medóin*, which was evidently borrowed into Scots after this development took place in Gaelic.

Outwith such special circumstances, place-names are generally adapted phonologically along with, although often at a slower pace than, the lexicon proper. An exception occurs in the occasional survival of relatively archaic instances of eclipsis – although, strictly, they are anomalous from a morphophonological, not phonological, point of view – whereby initial consonants were replaced by related sounds under certain grammatical conditions: (after the preposition *i*) *Meadarloch* < EG *i mBeinn Eadar Dhá Loch* (Eng. *Benderloch*); (after a gen. pl. article) Eng. *Achnagairn* < EG *Ach' na gCárn* 'the meadow of the cairns' (Beauly; after Watson 1926), besides Eng. *Achnacairn* < ScG *Ach' nan Càrn* (Argyll), with the same meaning; and (after a gen. pl. noun) *Cnoc O Dòmod* ('the knoll of *Uì Tòmod* (the descendents of **Tòmod*)', with a loan from the Old Norse man's name, *Hámund* acc. – South Shawbost, Lewis). (Further, see Watson [1904] 1976; Ó Maolalaigh 1998; Cox 2002a.)

LOANS

Language contact is a recurring feature in Gaelic place-name study, with names borrowed particularly from Pictish, Cumbric and Old Norse into Gaelic and from Gaelic into Scots.

Peairt (Eng. *Perth*) < Pict. **Pert* 'copse'; *Lannraig* (Eng. *Lanark*) < Pict. **Lanerc* 'clearing'; **Peofhair* (*Inbhir Pheothair* – Eng. *Inverpeffray*, Perth) < Pict. **Pevr* 'fair one (of a stream)'. It is not always possible to say whether a name contains a loan-name or a loan-word. For example, *Ceann Càrdainn* (Eng. *Kincardine*, Perth, etc.) may contain a loan-word from Pict. *carden* 'thicket' (and therefore mean 'the end of the thicket'), or may contain a Pictish loan-name. In the case of **Urchardan – Gleann*

Urchadain, Eng. *Glen Urquhart* – we are more likely to be dealing with a Pictish loan-name, **Ar Garden* ('by thicket', i.e. 'thicket-side', with initial mutation), because of its antiquity. Adamnan's form, *Airchartdan*, is most probably a gaelicisation of **Ar Garden*, i.e. Old Gaelic **Ar Charden* (with a change to the equivalent Gaelic mutation). The same morphophonological adaptation to Gaelic is seen in *Glaschu* < Cumbric **Glas Gou* ('green valley', with initial mutation of Cumbric **cou* 'hollow', cf. Welsh *cau*) > Scots *Glasgow*. Loan-shifts, involving part translation, also occur, e.g. Cumbric *Din Eitin* ('*Eidyn*'s fort' – the meaning of the specific is uncertain), yielding ScG *Dùn Èideann* and Scots *Edinburgh*, with the generic rendered according to the target language. (Further, see Watson 1926; Jackson [1955] 1980; Nicolaisen [1976] 2001.)

Old Norse loan-names are particularly frequent in the Outer Hebrides, less so along the western seaboard and in the Inner Hebrides. Distinctive forms of Old Norse (ON) loan-names in Gaelic include names in *-siadar/-seadar* < ON *sætr* 'farmstead; sheiling': *Laimiseadar* (pronounced *Laidhmiseadar*, with a diphthong; Eng. *Laimishader*, Lewis) < ON *Lamb-sætr* 'lamb-sheiling'; *-bost* < ON *bólstaðr* 'farmstead': *Siabost* (Eng. *Shawbost*, Lewis) < ON *Sæbólstað* acc. 'sea-farmstead'; *-aigh/-a* < ON *øy* 'island': *Beàrnaraigh* (Eng. *Bernera*, Harris etc.) < ON *Bjarnarøy* '*Bjǫrn*'s island, or the island of the bear', *Djùra* (Eng. *Jura*) < ON *Djúr-øy* 'deer-isle'; *-bhat* < ON *vatn* 'water': *Langabhat* (Eng. *Langavat*, Harris, etc.) < ON *Langavatn* '[the] long lake'; and *-dal* < ON *dalr* 'valley': *Rèinigeadal* (Eng. *Rainigadale*, Harris) < ON *Ræningadal* acc. 'the valley of the robbers'. (Oftedal 1954; Nicolaisen [1976] 2001; Oftedal 1980; Cox 1990a; Cox 1994; Gammeltoft 2000; Gammeltoft 2001; Cox 2002b.)

Scotticisation (anglicisation) of Gaelic place-names has been a concomitant part of the cultural assimilation of Gaelic Scotland by administrative powers and by Scots-speaking settlers for centuries. Distinctive forms of Gaelic loan-names in Scots include those in *bal-* < ScG *baile* 'village, etc.': *Ballantruan* (Banff) < ScG *Baile an t-Sruthain* 'the village of the stream'; *ach-/auchen-*, etc. < ScG *ach'*, *achadh* 'field, meadow': *Acharanny* (Arran) < ScG *Achadh na Rainich* 'the field of the fern', *Auchentaggart* (Dumfries) < ScG *Achadh an t-Sagairt* 'the field of the priest' – levelling is frequent with this element, e.g. *Auchenclech* (Aberdeen), contrast *Achnacloich* (Argyll etc.), both from ScG *Achadh na Cloich* 'the field of the stone'; *kil-* < ScG *cill*, *cille* 'church, etc.' (often with a saint's name): *Kilbarchan* (Renfrew) < ScG *Cill Bhearchain* 'Bearchan's church', *Kilmarnock* (Ayr) < ScG *Cill Mheàrnaig* ('Cill Mh' Eàrnaig') 'the church of my Ernóc'; *kin-* < ScG *ceann* 'head, end': *Kinneil* (Angus) < ScG *Ceann an Fhàil* 'the end of the [Antonine] wall'; *inver-* < ScG *inbhir* 'confluence; river-mouth': *Invernauld* (Sutherland) < ScG *Inbhir nan Allt* 'the confluence of the streams'; *ben-* < ScG *beinn* 'mountain, hill': *Benbuie* (Dumfries) < ScG *Beinn Bhuidhe* 'yellow mountain'. (Further, see Fraser 1973; Nicolaisen [1976] 2001.)

Gaelic loan-words, such as *ben* (< ScG *beinn* 'mountain, hill'), *craig* (< ScG *creag* 'rock') and *loch* (< ScG *loch* 'lake'), occur frequently in Scots place-names also.

FUNCTION

The function of a place-name is principally to denote a place or feature within a location. In other words, while a place-name may have an accessible lexical or dictionary meaning, it operates primarily on an onomastic semantic level. For example, *Srath Chluaidh* (Eng. *Strathclyde*) may mean literally the 'bottom land of the (river) Clyde', but it is generally understood to take in a greater geographical area and, at one time (1975–96), was an administrative area stretching from Tiree in the north to the Dumfries and Galloway border. (Further, see Nicolaisen 1977; Cox 1990b; Cox 2002a.)

Place-names were traditionally an integral part of the socio-economy and were used routinely, whether on the croft, in the moor or fishing. They also had an important role within the *cèilidh*, the gathering or visiting where news, songs and stories would be exchanged. They were frequently embedded within locally composed songs and, at times, found their way into the local renditions of traditional sagas (Meek 1998; Cox 2002c). Some would commemorate historical or pseudo-historical events, legends or myths, while others would simply be the peg upon which a tale or anecdote was hung. Although the lore of Gaelic place-names or *dinn-seanchas* has yet to be fully studied, various categories are discernible.

One category consists of derivational lore, focusing on the lexical or supposed lexical meaning of place-names. Names in this category may be given spurious etymologies. For example, *Abhainn Tuirc* (The Trossachs) is said to mean 'the river of the boar', an etymology based on the assumption that the specific is from Gaelic *torc* (gen. *tuirc*) 'boar'. Although the explanation is supported loosely by the erroneous tradition that *Na Tròiseachan* (Eng. *The Trossachs*) means 'bristly ground', *torc* here most probably means 'ravine'. Other names in this category arise from their features' physical characteristics: a channel through which the flood-tide runs east to west, which provides the best route northwards from Crinan (Argyll), is known as *An Doras Mòr* 'the great doorway'; a coastal rock formation has given rise to the name, *Leabaidh na h-Aon Ìghne* 'the bed of the solitary girl' (South Shawbost, Lewis) and its story of a jilted girl, who fell to her death. Yet others arise through misinterpretation: *Achadh Dùn Dòmhnaill* 'the field of *Dùn Dòmhnaill* (Dòmhnall's fort)' (Dundonnell, Lochbroom) has been reinterpreted as *Achadh Dà Dòmhnaill*, giving rise to the notion that there were two Donalds at one time here – although *Achadh an Dà Dhòmhnaill* might have been expected, were this the case.

Another category focuses upon the myth or legend behind a place-name: *Rocabarra* (or *Rocabarra fo Thuinn* 'Rockall beneath the waves'), as well as referring to Rockall, was one of several mythical islands to the west of Scotland and was renowned for its monsters and their evil designs on mankind. According to legend, the island has appeared twice and its next appearance will presage the end of the world: *Nuair thig Rocabarra ris, is dual gun tèid an saoghal a sgrios* 'When Rocabarra appears, the world is going to be destroyed' (Murchison 1988). In many cases, the lexical meaning of a name is used to authenticate the tradition, thus Fionn Mac Cumhaill, leader of the Fianna, is commemorated in names like *Uaigh Fhinn* 'Fionn's grave' (Glen Luss) and *Suidhe Fhinn* 'Fionn's seat' (Glen Fruin), all of which were part of a cultural infrastructure generated by the recitation of traditional tales on the *cèilidh* circuit (Meek 1998). Similarly, the tidal race, *Coire Bhreacain* 'the cauldron of Breacan' (Corryvreckan, Jura): Breacan, according to one tradition, was the grandson of Niall of the Nine Hostages, King of Ireland at the end of the fourth century; according to another, he was a Norwegian prince who fell in love with a princess of the isles. (An alternative explanation is that *breacan* is from the Gaelic adjective, *breac* 'spotted, speckled', and was used to describe the surface of the water here, a solution that allows for the appearance of *Coire Bhreacain* in both Scotland and Ireland – the same name-form occurs of a tidal race between Ireland and Rathlin – and perhaps describes the cross-currents better than the more fanciful *coire* [Cox 1998].) Many such tales depict dragons, goblins, giants and fairies and often attached themselves to stone circles or to single stones, e.g. *Clach Neacail* 'Nicol's Stone' (Mull; Maclean 1997), thrown by a giant, and *Clach an Truiseil* (Ballantrushel, Lewis; Cox 2002c), a petrified member of the Fianna.

Sub-sets of this last category are the historical and pseudo-historical traditions. The name *Tarbert* (Kintyre, Loch Lomond [Tarbet], etc.) is often translated 'place of portage', whereas it means literally 'isthmus'. The tradition is sustained partly by the saga references to Magnus Barelegs' dragging a boat from West Loch Tarbert over to Loch Fyne, whereupon he 'took possession of the land that then lay to the larboard', thereby designating Kintyre an island (*Heimskringla*, Anderson 1922 II, 113), and to King Haakon of Norway's dragging of boats from Arrochar on Loch Long over to Tarbet on Loch Lomond (*Hákonar saga Hákonarsonar*, loc. cit., 625). *Staca nan Gall* 'the stack of the foreigners' (Dalbeg, Lewis) records the wreck of a ship out of Wick: all those who made it to shore were killed by the locals, but the last to die managed to utter a curse that is thought to explain why the hamlet has such a small population to this day: *Daile Beaga, Daile Beaga/ Mas e beag e, mas e beag e/ Guma beag e, guma beag e:/ Cha bhi mac an àite athar,/ No nighean an àite màthar!* 'Daile Beag [the name of the village], if it be small, may it be small: no son shall succeed his father, nor daughter her mother!' (Cox 2002a). Administrative expediency is apparent in the inclusion of the foundation legend of the Columban monastery at Old Deer (Aberdeen) in the twelfth-century Gaelic notes in the *Book of Deer*, at a time when the written document was being seen increasingly as the only proper evidence of legal ownership.

Traditionally, *dinn-seanchas* was a phenomenon in flux, a perpetually changing process that was as much an affirmation of identity and place as it was a form of entertainment. (Further, see Cox 1998.)

ONOMASTICON

The Gaelic nomenclature of Scotland gives a valuable insight into the socio-economy, historical context and political history of the various communities that created it over the centuries. Significant categories include:

Natural features: among the commonest elements denoting natural features in the onomasticon – the mix and incidence of which may vary – are:

Access: *àth* 'ford', *bealach* 'pass', *beul* 'opening', *fadhail* 'ford', *tairbeart* 'isthmus'.

Declivities: *foithir* 'shelving slope', *leathad* 'hillside, slope', *leitir* 'slope'.

Depressions: *gil* 'ravine', *gleann* 'valley', *lag* 'hollow', *slug(aid)* 'gully'.

Eminences, precipices: *aodann* 'cliff, bluff', *bàrr* 'summit', *barran* 'summit', *beannan* 'mountain', *beinn* 'mountain', *càrn* 'cairn', *càrnan* 'hill, cairn', *cleite* 'mountain, cliff', *cnoc* 'hill', *creachann* 'mountain, hill', *creag* 'cliff', *creagan* 'hillock', *cruach* 'hill', *dùn* 'hillock, knoll', *meall* 'knoll', *mullach* 'summit', *sìthean* 'hillock, knoll', *tom* 'hillock, knoll', *tòrr* 'hill, knoll', *tulach*, 'hillock'.

Fissures, caves: *sgor* 'fissure, niche', *toll* 'hole', *uagha/uamha* 'cave'.

Identations: *bàgh* 'bay', *cala* 'bay', *camas* 'bay', *geodha* 'cove', *loch* 'fiord, bay', *tòb* 'creek'.

Islands, rocks, ledges: *bodha* 'reef', *carra(gh)* 'rock, boulder', *carraig* 'rock, cliff', *clach* 'stone, rock, boulder', *creag* 'skerry, rock', *eilean* 'island', *innis* 'island', *leac* 'flagstone, *palla* 'ledge', *sgeir* 'skerry', *staca* 'stack'.

Meadows, plains, plateaux: *achadh* 'meadow, field', *blàr* 'plain', *dail* 'meadow', *liana* 'flat meadowland', *machair* 'plain', *mòinteach* 'heath', *srath* 'strath, level ground by river'.

Narrows, current: *caolas* 'straits', *sruth* 'current'.

Peripheral: *ceann* 'head, end', *cùl* 'rear, back'.

Projections: *àird* 'headland', *corran* 'rounded headland', *gob* 'point', *rinn* 'point', *rubha* 'promontory', *sròn* 'point'.

Shoreline: *cladach* 'shore', *faoilinn* 'beach', *tràigh* 'beach'.

Water, water-logged land: *abhainn* 'river', *allt* 'stream', *alltan* 'streamlet', *bùrn* 'stream, burn', *eas* 'waterfall', *feadan* 'moorland stream', *fuaran* 'spring', *loch* 'lake', *lochan* 'small lake', *lodan* 'pool', *sruthan* 'stream'.

Elements descriptive of, or qualifying, natural features:

Colour: (light) *bàn* 'white', *buidhe* 'yellow', *dearg* 'red', *fionn* 'white', *geal* 'white', *glas* 'green'; (dark) *donn* 'brown', *dorch* 'dark', *dubh* 'black', *gorm* 'green', *liath* 'grey', *riabhach* 'brown', *ruadh* 'red, russet', *breac* 'speckled'.

Shape: *àrd* 'high, tall', *beag* 'small', *caol* 'narrow', *domhainn* 'deep', *leathann* 'wide, broad', *mòr* 'large', *reamhar* 'broad, thick'.

Relative location: *a deas* 'southern', *a tuath* 'northern', *a-muigh* 'outer', *an ear* 'eastern', *an iar* 'western', *a-staigh* 'inner', *ìo(chd)rach* 'lower', *ua(chd)rach* 'upper'.

Nature of terrain, vegetation, weather: *bog* 'boggy', *gainmheach* 'sand', *gaoth* 'wind', *garbh* 'rough', *grian* 'sun', *loisgte* 'burnt', *maoil* 'bare', *mòine* 'peat', *molach* 'lush', *sneachd* 'snow', *teine* 'fire, lightning'.

Settlement:

achadh 'meadow, field; farm or farmstead', *baile* 'piece of land; farm; village', *both* 'bothy, cell', *bothan* 'bothy', *caiseal/caisteal* 'fort, castle', *cill/cille* 'cell, church', *clachan* 'village', *croit* 'croft', *dabhach* 'portion of land', *dùn* 'fort', *dùnan* 'fort', *feòirling* 'farthingland', *làrach* 'site', *leth-pheighinn* 'half-penny land', *peighinn* 'pennyland', *peit/peite* 'piece of land, land holding, estate', *ràth* 'fort', *taigh* 'house', *tobhta* 'site'.

Cultivation:

Fields: *feannag* 'lazy-bed', *gead* 'parcel of land', *geàrraidh* 'enclosure, land around dwelling house', *gort* 'enclosure', *leas/lios* 'enclosure', *leòb* 'parcel of land'.

Crops: *arbhar* 'corn', *coirc* 'oats', *connlach* 'straw', *feur* 'grass', *tràthach* 'hay'.

Church related:

aifreann 'gift', *annaid* 'sanctuary, (mother) church', *bachall* 'crozier', *caibeal* 'chapel', *cailleach dhubh* 'nun', *cill/cille* 'cell, church', *cladh* 'graveyard', *comraich* 'sanctuary', *dìseart* 'retreat', *eaglais* 'church', *ìobairt* 'offering', *manach* 'monk', *ministear* 'minister', *neimhidh* 'church land', *reilig* 'graveyard', *sagart* 'priest', *teampall* 'temple, church', *tèarmann* 'sanctuary', *uaigh* 'grave'.

Other elements fall into such categories as flora and fauna; anthroponomy (personal names, nicknames, epithets, words for people by sex, age and other characteristics); husbandry; pastoral farming; fishing; trades, crafts and other occupations; law, custom and belief; and political history and institutions. (Further, see Cox 2002a.)

CHRONOLOGY

Gaelic place-names in Scotland date from the establishment of the Dalriadic colony in Argyll in the fifth century and the settlement of Dumfries and Galloway in the tenth century. A distribution map of the element *baile* illustrates the fullest extent of Gaelic-speaking settlement over the country, an expansion that was probably more or less complete by the eleventh century (see Figure 3.1).

The antiquity of names, however, is frequently impossible to judge. As regards written sources, 'Scottish tradition is centuries later than its English equivalent, for neither state documents nor monastic chartularies and registers begin much before the 12th or, more often, 13th centuries, and 14th and 15th-century spellings are quite frequently our earliest evidence' (Nicolaisen [1976: 19] 2001: 25). For the Highlands and Islands, documentary evidence is generally later still and, in many cases, does not begin until the nineteenth-century Board of Ordnance 6in:1m map. Indeed, a majority of names remain unrecorded and a large number, on account of socio-economic change, have no doubt been irretrievably lost.

Names may be dated absolutely, by supplying a *terminus ante* or *post quem*, and/or relatively, by dating them as early or late in relation to other names. Dating criteria may be external or internal, with broader (less specific) criteria yielding broader chronologies. External criteria may consist, for example, of maps, written sources, historical events, ecclesiastical history, demographic movements and mythology. Internal criteria are all linguistic in nature: morphological, phonological, lexical and structural. Under onomastic structure, for example, *Buaile Bheag Geàrr' na h-Aibhne* would be seen as later than *Geàrr' na h-Aibhne*, because the latter was used in the creation of the former. Under syntactical structure, certain types of names (not necessarily individual names) might be considered relatively early or late: specific-initial names, for example *Glas Bheinn* 'green mountain' (Assynt), as a type, are generally datable to before *c.*1200 – although this has to be treated with caution, because some such structures are still in use today. Similarly, periphrastic structures, such as *Peit a' Mhuilinn* 'the holding of the mill', are considered to be relatively late, although it is significant that they are already well established by the early twelfth century, as in *pett inmulenn* acc. (Book of Deer, *c.*1130; Watson [1904] 1976; Cox 2008). (Further, see Nicolaisen [1976] 2001; Nicolaisen 1977; Cox 2002a.)

RESEARCH AND INTEREST

Place-name study in Scotland began largely as an antiquarian pursuit and may be said to have begun formally with the publication of the twenty-one-volume *Statistical Account of Scotland* (1791–99). During the late nineteenth and early twentieth centuries – even before the development of the science of phonetics – Gaelic onomastics was put upon a sure footing, in particular by Alexander MacBain and William J. Watson. With the advent of phonetics, however, the discipline – insofar as it relied upon historical phonology – could be researched and taught upon a much more scientific basis. Since the Second World War, a steady stream of scholars have contributed to the field, especially W. F. H. Nicolaisen, Ian Fraser and Simon Taylor, as well as the late Magne Oftedal, whose main interest was Norse place-names in Gaelic Scotland. (Further, see Nicolaisen 2007.)

There have been attempts at formalising the collection of place-names on a nationwide basis, particularly the Place-Name Survey of Scotland within the School of Scottish Studies, University of Edinburgh (from the early 1950s). Ainmean-Àite na h-Alba was established in 2006 in order to provide a national gazetteer of Gaelic place-names, providing steerage in the spelling and use of names, as well as a database resource, with facilities for holding historical data and analysis, to promote the study of Gaelic place-names.

The Scottish Place-Name Society, founded in 1966, provides a welcome focus for extra-mural interest in place-names throughout Scotland, and the establishment of *The Journal of Scottish Name Studies* in September 2007 bears witness to the significant academic interest that there is in general in place-names relating to Scotland.

BIBLIOGRAPHY

Ainmean-Àite na h-Alba: http://www.gaelicplacenames.org/.
The Journal of Scottish Name Studies: http://www.clanntuirc.co.uk/ JSNS.html.
The Scottish Place-Name Society: http://www.spns.org.uk/.

Anderson, A. O. (1922), *Early Sources of Scottish History AD 500–1286*, 2 vols, Edinburgh and London: Oliver and Boyd.

Cox, R. A. V. (1990a), 'The Origin and Relative Chronology of *Shader*-names in the Hebrides', *Scottish Gaelic Studies* 16, pp. 95–113.

Cox, R. A. V. (1990b), 'Place-nomenclature in the Context of the Bilingual Community of Lewis: Status, Origin and Interaction', Proceedings of the 2nd International Conference on the Languages of Scotland (Glasgow 1988), in Derick S. Thomson (ed.), *Gaelic and Scots in Harmony*, Glasgow: Department of Celtic, University of Glasgow, pp. 43–52.

Cox, R. A. V. (1991), '*Allt Loch Dhaile Beaga*: Place-name Study in the West of Scotland', *Nomina* 14, 1990–1, pp. 83–96.

Cox, R. A. V. (1994), 'Descendants of *Bólstaðr*? A Re-examination of *bost* & Co.', Proceedings of the Annual Conference of the Scottish Society of Northern Studies (Ullapool 1988), in John R. Baldwin (ed.), *Peoples and Settlement in North-West Ross*, Edinburgh: The Scottish Society for Northern Studies, pp. 43–67.

Cox, R. A. V. (1998), 'Onomastic Luggage: Variability in the Onomastic Landscape', *Nomina* 21, pp. 15–28.

Cox, R. A. V. (2002a), *The Gaelic Place-names of Carloway, Isle of Lewis: Their Structure and Significance*, Dublin: Dublin Institute for Advanced Studies.

Cox, R. A. V. (2002b), 'Notes on the Question of the Development of Old Norse *bólstaðr* in Hebridean Nomenclature', *Nomina* 25, pp. 13–28.

Cox, R. A. V. (2002c), '*Clach an Truiseil*', *The Journal of Celtic Linguistics* 7, pp. 159–66.

Cox, R. A. V., 2008, 'The Syntax of the Place-names', in Katherine Forsythe (ed.), *Studies on the Book of Deer*, Dublin: Four Courts Press, pp. 309–12.

Forbes, A. R. (1923), *Place-names of Skye and Adjacent Islands: With Lore, Mythical, Traditional and Historical*, Paisley: Alexander Gardner.

Fraser, I. A. (1973), 'Anglicisation in Scottish Gaelic Place-names', *Onoma* 17, 1972–3, pp. 205–15.

Fraser, I. A. (1999), *The Place-Names of Arran*, Glasgow: The Arran Society of Glasgow.

Gammeltoft, P. (2000), 'Why the Difference? An Attempt to Account for the Variations in the Phonetic Development of Place-names in Old Norse *bólstaðr* in the Hebrides', *Nomina* 23, pp. 107–19.

Gammeltoft, P. (2001), *The Place-name Element* bólstaðr *in the North Atlantic Area*, Copenhagen: C. A. Reitzels Forlag.

Gillies, H. C. (1906), *The Place-Names of Argyll*, London: David Nutt.

Jackson, K. H. [1955] (1980), 'The Pictish Language', in F. T. Wainwright (ed.), *The Problem of the Picts*, Perth: Melven Press, pp. 129–60.

MacBain, A. [1922] (2003), *Place Names of the Highlands and Islands of Scotland*, William J. Watson (ed.), Glasgow: The Grimsay Press.

Maclean, C. (1997), *The Isle of Mull: Placenames, Meanings and Stories*, Dumfries: Maclean Publications.

Meek, D. E. (1998), 'Place-names and Literature: Evidence from the Gaelic Ballads', in Simon Taylor (ed.), *The Uses of Place-names*, Dalkeith: Scottish Cultural Press, pp. 147–68.

Murchison, T. M. (ed.) (1988), *Sgrìobhaidhean Choinnich MhicLeòid – The Gaelic Prose of Kenneth MacLeod*, Edinburgh: Scottish Academic Press for the Scottish Gaelic Texts Society.

Nicolaisen, W. F. H. [1976] (2001), *Scottish Place-Names: Their Study and Significance*, Edinburgh: John Donald.

Nicolaisen, W. F. H. (1977), 'Words as Names', Proceedings of the 12th International Congress of Onomastic Sciences (1976), *Onoma* 20, Part 1, 1977, pp. 142–63.

Nicolaisen, W. F. H. (1996), 'Gaelic -*ach* > Scots -*o* in Scottish Place Names', *Scottish Gaelic Studies* 17, pp. 278–91.

Nicolaisen, W. F. H. (2007), 'Place-names Studies in Scotland: A Brief History', *Scottish Place-name News* No. 23, Autumn 2007, 2; 'Addendum', idem No. 24, Spring 2008, p. 2.

Ó Maolalaigh, R. (1998), 'Place-names as a resource for the historical linguist', in Simon Taylory (ed.), *The Uses of Place-names*, Dalkeith: Scottish Cultural Press, pp. 12–53.

Oftedal, M. (1954), 'The Village Names of Lewis in the Outer Hebrides', *Norsk tidsskrift for sprogvidenskap* 17, pp. 363–409.

Oftedal, M. (1980), 'Scandinavian Place-names in Celtic Territory: An Attempt at a Linguistic Classification', in T. Andersson, E. Brylla, and A. Rostvik (eds), *Ortnamn och språkkontakt*, in *Norna-rapporter* 17, pp. 163–91.

Taylor, S. (2006), *The Place-names of Fife – Volume One: West Fife Between Leven and Forth,* Donington: Shaun Tyas.

Watson, A. and Allan, E. (1984), *The Place Names of Upper Deeside,* Aberdeen: Aberdeen University Press.

Watson, A. (1995), *The Ochils: Placenames, History, Tradition,* Perth: Perth and Kinross District Libraries.

Watson, W. J. [1904] (1976), *Place-names of Ross and Cromarty,* Inverness: Ross and Cromarty Heritage Society.

Watson, W. J. (1926), *History of the Celtic Place-names of Scotland,* Edinburgh.

Figure 3.1 Gaelic place-names containing baile.

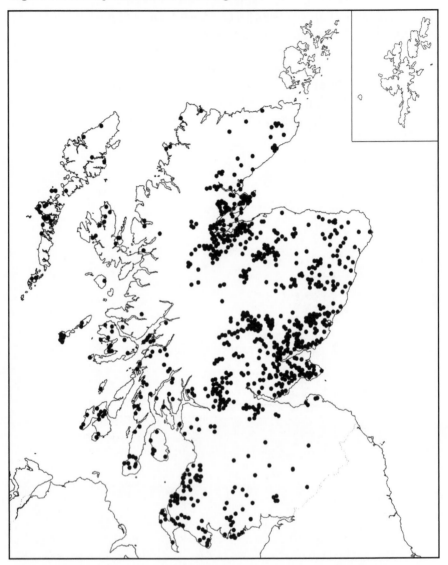

(Based upon W. F. H. Nicolaisen [1976: 137] 2001: 177. Printed with permission.)

CHAPTER 4

Language in Gaelic Literature

Moray Watson

INTRODUCTION

This chapter arises out of a growing realisation that an analysis of language has always been a central part of the criticism of Gaelic literature. In 1876, the pioneering literary critic John Stuart Blackie wrote: 'Had Robert Burns sung in Gaelic instead of Scotch, his works at the present day might have been as little known in Europe, or even in Edinburgh, as the satires of Rob Donn' (Blackie 1876: 26). A little over a century later, Donald John MacLeod wrote: 'Gaelic literature has only recently begun to escape from the diaglossic [*sic*] apartheid which confined it to home-neighbourhood domains in speech and to the expression of humour and sentiment in literature' (MacLeod 1987: 334). Before Blackie, after MacLeod, and throughout the intervening years, scholars have continued to engage with questions of language in relation to the literature. To some degree, this is because so much of the literature that was available for analysis was, in fact, poetry (Gillies 2006: 3). Even though poetry no longer forms the bulk of the literature being produced, and indeed perhaps has not always been 'the dominant form' since the 1960s (MacLeod 1987: 334), Gaelic criticism nevertheless continued to focus mainly on poetry until the most recent years (Kidd 2000: 67). In some ways, poetry lends itself most readily to linguistically based analyses. Because of its reliance on the notion of structure, poetry is a form that can be approached using stylistic techniques in an unself-conscious manner. Criticism of Gaelic poetry commonly addresses texts at linguistic levels, both in the macrostructure and at the levels of the various minutiae (examples include Thomson 1951, Thomson 1974, Wentworth 2000 and Gillies 2007). Critics discuss and debate grammar, orthography, graphology, lexis, etymology and philology, treating all of these things as legitimate foci for the analysis of literary works. At the same time, they work on deciphering the primary meanings and the nuances of texts, they unpick rhetorical codes, and they explain the rhythmic structures. And, as this chapter demonstrates, many of the techniques that scholars have used in elucidating poetry are also applicable to the other literary forms.

This chapter takes for granted the notion that original literature[1] can be classified as poetry, prose or drama, but also treats the *còmhradh* or 'conversation' as a genre in its own right. In a paper I intend to publish elsewhere, I demonstrate how the *còmhradh* differs from both prose fiction and drama in fundamental ways and, although it shares features with both, it can scarcely be thought of as one or the other (Watson forthcoming a). The term 'prose' can, of course, encompass not only the kind of fiction we think of nowadays as novels and short stories, but can include a wider range of work (see, for instance, Reid 1977: 30–42), including, in Gaelic, the 'readings' that became popular between the end of the nineteenth century and the beginning of the twentieth (MacLeod 1977: 209; Meek 2007: 260). The term 'prose' in its broadest definition also includes the (auto)biography, which is a genre that has found some success in Gaelic to date (MacLeod 1987: 333; Bateman 2007: 225–30). Given the limitations of space, this chapter largely avoids dealing with prose other than that which can be categorised as short stories or novels, but it is apparent that it would be worthwhile to undertake a thorough stylistic analysis of a much wider range of Gaelic literature, both in greater breadth and depth.

The chapter begins with a discussion of earlier forms of poetry, then moves on to the modern poetry, the dialogue, and, finally, prose and drama together. This is not to suggest that there is less to say about prose and drama: but, significantly less has been written about them to date, and so there is less existing critical ground to cover.

LANGUAGE IN EARLIER POETRY

In the introduction to his *Bàrdachd Ghàidhlig: Specimens of Gaelic Poetry 1550–1900* (1918), William Watson gives an account of the two main types of Gaelic poet who were active in the 350-year period his book surveys; Watson's typologies are still recognisable to a contemporary scholar, albeit with certain additions and modifications. The first group, he terms the 'Classic poets' (xvii–xviii and passim) and the second, the 'modern poets' (xix ff.). The two groups are chiefly distinguished by two main characteristics: their use of metrics and their use of language. Although he does touch on devices such as imagery and metaphor, Watson's main focus is on describing the linguistic and paralinguistic features of both types of poetry. He notes that:

The language of the modern poets is the current language of their day, the modern form, as developed in Scotland, of the ancient language which for so many centuries was common to Scotland and Ireland. In their use of the vernacular, they broke away, as did the modern Irish poets, from the literary dialect of the classical school, which contained many words and expressions already obsolete in common speech. (Watson 1918: xxii)

All of this is true, although the last part of the statement quoted here hardly goes far enough in describing the difference between the vernacular to which he refers and the classical, common language. The use of certain 'words and expressions' is the least of the difference between the forms of the language. The vernacular language of the sixteenth to the end of the nineteenth century differed markedly in syntax and morphology from the language used in the poetry described as classical, as is discussed in more detail by Ó Baoill in this volume. Watson himself notes that the classical poetry 'demand[ed] a very competent knowledge of the old style' (xxii). Although this 'very competent knowledge' would include an appreciation of metrical practices, rhetorical codes and literary function, it is also quite clear that he means that a most specialist understanding of the language is required. By contrast, 'anyone who knows [the] Scottish Gaelic' (xxii) of the twentieth century would have no difficulty in understanding a poem written in the vernacular style, even when written by a composer who also wrote in the classical form. Watson gives the reader little support in interpreting the language of the Early Modern poetry.[2] However, he lists the loan-words he has noted in the poems (which is a feature common to other collections of writings from the period). The noting of loan-words and influence from other languages reminds the reader that Watson and many of his contemporaries in the early days of the Celtic departments in the Scottish universities were, first and foremost, philologists, as regards their interests (Blackie 1876: ix–xi, 1–66, and passim), in several cases having come to Celtic via the Classics.[3]

On tone and lexical content, Watson finds the poetry of the eighteenth century (which is to say, vernacular or 'modern' poetry, for the most part) at times rather indelicate in comparison with his own sensibilities (Watson 1918: xxiv–xxv). Like Edward MacCurdy (1949–1950), Watson admires 'simplicity' (xxv and passim), although it is never entirely clear whether he means simplicity of language usage or of content, or both. However, he does aver that Gaelic 'artistry' requires 'precision, definiteness, completeness' (xxv). In his description of this quality of exhaustiveness (see also xxvi), Watson paints a picture of the typical Gaelic poet as craftsman first and artist second. He describes a certain wordiness that is a component of this exhaustiveness, and is associated in particular with compiling groups of adjectives. This practice dates back at least to the Middle Gaelic[4] period (xxvii), and it may be found even in poetry of the present day. (Some prose writers also experiment with it: notably, Norman Campbell and Duncan Gillies.[5]) In Watson's time, as now, it is appropriate to recognise this as a Gaelic literary technique. Like Watson, the modern critic must ask:

> whether the epithets add to the clearness and vividness of the description. If they do, the poet is justified: if they do not, or if they are merely a heaping up of synonyms, the art is bad. (Watson 1918: xxvii)

One of the major structural issues in relation to poetry is that of metre. Much of the Introduction to Watson's 1918 anthology dedicates itself to an explanation – albeit brief in relation to the vast potential size of such a description (see, for instance, Blankenhorn 2003) – of the metrical practices of the two types of poets under scrutiny. Watson's discussion of the 'modern' poets' metrics remains the most thorough analysis of the subject in relation to Scottish Gaelic to the present day,[6] although it is tempting to agree with Gillies, who wrote that the paper 'starts with sure-footed treatment of the classical poetry, but declines into uncharacteristic incomprehensibility in its vernacular sections' (Gillies 2006: 6, footnote 8). When Watson describes the stressed metres of the modern poets, it becomes clear that a thorough understanding of the prosody of the contemporary Gaelic is required in order to be able to appreciate properly the subtleties of the rhythms. For instance, the strophic metres (Watson 1918: xlii–li) have a good deal in common with Welsh *cynghanedd* in the sense that there can be mirroring patterns of sounds, but it is necessary to understand where the stresses must fall in order to be able to grasp the complexities of the patterns (consider, here, for instance, Watson's own comments on the intonational differences between Gaelic and Irish in his own day, xxxiv). Watson's discussion of stress patterning in the poetry leads him to touch briefly upon prosody in the language in general. In bemoaning what he calls the 'tyranny of the principal stress' (xxxiv), he descends into criticism of what he sees as a degeneration in the pronunciation of Gaelic, especially the varieties found in Lewis.[7]

In the Classical poetry, syllabic metre is a *sine qua non*. Knott (1934) describes these syllabic metres in some detail, and Ó Cuív (1973; also, 1966), among others, analyses them both in relation to the Early Modern language as a whole and in relation to other linguistic aspects of the poetry. Although their descriptions differ in places, which may be attributed partly to differences in interpretation or even expression, it is apparent that Watson, Knott and Ó Cuív are describing the same thing: that is to say, the syllabic poetry of both Scotland and Ireland belong to the same literary tradition. This finding is in keeping with the long-held contention of most scholars that the Classical poetry was part of a common, 'pan-Gaelic' cultural milieu (although, see, McLeod 1999 and 2004, for instance, for recent modifications on the old 'sea-divided Gael' perception).[8] It should be noted that the Introduction to *Bàrdachd Ghàidhlig: Specimens of Gaelic Poetry 1550–1900* is ambiguous about whether the book includes poetry of both Scotland and Ireland[9] (compare Watson 1918: xvii, xxi–xxii, xxv, xxviii, xxxiii, xxxiv, xliii, li, and liii), but it may be that Watson felt he was being clear enough by using a (Scottish) Gaelic phrase for the main title of the book.

Irrespective of the origin of a 'classical' poem, the metrics and the rhetorical codes (MacInnes 2006a)[10] are the two central features. The intricacies of some of the bardic metres appear highly complex, and the descriptions of them by scholars like Watson, Knott and Ó Cuív have the appearance of mathematical formulae. This contrasts with the freer metres of what Watson calls the 'stressed' rhythms of the eighteenth- and nineteenth-century vernacular verse. Where the bardic poetry would have been declaimed in performance, the vernacular verse would largely have been composed for singing (Gillies 2005: 632), which must explain the differences in the metrics (although see Ó Baoill and Ó Dochartaigh 2005, 2006 on the 'halfway house' style known as 'trí rainn agus amhrán'). A more stark contrast can be drawn with the twentieth-century verse, where Gaelic writers began to innovate with the form (Thomson 1990: 249). Thomson discusses the practices in the writing of Iain Crichton Smith and Donald MacAulay, alongside his own work. He shows that these poets actuated an evolution in Gaelic versification without, at first, entirely breaking with the tradition (292). The corollary of the evolution, however, seems to be that verse moved steadily further from the 'traditional' rhythms (both syllabic – already barely traceable even as an influence by the twentieth century – and stressed, which forms the backbone of 'village' poetry). Thus, in Thomson's own poetry, he adopts 'many novel developments in the use of rhythm ... including a simulation of speech-rhythms used to gain a range of effects' (293). This brings us to a discussion of the poetry of the twentieth and twenty-first centuries.

LANGUAGE IN CONTEMPORARY POETRY

Whyte (2002, 2006a, 2006b, 2007a) and, to an extent, Byrne (2008) show the kind of literary detective work that can be done when the scholar combines analysis of language with work on history, biography and the techniques of close reading and critical practice. These analyses are highly fruitful and considerably advance our understanding of the work of Sorley MacLean and Iain Crichton Smith, two of the major literary figures in the twentieth century.

Whyte's (2007a) work on the poetry of Derick Thomson[11] yields further results of linguistic interest, especially from a structural point of view. In particular, his suggestion of the term 'caption' (also Whyte 2005) to denote a style of Gaelic poetry may be highly beneficial to critics working on the writers who are often collectively known as the 'nua-bhàrdachd' poets.[12] He states that Thomson is the chief proponent (Whyte 2007a: 23 ff) of this style, and names Rody Gorman and Anne Frater as two others who have used the 'caption[/less] poetry' technique to good effect. In fact, as a structural device, what is noteworthy about the 'caption', as identified by Whyte here, is that its significance lies especially in the fact that it is often absent. Poems which fall into the category that Whyte describes, therefore, may usefully be contrasted with work by a poet such as Donald MacAulay,[13] who uses the epigram[14] to startling effect on a regular basis. If Thomson is the premier exponent of the 'caption'/less poem, MacAulay is Gaelic's leading epigrammatist. MacAulay's epigrams are self-conscious versions of the captions Whyte identifies as missing from poems by Thomson, such as 'Uiseag' or 'Cainnt nan oghaichean' (Whyte 2007a: 22–5). Thomson himself notes MacAulay's subtly powerful grasp of the structural devices of poetry (Thomson 1990: 294) and adds that: 'the rhythms, line-lengths and the weight of particular words, form a perfect expression of the poet's thought' (295).[15] The final line of 'An t-Seana Bhean' (MacAmhlaigh 1967: 61), for example, shows the effectiveness of his technique, driving home the closing part of the image of old age leaving both body and mind bereft of energy and ambition:

> 's do làmh anns a' bhalla)
> don aitreabh
> far an robh am maide-buinn air fàs na
> arrasbacan.
>
> Is shuidh thu an sin air do chathair.
> (MacAmhlaigh 1967: 61)

This same effect is augmented by both the choice of vocabulary ('crotach'; 'arrasbacan'; 'gun ghaoth a' dol eadar iad 's an talamh'), and also by the structure of the poem on the page (see, for instance, the fragmented punctuation, exemplified in the closing parenthesis which began in a previous stanza). The first stanza's shuddering structure echoes the halting steps of the old woman as she makes her way out to survey the lot. The enjambing of lines, and the positioning of the lines in relation to each other (such as their relative lengths), evoke the uncertainty of the old woman's balance. The poet's own reading aloud of the poem exemplifies this, but in a rather different way: he treats the first stanza as a single line (it is a single sentence) and places caesurae, first, where the formal punctuation lies and, second, where the pause matches the old woman's pause: for instance, he reads 'stad thu' and then waits while she waits.[16] The hiatus before the epigram then comes to match the moment of anticipation and release as the old woman lowers herself into her chair.[17] Listening to MacAulay reading the poem highlights the differences that are made possible by the different kinds of performance. The reader's performance of the poem must be informed by the physical structures of the marks on the page, especially on a first reading. The poet's performance may take this graphology into consideration, but may also express the same kind of synaesthetic effect by different means. At the same time, we must always temper any conclusions drawn about performance with the knowledge that performance is fluid and alterable: the poet may read the same lines differently for different effects (if consciously) or when different moods or whims take him (if less consciously). In comparison, the written word is relatively static (Fowler 1977: 76),[18] usually subject only to minor editorial changes at a later date; despite this, the reader's 'performance' of the text may vary and evolve over time.

Thomson's 'Anns a' Bhalbh Mhadainn' (MacThòmais 1967: 38) provides an example of what Whyte means by the 'caption', and it is not quite the same as a MacAulayan epigram. In the case of this poem, there are two seven-line stanzas. Whyte considers that they are in parallel construction, with the first setting the scene and the second 'broadening the field of reference immeasurably' (Whyte 2007a: 24). In the first stanza, there is a description of a snowy scene, where the sheep have been lost beneath the 'white blanket': it is a typical nature scene that would be in keeping with any Gaelic romantic lyric. The second stanza changes the reader's perception, however, and we see that the snow is a metaphor for the social, political and economic forces that have 'suffocated' the Gael: the sheep are, at the same time, a metonym for this selfsame thing. Thus, the second, 'parallel' stanza 'offers more explicit guidance in interpretation' (Whyte 2007a: 23). It directs the reader towards the poem's thematic content, first signalled in the word 'balbh' in the title. According to a reading of the first stanza only, 'balbh' is merely descriptive, adding to the image of the quiet after the storm. With the aid of the 'caption'-stanza, we realise now that the scene is also 'balbh' because there are no people there to talk.

Whyte considers that Thomson in particular has had a profound effect on some of the members of the younger generations of Gaelic poets. It is clear that, as he states, the idea of the caption can be traced in the writing of Anne Frater, among others. It is also clear that Thomson's pioneering use of free verse has now established itself as the norm, although poets like Meg Bateman and Myles Campbell[19] still experiment with both structure and form. In Bateman's case, she is prone to look into the Gaelic literary past – sometimes very far into the past – for inspiration. Another difference between the poetic eras lies in the poets' communicative intentions. The contemporary poets, following MacLean, Thomson and their peers, challenge the reader, both in terms of allusion and language, in a way that is reminiscent of modernism:

> Where the traditional poet seeks to enhance communication by playing on the expected, the modern poet ... demands engagement by subverting expectations. (Gillies 2005: 631)

Another point Whyte touches on in his article on Thomson's poetry is his own, Thomson's, and other writers', use of English in their Gaelic work (Whyte 2007a: 25–6). As he observes, the change of language can be used for deliberate effect, such as when Thomson subtly compares the social and cultural associations of English and Gaelic. Both Meg Bateman and Rody Gorman use the device, as well, perhaps for slightly different reasons. Whyte is inclined to offer what he describes as a 'weak defence' (26) for his own use of English in a single poem, which suggests the anticipation of potential censure. There is, indeed, the potential for suspicion, at least, among readers of Gaelic poetry, when they encounter the English language (McLeod 1998). Since the 1970s – with *Nua-Bhàrdachd Ghàidhlig: Modern Scottish Gaelic Poems* as one of the main templates – it has become a normalised position for Gaelic poetry to be presented with facing translations. Translation of poetry went on before the 1970s,[20] but it was less generalised, and non-Gaelic versions were not necessarily presented *en face* prior to that. By far the most common target language for the translation of Gaelic poetry is English. This is followed by Irish, and other languages are rarer. In some cases, however, it appears that the publication of Gaelic poetry is considered more viable by publishers if it is accompanied by either English or Irish.

As well as writing in 'macaronic' style, some Gaelic writers exercise their craft in writing entire works in English (see also Macleod 2007). These are in sharp contrast to writers like MacLean, Thomson and MacAulay, who published little poetry, if any, that was not in Gaelic. At least, this is true if we discount their translations of their own poems, although many of these translations may be considered to be of literary merit in their own right and, in some cases, have at least contributed to their reputations as important writers. Foremost among the writers who have also published in English in recent years has been Iain Crichton Smith.[21] Smith was unique among the major Gaelic writers in that, although prolific in Gaelic, he wrote considerably more English and had an international reputation among readers who perhaps were not even always aware of him as a Gaelic writer at all. He began his publishing career with a greater output in Gaelic than English, and was the first writer to produce a book of fiction that would be recognised as 'modern' short stories, when he published *Bùrn is Aran* in 1960. Always prolific, after his retirement:

> his output increased, especially in English. From the late-1980s, he wrote comparatively little Gaelic, having apparently come to a resolution regarding his sense of biculturalism. He also believed that he could no longer write naturally in Gaelic, having been away from the *Gàidhealtachd* for so long. (Watson 2009, internet resource)

Smith was exercised by his perception of biculturalism throughout his life. Not only was his sense of identity challenged by his native bilingualism (Smith 1989: 136), but he grew up in an area that left him feeling, in many ways, isolated from the rest of the world (see Smith 1986: 13–70, 73–83). This isolation was not necessarily a negative part of his perception, and his knowledge of two languages was something that he enjoyed and appreciated. However, he wrestled with the issues of bilingualism and bicultralism in an ongoing dialectic throughout his work over a period of thirty years. I have elsewhere argued that Smith's 1987 poetry collection *An t-Eilean agus an Cànan* represents his final major confrontation of all of these issues that were prevalent throughout his work (Watson 2006a). As early as 1984, Smith had expressed his envy for writers who could choose to be monocultural and could embrace a single language that would become their medium. His poem 'For Poets Writing in English over in Ireland' (Smith 1984b) expresses the sense of splitness that vexes the writer who is so reliant on language. Like MacAulay, Smith uses the structural potentialities of punctuation to emphasise the effect of the words. The splits between line *b* and line *c* and between lines *e* and *f* in the poem serve as an illustration of this: the sentence is interrupted by the gaps, mirroring the sense of groping uncertainty that is being expressed by the words themselves. Similarly, the parenthetically isolated strophes 'half-deaf' and 'half-blind' bring the reader up short, as if shunted into this world of impaired perception.

The most influential of all the twentieth-century poets, Sorley MacLean[22] was also troubled by the language issue (Watson 2008b).[23] As William Gillies has noted (Gillies 2005: 625), MacLean vacillated about whether or not to translate his poems into English. The decision to go ahead with the translations resulted in the poetry being critiqued by many commentators who knew little or no Gaelic. As Gillies (2005: 625), among others, has intimated, this caused a degree of unease among other commentators, who questioned the authenticity of literary criticism based entirely on translations. Both Gillies and Whyte have remarked on the contrast in criticism by those who had access to MacLean's poems only via the translations and the criticism of John MacInnes, whose linguistic and cultural background is closely aligned with MacLean's own. MacInnes himself expressed an unease about judgements based entirely on translations of MacLean's work, contrasting such judgements with what he calls 'realism' (MacInnes 1986: 137) and explaining how MacLean's achievement is so profound precisely because of what MacInnes calls his 'restorative work' (137) with the language. More explicitly:

> Simply by reading an English translation, no one could ever guess at the nature of MacGill-Eain's Gaelic diction. There is nothing very difficult – nor, in purely linguistic terms, anything very egregious – in the English. By contrast the original Gaelic exhibits virtually an entire spectrum of language. (MacInnes 1986: 137)

The implication here is that MacLean's language *is* difficult in Gaelic, and Gillies shares this view, at least in respect of the poem 'A' Chorra-ghritheach' (Gillies 2005: 631). According to Gillies, a concern with language was a central part of MacLean's craft:

> MacLean's practice follows that of the traditional poet in being supra-dialectal, and in his pleasure in careful and accurate usage, right down to correctness in case endings. (Gillies 2005: 636)

Gillies hints at a quasi-MacDiarmidan synthesis in MacLean's compilation of his vocabulary:

MacLean quarries and pillages words and meanings and nuances from all the sources available to him: local-dialectal, biblical-theological, and earlier literary sources, and ends up creating his own diction *de novo.* (Gillies 2005: 636–7)

Accordingly, this 'implies an attitude to language, and more particularly to literary language' (Gillies 2005: 637). MacLean's attitude to language is one thing, and the critics' attitude is another. The question of whether poetry, in general, can ever truly be understood, appreciated, or analysed when encountered only in translation has never been answered adequately or to everyone's satisfaction. In Gaelic, there is a further, related question, which pertains to the 'authenticity' of Gaelic writers' backgrounds when they come to write poetry. There remains a sense of distinction between the poetry of L1 speakers of Gaelic and L2 speakers, and Whyte suggests that literature by non-native speakers has not yet been accepted in Gaelic as having the same level of authenticity as the writing of native speakers (Whyte 2007b; Whyte 2005: 573). George Campbell Hay is perhaps one exception, but only to a degree (Whyte 2005), and even then because of the ambiguous nature of his acquisition of the language.

LANGUAGE IN THE 'CONVERSATIONS'

As Donald Meek has noted, the 'conversation' was a major cornerstone during the second important phase in the development of Gaelic prose writing (Meek 2007: 258). It is possible that the conversations have come into the prose via the poetic tradition, or that their development has been influenced by the poetry; according to John MacInnes, 'the verse dialogue is a form of fundamental importance' in Gaelic literature (MacInnes 2006b: 314; see also 302 and 303; see also Gillies 2005: 632). There is clearly also a parallel between the *còmhraidhean* and the dialogues that were being published in English(/Scots)-language magazines in the nineteenth century (MacCurdy 1949–50: 230). Sheila Kidd's reading of the first wave of the *còmhraidhean* as a form of social control (Kidd 2000; see also Kidd 2002) rings true. Donald John MacLeod (1977: 200–9) and others (such as Meek 2007) have seen the prose of the mid-nineteenth century as heavily influenced by the religious writing that had dominated the form since the sixteenth century. Much of what was being published up to and during this time (MacLeod 1977: 201–8; Blackie 1876: 313–31; MacNeill 1892: 222–53; MacLean 1904; MacLean 1912) consisted of translations of religious works.[24] According to Meek, some of the translators 'hugged their original texts to the point of exhaustion, and produced a ponderous style of profoundly theological Gaelic prose' (Meek 2007: 260; also Gillies 2005: 631 and MacLeod 1977: 206). This 'theological' style of prose found its way into the early *còmhraidhean*, of whom the Rev. Dr Norman MacLeod is the best-known author and publisher. MacLeod's son-in-law and fellow author, the Rev. Archibald Clerk, edited a collected volume of excerpts from MacLeod's and his own periodicals, entitled *Caraid nan Gaidheal* (1910 [1867]). The first of the three main sections in *Caraid nan Gaidheal* almost exclusively consists of some twenty-four *còmhraidhean*, which, MacCurdy claims, 'mirror the world of the Gael in microcosm' (MacCurdy 1949–50: 231). MacCurdy takes particular notice of the language of these *còmhraidhean*, which are marked by their 'Theocritean simplicity' (232), the 'bubbling sincerity of speech' (232) and by their sincerity and humour. These last qualities in particular seem to have made an impression on MacCurdy, as he repeats the assertion three times (twice on p. 231 and also on p. 232). MacCurdy regards the language of the *còmhraidhean* to be 'simple and sincere' (235) and finds 'solemnity in the simplicity of the concluding words' (242). Nevertheless, the didacticism (MacLeod 1977: 204) of MacLeod's expression does not escape MacCurdy's attention: he notes that the author 'fairly revels in the opportunity of giving information' (MacCurdy 1949–50: 233). Social control, as described by Kidd, is at the heart of this didactic tendency, and is aligned with MacLeod's instinct as a Christian minister, who regards his role to be one of educating people in their Christian duties. Despite this, MacLeod tends to be regarded as the person most clearly responsible for beginning the process of modernising Gaelic prose (MacLeod 1977: 206 ff; MacLeod 1987: 331; Watson 2008a: 573). As MacCurdy states: 'Norman Macleod's prose communicates to us a sense of the potentialities of the language as does that of no other writer' (MacCurdy 1949–50: 235).

Taking all of these views into account, there are several avenues for possible research on MacLeod's language, and on the *còmhraidhean* in particular. It may be fruitful, for instance, to examine the translatorese and other prose writings of the eighteenth and nineteenth centuries, analyse what it is that makes them so 'ponderous', and identify how the *còmhraidhean* mark a shift from that style.[25] Alternatively, it might be worthwhile examining the stylistic features of the first wave of *còmhraidhean* that Kidd identifies as being especially concerned about social control and comparing them with the second wave that Kidd has demonstrated as having almost the opposite function, that of social criticism. Since both types of text are what has sometimes been described as *operative* (Reiss 1981: 124),[26] it could be that they will be seen to share rhetorical and structural features, despite their markedly different content. On the other hand, they may differ structurally, separated as they are by around thirty years, during which time the Gaelic schools were promoting literacy in the language on a wider scale than ever before. Yet a third possibility which offers itself for scrunity is an investigation into the stylistic relationship between the *còmhraidhean* and the early drama and prose fiction dialogue that began to emerge between the end of the nineteenth century and beginning of the twentieth.

In an article currently being prepared for publication, I analyse the structure of the early, MacLeod wave of *còmhraidhean* and demonstrate that they share what is essentially a common formula (Watson forthcoming a). Following some of the early paradigms of Conversation Analysis, and employing the terminology of Harvey Sacks, Emanuel Schegloff and their associates (Sacks et al. 1974; Schegloff and Sacks 1973), I show how the Caraid nan Gaidheal *còmhraidhean* use repeated rhetorical patterns to create a dialectic that could be likened to the Socratic technique of Plato (cf. Kidd 2000: 68). There are five principal elements in the *còmhraidhean*, and these five almost invariably appear, in relatively predictable orders, in the twenty-four *còmhraidhean* collected in *Caraid nan Gaidheal*. The three main elements, which provide the framework for every dialogue, I have tentatively designated 'narratistic', 'extended (monologue)' and 'instigatory' features. The *còmhraidhean* begin with the 'narratistic' element, sometimes in conjunction with some of the related, lesser elements: the narratistic turns concern themselves with scene-building, as they effectively replace narrative (from prose fiction) or stage direction (from drama). The first speaker is usually the principal interlocutor, who may be identified as the author's spokesperson, bearing in mind Kidd's observation about the political motivations underlying the *còmhraidhean*. Typically, somewhere around the tenth turn, the first main instance of the instigatory feature will appear. A standard length of the *còmhraidhean* would place this first main disagreement (as most of the instigatory turns are) about a third of the way through the piece, but some *còmhraidhean* defy this length convention: the *Còmhradh nan Cnoc* on pp. 40–51 comprises some seventy-eight turns in all. This *còmhradh* has an instance of the instigatory element in turn four, but this attempt to initiate debate fails. The instigatory element returns in its 'usual' place, and this time it leads to the initiation of the debate. A possible area for future study would be to compare the dialogues with the early drama and the dialogue passages in the early prose fiction, as instinct suggests that they have a great deal in common with some of these features.

LANGUAGE IN PROSE AND DRAMA

In a number of papers (Watson 2007; Watson 2008a), I have shown that prose fiction was 'invented' or 'imported' into the language between 1870 and 1950. One of the marked features of the fiction of this period is its 'heavy reliance on dialogue' (Watson 2008a: 577):

> The dialogue takes the place of some of the techniques of formal realism, with narrative often making way for several pages of almost uninterrupted conversation. As a result, there is usually a lack of individuality in characters. (Watson 2008a: 577)

There are clear similarities in some of the language patternings used in the dialogue passages in the early prose fiction and the *còmhraidhean*, for instance. Given that dialogue is such a predominant feature in so many of the stories, it is very often possible to identify stylistic features of the stories as having stemmed from the *còmhraidhean*, or at least as having likely been influenced by them. In some ways, this is unfortunate, as the narrative passages are regularly the more successful parts of many of the stories; this is even more clearly the case with the three novels that were published between 1912 and 1923.[27] In all three of the 'early' novels, there is a tendency for dialogue to be stilted, lacking credibility, whereas there are some action and descriptive passages that are comparatively absorbing. The first Gaelic novel, John MacCormick's *Dùn-àluinn* (MacCormaic 1912), may serve to illustrate both of these points. The first chapter of the novel centres on the deathbed of the main character's mother. Long passages of speech – especially the incongruously loquacious speech of the dying mother (9–12) – are interspersed with some sharply drawn images, bringing together metaphor, metonymy, pathetic fallacy and other devices effectively and with comparative economy of expression (e.g. 14–15). Derick Thomson has suggested that the 'style, especially near the beginning, is reminiscent of MacPherson's Ossian' (Thomson 1990: 218). Both Thomson (1990: 218) and Ronald Black (Black 2003) find the social commentary expressed by the character of the minister to be the most interesting feature of *Dùn-àluinn*, but MacLeod wrote:

> MacCormick tries to give a rather anaemic adventure yarn some weight by interpolating a long diatribe by one of his characters against the Clearances, but he does so very clumsily; his writing, usually dependable if uninspired, here frequently slips into sheer bathos. (MacLeod 1977: 212)

Aside from the proto-socialist ideology and the attempt at social commentary, the section of the novel where the minister faces up to the landlord is important for two reasons: firstly, it represents the midpoint of the development of the only rounded character in any of the three early novels; and, secondly, it demonstrates better than any other passage how the *còmhradh* as a form evolved into the dialogue of early-century Gaelic fiction. The landlord's opening gambit in the exchange would equate well with the narratistic element in the paradigm suggested for analysis of the structure of the *còmhraidhean*:

> 'So, so,' arsa Dùn-àluinn; 'sin agaibh a nis an seann sionnach mór féin a tha dol feadh an t-sluaigh a' searmonachadh an còirichean air an fhearann. An còirichean! A chuideachd!' (MacCormaic 1912: 108)

This is narrative-like, in that it serves the function of scene-building. MacCormick has brought the characters together for a confrontation without fully explaining the background to their quarrel, or even sufficiently clarifying that they have a long-standing quarrel. Thus, the opening salvoes perform the function of narrative or stage-direction.

The whole turn from the minister amounts to six sentences in addition to the opening 'seadh'. This is an extended monologue, which relates to the 'extended' element in the *còmhradh* structure. The minister's instigatory element then initiates an 'adjacency pair' (Sacks, Schegloff et al. 1974: 710; Schegloff and Sacks 1973: 295 ff), in that he would expect the landlord character to respond to his offer to debate. The landlord gives him a dispreferred response, however, by treating the minister's earlier imprecation as the initiation of an adjacency pair:

> 'Cha 'n e 'n dreòlan, ach an deagh lann,' ars esan. (MacCormaic 1912: 109)[28]

While at all points this early part of the exchange (which continues for most of the rest of the chapter) is much more heated, more bad-tempered and more serious than the *còmhraidhean* of Norman MacLeod, even this brief sortie into comparing the structure of *Dùn-àluinn*'s dialogue with the *Caraid nan Gaidheal* conversations should show that there is considerable potential for further investigation here.

As was already suggested, it would be a useful development of the analysis of the structure of the *còmhraidhean* to explore whether or not it has any relationship with drama in Gaelic. Considering that drama has been as productive a form as the short story, and considering also that it has, in many ways, been a more popular medium of expression than fiction (Macleod and Watson 2007: 280–2),[29] Gaelic drama deserves substantially more attention than it has received so far. Aside from a Master's thesis by Antoinette Butler (1994) and some work by Michelle Macleod, it seems that very little has been done on any aspect of Gaelic drama. Macleod's 2008 paper points towards the very real possibility of using stylistic analysis as a way of elucidating the ways in which some Gaelic dramatists achieve their effects. In discussing Tormod Calum Dòmhnallach's play *Chan fhada gu madainn* (1986), Macleod shows how the sound patterns in the dialogue are intended to echo the sound of the action (Macleod 2008: 413). A good deal more work could be undertaken in this area, including, but not limited to, analysis of the speech structures, in comparison with the *còmhraidhean* and dialogue in fiction. The possibilities for comparison are clear: the *còmhraidhean* are based on dialogue, just as drama is; drama was developed at the same time as fiction, and in a similar 'deliberate' fashion (Macleod and Watson 2007: 280); drama was created by many of the same people who 'invented' prose fiction (Watson 2008a), but as a form it became comparatively more popular within the Gaelic community (Macleod and Watson 2007: 280). Like the *còmhraidhean*, Gaelic plays are almost all short – normally one act long – and this imposes certain structural limitations on them (again, like the *còmhraidhean*). As Macleod and Watson observe, in the case of one of the more 'modernist' plays (Fionnlagh MacLeòid's *Ceann Cropaig*, 1967):

> the enclosed space accentuates language that is often banal. This play's dialogue structure is certainly one of its most striking features. Short, sharp lines throughout highlight that communication problems lead to 'inauthentic existence', but that, by being more attentive to language, an individual may better comprehend his or her predicament. (Macleod and Watson 2007: 282).

This quotation provides a timely reminder that it is not just the structure of Gaelic literature that bears a linguistic interest: in a disproportionately high number of instances, even in a contemporary, postmodern cultural landscape, language is itself habitually a central theme of the writing. Given the minoritised and precarious position of Gaelic, and given the Gaelic community's situation, literally on the periphery of Europe (cf. Craig 1996: 11–30), it is easy to understand why this should be the case: Iain Crichton Smith's essay 'Real People in a Real Place', and other essays in his volume *Towards the Human* (1986), provide further insights into why language is such a crucial theme in Gaelic writing (see Macleod 2009). In any event, there are currently far more questions than answers regarding both the perception and the use of language in Gaelic literature. With drama, there are even more questions, as almost all the plays were written for production rather than publication, raising the question of whether this lends itself to a formulaic style or to innovation, or neither. It also raises the question of authorial control: with unpublished drama, written only for production – sometimes for a one-off competition – there must be the possibility of actors' ad libs or mistakes significantly altering the import of certain turns. While other literary forms also incorporate an element of authorial uncertainty (courtesy of editors, copy-editors, and the like), the play as produced provides an opportunity for these changes to be made without the writer's final approval or acceptance; and without any record of the alteration.

CONCLUSION

Because of the nature of this book, this chapter could touch on only a few of the aspects of the main genres in Gaelic literature. Even so, it should be clear by now that language has been a topic of special interest for scholars who have studied the literature, and it should also be clear that there is almost no limit to the work that can still be done, even if no more writings of any literary significance are published from now on.

On drama, for instance, it would be possible to investigate the interplay between characters, and discover whether the techniques of Conversation Analysis can go some way towards accounting for the popularity of the genre. Is drama popular because it uses a vernacular that is closer to what people recognise as the Gaelic they speak every day, as opposed to the literary language they see in the short story or novel? Or is the dialogue in drama more humorous or more 'natural', or is it more pointed? For instance, in his play *A' Chùirt*, Iain Crichton Smith uses the distinction between *thu* and *sibh* throughout as one way of underlining Patrick Sellar's alienation from the Gaelic community. There are other aspects to the speech patterns of the three main characters in this play that deserve analysis, to illuminate how Smith succeeds in depicting the gulf between their respective viewpoints. Similarly, in one short story, Norman Campbell uses dialogue with Anglicised structures and vocabulary in a young character in order to show the way the language is attenuating from generation to generation within a particular community (Watson forthcoming b), and in the Gaelic community in general. In the novel, language was an important issue from the beginning, and has continued to be so up to the present day (Watson 2007). Some authors have made deliberate efforts to mirror their own dialect, some have deliberately edged towards obscurantism, and others have attempted to emulate reality by mixing Gaelic and English in dialogue (one or two have even mixed the languages in the narrative).

In recent years, scholars have begun to understand that there is also a sociolinguistic side to the issue of language in literature (McLeod 1998; Watson 2007; but cf. Blackie 1876: 26 and ff.). Some critics have also contributed to the sociolinguistic aspect of the literature, perhaps unconsciously, by valuing the language itself, sometimes paying the work the backhanded compliment of praising the language while saying little about the quality of anything else. Donald John MacLeod took this sociolinguistic role a stage further, by coming to a conclusion also hinted at by Derick Thomson (1990: 249–99):

> *Deireadh an Fhoghair* is an exciting new work by a young writer.
> A language which could produce it is surely not a dying language.
> (MacLeod 1987: 335)

There are many other areas where linguistically informed criticism could be worth pursuing in the years to come. Scholars with an interest in perceptual dialectology may find stylistic analysis a fruitful avenue, both diachronically and synchronically (see again Watson 2007). Similarly, the analysis of the historical development of syntax, morphology and even phonology, to some extent, may also provide possibilities for research. Donald John MacLeod, among others, has suggested that another possibility might lie in comparing the language of the past century or so with the language in the vast store of verse and prose that have come down to us from the long-lasting Gaelic oral culture (MacLeod 1987: 333). This would be of particular interest, perhaps, to critics working on the writing of Duncan Gillies[30] or Sorley MacLean, both of whom have consciously drawn upon the oral tradition in their work. In any case, writers and critics of Gaelic literature retain an interest in language, both formally and thematically, and there is every sign that this will continue into the future.

BIBLIOGRAPHY

http://www.bbc.co.uk/scotland/alba/foghlam/larachnambard/lit_
crit/domhnall_macamhlaigh3.shtml (accessed 2 June 2009).

http://www.bbc.co.uk/scotland/alba/foghlam/larachnambard/
transcript_popup.shtml?video=44534099&audio=&author_
dir=domhnall_macamhlaigh&author_number=4&popup=yes
(accessed 2 June 2009).

Bateman, Meg (2007), 'The Autobiography in Scottish Gaelic,' in Ian
Brown, Thomas Owen Clancy, Susan Manning and Murray Pittock
(eds), *The Edinburgh History of Scottish Literature Volume 3:
Modern Transformations: New Identities (from 1918)*, Edinburgh:
Edinburgh University Press, pp. 225–30.

Bergin, Osborn (ed.) (1909), *Stories from Keating's History of Ireland*,
Dublin: Royal Irish Academy, reprinted many times in three
editions.

Black, Ronald (ed.) (1999), *An Tuil: Anthology of 20th Century Scottish
Gaelic Verse*, Edinburgh: Polygon.

Black, Ronald (Raghnall MacIlleDhuibh) (2003), Review of *Dùn-àluinn*,
The Scotsman, 5 December.

Black, Ronald (2007), 'Alasdair mac Mhaighstir Alasdair and the New
Gaelic Poetry', in Susan Manning, Ian Brown, Thomas Clancy and
Murray Pittock (eds), *The Edinburgh History of Scottish Literature
Volume 2: Enlightenment, Britain and Europe (1707–1918)*,
Edinburgh: Edinburgh University Press, pp. 110–24.

Blackie, John Stuart (1876), *The Language and Literature of the
Scottish Highlands*, Edinburgh: Edmonston and Douglas.

Blankenhorn, Virgina (2003), *Irish Song-craft and Metrical Practice
Since 1600*, Lewiston and Lampeter: Edwin Mellen Press.

Butler, Antoinette (1994), 'An Outline of Scottish Gaelic Drama Before
1945', unpublished MLitt dissertation, University of Edinburgh.

Byrne, Michel (2007), 'Monsters and Goddesses: Culture Re-energised
in the Poetry of Ruaraidh MacThòmais and Aonghas MacNeacail', in
Ian Brown, with Thomas Owen Clancy, Susan Manning and Murray
Pittock (eds), *The Edinburgh History of Scottish Literature: Volume
3: Modern Transformations: New Identities (from 1918)*, Edinburgh:
Edinburgh University Press, pp. 176–84.

Byrne, Michel (2008), '"A Moment of History": Iain Mac a' Ghobhainn agus "Dàin do Eimhir" Shomhairle MhicGill-Eain', *Caindel Alban; Fèill-Sgrìobhainn do Dhòmhnall E. Meek: Scottish Gaelic Studies* XXIV, pp. 97–114.

Campbell, Donald (1862), *The Language, Poetry, and Music of the Highland Clans*, Edinburgh: D. R. Collie and Son.

Chapman, Malcolm (1978), *The Gaelic Vision in Scottish Culture*, London: Croom Helm, and Montreal: McGill-Queen's University Press.

Clerk, Archibald (ed.) [1867] (1910), *Caraid nan Gaidheal: The Friend of the Gael: a Choice Selection of Gaelic Writings*, Edinburgh: John Grant,.

Craig, Cairns (1996), *Out of History*, Edinburgh: Polygon.

Fowler, Roger (1977), *Linguistics and the Novel*, London: Methuen.

Gillies, William (2005), 'Sorley MacLean's Gaelic Oeuvre: Writing in a Dying Tongue', in Marco Fazzini (ed.), *Alba Literaria: A History of Scottish Literature*, Venice: Amos Edizioni, pp. 625–40.

Gillies, William (2006), 'On the Study of Gaelic Literature', in Michel Byrne, Thomas Owen Clancy and Sheila Kidd (eds), *Litreachas & Eachdraidh: Rannsachadh na Gàidhlig 2: Glaschu 2002/Literature & History: Papers from the Second Conference of Scottish Gaelic Studies: Glasgow 2002*, Glasgow: Roinn nan Cànanan Ceilteach, pp. 1–32.

Gillies, William (2007), 'Merely a Bard? William Ross and Gaelic Poetry', in *Aiste: Rannsachadh air Litreachas Gàidhlig: Studies in Gaelic Literature* Vol. 1, pp. 123–69.

Kidd, Sheila M. (2000), 'Social Control and Social Criticism: The Nineteenth-century *còmhradh*', *Scottish Gaelic Studies* XX, pp. 67–87.

Kidd, Sheila M. (2002), 'Caraid nan Gaidheal and "Friend of Emigration": Gaelic emigration literature of the 1840s', *Scottish Historical Review* 81:1, pp. 52–69.

Knott, Eleanor (1934), *An Introduction to Irish Syllabic Poetry of the Period 1200–1600, With Selections, Notes and Glossary*, Cork and Dublin: Cork University Press.

Mac a' Ghobhainn, Iain (1966), *A' Chùirt*, Inverness: An Comunn Gaidhealach.

Mac a' Ghobhainn, Iain (1987), *An t-Eilean agus an Cànan*, Glasgow: Roinn nan Cànan Ceilteach, Oilthigh Ghlaschu.

MacAmhlaigh, Dòmhnall (1967), *Seòbhrach ás a' Chlaich*, Glasgow: Gairm.

MacCormaic, Iain (1912), *Dùn-àluinn: no An t-Oighre 'na Dhìobarach*, Glasgow: Alasdair MacLaren and Sons.

MacCurdy, Edward (1949–50), 'Norman MacLeod – "Caraid nan Gaidheal"', in *Transactions of the Gaelic Society of Inverness* XXXIX–XL, pp. 229–42.

MacGillÌosa, Donnchadh (2004), *Tocasaid 'Ain Tuirc*, Inverness: CLÀR (Ùr-Sgeul).

MacInnes, John (1986), 'Language, Metre and Diction in the Poetry of Sorley Maclean', in Raymond J. Ross and Joy Hendry (eds), *Sorley MacLean: Critical Essays*, Edinburgh: Scottish Academic Press, pp. 137–53.

MacInnes, John (2006a), 'The Gaelic Literary Tradition', in Michael Newton (ed.), *Dùthchas nan Gàidheal: Selected Essays of John MacInnes*, Edinburgh: Birlinn, pp. 163–83.

MacInnes, John (2006b), 'The Panegyric Code in Gaelic Poetry and its Historical Background', in Michael Newton (ed.), *Dùthchas nan Gàidheal: Selected Essays of John MacInnes*, Edinburgh: Birlinn, pp. 265–319 (orginally published in *Transactions of the Gaelic Society of Inverness* 50, pp. 435–98).

Mackinnon, Lachlan (ed.) (1956), *The Prose Writings of Donald MacKinnon 1839–1914, The First Professor of Celtic in the University of Edinburgh*, Edinburgh: Oliver and Boyd for the Scottish Gaelic Texts Society.

MacLean, Donald (1912), *The Literature of the Scottish Gael*, Edinburgh and London: William Hodge and Company.

MacLean, Magnus (1904), *The Literature of the Highlands*, Glasgow and Dublin: Blackie & Son Ltd., 1904.

MacLeod, Donald John (1977), 'Gaelic Prose', *Transactions of the Gaelic Society of Inverness* XLIX: 1974–76, Inverness, pp. 198–230.

MacLeod, Donald John (1987), 'Gaelic Prose', in Cairns Craig (ed.), *The History of Scottish Literature Volume 4: Twentieth Century*, Aberdeen: Aberdeen University Press, pp. 331–5.

Macleod, Michelle (2007), 'Gaelic Prose Fiction in English', in Berthold Shoene (ed.), *The Edinburgh Companion to Contemporary Scottish Literature*, Edinburgh: Edinburgh University Press, pp. 149–56.

Macleod, Michelle and Watson, Moray (2007), 'In the Shadow of the Bard: the Gaelic Short Story, Novel and Drama Since the Early Twentieth Century', in Ian Brown, Thomas Owen Clancy, Susan Manning and Murray Pittock (eds), *The Edinburgh History of Scottish Literature: Volume 3: Modern Transformations: New Identities (from 1918)*, Edinburgh: Edinburgh University Press, pp. 273–82.

Macleod, Michelle (2008), 'The Gaelic Plays of Tormod Calum Dòmhnallach', in Colm Ó Baoill and Nancy R. McGuire (eds), *Caindel Alban: Fèill-sgrìobhainn do Dhòmhnall E. Meek: Scottish Gaelic Studies* XXIV, Aberdeen, pp. 405–18.

Macleod, Michelle (2009), 'Language and Identity in Modern Gaelic Verse,' in Ian Brown and Alan Riach (eds), *The Edinburgh Companion to Twentieth-Century Scottish Literature*, Edinburgh: Edinburgh University Press, pp. 167–80.

McLeod, Wilson (1998), 'The Packaging of Gaelic Poetry', *Chapman* 89/90, pp. 149–51.

McLeod, Wilson (1999), 'Galldachd, Gàidhealtachd, Garbhchrìochan', *Scottish Gaelic Studies* XIX, pp. 1–20.

McLeod, Wilson (2004), *Divided Gaels: Cultural Identities in Scotland and Ireland c.1200–c.1650*, Oxford: Oxford University Press.

MacNeill, Nigel (1892), *The Literature of the Highlanders: A History of Gaelic Literature from the Earliest Times to the Present Day*, Inverness: John Noble, 1892.

MacThòmais, Ruaraidh/Derick Thomson (1967), *Eadar Samhradh is Foghar*, Glasgow: Gairm.

Meek, Donald E. (2003)(ed.), *Caran an t-Saoghail: The Wiles of the World*, Edinburgh: Birlinn.

Meek, Donald E. (2007), 'Gaelic Literature in the Nineteenth Century', in Susan Manning, Ian Brown, Thomas Clancy and Murray Pittock (eds), *The Edinburgh History of Scottish Literature Volume 2: Enlightenment, Britain and Europe (1707–1918)*, Edinburgh: Edinburgh University Press, pp. 253–66.

Newton, Michael (2006) (ed.), *Dùthchas nan Gàidheal: Selected Essays of John MacInnes*, Edinburgh: Birlinn.

Ní Annracháin, Máire (2007), 'Shifting Boundaries: Scottish Gaelic Literature after Devolution', in Berthold Shoene (ed.), *The Edinburgh Companion to Contemporary Scottish Literature*, Edinburgh: Edinburgh University Press, pp. 88–96.

Ó Baoill, Colm and Ó Dochartaigh, Cathair (2005, 2006), *Trí Rainn agus Amhrán*, Bridge of Allan: Clann Tuirc; first published in partial form by Lagan Press in Belfast, 1996.

Ó Cuív, Brian (1966), 'The Phonetic Basis of Classical Modern Irish Rhyme', *Ériu* 20, pp. 94–103.

Ó Cuív, Brian (1973), 'The Linguistic Training of the Medieval Irish Poet', *Celtica* 10, pp. 114–40.

Ó Maolalaigh, Roibeard (2006), 'On the Possible Origins of Scottish Gaelic *iorram* "rowing song"', in Michel Byrne, Thomas Owen Clancy and Sheila Kidd (eds), *Litreachas & Eachdraidh:*

Rannsachadh na Gàidhlig 2: Glaschu 2002/Literature & History: Papers from the Second Conference of Scottish Gaelic Studies: Glasgow 2002, Glasgow: Roinn nan Cànanan Ceilteach, pp. 232–88.

Reid, Ian (1977), *The Short Story*, London and New York: Methuen.

Reiss, Katharina (1981), 'Type, Kind and Individuality of Text: Decision Making in Translation', *Poetics Today*, 2:4, Translation Theory and Intercultural Relations, pp. 121–31.

Sacks, Harvey, Schegloff, Emanuel A. and Jefferson, Gail (1974), 'A Simplest Systematics for the Organization of Turn-taking for Conversation', *Language*, 50:4, pp. 696–735.

Schegloff, Emanuel A. and Sacks, Harvey (1973), 'Opening up Closings', *Semiotica* 8, pp. 289–327.

Smith, Iain Crichton/Mac a' Ghobhainn (1960), *Bùrn is Aran*, Glasgow: Gairm; 2nd edn 1974, excluding verse; 3rd edn 1987.

Smith, Iain Crichton (1984a), *The Exiles*, Manchester: Carcanet, and Dublin: Raven Arts Press.

Smith, Iain Crichton (1984b), *Selected Poems*, Manchester: Carcanet.

Smith, Iain Crichton (1986), *Towards the Human*, Edinburgh: MacDonald Publishers.

Smith, Iain Crichton (1989), 'The Double Man', in R. P. Draper (ed.), *The Literature of Region and Nation*, Basingstoke: Macmillan Press.

Thomson, Derick S. (1951), *The Gaelic Sources of Macpherson's 'Ossian'*, Edinburgh: Oliver & Boyd.

Thomson, Derick S. (1974), *The New Verse in Scottish Gaelic: A Structural Analysis*, Dublin: University College Dublin.

Thomson, Derick S. (2007), 'Scottish Gaelic Literary History and Criticism in the Twentieth Century', in *Aiste: Rannsachadh air Litreachas Gàidhlig: Studies in Gaelic Literature* Vol. 1, pp. 1–21.

Thomson, Derick S. [1974] (1990), *An Introduction to Gaelic Poetry*, Edinburgh: Edinburgh University Press.

Watson, Moray (2006a), 'Dualchasan a' bualadh ri chèile', *Gath* 2, pp. 40–4.

Watson, Moray (2006b), '"Dh'fhiosraich mi Céitean"', in Wilson McLeod, James E. Fraser and Anja Gunderloch (eds), *Cànan & Cultar/Language & Culture: Rannsachadh na Gàidhlig 3*, Edinburgh: Dunedin Academic Press, pp. 129–36.

Watson, Moray (2007), 'Language in the Development of the Gaelic Novel', *Northern Scotland* 26.

Watson, Moray (2008a), 'Argyll and the Gaelic Prose Fiction of the Early Twentieth Century', in Colm Ó Baoill and Nancy R. McGuire (eds), *Caindel Alban: Fèill-sgrìobhainn do Dhòmhnall E. Meek: Scottish Gaelic Studies* XXIV, Aberdeen, pp. 573–88.

Watson, Moray (2008b), 'Sorley MacLean', http://www.litencyc.com/php/speople.php?rec=true&UID=4975.

Watson, Moray (2009), 'Iain Crichton Smith', http://www.litencyc.com/php/speople.php?rec=true&UID=4117.

Watson, Moray (forthcoming a), 'Monologue, Rhetoric and Dialectic: How Caraid nan Gaidheal Structures a *Còmhradh*'.

Watson, Moray (forthcoming b), 'Cuirp Ghleansach Dhubh: An Saoghal ann an Uirsgeul na Gàidhlig', in Niall O'Gallagher and Peter Mackay (eds), *Sùil air an t-Saoghal*, Skye: Clò Ostaig.

Watson, William J. (1918), *Bàrdachd Ghàidhlig: Specimens of Gaelic Poetry 1550–1900*, Inverness: An Comunn Gaidhealach.

Watson, William J. [1915] (1929), *Rosg Gàidhlig: Specimens of Gaelic Prose*, printed for An Comunn Gaidhealach by Alexander MacLaren and Sons, Glasgow.

Wentworth, Roy G. (2000), 'An Dàrnacha Beum ann an Òrain na Gàidhlig', in *Scottish Gaelic Studies* XX, pp. 117–46.

Whyte, Christopher (ed.) (2002), *Dàin do Eimhir* by Somhairle MacGill-Eain, Edinburgh: ASLS.

Whyte, Christopher (2005), 'The Gaelic Poetry of George Campbell Hay: Defence from Recent Strictures', in Mario Fazzini (ed.), *Alba Literaria*, Venice: Amos Edizioni, pp. 565–76.

Whyte, Christopher (2006a), 'Sorley MacLean's "Dàin do Eimhir": New Light from the Aberdeen Holdings', in Michel Byrne, Thomas Owen Clancy and Sheila Kidd (eds), *Litreachas & Eachdraidh: Rannsachadh na Gàidhlig 2: Glaschu 2002/Literature & History: Papers from the Second Conference of Scottish Gaelic Studies: Glasgow 2002*, Glasgow: Roinn nan Cànanan Ceilteach, pp. 183–99.

Whyte, Christopher (2006b), 'Sorley MacLean's "An Cuilthionn": The Emergence of the Text', in Wilson McLeod, James E. Fraser and Anja Gunderloch (eds), *Cànan & Cultar/Rannsachadh na Gàidhlig 3*, Edinburgh: Dunedin Academic Press, pp. 111–27.

Whyte, Christopher (2007a), 'Derick Thomson: The Recent Poetry', in *Aiste: Rannsachadh air Litreachas Gàidhlig: Studies in Gaelic Literature* Volume 1, pp. 22–37.

Whyte, Christopher (2007b), 'Confessions of a Chinese Beetle or, Reflections on Writing Poetry in Gaelic in the Twenty-first Century', in Sheila Kidd (ed.), *Glasgow: Baile Mòr nan Gàidheal/City of the Gaels*, Glasgow: Roinn na Ceiltis, Glasgow University, pp. 228–38.

Widdowson, Henry (1972), 'On the Deviance of Literary Discourse', *Style* 6:3, pp. 294–306.

NOTES

1 I am using the term 'original literature' here to make it clear that I am not dealing with the folk tale, legend, mythology or any other genre of anonymously composed or 'traditionally' transmitted 'literature'. Similarly, I am not dealing with literature in translation. It may be that a convincing case can be made for using stylistic techniques to analyse the artefacts of the oral culture, and it is perfectly clear that these techniques can be fruitful when analysing translations. Neither of these is my concern in this short chapter, however.

2 Cf., for instance, Bergin's selected edition of Keating's *Foras Feasa ar Éirinn* (Bergin 1909), *Stories from Keating's History of Ireland*, which is prefaced by a short description of several aspects of the language of the text, especially information on verb forms.

3 This is a rather sweeping statement, of course, and it should be noted that Watson's immediate predecessor in the Chair at Edinburgh, Donald MacKinnon, contributed significantly to Gaelic literary criticism at the time (See Meek 2007: 260, and see Mackinnon 1956). Similarly, Magnus Maclean, first Celtic lecturer in Glasgow, made important contributions to our appreciation of Gaelic literature (MacLean 1904, in particular). It may be a rather useful generalisation, however, in light of the direction of Celtic in Scotland throughout the twentieth century.

4 Called by Watson, and known conventionally as, the Middle Irish period. Colm Ó Baoill deals with the naming of earlier manifestations of the Goidelic languages in this volume.

5 They publish under the Gaelic versions of their names: Tormod Caimbeul and Donnchadh MacGillìosa, respectively. Campbell is also known more familiarly as Tormod a' Bhocsair.

6 See Ó Baoill and Ó Dochartaigh (2005, 2006) on the 'song' metres in relation to the syllabic metres.

7 English does not escape his disapproval here, either, with his disdain primarily directed at the dialect in the South, which he describes as 'a mere jargon' (Watson 1918: xxxiv).

8 See Ó Cuív, *Seven Centuries of Irish Learning* (1961), for an insight into how Irish scholars have, in the past, sometimes treated the Scottish part of the tradition dismissively. It is notable that the phrase ('sea-divided Gael') is part of Watson's vocabulary, too (1918: xxviii).

9 No mention is made of Manx, and there is no hint as to whether or not the Classical, common tradition ever reached that island. The only indication that the language even exists comes in a single note in the glossary.

10 There is a new book in progress by Pía Coira which will analyse the rhetorical codes of around 800 poems in some detail.

11 Thomson publishes his poetry under the Gaelic version of his name: Ruaraidh MacThòmais.

12 The designation refers to Donald MacAulay's 1976 anthology *Nua-Bhàrdachd Ghàidhlig: Modern Scottish Gaelic Poems*, which drew together the work of Sorley MacLean, George Campbell Hay, Derick Thomson, Iain Crichton Smith and MacAulay himself. These five were among the leading literary lights in the second half of the twentieth century. Subsequent to the anthology's publication, they have commonly been thought of as a 'group', even though there is no significant evidence to suggest that they thought of themselves in this way. Clearly, they identified with each other's work, in the sense that each recognised at least some

of the others as major writers, but I have argued elsewhere that it would be prudent to bear in mind that they were not, in any way, a conscious 'movement', aside from the fact that they were all aware of one another as fellow 'modernisers' (Watson 2006b).

13 MacAulay publishes his poetry under the Gaelic version of his name: Dòmhnall MacAmhlaigh.

14 I am here defining 'epigram' as the final section of a poem (rather than as a complete poem in its own right); most often, in MacAulay's case, taking the form of a closed couplet separated by a line break.

15 Iain Crichton Smith notes that 'One of his [i.e. MacAulay's] aims seems to be to eradicate the sometimes false music of Gaelic so that he can make statements which will not seduce the ear from their truth' (Smith 1986: 105).

16 The reader may listen to MacAulay reading this poem at the Làrach nam Bàrd site: http://www.bbc.co.uk/scotland/alba/foghlam/larachnambard/lit_crit/domhnall_ macamhlaigh3.shtml.

17 Note that the word used for 'chair' ('cathair') has particular connotations for the poet. As he explains, it is a key point in understanding the poem and its theme of 'inbhe' (status): http://www.bbc.co.uk/scotland/alba/foghlam/larachnambard/ transcript_popup.shtml?video=44534099&audio=&author_dir=domhnall_ macamhlaigh&author_number=4&popup=yes (accessed 2 June 2009).

18 Fowler states that 'Language is a powerfully committing medium to work in' (1977: 76).

19 Campbell publishes his poetry under the Gaelic version of his name: Maoilios Caimbeul.

20 See MacAmhlaigh (1967) and MacThòmais (1967), two works already consulted here, as examples of a common way of incorporating translations into books of Gaelic poems before the fashion for facing translations took hold. The translations are demoted to the back of the book, and not all poems are translated.

21 Smith published under both the English version of his name and also, when writing Gaelic, as Iain Mac a' Ghobhainn.

22 MacLean published under the Gaelic version of his name, which has appeared with more than one spelling, but is usually 'Somhairle MacGill-Eain' (the Anglicised version of his surname appears with both the capitalised and lower-case L, sometimes within the same publication).

23 Michel Byrne has noted that MacLean 'questioned the relevance of creating literature in a 'dying tongue'' (Byrne 2007: 176), and Gillies (2005) also picked up on this phrase.

24 Although there has been a tendency to see the nineteenth century as a period of poor literary quality (implied, for instance, throughout the relevant section in MacLeod 1977: 201–8), scholars like Meek (2003, 2007) and MacInnes (2006a: 173–81) have convincingly argued against this. The tendency seems not unlike – and almost definitely related to – the tendency of earlier generations of Scottish literature commentators to disparage the Kailyard and other aspects of non-Gaelic Scottish literature.

25 In the first còmhradh recorded in Caraid nan Gaidheal, the character Eoghan complains that Gaelic religious writing is usually too 'domhain' for him to get much out of it. His interlocutor Lachann explains that this is because these writings are usually translated from English, suggesting that the act of translation has resulted in obscurity, which confirms that MacLeod himself was aware of this problem (Clerk 1910: 11).

26 'The communication of content with a persuasive character' (Reiss 1981: 124).

27 Although, unlike many of the texts of the period, *An t-Ogha Mór*, the second novel, has far more narrative and a much more 'normal' balance between narrative and dialogue. Similarly, the third novel, *An Cailin Sgiathanach*, has a better balance of narrative and dialogue: however, there are very long passages which are highly reminiscent of the *cómhraidhean*.

28 Note also MacCormick's predilection for puns, which is prevalent.

29 It thus fulfils Donald John MacLeod's criterion of pleasing the 'man on the croft' (MacLeod 1977: 225).

30 Gillies publishes his work in his Gaelic name, Donnchadh MacGilllosa.

CHAPTER 5

A' Ghàidhlig an Canada: Scottish Gaelic in Canada

Kenneth E. Nilsen

INTRODUCTION

By the second half of the nineteenth century, Scottish Gaelic was the third most widely spoken language in Canada after English and French. This essay will provide an overview of immigration by Gaelic-speaking Highlanders to Canada from the 1770s to the twentieth century with reference to the use of the language in the new country. Many historians have dealt with the reasons for emigration from the Highlands and the reader may wish to consult some of the in-depth studies.[1]

Although the story of Highland emigration to Canada dates principally from the 1770s on, the first Scottish connection to Canada occurred a century and a half earlier. In 1621 Sir William Alexander obtained from King James VI/I a charter for the territory of Nova Scotia. This consisted of a vast area between New England and Newfoundland and included present-day Nova Scotia, New Brunswick and Prince Edward Island. It was the region known to the French as Acadie. In 1629 James Stuart, Lord Ochiltree, landed with sixty colonists on the shore of Cape Breton at Baleine, near present-day Louisburg, and began construction of a fort on the site. Within two months, this fledgling colony was attacked by a French fleet under Captain Charles Daniel who captured the Scots and brought the majority of them to England where they were set free but Lord Ochiltree and several others were taken as prisoners to Dieppe, France. Another fledgling Scottish colony on the mainland of Nova Scotia under the leadership of Sir William Alexander's son, also a Sir William Alexander, met with a similar fate in 1632. It may be impossible to determine whether any of these early Scottish colonists were Gaelic speakers but in any case, in 1632, under the terms of the Treaty of Saint Germain-en-Laye, control of Acadie/Nova Scotia was returned to France.

MIGRATION

Over the course of the next century, control of the region would change hands several times between England and France. In 1713, the Treaty of Utrecht ceded mainland Nova Scotia to England and left Île Royale (Cape Breton) and Île Saint Jean (Prince Edward Island) under French rule. British presence in the region was negligible until the 1740s. The first major British move into Nova Scotia was marked by the establishment of Halifax as capital in 1749. In the 1750s hostilities between Britain and France resumed in the Seven Years' War. It was during this time that the Acadian population was removed and sent into exile, an episode known in French as 'le grand dérangement'. In 1758 British forces captured the French fortress at Louisburg in Cape Breton. Included among the British were the 78th Fraser Highlanders who, the following year, were active at the battle at the Plains of Abraham in Quebec. Along with the Fraser Highlanders was their minister Reverend Robert MacPherson who, along with a number of the troops, remained in Quebec at the end of the war in 1763.

Once Acadie had been cleared of Acadians, the region was open to colonists from Britain and British colonies. The first Highlanders to settle in the region came from Perthshire to the Island of St John (later Prince Edward Island) in 1770 (Bumsted 1982: 56). A more notable settlement in the island occurred two years later when Highlanders from Clanranald estates emigrated in a scheme organised by Glenaladale with the backing of the Catholic church in Scotland. This consisted mainly of Catholics who were motivated to emigrate at least in part due to religious persecution. They sailed on the ship *Alexander* in May 1772 and were followed a year later by Glenaladale himself, known in Gaelic as *Fear a' Ghlinne* (Bumsted 1982: 57 ff).

In 1773 the first influx of Highlanders to Nova Scotia arrived on the ship *Hector* in Pictou with nearly 200 passengers. They had boarded the ship at Loch Broom and came mostly from Ross-shire and Assynt, and to a lesser extent from East Sutherland, Beauly and Inverness. The voyage took two and a half months. These immigrants had not been forced to leave Scotland but many were dissatisfied with what they considered to be high rents and had been enticed by the descriptions given by emigration agents (Bumsted 1982: 61 ff).

In 1784, after the American Revolution, a group of Highlanders who had emigrated to the Mohawk Valley region of New York in 1773, moved to Glengarry township in what would become Upper Canada in 1791 and is now part of the province of Ontario (Bumsted 1982: 67; McLean 1991: 82 ff). Among the immigrants to the Mohawk Valley who later moved on to Canada were Simon MacTavish who became one of the founders of the Northwest Company and Alexander MacKenzie, the explorer and fur trader. Throughout the course of the nineteenth century, many Gaelic speakers would be involved in the North American fur trade. Some of these men took Indian wives and there are reports that the children of some of these unions were fluent in several languages, including Gaelic.

In the early 1790s there were several groups of Highlanders, including many Catholics, who emigrated to Nova Scotia, Prince Edward Island and Glengarry. In 1790 ninety Highlanders left Morar, Arisaig, Glengarry and Eigg and journeyed to Glengarry, Canada. In the same year two ships brought a total of 328 passengers to Prince Edward Island and in 1791 four vessels brought 1300 emigrants to Pictou, Nova Scotia. This group arrived in Pictou in September, wintered there, but later ventured east into Antigonish County on the Nova Scotia mainland just west of Cape Breton Island (Bumsted 1982: 74).

Thus by 1800, there were three major Gaelic-speaking areas in British North America: Pictou and Antigonish, Nova Scotia; Stanhope and Scotchfort on the north shore of Prince Edward Island; and Glengarry, Upper Canada. These areas continued to receive sporadically additions to their Highland population over the course of the next half-century.

Although many of those who emigrated before 1800 had done so of their own volition, there were instances of individuals who had been 'cleared' from their holdings or at any rate threatened with eviction. Such was the case of the emigration in 1785 and 1786 from the Glengarry Estates when tenants were about to be evicted from their land and emigrated to Glengarry in Canada (McLean 1991: 102–8).

Many of these early emigrants paid for their own passage. Some oral traditions collected from Donald Cameron of Antigonish County, Nova Scotia refer to emigrants and their monetary resources. Cameron's own maternal great-great-grandfather Murdoch MacRae, who emigrated from Kintail to Antigonish early in the nineteenth century was known in Gaelic as *Murchadh nan Ciad* because of the comparatively large amount of money he brought with him to Nova Scotia.[2] Another tradition tells of an anonymous woman who was asked by a male acquaintance of hers how she had protected her funds on the voyage to the New World. Donald Cameron explained:

> There were thieves on the boats coming over, some people had left their money behind in Scotland and had it sent over later. One woman wouldn't do that. She hid the money. She was telling this to a man who asked her where she had hidden it. She took

him aside and said, 'A dh'ìnnse dhut na fìrinn, chuir mi suas 'nam dhrathais e.' To which the man replied, 'Bha thu cho gòrach. Sin a' chiad àit' a chuirinn mo làmh!'[3]

Some Highlanders who had landed in Pictou in the 1790s and moved eastward to Antigonish gradually made their way further east to Cape Breton Island. Indeed, Michael MacDonald, who emigrated to Prince Edward Island in the 1770s, is reputed to have spent the winter of 1775 in the area of Judique, Cape Breton where he composed the song, 'O, 's àlainn an t-àite' (MacDonell 1982: 58). A gravestone for Sarah McInnis (née MacDonald) in the Catholic cemetery on Verona Island in the State of Maine reads, 'Sarah, wife of Lauchlin McInnis, died Dec 31, 1868, AE 70 yrs, a native of Cape Britton Isle', indicating that Highlanders were on the island before 1800. The first recorded landing of Highlanders directly on Cape Breton, however, was in August 1802 when a ship arrived at Sydney with 299 passengers from the Highlands on board (Hunter 1994: 124). This was the beginning of an influx that would eventually make Cape Breton one of the most Gaelic regions outside of Scotland.

The early years of the nineteenth century saw a large flow of Highland emigration to America. Estimates vary from 6000 emigrants in 1802 to 20,000 in 1804. Highland lairds were alarmed at this outpouring of population and feared it would mean an end to their supply of cheap labour. The government too was distressed by this depopulation and moved in July 1803 to legislate the Ships' Passengers Act, a law that ostensibly aimed to improve conditions on transatlantic vessels but which, in fact, by raising the cost of passage, prevented many would-be emigrants from leaving. One obvious result was that those who could afford the new higher rates were undeterred from leaving while the poorer members of society were left behind.

An interesting figure to emerge in the debate around emigration was Lord Selkirk.[4] He had a genuine interest in improving the lot of Highlanders and was convinced that emigration to British North America was the answer. He even learned Gaelic, travelled to North America, bought lands there and initiated several emigration projects. In the first of these he led 800 from Skye, Uist and Mull to Prince Edward Island in 1803 (Bumsted 1982: 146–7). Later endeavours of his brought additional emigrants to Prince Edward Island, to Baldoon in Upper Canada and to Red River in Manitoba. This latter scheme involved a number of individuals from Kildonan, Sutherland who had been the victims of the notorious evictions of 1813.

Emigration continued, but due to the Ships' Passengers Act, at a reduced rate. By the end of the Napoleonic Wars in 1815, Highland landlords who had been profiting from the kelp industry witnessed dramatic declines in their income due to the reduced demand for their product. Many of them sought to increase the profitability of their holdings by introducing extensive sheep-farming. This necessitated the removal of their tenants to make room for sheep-runs. The government rescinded the Ships' Passenger Act and soon major evictions led to large-scale emigration. It is estimated that between 1815 and 1840 20,000 Gaelic speakers emigrated to Nova Scotia. In the 1840s Cape Breton suffered from the potato blight which also ravaged Ireland and the Highlands. After this time evidence for Highland emigration to Cape Breton is very sparse. One family of MacKenzies from Lewis is known to have settled in Ross' Point, Boulardrie Island, Cape Breton in the 1880s.[5] Rory MacLeod and his family from Berneray, Harris emigrated to Framboise, Cape Breton as late as 1906. Their departure was commemorated in song by the local Berneray bard Eachann Ruadh MacFhionghain.[6]

During the first half of the nineteenth century there were clearances throughout the Highlands that led to emigration to Canada. For instance, in the late 1820s the Duke of Hamilton cleared his lands on the Isle of Arran. A percentage of these displaced Arraners emigrated to Quebec and eventually settled in the Eastern townships in the region of Megantic (Little 2000: 3–30).[7] Several decades later the area was settled by emigrants from the Isle of Lewis (Bennett 1998).

In 1834 the Marquis of Breadalbane had extensive clearances carried out on his properties in Perthshire. Many of those cleared made their way to a new section of Ontario named North Easthope in what is now Perth County. Alexander MacKenzie in his *History of the Highland Clearances* published in 1884 and 'altered and revised' in 1914 says this about the Breadalbane clearance:

> What came of the dispersed? The least adventurous or poorest of them slipped away into the nearest manufacturing town, or mining districts where there was a demand for unskilled labourers. There some of them flourished, but not a few of them foundered. The larger portion of them emigrated to Canada, mainly to the London district of Ontario, where they cleared forest farms, cherished their Gaelic language and traditions, prospered, and hated the Marquis more, perhaps, than he rightly deserved when things were looked at from his own hard political-economy point of view. (MacKenzie 1914: 277)

Other sections of Ontario were settled by Gaelic speakers in the following decades. The area around Orillia, some forty miles north of Toronto saw an influx of Gaels from Islay and Coll in the 1830s and 1840s.

RELIGION AND EDUCATION

Most of the Gaels emigrating either brought a Gaelic-speaking clergyman with them or did their utmost to obtain the services of one. Reference has already been made to Reverend Robert MacPherson who accompanied the 78th Fraser Highlanders to Nova Scotia and finally to Quebec. In 1772, among the 210 passengers of the Glenaladale group that came to Prince Edward Island was Father James MacDonald. Reverend James MacGregor arrived in Pictou in 1786 to serve the needs of that region's Presbyterians. The 520 Glengarry people who came to Canada in 1786 were accompanied by Father Alexander Macdonell (Bumsted 1982: 73). Alexander MacKenzie notes that:

> A large swarm from Breadalbane, Lochearnhead, and Balquhidder went off to Nova Scotia about 1828, and got Gaelic-speaking ministers to follow them. In 1829 a great number of Skyemen from Lord Macdonald's estate went to Cape Breton, where Gaelic is the language of the people and pulpit to this day. (MacKenzie 1914: 274)

Many settlements, however, were not so fortunate and had to depend on rare visits by missionaries for their spiritual needs. Canadian religious journals of the nineteenth century such as *The Canadian Christian Examiner and Presbyterian Review* (Niagara, U.C. = Upper Canada), *The Ecclesiastical and Missionary Record for the Presbyterian Church of Canada* (Hamilton, U.C.), *The Canada Presbyterian* (Toronto) and a host of others contain numerous reports by missionaries which provide valuable information regarding the use of Gaelic in various communities. One such report written by Peter Ferguson (see Whyte 1986: 92) appeared in the June 1837 issue of *The Canadian Christian Examiner and Presbyterian Review*. The six-page account details the places around Lake Simcoe visited by Ferguson and his fellow missionary William McKillican (Whyte 1986: 262)[8] in January, 1837. It also treats the question of the difficulty some of the Highland settlements had in securing the services of a suitable minister. The excerpt below will serve to illustrate the style of these reports:

Missionary and Ecclesiastical Intelligence.
Missionary Visit within the Rounds of the
Presbytery of Toronto.
To the Editor of the Christian Examiner,-
In compliance with a request of the
Presbytery of Toronto, I have sent you the following
communication, containing the outlines of a Missionary Tour
on which the Rev. Mr. McKillican and myself were sent out, in
January last, by their appointment.

The field of our mission was the country around Lake
Simcoe. On the 6th of that month, we set out together, from
W. Guillimburg, for the townships of Thorah and Eldon, on the
south of that lake.... On Sabbath I preached at Beaverton to a
numerous and interesting auditory. The house in which the
people assembled was large and commodious... They collected
from Eldon, on the east, and Mona, on the north of Thorah. As
most of them were Scotch Highlanders, two discourses were
preached – the one in English and the other in Gaelic. On the next
day I attended to the appointment made in Eldon... Here, too, the
services were conducted, as at Beaverton, in both languages, and
for the same reason... From Eldon I went on the next day to the
southern extremity of Thorah, and preached at Mr. Cameron's to
a considerable number of people... There also the services were
conducted in English and Gaelic. The parts of Thorah and Eldon
which the writer visited, are well settled, and the settlers, few
excepted, are in connexion with the Church of Scotland. Since
their settlement there, they have made several movements to
secure a settled clergyman among them; but hitherto without
success. More than once, many of them have been made dupes
of designing men, that came among them, pretending that they
were ministers in regular standing with their Church. The last
of them was a Mr. Alexander Campbell, formerly minister of the
Parliamentary Church Portnahaven, Islay, Scotland; but who was
deposed, in 1834, from the office of the ministry, for immoral
conduct. Soon after, or about the time of his deposition, he came
to this country, and settled in Eldon ...

On the 13th, we proceeded as far as the north side of
Kempenfelt Bay, on Lake Simcoe ... The following day, being the
Sabbath, Mr. McKillican preached in English and Gaelic ... On
that Sabbath I visited the Scotch settlement in the township of
Nottawasaga, which is ten miles farther to the west ... The service

throughout was conducted in the Gaelic language, the audience, without an exception, being from the Highlands of Scotland ... Peter Ferguson, Esquesing, 25th May, 1837.[9]

The nineteenth century is sometimes referred to as the century of the Protestant Crusade. Many Protestant organisations in Britain, Ireland and North America worked actively to proselytise Roman Catholics. In the United States, the American and Foreign Christian Union in the 1850s, as a reaction to the large influx of Irish Catholic immigrants, hired Irish-speaking apostates from Catholicism to proselytise Irish-speaking immigrants in New York, Boston and Philadelphia and other major American cities.[10] Similar work was carried on among Gaelic speakers in Canada also. In 1853, at the third session of the Baptist Nova Scotia Eastern Association, 'Rev. Richard McLearn proposed a mission to the Gaelic population of Cape Breton, which numbered more than 20,000, mostly Roman Catholics. Elder Hugh Ross was appointed missionary to those people, under the auspices of the Domestic Missionary Board' (Bill n.d.: 628). Three years later at the sixth session it was reported that '[t]he Gaelic Mission in Cape Breton was extending the influence of truth. The missionary, during the past year, organised a baptised Church of twelve members at Schooner Pond, six of whom were baptised by himself' (644). A report of the Synod of Montreal in *The Home and Foreign Record of the Canada Presbyterian Church* for May, 1872 makes mention of a proposal for a similar initiative:

Synod of Montreal
This Synod met at Belleville, Ont., within John Street Presbyterian Church on Tuesday the 6th of May ... An Overture from the Presbytery of Montreal was presented, praying the General Assembly to establish a Mission to the Gaelic-speaking Roman Catholics of the county of Glengarry, in the Province of Ontario. The Synod unanimously agreed to transmit said Overture with special recommendations.[11]

In addition to religion, education was an important concern for Highland immigrants but evidence for the teaching of Gaelic is sparse. Rev. Norman MacLeod of St. Ann's, Cape Breton, is a notable example of a teacher who did use Gaelic in his school in the 1820s–40s. According to his biographer, 'Although he was equally fluent in both languages he taught the common school in Gaelic' (MacPherson 1962: 78). The topic of teaching in Gaelic was raised in a petition put forth by Fr. Colin Grant, parish priest of Arisaig in Antigonish County (formerly County of Sydney), to the Nova Scotia House of Assembly in early 1836:

A Petition of the Rev. Colin P. Grant and others, residing on the Gulf Shore, in the Upper District of the County of Sydney, was presented by Mr. Dickson and read, praying that in considering the subject of Schools, provision may be made for a Gaelic school in that Settlement – a large number of the Inhabitants there speaking no other language.[12]

Within a few months Alexander MacGillivray, author of *Companach an Oganaich*, was teaching Gaelic in his school as indicated by this note in the Pictou *Bee* (Vol. 2:1, p. 6, 25 May 1836), 'An examination [was held] in [the] school room at Arisaig on the 16th inst. when upwards of 50 English, 3 Latin, and 5 Gaelic pupils received instruction under ... Alexander McGilvray, late from St. Andrews College, P. E. I. Island.' In the same year Gaelic was apparently being taught to some students in Megantic, Lower Canada as Quebec was then known.[13]

In 1841 the Nova Scotian administration enacted a law which stated: 'Any school in which the ordinary instructions may be in the French, the Gaelic, or the German language, is to be entitled to participation in the public money, equally with those where the English only is used' (Sec. 12, Act 1841).[14]

Although instruction in Gaelic may not have been offered at the college level in the early days of immigration, some of the theological seminaries did offer bursaries for accomplishments in Gaelic. Thus the Theological College of the Presbyterian Church of Canada in Toronto offered a bursary in 1845 to a successful candidate for 'Repetition and Explanation of the Shorter Catechism, in Gaelic, in connexion with fluency and propriety of pronunciation in that language.'[15]

The Presbyterian College of Montreal, founded in 1865, had a good deal of Gaelic activity in the final decades of the nineteenth century. As early as 1872, the College listed $30 scholarships donated by John MacKenzie of Lennoxville for the best and second best examinations in Gaelic.[16] In March 1872 *The Canada Presbyterian* noted:

A Gaelic service has recently been instituted in Montreal by the Gaelic-speaking students of the Presbyterian College in that city.

It is held in Stanley street Church on the Sabbath afternoon, and is attended by large numbers of the class for whom it is designed. Messrs. Mathieson, McLean and Morrison are the students who conduct it in turns.[17]

In November, 1879 *The Canada Presbyterian* had the following item:

Students' Missionary Society of Montreal Presbyterian College. The annual meeting of the Students' Missionary Society was held on the 27th ult., in lecture-room No. 3, at 7:15 p.m, Mr. Charles McLean, and Vice-President, in the chair ... Mr. Chas. McLean gave a very interesting account of the Gaelic work carried on by him under the auspices of the Society in conjunction with several other Gaelic-speaking students in the city.[18]

In February, 1881 *The Canada Presbyterian* announced that the Rev. Dr McNish[19] was delivering a course of lectures at the College 'on the Gaelic language and literature, which are spoken of most favourably by the Montreal press'.[20] Rev. McNish was to continue as Gaelic lecturer for at least the next fifteen years. In December, 1896 an article in *The Canadian Presbyterian* about the College stated:

One distinctive feature of the institution is its lectures on Gaelic Literature, continued for some fifteen years by the Rev. Dr MacNish, of Cornwall, one of the best Celtic scholars in the Dominion. He has secured for the College a number of scholarships to be competed for annually in this department. A special appeal is being made at the present time for means to endow this lectureship. The ministers of one hundred and twenty congregations of our Church still require Gaelic for the efficient discharge of their duties.[21]

Queens University in Kingston, Ontario had a large number of Gaelic-speaking students in the nineteenth century. The college also had Gaelic and Ossianic societies and articles in Gaelic were occasionally printed in its student paper. There was also a Gaelic scholarship yet despite all this interest in the language there is no evidence to indicate that Gaelic was offered as a subject of instruction.

In 1891 St Francis Xavier College in Antigonish, Nova Scotia offered a Gaelic class taught by D. M. MacAdam, a native Gaelic speaker from East Bay, Cape Breton, who was ordained a priest in 1893 and who would go on to be a major figure in the Gaelic life of Nova Scotia until his untimely death in August 1924. St Francis Xavier has continued to have Gaelic as a part of its curriculum to the present day. In 1958 St Francis Xavier University established a Celtic Studies Department and continued to expand with the establishment of the Sister Saint Veronica Chair in Celtic Studies in 1983 and the Ben Alder Chair in Celtic Studies in 2000. Its Celtic Studies Department today is the only such department in North America which emphasises the teaching of Scottish Gaelic.

EARLY PUBLISHING

The 1830s mark the beginning of Gaelic printing in British North America with items being published in 1832 in Pictou, Nova Scotia and Charlottetown, Prince Edward Island. Soon other works in Gaelic were printed in Toronto, Montreal and Kingston, Ontario (for a more detailed description see Nilsen 2002: 127–40). Indeed, in 1840 there appeared in Kingston a newspaper titled Tourist of the Woods and Emigrants Guide with the Gaelic subtitle *Cuairtear nan Coillte* which occasionally contained Gaelic articles and poetry. Interesting items include two letters by 'Aulaidh MacFhearchar', apparently translated to Gaelic ('air a h-eadar-theangachadh'), in which the writer speaks of his voyage to Canada (Cuairtear nan Coillte, 7 February 1842, p. 3) and of his early days in the new country (Cuairtear nan Coillte, 14 February 1842, p. 3).

In the following decades a number of religious works were published in British North America. In 1851 John Boyd of Antigonish published a Gaelic monthly *An Cuairtear Og Gaelach*. This ceased publication after one year and Boyd started publishing the weekly *Casket* which at first had four pages of Gaelic and four pages of English. The Gaelic content was soon reduced to a single column and for years at a time Gaelic would be completely absent from the paper. The jewel of Gaelic publishing in Canada was *Mac-Talla* published by Jonathan MacKinnon in Sydney, Cape Breton from 1892 to 1904. This paper was completely in Gaelic and had subscribers throughout the world.

HIGHLAND EMIGRATION TO THE CANADIAN PRAIRIES

By the last two decades of the nineteenth century Canada was eager to entice Europeans to come to settle in the Prairie provinces. Thousands of settlers did come including in 1883 and 1884 a number of emigrants from South Uist and Benbecula who settled in Wapella, west of Winnipeg.[22] In 1887 Malcolm McNeill obtained British government assistance to transport a group from Lewis to settle in Killarney, Manitoba. In 1888 another 200 Lewismen emigrated to Saltcoats, Manitoba.

After the turn of the twentieth century, Canada still wanted to attract more immigrants and even published a booklet in Gaelic *Machraichean Móra Chanada* in an attempt to encourage more emigration from Gaelic Scotland. In 1923 the ship *Metagama* carried several hundred Lewis people to Canada who settled in Ontario. In the same year the ship *Marloch* took several hundred Uist immigrants across under the leadership of Fr Andrew MacDonell. This group settled in Alberta as did a later group also brought out by Fr MacDonell. This marked the last organised attempt to establish a Highland community in Canada. After the Second World War emigration of Gaelic speakers to Canada would be to major urban centres such as Vancouver, Toronto and Montreal.

GAELIC IN NOVA SCOTIA: TWENTIETH CENTURY TO THE PRESENT

At the turn of the twentieth century eastern Nova Scotia, including the island of Cape Breton, was undoubtedly the most Gaelic region of Canada. Jonathan Dembling has estimated that there were c.50,000 Gaelic speakers in Nova Scotia in 1901 (Dembling 2006: 207). But already outmigration to cities such as Boston, Detroit and Toronto had dramatically changed the traditional farming communities. The use of Gaelic declined rapidly in the Nova Scotia mainland counties of Pictou, Antigonish and Guysborough so that by the 1980s there were very few fluent mainland Gaelic speakers. Gaelic continued to be strong in some communities in Cape Breton up until the Second World War after which few families passed the language on to their children.

A number of efforts were made to maintain the language. The Antigonish *Casket* had a weekly Gaelic column from 1920 to 1944 edited by Monsignor Patrick Nicholson of St Francis Xavier University. Nicholson, a native Gaelic speaker from Beaver Cove, Cape Breton, had taken Gaelic classes while a student at St Francis Xavier taught by Rev. Alexander MacLean Sinclair, a pioneer of Celtic Studies in Nova Scotia. There was a number of periodicals including *Fear na Céilidh* and *Mosgladh*. Several papers in Sydney, Cape Breton carried weekly Gaelic columns. In 1938, the Gaelic College was established at St Ann's near Baddeck in Cape Breton to offer summer courses in Gaelic and Scottish culture.

Starting in the 1930s and continuing into the 1990s, John Lorne Campbell and his wife Margaret Fay Shaw visited Nova Scotia and were the first to begin major recording projects of Nova Scotia Gaelic. Their visits were important in making Nova Scotians realise the value of their Gaelic traditions. Dr Campbell's work resulted in the book *Songs Remembered in Exile*. Another visitor to Nova Scotia was Charles Dunn who made recordings in Nova Scotia and published the classic *The Highland Settler: A Portrait of the Scottish Gael in Nova Scotia*.

After the Second World War Major C. I. N. MacLeod, who had studied Celtic at university in Glasgow and Edinburgh, came to Nova Scotia from Scotland and soon became an important figure in Gaelic circles. For a while he taught at the Gaelic College and was later appointed by the Province as Gaelic advisor. In the early 1950s he published weekly Gaelic articles in the New Glasgow *Eastern Chronicle* and the Antigonish *Casket*. He began recording Gaelic speakers and, with the folklorist Helen Creighton, published *Gaelic Song in Nova Scotia*. In 1958, St Francis Xavier University established a Celtic Studies Department and hired Major MacLeod to be department head. MacLeod published two volumes of Nova Scotia material *Sgialachdan a Albainn Nuaidh* and *Bàrdachd a Albainn Nuaidh*.

Major MacLeod died in 1977 and his position was taken up by Sr Margaret MacDonell, a native Gaelic speaker from Judique, Cape Breton with a doctorate in Celtic Studies from Harvard University. Sr MacDonell was instumental in obtaining a grant from the Canadian Multicultural Directorate to have the Gaelic folklore of Cape Breton recorded. John Shaw, who later received a doctorate in Celtic Studies from Harvard, was hired to collect Gaelic folklore throughout Cape Breton Island. An early result of this project was the book *Luirgean Eachainn Nìll*, a collection of the folk tales of Hector Campbell of Judique, edited by Sr MacDonell and John Shaw. The collecting project lasted for five years and resulted in obtaining over 2000 folklore items, of which one thousand are songs. This material has now been digitised under the name Gaelstream/Sruth nan Gaidheal and is available on the world wide web at www.gaelstream.ca. John Shaw has also published three books from this material: *Sgeul gu Latha/Tales until Dawn*, the folklore of Joe Neil MacNeil; *Brìgh an Òrain*, the songs and stories of Lauchie MacLellan; and *Na Beanntaichean Gorma*, a collection of folk tales.

In 1983 Sr MacDonell published *The Emigrant Experience: Songs of Highland Emigrants in North America*. She was also responsible for obtaining for St Francis Xavier University a multicultural ethnic chair, the Sister Saint Veronica Chair in Gaelic Studies. In the year 2000, a generous philanthropist endowed another chair in the Celtic Studies Department which has been named the Ben Alder Chair of Celtic Studies. In 2008 the department hosted *Rannsachadh na Gàidhlig 5*, the first time this Scottish Gaelic conference was held outside of Scotland. The department has a complement of three full-time positions and has been responsible for teaching Gaelic to many of the younger generation who are now actively involved in the province's Gaelic movement. The library at StFX houses one of the finest Celtic Studies collections in North America.

A number of institutions throughout the province promote Gaelic. The language is taught at Saint Mary's University in Halifax and Cape

Breton University in Sydney. Cape Breton University is also home to the Beaton Institute which has a large collection of Gaelic recordings from the early 1970s. A number of primary and secondary schools include Gaelic as a subject in their curriculum. The Highand Village in Iona, Cape Breton has a long record of promoting Gaelic events as does the Gaelic College at St Ann's. In Halifax A' Sgoil Ghàidhlig offers a variety of Gaelic classes. The Atlantic Gaelic Academy also offers classes at various locations throughout the province. Comhairle na Gàidhlig, Alba Nuadh/ The Gaelic Council of Nova Scotia supports a wide array of Gaelic events. Nova Scotia can even boast a Gaelic bookseller and publisher *Sìol Cultural Enterprises* whose most recent publication is a collection of the poetry of Alexander MacDonald, the bard of the Keppoch, Antigonish County, edited by Trueman and Laurinda Matheson. Another collection of Nova Scotia poetry is *As a' Bhràighe/Beyond the Braes, the Gaelic Songs of Allan the Ridge MacDonald, 1794–1868* edited by Effie Rankin.

In recent decades, some individuals have been involved in recording video interviews with Nova Scotia's Gaelic speakers. Starting in Boston, Massachusetts in 1983 and in Nova Scotia since 1984, I personally have videotaped more than eighty of the province's Gaelic speakers. This archive comprises more than a hundred hours of video interviews. In 1995–6 Peter Murphy of Seabright Video and I conducted the StFX Gaelic Video Project in which twenty-eight individuals were interviewed providing a further twenty-eight to thirty hours of recordings. More recently the Gaelic Council of Nova Scotia sponsored a video project named 'Cainnt mo Mhàthar' in which twenty-five to thirty Gaelic speakers were recorded. Excerpts from this project can be viewed on the world wide web at www.cainntmomhathar.com.

One of the most encouraging signs in recent years has been the establishment by the government of Nova Scotia of an Office of Gaelic Affairs with its main office in Antigonish. This office has been a major supporter of Gaelic initiatives such as the widespread establishment of TIP (Total Immersion Plus) classes in many communities in the province. The CEO of the Office of Gaelic Affairs is Lewis MacKinnon, an accomplished Gaelic singer, who has just published a collection of his own poetry *Am Famhair/The Giant.*

Although the number of native Gaelic speakers in Nova Scotia may hover around 100 at the time of writing, this province remains and will remain one in which the Gaelic language has an important presence.

BIBLIOGRAPHY

Abstract of the Acts of the Province of Nova-Scotia, Respecting Schools,
    prepared by order of the Central Board of Education. Halifax:
    Printed at the Novascotian Office June, 1841.

American and Foreign Christian Union Journal (1850–3), New York.

Bennett, Margaret (1998), *Oatmeal and the Catechism: Scottish Gaelic
    Settlers in Quebec,* Edinburgh: John Donald.

Bill, Rev. I. E. (n.d.), *Fifty Years with the Baptist Ministers and Churches
    of the Maritime Provinces of Canada,* St John, N.B. Printed by Barnes
    and Company.

Bumsted, J. M. (1982), *The People's Clearances: 1770–1815,* Edinburgh
    and Manitoba: Edinburgh University Press.

*Continuation of the appendix to the XLVth volume of the Journals of the
    House of Assembly of the province of Lower Canada, second session of
    the fifteenth provincial Parliament,* (Québec): King's Printer, 1836,
    Page 00–62.

Dembling, Jonathan (2006), 'Gaelic in Canada: New Evidence
    from an Old Census,' in Wilson McLeod, James E. Fraser and
    Anja Gunderloch (eds), *Cànan & Cultar/Language & Culture
    Rannsachadh na Gàidhlig 3,* Edinburgh: Dunedin Academic Press.

Dunn, Charles W. (1953), *Highland Settler: A Portrait of the Scottish
    Gael in Nova Scotia,* Toronto: University of Toronto Press.

Hunter, James (1994), *A Dance Called America: The Scottish Highlands,
    the United States and Canada,* Edinburgh: Mainstream Publishing.

Journal of the Proceedings of the Nova Scotia House of Assembly, 1836,
    p. 960.

Little, J. I. (2000), 'From the Isle of Arran to Inverness Township:
    A Case Study of Highland Emigration and North American
    Settlement, 1829–1834', *Scottish Economic & Social History,* 20:1.

MacDonell, Margaret (1982), *The Emigrant Experience: Songs of
    Highland Emigrants in North America,* Toronto: University of
    Toronto Press.

MacKay, Donald (1980), *Scotland Farewell: The People of the Hector,*
    Toronto: McGraw-Hill Ryerson.

MacKenzie, Alexander (1914), *History of the Highland Clearances,*
    Glasgow, 2nd edn.

MacPhee, Hugh (1969–70), 'The Trail of the Emigrants', *TGSI* XLVI, pp.
    213–16.

McLean, Marianne (1991), *The People of Glengarry: Highlanders in Transition, 1745–1820*, Montreal and Kingston: McGill-Queen's University Press.

McPherson, Flora (1962), *Watchman Against the World: The Story of Norman MacLeod and his People*, London: R. Hale.

Meek, Donald E. (1988), 'Evangelicalism and Emigration: Aspects of the Role of Dissenting Evangelicalism in Highland Emigration to Canada', in Gordon W. MacLennan (ed.), *Proceedings of the First North American Congress of Celtic Studies, Ottawa, 1986*, Ottawa.

Nilsen, K. (2002), 'Some Notes on Pre-*Mac-Talla* Gaelic Publishing in Nova Scotia (with References to Early Gaelic Publishing in Prince Edward Island, Quebec and Ontario)' in Colm Ó Baoill and Nancy R. McGuire (eds), *Rannsachadh na Gàidhlig 2000*, Aberdeen: Aberdeen University Celtic Department.

The Canada Presbyterian, New Series, 2:19, 7 March 1879, p. 301.

The Canada Presbyterian, New Series, 3:1, 7 November 1879, p. 12.

The Canadian Christian Examiner and Presbyterian Review, 1:4, June 1837, pp. 122–8.

The Ecclesiastical and Missionary Record for the Presbyterian Church of Canada, 2:3, Hamilton, October 1845, p. 128.

The Home and Foreign Record of the Canada Presbyterian Church, 11:5, May 1872.

Whyte, Donald, (1986) *A Dictionary of Scottish Emigration to Canada before Confederation*, Ontario Genealogical Society.

NOTES

1 A short list of reference works would include: Bumsted 1982, Dunn 1953, Hunter 1994, MacDonell 1982, MacKay 1980, McLean 1991.

2 From videotaped interview with Donald Cameron recorded by Kenneth Nilsen on 26 April 1986.

3 Ibid.

4 Referred to as 'Selkirk na bàighe' in Rory Roy MacKenzie's poem 'An Imrich.' See MacDonell (1982): 112–15.

5 Information from Dr John Hickey of Antigonish whose grandmother Catherine MacKenzie was an infant when her family emigrated to Cape Breton from Lewis.

6 The song was sung to me in videotaped interviews by the bard's son, Duncan MacKinnon on Berneray in June 1987 and by John MacLeod, Rory MacLeod's nephew, who lived in Lowell, Massachusetts, in August 1987. Two verses of the song are:

A Ruairidh ghrinn, a nàbaidh, a Leòdaich bhlàth 's a charaide,
Tha còmhnaidh anns a' cheàrn seo bho'n thàinig mi air m'aineol ann.
A bheil thu dol gar fàgail is a' cur do chùl gu bràch 'nis
ri Eilean uaine Bheàrn'raidh a dh'àraich 'na do bhalach thu?

Nuair a gheobh thu cuairt air tìr ann, na dìochuimhnich do charaide
Fiach gum bi thu sgrìobhadh 's ag ìnnse dhuinn mu Chanada
'S gheobh thu naidheachd Bheàrn'raidh is litir bho do nàbaidh
le rann de dh'òran Gàidhlig bheir gàireachdaich fad seachdain ort.

7   A small number of Arran people had previously emigrated to the Restigouche
    region of New Brunswick in 1820.
8   This William McKillican is not to be confused with the Baptist William McKillican
    of Lochiel Township, Glengarry County, Ontario on whom see Meek (1988, pp.
    15–36).
9   *The Canadian Christian Examiner and Presbyterian Review* 1:4, June 1837, pp. 122–8.
10 Various issues of the *American and Foreign Christian Union Journal*, 1850–1853
    (New York).
11 *The Home and Foreign Record of the Canada Presbyterian Church* 11:5, May 1872: p.
    176.
12 *Journal of the Proceedings of the Nova Scotia House of Assembly*, 1836: p. 960.
13 In response to a question regarding what languages were being taught in schools
    in his riding, John G. Clapham, Esquire, Member for the County of Megantic
    (Quebec) responded: French only, none; three French and English; fifteen English
    and some Gaelic (*Continuation of the appendix to the XLVth volume of the Journals
    of the House of Assembly of the province of Lower Canada, second session of the
    fifteenth provincial Parliament*, 00–62, (Québec): King's Printer, 1836.
14 *Abstract of the Acts of the Province of Nova-Scotia, Respecting Schools*, prepared by
    order of the Central Board of Education. Halifax: Printed at the Novascotian Office
    June 1841, p. 15.
15 *The Ecclesiastical and Missionary Record for the Presbyterian Church of Canada*,
    2:3, Hamilton, October, 1845: p. 128.
16 *The Home and Foreign Record of the Canada Presbyterian Church*, 11:5, May 1872,
    p. 147.
17 *The Canada Presbyterian, New Series*, 2:19, 7 March 1879, p. 301.
18 *The Canada Presbyterian, New Series*, 3:1, 7 November 1879, p. 12.
19 Donald Whyte's *A Dictionary of Scottish Emigration to Canada before Confederation*
    indicates that Neil MacNish was a native of Argyllshire who studied at the
    University of Edinburgh where he graduated with a BD in 1869. He also studied at
    Glasgow and Toronto and was a Gaelic scholar.
20 *The Canada Presbyterian*, 9:6, 11 February 1881, p. 92.
21 *The Canadian Presbyterian*, 25:51, 16 December 1896, p. 816.
22 See MacPhee (1969–70, 213–16), where several verses by two Benbecula
    emigrants are given. The following give an idea of the tone of these verses:

'Nuair a ràinig sinn talamh a' gheallaidh
Reothadh ann cho cruaidh ri sgalaidh;
Còrr is dà throigh dheug 'san talamh –
'S cha bhiodh seangan beò ann.

Dh'fhoighneachd mi do Dhòmhnall MacChaluim,
"Cuin thig an deigh as an talamh?"
Thuirt e rium le gruaim, "A charaid,

Fanaidh e ri d' bheò ann."
See also MacDonell (1982: 149 ff).

CHAPTER 6

Hebridean and Mainland Dialects

Seosamh Watson

INTRODUCTION

In marked contrast to Ireland where a modern standard literary Gaelic language was created as a result of government action, such a goal has been achieved in Scotland through the onward march of time which has seen the dialects of the north, east and south progressively disappear, leaving the field to the language of the Western Isles and Skye. The latter dialects are essentially very similar to those of the adjacent west coast and, in view of the significant literary inheritance of this whole area from the seventeenth century to the present day, the dominance of a standard dialect from this region is, no doubt, fitting. As in the case of the Irish *Caighdeán,* or standard language, of course, such a norm relates to matters orthographic and morphological, with native speakers from the various areas being free to adhere to the phonology of their own dialect. In contrast to the dialects of the west, which are characterised as more conservative, those of the eastern highlands are progressive in nature and are marked in the various categories by a number of features of phonology, morphology, syntax and lexicon which are largely unfamiliar on the west coast and in the isles. Considerations of space make it impossible to provide an exhaustive treatment of all of the dialects involved and so attention is directed here to certain salient features which distinguish some varieties of Gaelic spoken in the regions just referred to. The data discussed here are, of course, drawn in the main from the standard published linguistic accounts and relate, therefore, to the speech of previous generations before certain of the dialects had become extinct or the full impact of English mass media had made itself felt on others.

PHONOLOGY

The system for stressed vowels portrayed in Tables 1 and 2 (after Oftedal 1956: 43–4) may be taken as typifying Lewis, together with parts of Skye and adjacent areas of the west coast. Within the Gaelic dialects of this region there are a number of differences to be found at the sub-phonemic level. A very familiar case in regard to the vowel system is that of the *u*-phoneme, the fronted articulation of which found over much of Lewis is quite distinct from the articulation of other areas, and which has been described by Borgstrøm (1940: 32) as 'rather like that of a Norwegian *u*-sound'. This scholar conducted a survey in regard to 102 items from N. Lewis to Barra and has remarked (Borgstrøm 1940: 227) 'the largest bundle of isoglosses in the Outer Hebrides, is the one ... separating Harris from Lewis', an assessment now undergoing revision in the light of the publication of the *SGDS* data (Watson 2007a).

Table 1 Vowel system: monophthongs

	Front unrounded	Non-front unrounded	Back rounded
High	i	ɯ	u
Mid	e	ə	o
Lower-mid	ɛ	a	ɔ

A particular lexeme may vary from dialect to dialect in regard to its phonemic composition, e.g. *doras*: Lewis, ER[1], ES **darəs** vs Harris-Uist **dɔrəs**. A notable study in relation to this particular aspect of dialect differentiation is, of course, that of Jackson (1968, further refined by Ó Maolalaigh 2003: 262–3) on the 'breaking' of inherited long *ē* into an *i*-diphthong, affecting forms such as *beul* 'mouth', *feur* 'grass', *Seumas* 'James'.

Table 2 Vowel system: diphthongs

Closing			Opening	
i-diphthongs		**u**-diphthongs		
ei	ui	ɔu	iə	uə
əi	ai	au	ia	ua

Individual vowel phonemes may, however, exist in certain dialects which are absent in others, as in e.g. ɛu *gleann* 'valley', which contrasts with **au**, as in *gann* (both diphthongs also with nasalisation), in a number of western dialects, but which does not exist in Lewis, Harris or eastern varieties. Features Borgstrøm (1940: 237) viewed as separating Lewis from Harris and the S. Hebrides are the appearance of a vocalic element, e.g. ɛ or ᶖ, as opposed to **j** (this latter absent post-consonantally), in sequence before ɔ(ː), orthographic *eo, eò,* cf. *deoch* 'drink', *eòin* 'birds', together with a related isogloss (Borgstrøm 1940: 242) involving the presence of ᶖ in sequence with **u**(ː), orthographic *iu, iù,* cf. *iuchair, triùir.* With the evidence of the finer mesh of net-points presented in *SGDS* it is now clear (Watson 2007a: 256) that some areas in Lewis are in agreement with Harris in regard to these features. Data from the same source make it clear that adjacent west coast dialects divided in similar fashion between the two realisations, while eastern forms generally do not exhibit the vocalic element preceding a back vowel in such forms. Nasalisation of vowels is, of course, phonemic in Gaelic and it is to be noted that there is variation from dialect to dialect as to which vowels may be nasalised and the lexemes which contain such vowels. In some eastern Gaelic dialects the distinction between mid vowels of varying heights disappears in the case of long vowels, e.g. *dòrn ~ bó:* Lewis-Barra ɔː ~ oː: ER, ES ɔː.

The distribution of ə as between the different dialects is deserving of particular comment. Both Borgstrøm (1940: 50–2) and Oftedal (1956: 149–50) have dealt with the phenomenon – dubbed 'caducous schwa' by the latter – whereby ə in word-final position following voiceless consonants, e.g. *oidhch(e)* 'night', is lost in pausa or in sentence-final position. In eastern dialects, however, it is known (Watson 1985) that the situation is significantly different, inasmuch as this element is commonly absent after voiced consonants also and following historical hiatus, nor is it generally present in sentence-internal position, e.g. ER *'s aithn(e) domh* 'I know'. Oftedal notes that the same element tends to be lost not only in enclitic forms, but also in pausa and in sentence-initial forms of preclitics and this would appear to be widespread in the language, e.g. *an-dé, a-rithist, a-riamh* (*SGDS* s.v.). In addition to its loss in these positions, there is a general tendency in eastern dialects for the vowel to disappear from preclitics in sentence-internal position also, cf. ER *na brogaich (a') tighinn (a-)steach* 'the boys coming in' (Watson 2007a: 91). Indeed, there is also a tendency in these same dialects for the vowel to be elided in lexemes generally as the result of internal syncope, cf. ER *urr(ai)nn* 'able', *òn(a)rach* 'lonely'. There are certain situations in which ə is found in other dialects where the eastern dialects referred to show **a,** as, for instance, in position beside a velar fricative: ER *dochar* 'wrong', *bodach, leabchan* 'beds', *dor[a]ch.* In the last case the vowel of the unstressed syllable is, of course, unhistorical, having arisen as a svarabhakti, or epenthetic, vowel through the conjunction of certain classes of consonant.

The manner of realisation of the svarabhakti vowel itself constitutes an interesting boundary between Scottish Gaelic dialects in the north, as elsewhere. In some eastern dialects, as in other regions on the periphery, a situation exists similar to that found in most Irish dialects, in that ə has evolved either totally, as in ER, ES, or in part, cf. EP (cf. Ó Murchú 1989: 92–6), as e.g. in *ainm,* or else the vowel has been modified to **i,** cf. *mairbh,* or **u,** cf. *dearbh,* through the influence of the consonantal environment. Over much of Gaelic-speaking Scotland the svarabhakti vowel which has developed echoes, or is influenced by, the quality of vowel in the preceding syllable, cf. *tarbh:* ₁**a-a**₎ *tairbh:* ₁**ə-i**₎. The syllabic structure is here distinguishable from other ostensibly similar syllabic sequences in that the vowel pair in question exhibits features of stress and intonation typical of a single syllable, cf. *ainm* vs *anam.* The question of vowel-length in such syllables has been analysed, within a general treatment, in terms of morae by Ternes (2006: 89–91) who classifies them together with long vowels and diphthongs. The same scholar draws attention to the distinction made in WR Gaelic (which exists elsewhere, though perhaps only vestigially, cf. Dorian 1978: 59–69) between the latter long vocalic elements and others which derive from sequences of vowels previously separated by hiatus of various origins. The pre-existence of a syllabic boundary is now indicated, therefore, in such dialects by means of a vowel length which is intermediate, as in e.g. *sithinn,* between a short vowel as in *sin,* and a long one as in *seinn.* In other dialects of the west referred to here the transition between the two syllables continues to be marked. This is generally signalled through audible action, usually a glottal stop, though sometimes the latter may be replaced by a glottal fricative or approximant of a voiceless or voiced variety (Watson 1996: 376–82; Ternes 2006: 87). In the dialects of Lewis, this glottal action may or may not be present and transition is marked, as also noted for WR (Ternes 2006: 129–39) through a tonal distinction according to which words containing vowels in hiatus are to be categorised along with disyllables rather than as monosyllables, a feature which has, likewise, been observed in an eastern variety of Gaelic also (Dorian 1978: 59).

A propos of hiatus, it is interesting to observe how frequently, in the case of western dialects, the phenomenon of vowel harmony features (Watson 1999: 347–59 for references and discussion), in that ə in a syllable following that bearing the stress is replaced by a tonic vowel, mirroring the pattern described for svarabhakti vowels. Examples are: **u-u**: *crudha*, **o-o**: *ogha*, **ɛ-ɛ**: *leatha.* In a hiatus environment also, as observed in the same treatment (Watson 1999: 353), ə may, alternatively, be absorbed in the vocalisation of a preceding historical fricative, thus causing a shift in the historical syllable boundary, cf. **a-i**: *laighe*, **e-u**: *leabhar*, **u-i**: *buidhe.* Studies of eastern dialects, such as ER, show that ə following historical hiatus, if not lost, as in final open position in the case of *leatha, buidhe,* will merge with the vowel preceding the hiatus and this, in such circumstances, may evolve into a diphthong, as, e.g. **ia**: *nighean, tighearna,* or lengthened vowel, cf. **a:** *adhar,* **e:** *leathar.* The hiatus involved may be inherited from the early period, as in the first instance, or subsequent in origin, as illustrated by the second example, where it arises through the loss of an historical fricative or approximant.

Stop consonants constitute a centrally important topic in Scottish Gaelic phonetics, where there exist typically a fortis, and a corresponding lenis, category. Both classes are generally realised as voiceless plosives (but see the discussion of initial mutations below) although certain eastern dialects (Dorian 1978: 40–2) may register non-fortis voiced consonants in certain positions, as, e.g. **ḅ**: *obair,* **ḍ**: *bradan,* **ǧ**: *eaglais.* The fortis class is aspirated initially and in postvocalic position within stressed syllables was preceded by a feature of preaspiration or voiceless friction; in unstressed position, however, and following stressed long vowels the lenis category is often found in place of the fortis; and certain eastern dialects show lenis stops intervocalically after stressed vowels also, e.g. ER **g'**: *chreiceadh,* **b**: *tapaidh,* **d'** *itean.* In Lewis dialects, as is well known, such preaspiration characterises the plosive consonant itself, while in very many other dialects of the west it commonly takes the form of an independent consonant phoneme, generally speaking **x** or **ç** before velar stops and **h** elsewhere, although in mainland areas further south, e.g. N. Inverness-shire, **x** or **ç** are found before non-velars, e.g. *slat, tapaidh, tuiteam* (see Ó Maolalaigh 2003: 261–2, for a fuller treatment). In numerous varieties of Gaelic such a phoneme may also appear in position following a vibrant or liquid, e.g. *corca, olc.* Borgstrøm (1940: 227–44) in his survey indicated this to be a feature of dialects south of Lewis and Harris, both of which, he reports, instead of presenting such a consonantal cluster, de-voice the liquid or vibrant involved. On the basis of his survey Borgstrøm proposed a boundary in regard to this feature between the two regions mentioned. The *SGDS* data, however, have since shown that the situation is more complicated, since some Harris dialects do, in fact, present the cluster in question (Watson 2007b: 260–1).

The nature of clusters in general constitutes a further vital diagnostic in regard to Gaelic in Scotland. We may consider the distribution, for instance, of those consisting of vibrant + sibilant + stop. Their existence may, in the first place, be taken as typical of all varieties of Gaelic, apart from the extreme south-western periphery. Not all of those dialects in which they occur permit them, however, within unstressed syllables. They do not feature here, for example, in the north or north-east, and it is interesting to note, within the Western Isles, that this is the situation only in Lewis and southern S. Uist. The cluster is, moreover, of more frequent occurrence in those dialects in which it occurs as reflex of historical –rd as well as of –rt, which is the case for the region between these two areas. This is the situation which prevails also in the Inner Isles, over most of Mull, in eastern Skye and on the west coast between these two islands (see Figure 6.1).

The extent to which palatalisation affects both single consonants and clusters likewise varies between dialects: the phenomenon, in synchronic terms, does not affect labials in Scottish Gaelic and the distinction may be unknown in certain dialects for other consonant classes in particular environments, e.g. in the case of velars before high front vowels in the east: *cinn* (Dorian 1978: 41–2); and, for initial clusters of stop + liquid/vibrant, palatalisation of the second member is reported only on the northern and southern peripheries of the Western Isles (Watson 2007b: 263, 272–3). Among features selected for comparative study by Borgstrøm in his analysis was the treatment of clusters consisting of vibrant (+ sibilant) + stop. In numerous dialects the vibrant here has – or had – a retroflex articulation, which affected also in varying fashions the articulation of a following element. Sometimes the vibrant has disappeared, leaving a retroflex stop (in parts of S. Uist the disappearance seems to have resulted in neither sibilisation or retroflexion, cf. *àrd* **ä:d̯**). In clusters which show a vibrant this is not subject to palatalisation, but a following element may or may not be and, with *SGDS* reporting palatalised stops at Harris points as against retroflex in Lewis, the isogloss boundary there reported by Borgstrøm (1940: 236) is validated in this case. There is a similar division in the case of other northern dialects generally but, according to *SGDS* data, where the cluster exhibits a sibilant this will not be palatalised in the dialects in question.

Reflexes of historical voiced labial and velar fricatives vary from dialect to dialect. Indeed, there are sometimes competing forms within a single dialect, cf. ER *fiadhaich* **fiʁiç** ~ **fiʁviç**. Internally we may find a fricative or continuant, or that a vowel sequence, with or without hiatus, has developed. An examination in the *SGDS* data of the form just cited illustrates this. The former reflex is, apart from sporadic occurrences elsewhere, found from northern and western Skye right round the north and west of the mainland as far as the head of the Great Glen, with the other dialects presenting the alternative option. The pattern varies, of course, according to the lexeme examined, cf. *abhainn, feadhainn, Samhainn,* etc. Historical non-palatalised labial fricatives in intervocalic position have generally left evidence in segmental form, except in north-west Skye and Raasay where hiatus is found, cf. *Samhainn* pt 115 **sã-ɪŋ**. That historical fricatives tend more generally to disappear intervocalically in svarabhakti syllables can be discerned from an inspection of *SGDS* data for, e.g. *gainmheach* or *dh'fhalbhadh.* In such a case an epenthetic vowel related in quality to the one preceding hiatus will generally be present, except in certain north-eastern dialects where the unhistorical vowel may be absorbed in that of a following syllable. In some of these, historical finals in –*l/ rbh, -amh, -adh* have resulted in final **u, u̧**, e.g. *marbh* **maru,** *balbh* **balu,** *fiadh* **fix̧u̧**.

MORPHOPHONEMICS

In Tables 3 and 4 (after Borgstrøm 1940: 173) will be found patterns of initial lenition and nasalisation typical of Lewis dialects.

Table 3 Initial mutations: aspirated stops

Radical	p	t	t′	kʰ	k′
Nasalised	m'	Nʼʰ	Nʼʼʰ	ŋʼʰ	ŋʼʼʰ
Lenited	f	h	h, hi̱	x	ç

The manner in which the **nasal mutation** is effected is a feature which distinguishes these and a few neighbouring dialects from the majority. In the case of most varieties of Gaelic the stop element is preserved. The outcome in some areas may be a pre-nasalised stop, with the nasal element subject to reduction and frequently lost. The fortis characteristic distinguishing one of the classes of stops disappears, but the distinction between the two classes is sometimes preserved, as in the S. Hebrides, for example, because the stops which replace them take the form of aspirated lenis stops, e.g. *an taigh* əᴺd̥‘øj vs *an dùthaich* əⁿḍu:hiç (Borgstrøm 1940: 182). Voicing may occur in the case not only of the mutated lenes but also with the mutated fortes, as in WR (Ternes 2006: 10). The latter (18) indicates that aspirated lenes are typical only of conservative speakers in the dialect just referred to. The category of aspirated lenes probably existed in the past in certain east coast dialects also, such as ER, ES (Dorian 1978: 71–2) where both classes have now fallen together under mutation, being represented in each case by the equivalent voiced unaspirated stop: *an cat* ən ĝatʰ : *an geata* ən ĝɛtʰ. Where initial *t-* has been prefixed word-initially, as required by the rules of grammar, this is likewise subject to nasal mutation, e.g. *an t-earrach.* In the eastern dialects just referred to, the prefixed form may be gener-alised for use following the article, which explains diachronically the situation referred to by Dorian (73–5) where initial **j** in lexemes such as *earrach* is mutated to **ʤ**. This scholar also records in her discussion the tendency for **ʃ** to be mutated in the same fashion and notes, as well, that **s** may be mutated to **ḍ**. Furthermore, in mainland dialects initial **f** may be mutated to **v** and **s** to **z**, e.g. EP (Ó Murchú 1989: 113–14) *an solas* **nzɔɫs**, *am fasgadh* **mvasgɑ**. The area affected by the former feature has been observed to be the more extensive (Watson and Clement 1983: 401): 'The area of dialects with z is crescent-shaped, having Braemar as its northern point and extending through Perthshire and ending east of Lochgilphead on Loch Fyne. The area of v from f is wider, including most of south-west Argyll as well as the area described for z.'

Table 4 Initial mutations: unaspirated stops

Radical	b	d	d´	g	g´
Nasalised	m'	N'	N''	ŋ'	ŋ''
Lenited	v	ɣ	j, i̯	ɣ	j, i̯

As far as the **lenition** of consonants is concerned, distinctions are particularly to be noted in regard to the categories of liquids, nasals and vibrants, and also in respect of those consonantal clusters in which such consonants participate. It should be pointed out in the first instance that particular western dialects show quite conservative inventories of consonants. Certain Lewis dialects, for example (Oftedal 1956: 45), have 4 *l*-phonemes (**L, L´, l, l´**): 3 *n*-phonemes: (**N, N´, n**); and 3 *r*-phonemes (**R, r r´**); as against 3: 2: and 1 respectively in ES (Dorian 1978: 44–5), with similarly reduced systems noted elsewhere, cf. Borgstrøm (1941: 37) for north-east Skye. In regard to lenition of fortis sonorants within the Western Isles dialects, scholars have noted differences: Borgstrøm (1940: 78), for example, records in the case of Bernera, Lewis, both **N** and **N′** leniting as **n**; **l** as the lenited form of **L** and **L′** and **r** appearing for lenited **R**; Oftedal (1956: 166–7) indicates for Leurbost in Lewis, that **L** and **N** do not normally lenite while Borgstrøm (1940: 174) reports for the S. Hebrides that **L** – though not **N** – is immutable. For WR Borgstrøm (1941: 102) reports lenition of **N** and **N′** to **n**, while in the case of Skye (45–6) all sonorants except **L** may be lenited, though this is said not to be universal with the younger generation. Dorian (1978: 68–9) notes that simple sonorants are unaffected by lenition in ES. Such is the case also, in my experience, in ER; and evidence from Ó Murchú (1989: s.v. Lexicon) would indicate that this is so in EP as well. As far as lenition of clusters containing sonorants is concerned we note the following situation. Oftedal (1956: 167–8) for part of Lewis records lenition of **sN** and **ʃN′** as **n**; of **sL** as **L**, and **ʃL′** as **l′**; of **sdr** (< *sr) as **r**; and of **tr** as **hr**, which is in agreement with Borgstrøm's (1940: 78) accounts of another Lewis dialect and S. Hebridean varieties (164, 174). Borgstrøm (1941: 41–2) indicates as the lenited forms in such instances aspirated sonorants (transcribed **nh; Lh, l′h** respectively and **ɽh**) for Skye dialects except the north-east which, like the Western Isles, only aspirates in the case of **tr**. WR is reported by the same source as being in agreement with the former region in Skye, having aspiration in lenited **r-** and **n-**clusters. No data are provided by the source in question for Skye or WR in the case of **l**-clusters, but Ternes (2006: 63) confirms aspiration here also in the case of the Applecross dialect. Dorian's (1978: 70–1) account of ES shows use of the mutation in decline but with unaspirated, rather than aspirated, forms as the norm – though some older speakers aspirated occasionally in the case of **tr**. EP (Ó Murchú 1989: Lexicon) shows aspirated sonorants for **tr**, s.v. *treabh*; unaspirated for **sr** in nouns; unaspirated ~ no mutation for **sL**; and no mutation in the case of initial **sN, sn** in verbs.

A feature of a number of northern and eastern dialects is, of course, verbal lenition in the case of initial *f-* following the particle *nach*, as in the Western Isles (Borgstrøm 1937: 186; Borgstrøm 1940: 109, 193); in WR, e.g. *nach fholbh* (Wentworth 2003: 524); in ER, e.g. *nach fhaithnich thu;* in ES, featuring **nax, (n)ax** (Dorian 1978: 136); and in EP (Ó Murchú 1989: Lexicon s.v. *faic*), e.g. the irregular verbal form *nach fhaiceadh.* Lenition of initial *f-* after the verbal particles *an, gun* has been noted in EP (Ó Murchú 1989: Lexicon s.v. *fàg, faigh, faic*) in the case of regular verbs: *fàg,* cf. fut. dep. **nɑːg u,** cond. dep. **nɑːgəx u** and also of the irregulars *faic:* fut. dep. **nɛ̃x′g′ u, gə nɛ̃x′g′,** past dep. **nãxg u,** cond. dep. **gə nɛ̃x′g′əɣ,** and *faigh:* fut. dep. **no, gə no,** cond. dep. **gə noəx.**

In ER past dep. *faca,* and sometimes cond. dep. *faiceadh, faigheadh,* may be lenited after *an* or *gun.*

The distribution of initial **h- prefixation** also varies between dialects. This is known to affect vowel initials after *mana* 'unless' in Lewis (Borgstrøm 1940: 111; Oftedal 1956: 260) and the S. Hebrides (Borgstrøm 1940: 193), as also in Skye and WR (Borgstrøm 1941: 55, 118) but this is not the case in ER or ES (Dorian 1978: 123). Though affecting only vowel initials historically, as is still the case in a number of varieties of Gaelic, its use in Lewis after *mana* 'unless' with verbs in radical initial **f-** is reported by Borgstrøm (1940: 109) and Oftedal (1956: 260). This is not so in the S. Hebrides (Borgstrøm 1940: 192–3) where the initial in question is unaffected after the corresponding particle *mara,* or, in Skye according to Borgstrøm's (1941: 46) material, though it is recorded for WR in the latter source (118–19), as confirmed by Wentworth (2003: 392), cf. **marə har′iç** *mara h-fhairich.* Such is not the case, however, in the eastern mainland areas of ER and ES (Dorian 1978: 123) where, on the other hand, the **f-** is lenited after ER **mər**, ES **mər, mə(n)**, cf. also EP (Ó Murchú 1989: 370) from where the following instance is noted: **mər no α** *maran fhaigh e,* together with an example with vocalic initial: **mər nɔ:l u** *maran òil thu.* In those dialects in which initial **f-** is affected by the **h**-mutation this generally applies to irregular verbs also, as in the case of the fut. and cond. of *faigh,* and *faic,* cf., for E. Lewis (Oftedal 1956: 243), **manə hã** *mana h-fhaigh,* **manə hɛ̆k′** *mana h-fhaic,* respectively, with comparable forms recorded in data from WR (Borgstrøm 1941: 121–2). Dialects differ, likewise, in regard to the form of the verbal particle *mur, man(a), mas, mus* 'before', as to whether a mutation follows or not and, if so, as to its nature. In Lewis, where the particle in question is **mas**, Borgstrøm (1940: 109) notes lenition of a following initial **f-**, which does not occur in the S. Hebrides (192). Here the nasal mutation after the corresponding form **man** does not affect **f-**. The same authority (1941: 118), which presents no data specific to Skye, indicates a radical initial only following the WR form **mas**. Wentworth's (2003: 65) data which contain also the forms **mə, ma, məs**, would appear to support this claim, although he has an entry only under **mə: mə ′fe:m** *mu feum.* In ES (Dorian 1978: 136–7), where we find the forms **məs, mə(n)** and **mər** – and a degree of merging with **mə(n), mər** 'before'– as well as nasalisation after forms of the particle, lenition of **f-** has also been recorded after, e.g. **məs** and **mər**. In ER also, where there has been similar merging with **mər, mə** 'unless', lenition of initial **f-** in *faic,* cond. dep. *mur fhaiceadh,* is noted; as likewise in EP (Ó Murchú 1989: 377) in the case of *faigh* after **məs**: fut. dep. **məs əj αʃ** *mus fhaigh eise,* though lenition is lacking in the case of a regular verb: **məs fɔL·w α** *mus falbh e.*

MORPHOLOGY AND SYNTAX

The morphology of the **noun and adjective** is not, generally speaking, seen to vary a great deal as between the most conservative western dialects. In regard to Class 1 nouns, Borgstrøm (1940: 180) notes that the gen. sg. and nom. pl. are marked by palatalisation of final consonant in Hebridean dialects south of Lewis, a region which shows for nouns in −an[2] non-palatalised nasal in the gen. sg. and suffixing of morph -ən in the pl. In Skye (Borgstrøm 1941: 47, 49) palatalisation is the norm in the former instance, while both forms are found in the second; and in WR (104, 107) -ən is restricted to instances where 'the consonant preceding −an and -ən is not palatal'. The usual pl. formation with −an is also -ən in some eastern dialects, where the termination is realised as a syllabic nasal (Dorian 1978: 86–7; Ó Murchú 1989: 120). A further distinction between Lewis and more southerly dialects, as well as those of Skye and parts of the western mainland is the appearance in these latter areas of a gen. sg. fem. in final -əɣ in the case of monosyllabic or syncopated Class 2 nouns, cf. *(muir:) maradh, (bainis:) bainseadh* (Borgstrøm 1941: 47). In Lewis the corresponding morpheme -ə appears consistently only before a following initial consonant (Borgstrøm 1940: 88), while in the S. Hebrides -ə is found instead of -əɣ before the initial consonant of a following adjective, with the latter instead acquiring the -əɣ termination, cf. *fear na làimhe bigeadh* (Borgstrøm 1940: 186). In WR, within Class 2, a dat. morpheme −i is recorded (Borgstrøm 1941: 105): *gaoithe* ĝɯ:hi, *cloiche* kʰLɔhi, which may have arisen on account of the influence of the fricative preceding a -ə, cf. forms such as *cnàimhean* kʰra:`in, *ghabhadh* ɣa`uk in the same dialect (107, 119). Oftedal (1956: 196) notes the tendency in Leurbost, Lewis, for gen. to be replaced with nom. but records no separate dat. sg. fem. for this class. Borgstrøm (1940: 89), however, notes the existence of this case in Bernera Gaelic where it is marked by palatalisation of final, though its restricted distribution receives comment. There is also a certain category of lexeme, e.g. *coille,* listed in Class 2 for Barra by Borgstrøm (1937: 162), for which is recorded a dat. sg. morpheme −i. This ending, which would have been restricted originally to consonantal stems, can be seen to have spread to additional classes, and is also found in other regions, as in *litidh* Skye, Borgstrøm (1941: 47). In a number of western dialects the morpheme in question is, rather, -iç and Ó Maolalaigh (1999) has explained the distribution of this in terms of hyperdialectalism. In WR, even though traditional inflexional categories continue to function, inherited oblique forms have sometimes replaced historical nominatives, of which process the following will serve as instances in the case of the noun: *teangaidh* (Borgstrøm 1941: 70), *leas [lios,* gen. *leasa]* (104), *cloinn, làimh* (105), *meal [meala,* for *mil]* (126). This is so also for the eastern dialects discussed here where inherited inflexion survives in respect of nouns and adjectives for the most part only in fixed phrases and expressions such as: ER *Oidhch[e] na Shamhn[a]* (sic), *amadan an danais!, seasamh na mor [mara]*; ES *leabaidh-m(h) uill, taigh-shalais [solais], sgoth sheòlaidh* (Dorian 1978: 85); EP *galar a' bhàis, muc mar [mara], fear an taighe* (Ó Murchú 1989: 348, 375, 411). In such dialects instances of historical oblique forms such as the following in use as nominative may be noted: ES *fradhaidh [rabhadh], meangain, Eachainn, gobhainn, fearainn, salainn, neòlach* (Dorian 1978: 154–5, 166–7, 171); EP *aighearaich, aitimh, amhaich* (Ó Murchú 1989: 277–8, 281); ER *feamainn, gainmhich, taghlaich [teaghlach], craicinn, taoibh.* In the same way that adjectives also have been affected, cf. ER *falaimh, ullaimh, deis [deas],* so adverbs and adverbial phrases have similarly been influenced, e.g. ER *a-màraich, Dihaoinibh, air adhairt, an tosaich* (Watson 2007a: 37). Similar instances in the case of noun pls. which may be noted are ES: *fiachaibh, naimhdibh, ceudaibh, rìghribh, sùsanaibh* (Dorian 1978: 88) and ER: *daoinibh, speuraibh.*

As previously mentioned, such eastern dialects for the most part no longer mark genitival relationship morphologically. Where two nouns are so linked, word order will indicate the connection, e.g. ER *meall feòil,* generally also with the required initial mutation in the case of the article, as ER *Là a' Bhreitheanas, tìom an fhoghar, barr an t-sròin.* The connection may also be expressed through the use of *aig:* ER *na cluaisean aig an t-each, an t-sealladh aig an t-sùil;* and this is common also where the noun is governed by a pronoun: ER *na sliastan agam.* In the case of compound prepositions in certain eastern dialects, instead of the possessive adjectival form of the pronoun, a personal pronoun may serve, ER: *nam aghaidh ~ an aghaidh mi,* EP *am measg iad uile* (Ó Murchú 1989: 357); ES *orn [air shon] thu (~ air do shon)* (Dorian 1978: 114). A simple personal pronoun may also, as alternative to a possessive form, be used as complement to a verbal noun phrase involving *ag* in ER: *a' leantainn mi, a' faicinn aid,* and in other dialects of the east, such as ES *[a'] loisgeadh aid, [a'] glanadh aid* (Dorian 1978: 96). EP Gaelic (Ó Murchú 1989: s.v. Lexicon), on the other hand, like western dialects, favours the construction whereby a possessive adjective is prefixed to the verbal noun. The prefixing element is generally a variant form of a preposition and this is a point on which the dialects divide. As reported by both Borgstrøm (1940: 101–2) and Oftedal (1956: 213), *gha* is the regular prefixer in Lewis, which is the case in much of WR also (Borgstrøm 1941: 113), apart from Duirinis where the latter notes the use of *na* instead. In the S. Hebrides (Borgstrøm 1940: 240), as in Skye (Borgstrøm 1941: 52), the usage is *ga,* which is also the case in EP and, as previously noted, insofar as the construction is found, in ER, e.g. *ga mo thuigeil.*

A further point on which dialects diverge is the forms of the 1 and 2 pl. possessive adjectives which are found not only in this construction but also in others which are represented in all the dialects, namely with *an* and, likewise, following *air* in perfect or passive constructions. As has been made clear in respect of the forms in question by Borgstrøm (1940: 101–2, 187–8, 241–2), the S. Hebrides show **ər n-** (**ɣar n-** when compounded with *gha*), while Lewis and Harris here agree on an alternative mutation, viz. **ər h-** (**ɣa:r h** when compounded with *gha*),[3] which is also that found in N. Skye (Borgstrøm 1941: 53). WR, on the other hand, has **nə h-** here, which yields **ɣanə** as prefixed pronominal. In both ES (Dorian 1978: 97) and ER **nə** is, likewise, the form of the adjectives in question, e.g. ER *gabhaibh na h-anail!* EP (Ó Murchú 1989: 78), on the other hand, shows a form with final *–r,* namely **nər h-** (though **nə h-** is also reported). There is a great deal of variety between dialects in regard to other pronominal forms, particularly in the case of the 3 sg. m. and 3 pl. personal pronouns. Oftedal (1956: 209) records **aʃiN´** as the emphatic form for Leurbost in the first case, and Borgstrøm (1940: 100, 187) **æʃiN´**, for Bernera and Harris with **æʃin** in Skye (1941: 52), as against S. Hebrides **esən**. EP (Ó Murchú 1989: 334) has **aʃ, ɛʃ**; WR **æʃə** (Borgstrøm 1941: 112); ER **ɛʃ** and ES **e:ʃ** (Dorian 1978: 95). The corresponding pl. forms (from the same sources) are as follows: Leurbost **a:sən** (together with the dissyllabic emphatic forms **i-ad, e-ad**); Bernera ˌiəˌdsən; Barra **a:sən, ædsən**; Skye (no data provided), WR **ædsə**; ER, ES (Dorian 1978: 95) **e:d´əs**, EP **a:ds, ɛ:ds** (cf. also stressed **a:d´**). Unexpected final palatalised stop in 3 pl personal pronoun of ER, WR, ES, EP (Watson 2007a: xl; Borgstrøm 1941: 112; Dorian 1978: 95; Ó Murchú 1989: 357) vs non-palatalised consonant of other dialects may be due to the influence of the historical verbal termination *–id.*

Within the category of prepositional pronouns, the 3 sg. fem. and 3 pl. are forms which distinguish different varieties of Gaelic, as Borgstrøm (1941: 238) noted when he chose to compare Western Isles dialects, using *bho* as exemplar. His data show, in both cases, forms in final *–hpə* from Harris to S. Uist. For the fem. pron. Bernera shows **foç(ə)**, and Barra **ɣuəˌçɔ̃**, while the pl. forms are, respectively, Bernera **foh(ə)** ~ **fohp(ə)**, Barra **ɣˌuəˌxɔ̃**. Final morph with labial element is also found in the case of the prepositions *fo,* and *ro, tro* (with forms of the latter preposition subsumed in the preceding one in the case of S. Hebridean and some Skye dialects). Data from Oftedal (1956: 220–2) for eastern

Lewis, on the other hand, register the labial morpheme in the items in question and data from *LASID* (Q.1012 pt e) would appear to indicate its presence in N.W. Lewis also. It is likewise in evidence in Skye, apart from the N.W. of the island, while on the mainland, though labial forms are noted for EP (Ó Murchú 1989: Lexicon s.v. *bho, fo, roimh, troimh*), the series without this element is found elsewhere, cf. WR where there are forms in **h-**, Borgstrøm (1941: 115–17); ER; and ES (Dorian 1978: 112–13): **fɔi, fɔ; vɔi, vɔ; rɔ̃, rɔ̃ĩ; trɔ̃ĩ, trɔ̃ ad´**, respectively. In the case of another preposition, *an,* the vowel which appears in most of the personal forms (1, 2 sg. and 1, 2, 3 pl.) serves to distinguish various dialects. The distribution here is particularly interesting since, as Borgstrøm (1940: 105, 190) indicates, Harris with **a** stands apart from both Lewis and the rest of the S. Hebrides which show **u**, as also do N. and S. Skye (Borgstrøm 1941: 53). In the case of mainland dialects EP (Ó Murchú 1989: 283–4) shows **a** (~ **ɔ**).[4] This is also the case for ES (Dorian 1978: 112) and W. Sutherland, *LASID* (Q.103 pt g), while ER and WR (Borgstrøm 1941: 115–16) both have **u**, in which areas also forms of *mu* (**uməm** etc.) may sometimes replace those of *an.*

An examination of the morphology of the regular verb indicates that in the indep. fut. the 3 sg. termination is recorded as **-i** (*-idh*) by Borgstrøm (1940: 108–11), for Bernera and the S. Hebrides (192–3) and it is this **-i** morpheme which Borgstrøm (1941: 54–5) has recorded for Skye dialects also. Oftedal (1956: 236), for Leurbost, reports -i in citation forms or careful speech but -ə elsewhere, and notes that -əs, the regular relative form, is used as indep. form with the fem. pronoun *i,* the final sibilant of the verb here reflecting earlier *sandhi* with E.Ir. fem. pron. *sí.* For WR dialects Borgstrøm (1941: 117–18) notes, as confirmed by Oftedal, the use of -ə and -i according to the environment, but also records -əs as indep. form with following noun or pronoun. Some unusual variant forms have been produced in this dialect through the influence of a preceding fricative on ə in these particular terminations (118), cf. 'ihis ə 'vo: *itheas a' bhó,* L´ˌiaˌ`us a *leughas e* vs L´ˌiaˌvi *leughaidh* (affirmative response). Dorian (1978: 121), in the case of ES, has a similar record for -ə and -i forms, but notes indep. -əs as excluded from use with 1 sg. and 1, 2 pl. pronouns. For ER the situation is similar, though I have certainly also heard -əs in use at least with 1 sg. pron., viz. *canas mise.* The position in regard to EP (Ó Murchú 1989: Lexicon s.v. *dùn*), allowing for loss of vocalic final of the historical termination *-idh* before following initial of noun or pronoun, e.g. **du:n mi, du:n ʃin, du:ns a, du:ns ad´**, appears to have a certain amount in common with ES, but we may note that in the former area use of the **-s** morpheme is optional in the case of the 2 sg. form (s.v. *buail*), viz. **bu·əl**

~ **bu·əls u** *buail(idh)* ~ *buaileas thu.* As item no. 24 (*bhitheamaid*) in his Western Isles questionnaire Borgstrøm (1940: 233, 238), includes the use of a synthetic vs analytic form in the case of the cond. 1 pl. form which he designates, cf. *bhitheadh sinn* vs *bhitheamaid,* as an important isogloss boundary between Lewis on the one hand and Harris plus the remainder of the S. Hebrides on the other. Skye, the same authority (1941: 55, 58) reports, agrees with the latter group, while WR, like Lewis, he notes, employs analytic forms. Analytic forms are found in the dialects of ER and ES (Dorian 1978: 118), e.g. **xuru ʃin´** *chuireadh*[5] *sinn,* as, likewise, in EP (Ó Murchú 1989: Lexicon s.v. *dùn*): **ɣu:nəx ʃin** *dhùnadh sinn,* and *LASID* (QQ.501, 585 pt e) seems to indicate this to be the case for W. Sutherland also.

In regard to the morphology of irregular verbs, it is to be noted that, while a number of dialects present separate forms in the fut. indep. of *their* and *thoir* respectively, e.g. Skye and WR (Borgstrøm 1941: 56, 122), EP (Ó Murchú 1989: 273, 415), ER and Lewis (Oftedal 1956: 251–2), which shows **heð** and **veð, feð** – though the former is regularly replaced by *canaidh* in the two latter areas – forms of the verbs in question merge in the S. Hebrides, e.g. **fer´, fer´i** *bheir(idh).* In ES (Dorian 1978: 128), as in ER, the future of the former verb is supplied by *can.* In the case of irregular verbs in general, there is an impressive range of different verbal forms found over the various dialects so that attention is directed here to a selection only, dealing first with verb-initial variation. In the case of the substantive verb, it is to be noted that certain dialects show that the initial of the present affected by the nasal mutation is **b-**, rather than **v-**, as in ES (in one of three villages, Dorian 1978: 118) **bel** *beil,* as well as W. Sutherland (*LASID* Q.421 pt e), both ER and WR (Borgstrøm 1940: 121), and Lewis (Oftedal 1956: 243), though in the latter two areas (cf. Borgstrøm 1941: 114) we note also *bheil* which is the regular form in other areas, such as the S. Hebrides and EP (Ó Murchú 1989: 293). An unhistorical initial labial stop of this nature is, of course, familiar in the case of other irregular verbs, in future and conditional forms, e.g. ER (Watson 2007a: xlii), and ES (in one village out of three, Dorian 1978: 125–6). In these latter areas the morphemic marker **d, də** commonly found before dep. past tense forms with regular verbs and the irregular *dean,* as in *d'rinn,* appears also in *bi*: past dep. **xa tro** (118), and also in *thèid:* cond. dep.: **traxu** (124), the form found also in WR: **dʒrɛxək** (Wentworth 2003: 312). However, as this latter source shows, the cond. in WR may be based on more than one stem, and another form cited there is **je-ək** *dheigheadh* (dep. **dʒ´e-ək**). While Borgstrøm (1940: 233) has identified *dheigheadh* vs *rachadh* as an isogloss boundary between Lewis and Harris on the one hand and the remainder of the S. Hebrides on the other, with which latter area Skye would seem to go (Borgstrøm 1941: 56), data on the mainland dialects referred to, indicate that there is variation in the cond., not only between *rach-* and *dheigh-*, but that a third stem, *reagh-*, comes into play as well: WR **r´e`ǝk** *reaghadh* (dep. **ḑre`ǝk**) (Borgstrøm 1941: 121), ES (Dorian 1978: 124) **heu, reu, d´eu**. In contrast to Western Isles and Skye **xa(:)j** *chaidh*, the past indep. of the verb in question also shows significantly different forms in some of these mainland areas. In WR **xa(:)r** is found (Borgstrøm 1941: 121; Wentworth 2003: 312), while in ER and ES (Dorian 1978: 124) the form is **ɣa** (and the same voiced initial segment is found in **ɣ₁ua₁l** *chual,* past indep. of *cluinn,* in these last two regions). In dialects of Skye (Borgstrøm 1941: 56), as likewise in Barra (Borgstrøm 1937: 193), **ḑ´ax** *deach,* past dep. of *thèid,* has been observed to have a long citation form, **ḑ´axi** *deachaidh,* and this is stated to be the case also for *faic: chan fhacaidh,* and *cluinn: chualaidh.*

    Within the adverbial category, in regard to those members most commonly used to indicate location, *an seo, an sin,* and *an siud* a good deal of diversity is to be noted – even excluding here the various suffixes which may be added, e.g. WR **-ɔxkiN´** (Wentworth 2003: 788). In the Western Isles, for example, the forms cited are as follows: Leurbost Lewis: **aNǝ´ʃɔ, aNǝ´hjɔ, (ǝ)´ʃɔ; aNǝ´ʃin, (ǝ)´ʃin, aNǝ´hîn, aNǝ´hid** (Oftedal 1956: 214); Bernera Lewis: **(ǝ)ʃɔh, aNǝ´hi̯ɔh; (ǝ)ʃæn, aNǝ´hæn; (ǝ)ʃiḑ, aNǝ´hiḑ** (Borgstrøm 1940: 102); (no paradigms are supplied for Barra in Borgstrøm 1937: 179; Skye, Borgstrøm 1941: 52; or Harris, Borgstrøm 1940: 188, though the adjective corresponding to the second form of the trio is recorded as **ʃɛn** for the last region). For WR the following are on record: **aNǝ ~ aNa ´ʃɔʰ, ǝ´ʃɔʰ; aNǝ´ʃîn, ǝ´ʃîn, ʃîn; aNǝ´ʃit, ǝ´ʃit, ʃit** (Wentworth 2003: 355); in ER: **anǝ´ʃɔ, ʃɔ; anǝ´ʃin, ´ʃin; anǝ´ʃiḑ, ʃiḑ;** for ES: **anǝ´ʃɔ, ʃɔ; anǝ´ʃǝn, ´ʃǝn; anǝ´ʃǝd, ´ʃǝd** (Dorian 1978: 100); and in EP the forms **nd´ɔ, nd´ɛn (nd´in)** (Ó Murchú 1989: 284–5). Continuing with adverbs, a further distinction in the lexicon is to be noted with regard to how location and direction are signified. In the Western Isles 'up' and 'down' are indicated by the forms *suas, sìos; a-nuas* (direction) and *shìos, shuas* (location), cf. Lewis (Borgstrøm 1940: 103). For the eastern Highlands, on the other hand, Dorian (1978: 109) has observed: '/siǝs/ and /suǝs/, which in western dialects usually mean 'up' and 'down', are used in ES to mean 'east' and 'west' respectively'; and this is certainly true as well for ER **siǝs** (*sic* **s-** in both dialects), **suǝs**, as well as in the case of the EP (Ó Murchú 1989: 402, 409) forms. The adverbials used in ES for 'up' and 'down' respectively are: **hurǝd** *thurad* (location), **(ǝ) no:rd** *an àirde* (direction); **stã:n** *a-stàn* (location), (ə) **vã:n** *a-bhàn* (direction), forms comparable to which are found in ER and EP (Ó Murchú 1989: 292, 424).

LEXICON

In a limited survey like this not much space can be devoted to matters of Lexicon proper. A very few distinctions in core vocabulary, however, may be briefly noted, such as *bùrn* 'fresh water' in Lewis, Harris (Borgstrøm 1940: 231), Skye (Holmer 1938: 132, *recte* part of), ES (ER, EP *burn*) vs *uisge* in WR, S. Hebrides and the western mainland. While this example illustrates a largely north-south divide, there are others which mark off the eastern periphery from the rest, such as *nodha* 'new' (vs *ùr*) which appears in ES, ER and EP. *Treabhair* (vs *taighean*) as pl. of *taigh* is, on the other hand, confined to the north-eastern highlands (Dorian 1978: 88), and in the useful Appendices supplied by the same scholar (151–71) there are numerous other items known also from the ER lexicon, if apparently unfamiliar elsewhere, e.g. *(n)iochd* 'ghost', *pioc- tar* 'picture', *pollach* 'cod', *tailb* 'oarlock', etc. A feature of such eastern dialects is, of course, the number and nature of the Scots borrowings they contain, as illustrated in Dorian's lists where we note such forms as *frachd* 'a pair of pails', *rùlaidh* 'lead pencil', *spilcnis* 'split peas', *nobsaidh* 'fish soup', etc.; and from my own ER material I cite the following instances, by way of illustration: *laidhbeal* 'certificate', *lòrn* 'shoe', *robh* 'roll', *sguil* 'basket', *slais* 'whip', *slop* 'fisherman's shirt', *sguitear* 'ladel', *tobha* 'rope', *tomaidh* 'loaf'. However, until collections comparable in scope to that of Wentworth (2003) for WR are carried out elsewhere lexical comparisons such as this must remain somewhat speculative. It is, needless to say, of the utmost importance, therefore, that this and other vital linguistic work remaining to be undertaken among traditional Gaelic language communities in the diminishing number of areas where this continues to be feasible be carried out without delay.

Figure 6.1 Distribution of epenthetic -s-

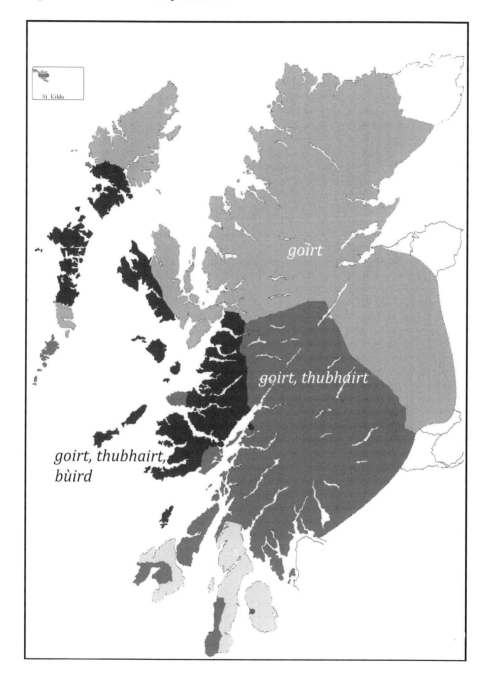

BIBLIOGRAPHY

Borgstrøm, C. Hj. (1937), 'The Dialect of Barra in the Outer Hebrides', *Norsk Tidskrift for Sprogvidenskap* 8, pp. 71–242.

Borgstrøm, C. Hj. (1940), *A Linguistic Survey of the Gaelic Dialects of Scotland I: The Dialects of the Outer Hebrides*, Oslo: H. Aschehoug and Co.

Borgstrøm, C. Hj. (1941), *A Linguistic Survey of the Gaelic Dialects of Scotland II: The Dialects of Skye and Ross-shire.* Oslo: H. Aschehoug and Co.

Dorian, N. C. (1978), *East Sutherland Gaelic. The Dialect of the Brora, Golspie, and Embo Fishing Communities*, Dublin: Dublin Institute for Advanced Studies.

Holmer (1938), *Studies on Argyllshire Gaelic*, Uppsala: Almqvist and Wiksells.

Jackson, K. H. (1968), 'The Breaking of Original Long *ē* in Scottish Gaelic', in J. Carney and D. Greene (eds), *Celtic Studies: Essays in Memory of Angus Matheson, 1912–1962*, London: Routledge and K. Paul, pp. 65-71.

LASID Wagner, H. and Ó Baoill, C. (eds) (1969), *Linguistic Atlas and Survey of Irish Dialects*, Vol. 4, Dublin: Dublin Institute for Advanced Studies.

Ó Maolalaigh, R. (1999), 'Transition Zones, Hyperdialectalisms and Historical Change: The Case of Final Unstressed *–igh/-ich* in Scottish Gaelic', *Scottish Gaelic Studies* 19, pp. 195–233.

Ó Maolalaigh, R. (2001), 'Forás na ndeirí díspeagtha *–ean* agus *ein* i nGaeilge na hAlban', in B. Ó Catháin and R. Ó hUiginn (eds), *Béalra: aistí ar theangeolaíocht na Gaeilge*, Maynooth: Sagart.

Ó Maolalaigh, R. (2003), 'Review article: *The Gaelic of Islay*', *Scottish Gaelic Studies* 21, pp. 255–68.

Ó Murchú, M. (1989), *East Perthshire Gaelic*, Dublin: Dublin Institute for Advanced Studies.

Oftedal, M. (1956), *The Gaelic of Leurbost, Isle of Lewis*, Oslo: Norwegian Universities Press.

SGDS Ó Dochartaigh, C. (ed.) (1994–7), *Survey of the Gaelic Dialects of Scotland*, Vols 1–5, Dublin: Dublin Institute for Advanced Studies.

Ternes, E. (2006), *The Phonemic Analysis of Scottish Gaelic.* Dublin: Dublin Institute for Advanced Studies.

Watson, A. and Clement, R. D. (1983), 'Aberdeenshire Gaelic',
   Transactions of the Gaelic Society of Inverness 52, pp. 373–404.
Watson, S. (1985), 'Caducous and Fallen Vowels in Irish and Scottish
   Gaelic', *Ériu* 36, pp. 125–36.
Watson, S. (1996), 'Hiatus-filling /h/ in Irish and Scottish Gaelic
   Dialects', *Scottish Gaelic Studies* 17, pp. 376–82.
Watson, S. (1999), 'Aspects of Some Nova Scotian Dialects', in R. Black,
   W. Gillies and R. Ó Maolalaigh, *Celtic Connections: Proceedings of the
   Tenth International Congress of Celtic Studies,* Vol. 1, pp. 347–59.
Watson, S. (2007a), *Saoghal Bana-mharaiche,* Ceann Drochaid: Clann
   Tuirc.
Watson, S. (2007b), 'Borgstrøm's Word-list Revisited: Lewis and
   Harris', in J. E. Rekdal and A. Ó Corráin (eds), *Proceedings of the
   Eighth Symposium of Societas Celtologica Nordica,* pp. 249–74.
Wentworth, R. (2003), *Gaelic Words and Phrases from Wester Ross/
   Faclan is Abairtean à Ros an Iar,* Inverness: CLÀR.

NOTES

1 ER data, unless otherwise stated, are from the writer's own field collection.
2 For discussion of this and related diminutive suffix morphemes see Ó Maolalaigh
   2001.
3 See Oftedal (1956: 213) re. vowel length in this case.
4 3 sg. m. and 3 pl. forms may have a diphthong.
5 [u] in these dialects being a regular reflex of hist. *–adh.*

CHAPTER 7

The Gaelic Language-Group: Demography, Language-Usage, -Transmission, and -Shift

Kenneth MacKinnon

INTRODUCTION: OVER A CENTURY OF DEMOGRAPHIC DECLINE 1881–2001

At the end of the nineteenth century, Gaelic was widely spoken in Scotland over the whole of the Highlands, Hebrides and Clyde Islands. There were also sizeable numbers of Gaelic speakers in Canada – particularly in eastern Nova Scotia – and their numbers were suggested as comprising some 75,000 in the later nineteenth century (Stephens 1976). These numbers had declined to 24,000 in 1931 when the Canadian census first asked a question on Gaelic, and to 1500 in 1971. More detailed census analysis is reported in MacKinnon (2001a). The present author also undertook detailed surveys of Gaelic communities in Cape Breton Island in the mid-1970s, which are reported in MacKinnon (1996).

In Scotland a question on Gaelic (whether it was 'spoken habitually') was asked for the first time in 1881, and a total of 231,594 speakers was recorded, comprising 6.76% of the national population. The shortcomings of this process were improved upon ten years later with a written question on the census form ('can you speak Gaelic'). On this definition numbers ostensibly increased to 254,415 (some 6.84% of the national population). Some weakening of the language was, however, already becoming apparent along the eastern Highland fringes from Caithness to the Clyde Islands. However, proportions speaking Gaelic registered over 70% of local populations in the Hebrides, western coastal parishes and even some central areas. The proportion of 70.7% is critical for predominant potential language-use. It represents the 50% chance level of local Gaelic speakers meeting and using their language together. These levels for successive censuses are shown in Figure 7.1.

By 1891, migration was bringing substantial numbers of Gaelic speakers to Lowland industrial areas. The proportion of Gaelic speakers in Highland areas at the end of the nineteenth century was already showing a decline from 87% to 77%. During the twentieth century this proportion was maintained above 70% until 1961, but by 2001 had reached 56%. The changing situation is detailed in Figures 7.2 and 7.3. It will be apparent too that over this period the language-group has declined rapidly to 58,652 speakers of three years or older. This total represented 1.20% of the national population in 2001, and a decrease to 23.05% of the number in 1891. In this process of decline the only ostensible increase was in 1971 when questions on reading and writing Gaelic were asked for the first time. A summary for Gaelic speakers by area of residence is shown in Figures 7.4 and 7.5.

By 2001, it was becoming clear that Gaelic populations in Lowland areas are approaching half the total, and that these numbers are increasing in east coast areas with new industries, administrative, financial and residential centres. However, numbers of Gaelic speakers declined in old central belt industrial areas, with more substantial decreases in the Highlands and Hebrides.

There are many reasons for the rapid decline of Gaelic from at least the end of the nineteenth century. One of the most basic is that the language had very little institutional place in Scottish society and had developed few distinctive institutions which might have secured a place for it in the lives of its speakers. A system of Gaelic schools which used the language as a teaching medium and taught Gaelic literacy was superseded from 1872 by a national system in which Gaelic had little or no place. This might have seemed appropriate to enable Gaelic speakers to 'get on' in a non-Gaelic-speaking world but it also reinforced the impressions generated in this period that Gaelic 'held you back', interfered with mental function, and was generally backward looking. Although a questionnaire on Gaelic in schools was circulated to Highland school boards in 1876 with a majority in favour, nothing much resulted (Withers 1984: 158). However, Gaelic was recognised as a 'specific subject' in 1876 (Smith 1983: 260), but it was decades before it really achieved similar recognition to other languages. From 1882 it was possible to study Gaelic as part of a university degree in Celtic.

Outwith education, the cultural organisation An Comunn Gaidhealach (founded in 1891) specifically avoided any sort of political engagement and concentrated on running Gaelic cultural festivals: the local and national Mòds. With the achievement of crofting legislation in 1886, the Highland Land League which had 'the language' in its motto failed to do anything further on its behalf. The only institution in which

Gaelic featured apart from home and community in this period was the Church. However, as Gaelic weakened, so too did the place of Gaelic in religious life: the churches featured the language instrumentally solely as a medium for worship and mission. Its intrinsic spiritual values were scarcely realised – unlike Welsh in church life in Wales (Davies 1970; see Macleod in this volume for more on language in society).

Throughout the twentieth century the processes of industrialisation continued to produce substantial migration from Highlands and Hebrides to Lowland industrial centres. Reverse flows of professional, administrative and managerial personnel further weakened Gaelic in its home areas, and meant that English became even more dominant in social and official life. Two world wars speeded up the rate of economic and social change and it is quite apparent that the First World War took a particularly heavy toll on Gaelic speakers, especially in terms of losses at sea and of Highland infantry. The contraction of the language as a language of upbringing is also readily apparent, indicating acute demographic deficit as compared with the non-Gaelic population. The interwar period witnessed substantial migration overseas, especially from the Hebrides. The demographic effects of these processes can still be felt today, and can be seen in the population profiling of Gaelic language abilities discussed below.

GAELIC LANGUAGE ABILITIES AND POPULATION PROFILES

Questions on reading and writing Gaelic, which have been asked since 1971, indicate the success of teaching Gaelic literacy in Gaelic areas schools since the late 1950s. In the 1970s and 1980s Gaelic as a second language was also introduced into Highland primary schools in many areas. With the creation of the Western Isles authority (Comhairle nan Eilean) in 1975, a bilingual education scheme was introduced, extended in 1978 and was to have been applied in all schools from 1981.

From 1985, following a very successful experience with developing pre-school Gaelic playgroups or *cròileagain,* Gaelic-medium units were established in two primary schools in Glasgow and Inverness. From these beginnings, Gaelic-medium education (GME) expanded to sixty primary schools, with 2256 pupils by 2009/10. Despite these developments, it remains the case that Gaelic-medium secondary education remains relatively undeveloped, with a considerable drop in pupil numbers on transfer from primary. However, it is clear that although the Gaelic-medium sector is still small and lacking effective secondary development it is making a difference. Their effects, together with other forms of Gaelic education, can be seen in the population profile in Figure 7.6. (For more on the development of education, see Macleod in this volume.)

Although Gaelic education in its various forms is making a difference to the viability of local Gaelic populations, it is not at a sufficient scale to overcome losses from natural decrease and migration. Populations need at least a third of their number under 25 for potential population growth to occur and for viability to be possible. Scotland itself has fallen below this norm, and the main Gaelic areas and their Gaelic populations especially so. In 2001, only 19.4% of Gaelic speakers in the Western Isles were aged under 25 – compared with 39.2% of non-Gaelic speakers, and as compared with 16.4% in areas with no Gaelic school education. In terms of this viability index, Argyll & Bute and Highland were doing rather better with 26.3% and 25.2% respectively. However, if the development of Gaelic education is seen as the main plank in Gaelic language-planning policy these figures indicate that there is a considerable further development needed to bring them above 33.3%.

A further question, on understanding Gaelic, was asked for the first time in the 2001 census. With the development of the Gaelic broadcast media in the later twentieth century and into the twenty-first, this provided essential baseline data for media audience assessment. The development of the Gaelic media, and Gaelic education in this period, has provided two important domains of use and presence of the language in society. For all ages there were 58,969 actual speakers *as such*, and 7094 persons without speaking ability but able to read and/ or write Gaelic. These may be understood as persons who had learned Gaelic through written media, e.g. as a second-language learner at school, or as an adult education learner. There were also 27,219 persons able to understand but not speak, read or write Gaelic. These may be understood as 'semi-speakers', persons who had become familiar with Gaelic through family or community experience but whose educational experience had not developed this into confident speaking, reading or writing abilities. In terms of language-planning or Gaelic education strategies, both categories are to be found within school ages in all areas and thus represent the most accessible cases for language acquisition.

The age-profile for Gaelic language speakers nationally is illustrated in Figure 7.7, and shows sharp decline by age compared with non-Gaelic speakers. The effects of Gaelic education policies do show up even at this level. They become more apparent in Figure 7.8: the aggregate of the Argyll & Bute, Highland and Eileanan Siar education authorities. The effects of migration in the late teens and early twenties are very apparent in all these areas. It is also very noticeable in the aggregate for Gaelic speakers in Lowland education authority areas with Gaelic-medium education in Figure 7.9 that amongst younger age-ranges there is a marked peak in the 20–24 age-group – precisely the age-group in which numbers fall away after the school years in the Highlands and Hebrides areas. Sharp decline of Gaelic language abilities is apparent in areas without Gaelic-medium education as shown in Figure 7.10.

MIGRATION, FAMILY FORMATION AND LANGUAGE-TRANSMISSION

Migration thus continues to play a key role in the prospects for Gaelic language-maintenance. Scottish society has become increasingly mobile – and Gaelic speakers have become almost as mobile as the rest. In 1990–1 the annual migration rate (i.e. the proportion of persons moving home) had become 10.4%, and for Gaelic speakers 8.9%. Ten years later these proportions had risen to 11.6% and 11.1% respectively. The mobility of Gaelic speakers – and most especially of younger Gaelic-speaking adults – means that life-chances bring Gaelic- and non-Gaelic-speaking potential spouses together at an ever-increasing rate. Not only are Gaelic speakers moving into non-Gaelic-speaking areas, but non-Gaelic speakers are moving into Gaelic-speaking areas at an ever-increasing rate as well.

This means that family formation between Gaelic-speaking and non-Gaelic-speaking adults is taking place also at an ever-increasing rate. If policies are to be made for Gaelic speakers in society, then this must be understood as being made for a society and for Gaelic speakers who are very much on the move. These movements at over 11% annually mean that over a decade they add up to more than the equivalent of the total population of all Gaelic speakers. Modern Scotland, and its Gaidhealtachd, are no longer the settled, static world of past generations.

The clear implication of this socio-economic fact of modern life is that if policies are to be made for Gaelic in the family, these policies must address the fact that by 2001 fewer than half of all Gaelic speakers lived in entirely Gaelic-speaking households (estimated at 46.3%.) These comprised an estimated 12,792 persons living in couple households (21.8% or just over one in five out of 58,652 Gaelic speakers aged three or over), an estimated 1725 living in lone parent households (2.9%), 11,404 single Gaelic speakers living alone (19.4%), and an estimated 1220 Gaelic speakers living in all-Gaelic multiple households (0.9%) (estimated from GROS 2008). In all families where all adults were Gaelic-speaking, some 58.8% of their children spoke Gaelic, and these families contained an estimated 29,995 or 51.1%% of all Gaelic speakers. This situation has clear implications for language transmission within the family. Without strong supportive institutions outwith the family, such as education, social and cultural life, and the media, Gaelic language-reproduction amongst the present and coming generations will rapidly diminish and cease. These figures also have implications for television subtitling policy. Unless Gaelic programmes are subtitled in English they will not be considered as 'suitable family viewing' in the vast majority of households with Gaelic speakers, and Gaelic programming will not be selected.

Family structures today are no longer merely and typically a married couple and their 2.4 or so offspring. In present-day society the family takes many diverse forms, and the fortunes of Gaelic in family life are similarly various. It is very noticeable that, in the Western Isles (Eileanan Siar), which is the principal remaining Gaelic-speaking area, families with all adults speaking Gaelic comprised only 42.7% of all families with Gaelic-speaking adults in 2001, and 29.7% of all families in total. Some 46.8% of their children aged 3–15 were Gaelic-speaking. In Skye and Lochalsh, which was the next strongest Gaelic area in 2001, families with all adults speaking Gaelic comprised 25.9% of all families with Gaelic-speaking adults, and 9.9% of total households in the area. Although actual numbers were much smaller, some 76.4% of their children aged 3–15 were Gaelic-speaking.

In the remainder of the Highlands in 2001 families all of whose adults were Gaelic-speaking comprised 26.3% of all families with Gaelic-speaking adults, and in the rest of Scotland this proportion was 28.2%, with 61.6% and 54.3% respectively of their children aged 3–15 speaking Gaelic. In these areas, of course, Gaelic-speaking families comprised only a small proportion of all families in total. However, as has been seen above, in 2001 20.4% of all Gaelic speakers resided in the mainland Highlands, and 43.8% in the Lowland area. Thus almost two-thirds of all Gaelic speakers now live within essentially non-Gaelic-speaking communities, and for whom their only Gaelic everyday contacts were within the family or from the Gaelic media. This fact too has important implications for the future of the language. Left to itself it is a problem which will swiftly hasten the demise of the language. On the other hand it presents a challenge to language planners and an opportunity for providers of the Gaelic media. Regarded in this way there are Gaelic families throughout Scotland and each one is a mini-Gaidhealtachd. In 2001 they were still bringing up a majority of their children to become Gaelic speakers. With such residual strengths, can the Gaelic arts, the Gaelic media, Gaelic education institutions and Gaelic social networks effectively link these scattered Gaels together and provide the basis for effective reproduction of the language-group in the forthcoming generation?

GAELIC LANGUAGE-USE IN FAMILY LIFE

Although the Gaelic-speaking couple-family is now in a minority of family types (even amongst families with Gaelic-speaking adults), the majority of their children were still Gaelic-speaking in 2001, even in Lowland situations, and this is a residual strength which can be built upon. Gaelic has been maintained as a family language, even if there have been few formal supports and encouragements. Over recent decades there have been a number of research initiatives which have looked at actual language-usage in family domains. These have chiefly been in Gaelic-speaking areas such as the Western Isles and Isle of Skye. However to date there has only been a single research study of Gaelic speakers nationally, namely the Euromosaic survey in 1994/5.

The results in three successive surveys at approximately ten yearly intervals for family language in the Western Isles are presented in Figure 7.11. The decline of Gaelic within the four-generational families of contemporary respondents is abundantly apparent, as is the decennial decline between each successive survey. This indicates the situation of rapid language-shift experienced in the Western Isles between the successive surveys: the Language Maintenance and Viability Survey in 1986/7 (MacKinnon 1988, 1991, 1994, 2000), the Euromosaic Survey in 1994/5 (MacKinnon 1998, 2001b), and the Western Isles Language Plan Project (WILPP) in 2004/5 (WILPP 2005, MacKinnon 2006, forthcoming a, forthcoming b). The rapid decline of Gaelic usage amongst children themselves is particularly noticeable.

The maintenance of Gaelic amongst Western Isles children had been quite stable in the 1971 and 1981 censuses with 67.1% and 67.7% of children aged 3–15 returned as speaking Gaelic. Between 1975 and 1981 the Primary Bilingual Education Project was being developed by the newly created education authority, and by 1981 the project was intended to be extended to all schools. In the subsequent censuses the proportion of 3–15s returned as speaking Gaelic declined to 49.3% in 1991 and to 46.6% in 2001. After 1981 the authority changed its policy to one of introduction of primary Gaelic-medium units. These were slow to develop and by 1991 only 7.2% of primary pupils were being educated in them. This proportion rose to 26.3% in 1998/9, and stood at 26.5% in 2009/10. Without robust supportive policies in education, as have been developed in Wales, powerful local socio-economic factors such as migration, family formation between language-groups, and the hegemony of English-medium media, commercial life and administration will continue to reduce the incidence of Gaelic language-use and transmission within the family.

The Euromosaic project undertook a study of language-use amongst Gaelic speakers throughout Scotland in 1994/5. It was part of a wider survey of lesser-used languages in the then European Union. To date it is unique as the only national survey of Gaelic language-use so far attempted. The survey was quota-sampled by age, gender, occupation and area. There were 130 respondents in the Western Isles and 192 in the rest of Scotland. It was thus fairly small-scale and methodologically limited. It deserved to have been the pilot study for a more comprehensive and methodologically thorough investigation of language-use and attitudes. However, comparison of the two sub-samples regarding family language-use is instructive. The chiefly mainland sample is very similar in pattern of response to the Western Isles Gaelic-area sample insofar as prior generations is concerned, since most mainland Gaelic speakers are of island origin. Results, though, in terms of exchanges between present-day partners and their children, clearly show weaker results for Gaelic amongst the mainland sample – although the results for the island sample in these respects is by no means robust.

Taken altogether these survey results for Gaelic use in the family call for strong, supportive and urgent policies for Gaelic in the family from Gaelic language-planning and development bodies.

GAELIC LANGUAGE-USE IN COMMUNITY LIFE AND THE MEDIA

The above surveys also undertook an investigation into the use of Gaelic in local community life and in the uptake of Gaelic media. In general terms crofting, religious life, local social events, local community figures such as nurses, clergy and teachers, and township business are strongly featured. It can be seen, however, that in Skye these aspects though still quite strongly Gaelic were weakening compared with the Western Isles. In respect of Gaelic media uptake Gaelic speakers in both sub-samples showed strong demand for Gaelic broadcast media, more moderate readership of Gaelic in newspapers and weak readership of Gaelic books – even weaker Gaelic letter-writing practice (see MacKinnon 1988, 1991).

Similar questions were asked of Western Isles Gaelic speakers in the Euromosaic Survey 1994/5 and the Western Isles Language Plan Project 2004/5. In ten years there had been considerable slippage in extent of use of Gaelic in the community. It was not considered worthwhile asking concerning the twelve weakest or minimally responded aspects in 1994/5 ten years later. These chiefly lay in the commercial and administrative spheres in which English predominated. Moderate aspects of use of Gaelic in 1994/5 had chiefly become lower or minimal use levels in 2004/5. However, even for the strongest aspects, such as with local clergy, councillors, for shopping and car business, with teachers and hairdressers, Gaelic was only reported as actually being used between 50% and 25% of conversational exchanges. If the adoption of a Gaelic Plan by the local authority in 2008 is to have any chance of successfully retaining the Western Isles as an actual Gaelic-using community, it will need to turn this situation around as a matter of urgent priority.

PROSPECTS FOR A GAELIC FUTURE

The past decade has witnessed belatedly and at long last the creation of institutions for Gaelic which would have been appropriate a century earlier (for details, see the chapters by Dunbar and Macleod in this volume). With these developments Gaelic achieved the infrastructure which it had long lacked – but it is a moot question whether this has been created too late or in the nick of time. This chapter has attempted to review the reasons and causes for the rapid decline of Gaelic since at least the late nineteenth century. Powerful socio-economic forces have brought this about and any strategy for the future of the language cannot afford to ignore them. Indeed it must live with them, and if possible make use of them.

The Gaelic character of even the strongest areas for the language – such as the Western Isles and Isle of Skye – continue to be under threat. Their local authorities were amongst the first to be called upon to formulate local Gaelic plans in 2008. If they are to stand any chance of success it will need the local authorities fully to understand the socio-economic processes which are affecting the language and its speakers. Robust measures will need to be undertaken – especially in education. At present Gaelic education is functioning at nowhere near the level necessary effectively to support what are predominantly now mixed-language Gaelic families, and to undertake the function of language reproduction which the family by itself is now no longer capable of doing. It will need a quantum step-change to transform and expand the system. Although recent years have seen expanded initial training (from 2008) and distance-learning in-service professional update (from 2006), the problem of teacher supply continues to hold back the development of Gaelic education (now more effectively nationally co-ordinated). The idea of virtual Gaelic classrooms was floated with the establishment of the dedicated all-Gaelic all-through school in Glasgow in 2006. This, coupled with imaginative development of new interactive electronic media and Gaelic educational television, may provide new ways forward. A dedicated Gaelic television channel BBC Alba and a reformulated Gaelic media authority MG Alba both commenced in 2008.

Gaelic will continue to need a territorial base – but its existing bases do not have the demographic resources effectively to reproduce the language at a scale to overcome natural decrease and migration. However, Gaelic urgently needs the creation of a new Gaelic community based upon new social networks. We may already be seeing these develop around the growth-points of education, media, arts and entertainments. Will these be sufficient to provide a basis for the language-group to be maintained?

BIBLIOGRAPHY

Davies, P. et al. (n.d. circa 1970), *The Christian Value of the Welsh Language*, Swansea: Gwasg John Penry.

General Register Office (Scotland) (2008), '2001 Census Scotland: Family Types by Gaelic language', Special tabulation for Welsh Language Board (Hywel Jones).

MacKinnon, K. (1988), 'Gaelic Language-maintenance and Viability in the Isle of Skye', report to Economic and Social Research Council. Published Hatfield Polytechnic Business and Social Sciences Reports Series No. BSSR 17, Hatfield: Hertis Publications.

MacKinnon. K. (1991), 'Language-maintenance and Viability in Contemporary Gaelic-speaking Communities: Skye and the Western Isles Today (From Survey and Census Data)', paper to Eighth International Symposium on Language Contact in Europe 18–24 September 1988, Douglas, Isle of Man. Published in: P. S. Ureland and G. Broderick (eds), *Language Contact in the British Isles*, Tübingen: Niemeyer, pp. 495–534.

MacKinnon, K. (1994), 'Gaelic Language-use in the Western Isles', in A. Fenton and D. A. MacDonald (eds), *Studies in Scots and Gaelic: Proceedings of Third International Conference on the Languages of Scotland*, Edinburgh 25–27 July 1991, Edinburgh: Canongate, pp. 123–37.

MacKinnon, K. (1996), 'Cape-Breton–Western Isles: Transatlantic Resonance of Language and Culture', Chapter 19 in P. S. Ureland and I. Clarkson, *Language Contact across the North Atlantic*. Tübingen: Niemeyer, pp. 363–86.

MacKinnon, K. (1998), 'Gaelic in Family, Work and Community Domains: Euromosaic Project 1994/95', in J. D. McClure (ed.), *Scottish Language, No .17 1998, a Selection of Papers Presented at the Fifth International Conference on the Languages of Scotland and Ulster, Aberdeen 1–5 August 1997*, Association for Scottish Literary Studies, pp. 55–69.

MacKinnon, K. (2000), 'Gaelic Language Usage in the Community and Media: Western Isles of Scotland 1987–88', in P. W. Thomas and J. Mathias, *Developing Minority Languages, Proceedings of the Fifth International Conference on Minority Languages*, University of Wales: Cardiff 5–9 July 1993, pp. 614–31.

MacKinnon, K. (2001a), 'Gaelic in Canada: Haki's and Hekja's Inheritance in "The Land of Promise"', in P. S. Ureland (ed.), *Global Eurolinguistics: European Languages in North America – Migration, Maintenance and Death*, Tübingen: Niemeyer, pp. 19–48.

MacKinnon, K. (2001b), 'Identity, Attitudes, and Support for Gaelic Policies: Gaelic Speakers in the Euromosaic Survey 1994/95', in J. M. Kirk and D. P. Ó Baoill (eds), *Language Links: The Languages of Scotland and Ireland*, Belfast: Queen's University Press, pp. 177–86.

MacKinnon, K. (2006), 'The Western Isles Language Plan: Gaelic to English Language Shift 1972–2001', in Wilson McLeod (ed.), *Revitalising Gaelic in Scotland: Policy, Planning and Public Discourse*, Edinburgh: Dunedin Academic Press, pp. 49–72.

MacKinnon, K. (forthcoming a), 'Gaelic Usage in the Western Isles: Euromosaic 1994/5, Census 2001, and the Western Isles Language Plan Project 2004/5', paper to Language and Politics Symposium, Queen's University Belfast, 7–9 November 2007.

MacKinnon, K. (forthcoming b), 'Gaelic Speakers' Attitudes Towards Language Issues in the Western Isles: Euromosaic Survey 1994/5, and the Western Isles Language Plan Survey 2004/5', n.p.

Smith, J. A. (1983), 'Gaelic Teaching in Schools', in D. S. Thomson (ed.), *The Companion to Gaelic Scotland*, Oxford: Blackwell, pp. 259–62.

Stephens, M. (1976), *Linguistic Minorities in Western Europe*, Llandysul: Gomer Press.

Western Isles Language Plan Project (WILPP) (2005), 'Research and Outcomes of Phase 1 of the Project; Final Report', Stornoway: Lews Castle College.

Withers, C. W. J. (1984), *Gaelic in Scotland 1698–1981: The Geographical History of a Language*, Edinburgh: John Donald.

Figure 7.1 Gaelic speakers by area of incidence 1881–2001

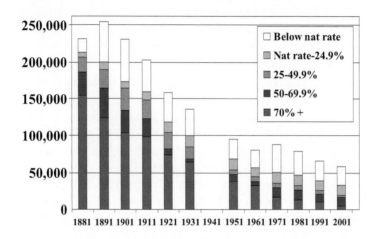

Figure 7.2 Gaelic speakers in Highland and Lowland areas 1881–2001 – numbers

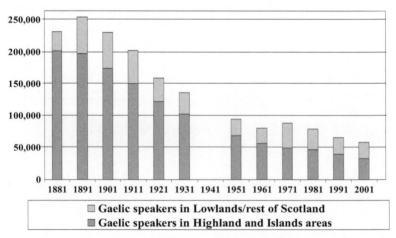

Source : GROS 1931 Census, Table 54; 1961 Gaelic Report Table 3; 1971 Gaelic Report, Table A; 1981 Census LBS, p. 9, Table 40; 2001 Gaelic Report, Tables 1, 3.

Figure 7.3 Gaelic speakers in Highland and Lowland areas 1881–2001 – proportions

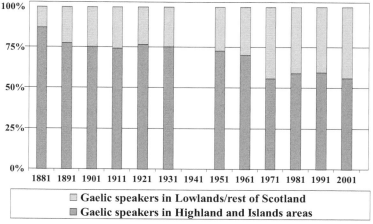

☐ **Gaelic speakers in Lowlands/rest of Scotland**
■ **Gaelic speakers in Highland and Islands areas**

Source: GROS 1931 Census, Table 54; 1961 Gaelic Report Table 3; 1971 Gaelic Report, Table A; 1981 Census LBS, p. 9, Table 40; 2001 Gaelic Report, Tables 1, 3.

Figure 7.4 Gaelic speakers by area of residence 1891

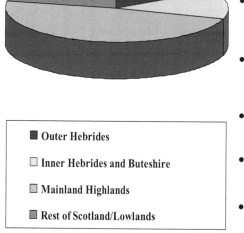

■ Outer Hebrides

☐ Inner Hebrides and Buteshire

☐ Mainland Highlands

■ Rest of Scotland/Lowlands

In 1891 of all Gaelic speakers:

- 41,742 or 16.41% of all Gaelic speakers aged 3+ were located in the Outer Hebrides;

- 33,851 or 13.30% were located in the Inner Hebrides and Buteshire;

- 121,970 or 47.94% were located in the mainland Highlands; and

- 56,852 or 22.35% were located in the rest of Scotland/Lowlands.

- In 1891 Gaelic speakers totalled 254,415 or 6.84% of Scotland's 3+ population of 3,721,778.

Figure 7.5 Gaelic speakers by area of residence 2001

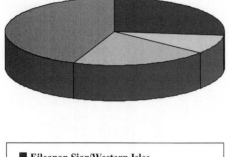

In 2001 of all Gaelic speakers:

- 15,723 or 26.81% of all Gaelic speakers aged 3+ resided in the Western Isles/Eileanan Siar;

- 5,301 or 9.04% resided in the Inner Hebrides and the Clyde Islands;

- 11,956 or 20.38% resided in the mainland Highlands; and

- 25,672 or 43.77% resided in the rest of Scotland / Lowland area.

- In 2001 Gaelic speakers totalled 58,652 or 1.20% of Scotland's 3+ population of 4,900,492.

■ Eileanan Siar/Western Isles

□ Inner Hebrides and Clyde Islands

□ Mainland Highlands

■ Rest of Scotland/Lowlands

Figure 7.6 Population Profiles: Gaelic and non-Gaelic speakers Census 2001 Scotland

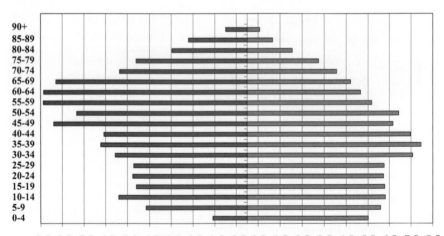

Source: GROS special tabulations 30.05.08; 15.07.09

Figure 7.7 Scotland 2001 Census: persons with Gaelic language abilities – numbers

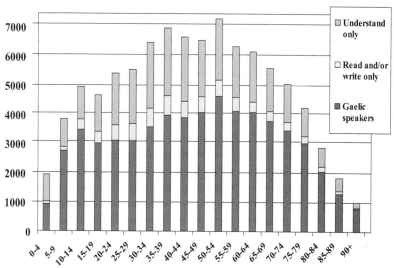

Source: GROS Census 2001 Scotland, Special Tabulations, Census Customer Services, 11.06.08

Figure 7.8 Highlands and Hebrides 2001 Census: persons with Gaelic language abilities – numbers

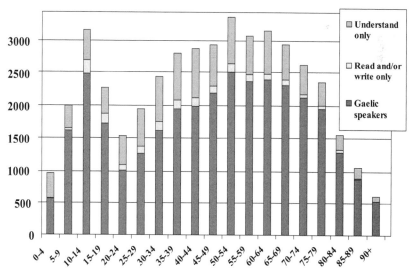

Source: GROS Census 2001 Scotland, Special Tabulations, Census Customer Services, 11.6.08

Figure 7.9 Lowland education authorities with G.M. Education 2001 Census: persons with Gaelic language abilities – numbers

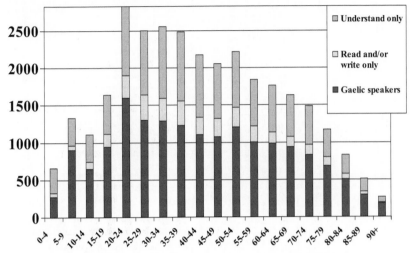

Source: GROS Census 2001 Scotland, Special Tabulations, Census Customer Services, 11.06.08

Figure 7.10 Education authorities without Gaelic Medium Education 2001 Census: persons with Gaelic language abilities – numbers

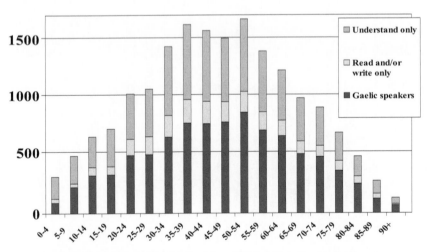

Source: GROS Census 2001 Scotland, Special Tabulations, Census Customer Services, 11.06.08

Figure 7.11 Intergenerational language-shift: Western Isles' Gaelic speakers at successive surveys: 1986/8 (N=224), 1994/5 (N=130), and 2004/5 (N=254)

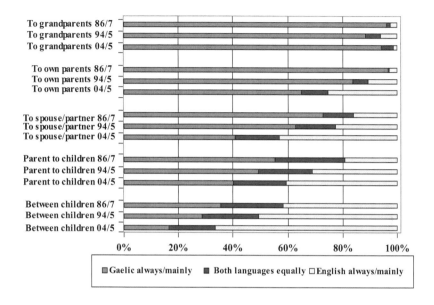

CHAPTER 8

Language Planning

Robert Dunbar

INTRODUCTION[1]

In their text on language planning, Kaplan and Baldauf note that '[i]n its simplest sense, language planning is an attempt by someone to modify the linguistic behaviour of some community for some reason' (Kaplan and Baldauf 1997: 3). A slightly different and more technical definition is offered by Cooper, in another important contribution to the literature: '[l]anguage planning refers to deliberate efforts to influence the behaviour of others with respect to the acquisition, structure, or functional allocation of their language codes' (Cooper 1989: 45). However, both definitions convey the sense that language planning involves efforts by some actor or actors to influence the linguistic behaviour of some group of people.

Understood in this way, language planning has undoubtedly been engaged in by political communities since the earliest of recorded times (Kaplan and Baldauf 1997: ix–x), and it has played a crucial role in the formation of the modern nation state: since the late eighteenth century, governments have frequently sought to develop a standard language and to disseminate it throughout the population as a whole as a means of fostering a common citizenship and identity (May 2001: 52–90; Wright 2004: 42–68). Such language planning has usually had serious negative consequences for other languages used by the population of the particular state.

Until quite recently, for example, British language policy provided for the use of English as the sole means by which public affairs was conducted, and promoted the acquisition and ever greater use of English as the common language of the British people. By ensuring that successive generations of Gaelic speakers were fully fluent in English, by restricting the domains[2] in which Gaelic could be used, and by ensuring that only English would be used in the most prestigious domains, the prevailing language policy contributed greatly to the sharp and ongoing reduction in numbers of Gaelic speakers (see MacKinnon in this collection).

In this chapter, however, language planning in support of Gaelic, rather than language planning which has operated against it, will be considered. The focus will be on language planning activities of public institutions, where most developments have taken place only in the last thirty years or so. Reference will, however, also be made to the efforts of private and voluntary institutions and organisations, as well as the work of individuals, as they have also played an important part in the story of language planning in support of Gaelic.

LANGUAGE POLICY AND LANGUAGE PLANNING

While, as noted, humans have engaged in language planning since time immemorial, the study of language planning[3] is a recent development, emerging as a branch of sociolinguistics in the late 1950s. In recent years, increasing attention has been focused on the role of language planning in maintaining linguistic diversity, and on the global spread of English (Ricento 2006: 10–23).

The terms 'language policy' and 'language planning' are often used together and, indeed, occasionally almost interchangeably in the literature, raising the question of whether there is a difference between them. There is a sense that the two terms do, or should, distinguish between different phenomena, but the distinctions suggested are not always particularly satisfying. Referring back to the definitions with which this chapter started, we saw that language planning involves efforts by an actor or actors to influence the language behaviour of some group of people. Language policy could be understood as the goals which these actors wish to accomplish when they seek to influence language behaviour of the group.

Language policy goals could be understood in terms of a continuum, ranging from the promotion of complete linguistic uniformity (implying the assimilation of linguistic minorities) at one extreme, to the promotion of maximum linguistic diversity at the other (often through autonomy regimes for the linguistic minority allowing it to take strong measures of support for the language), with various forms of integration (implying the toleration of linguistic diversity) and, in some models of integration, its facilitation to a certain degree, in between.[4]

Frequently, the language policy of the state (or a sub-state unit such as a province, region or autonomous community) is made explicit (or overt) through constitutional provisions, legislation, or policy pronouncements. Often, however, language policy is implicit (or covert), in that it can only be determined by the actual language practices engaged in by the actor. Whether implicit or explicit, though, all actors have a language policy. Furthermore, it must be borne in mind that there are often significant differences between an actor's explicit/ overt language policy and the implicit/covert one which it actually follows (Shohamy 2006: 50–2).

With regard to language planning itself, there are three types of activity that are now generally accepted in the literature: corpus planning, status planning and acquisition planning. 'Corpus planning' involves modifying the language itself, such as 'coining new terms, reforming spelling, and adopting new script[5] ... in short, to the creation of new forms,[6] the modification of old ones,[7] or the selection from alternative forms in spoken or written code' (Cooper 1989: 31). Corpus planning also often includes the development of dictionaries and grammars, and even the development of a written literature. Corpus planning is particularly important for minoritised languages such as Gaelic because, as they are often excluded from important domains, they often lack relevant specialist terminology, and registers and styles appropriate to such domains.

By contrast, 'status planning' has to do with modifying the functions which a particular language is meant to serve (or, to put it another way, modifying the domains in which a language is used). It therefore relates to the social (and political) position of the language (Cooper 1989: 32–3). Status planning has often played a significant part in the decline in minority languages: the choice of a particular language as an official language usually meant the exclusion of other languages from important or 'high' domains. As the name implies, status planning also relates to the prestige of a language, and by reserving to a particular language important domains, its prestige, and its actual and perceived utility, is enhanced, and that of others is diminished. This tends to lead to the displacement of other languages by the more prestigious one in more and more domains, resulting in 'language shift': 'the change (gradual or not) by... a speech community from the dominant use of one language... to the dominant use of another language in almost all spheres of life' (Pauwels 2006: 719). Status planning for minority languages such as Gaelic is concerned with reclaiming domains from the socially dominant language.

Sometimes reference is made, in the context of language planning for minority languages, to a fourth type of language planning, 'use (or usage) planning' (Welsh Language Board n.d.). In fact, use planning subsumes many aspects of what status planning is concerned with: the encouragement of the practical use of the language in a greater number of domains. When the concept of use planning is used, status planning tends to refer to planning to enhance the prestige (through both visibility and audibility and consequently the symbolic value) of the language.

Finally, there is 'acquisition planning' (Cooper 1989: 33–4), which concerns planning for the increase in the number of users – speakers, writers, listeners, or readers – of the language. Obviously, the school (and other formal educational institutions) are important settings for acquisition planning, but a language is first acquired in the home and local community, and language skills are enhanced by institutions other than educational ones, particularly the media. Acquisition planning therefore also involves planning activities outside of the educational system. Acquisition planning is of particular importance to minority languages, as they tend to suffer ongoing losses in numbers of users, often due in part to their exclusion from the education system.

LANGUAGE POLICY AND PLANNING FOR MINORITY LANGUAGES

Gaelic, like other minority languages, faces a number of overlapping sociolinguistic problems. Because of the education policies which have been pursued in Gaelic-speaking areas, virtually all Gaelic speakers are bilingual, and, indeed, for many, at least certain linguistic skills may be stronger in English than in Gaelic. Gaelic speakers also find themselves in a diglossic situation. They will use English in certain domains, particularly higher status, more formal ones, either because institutions operating in those domains use only English, or because Gaelic speakers are simply accustomed to using English in such domains because of the traditional dominance of English. However, they will use Gaelic in other domains, particularly lower status (but as we shall see, not unimportant) domains, such as within the family and neighbourhood.

Crucially, however, such diglossia tends to be unstable. Because of the low status associated with the minority language, and the language beliefs which such status instils in its speakers, they tend to use their native language less and less even in lower, informal domains. Crucially, where they believe that the language will be of no practical benefit – or may even constitute a detriment – to their children's advancement, speakers of a minority language will simply not pass it on, resulting in a failure of 'intergenerational transmission' within the home. Diglossia also becomes unstable because, increasingly, speakers of the minority language live in mixed-language home and community environments in which there is a presence of unilingual speakers of the majority language, due to the breakdown in intergenerational transmission and, often, to the arrival in the community of non-speakers (frequently, state functionaries are amongst the first and most important arrivals, in terms of their linguistic impact). Density of the minority language-speaking population becomes an important issue: where speakers of the minority language are scattered, or where they make up a decreasing percentage of the local population, they are increasingly likely to be dealing with non-speakers of the language even in 'lower', informal domains, contributing to further 'language shift' away from the minority language.

The single most important contribution to our understanding of what should be done to address 'language shift' has been that of Joshua Fishman, whose 1991 *Reversing Language Shift* is the seminal work in the field. In it, Fishman laid out his 'Graded Intergenerational Disruption Scale' ('GIDS'), an eight-stage scale for determining the degree to which a minority language is threatened, with stage eight representing the highest degree of threat and stage one representing the lowest.[8] GIDS also provides insights into what sort of planning should be engaged in to reverse the shift by speakers away from the language.

The goal at stages eight through five is to attain a stable diglossia. Crucial to this is his Stage 6, at which the language is being 'transmitted intergenerationally': parents pass it on to their children in the home, and it is 'the normal language of informal spoken interaction between and within all three generations of the family'. At this stage, Fishman says, there needs to be 'demographic concentration' and 'institutional reinforcement': by the former, he means concentrations of families in which intergenerational transmission is occurring in the same neighbourhoods, so that the language becomes 'the language of interfamily interaction, of interaction with playmates, neighbors, friends and acquaintances'; by the latter, he means neighbourhood institutions such as 'local economic, religious, cultural and recreational units', institutions which also play an important part in ensuring the daily use of the language as a normal means of communication. Planning at this stage should focus on measures to assist families in achieving intergenerational transmission, and building demographic concentrations and supportive local institutions; simply, planning should aim at measures which allow increased use of the language in daily life in lower, more informal domains. Fishman cautions, however, that this is a difficult stage: it 'involves the informal daily life of a speech community' and as such, 'it is difficult to plan (planned informality is a contradiction of sorts)' (Fishman 1991: 92–5).

Initiatives at stages 4 to 1 involve school instruction through the medium of the minority language, the expansion of its use in the workplace, the expansion of its use in the local or regional mass media and governmental services, and its presence in higher education, the mass media and governmental operations at the national level. Fishman warns, however, that unless Stage 6 is attained, efforts at these higher levels will result in failure to address language shift, and that planning initiatives at these higher stages should aim at reinforcing Stage 6 (Fishman 1991: 81–121).

While Fishman has tended to dominate thinking about language planning for minority languages, other approaches to the issues involved have more recently emerged. For example, the Catalan language planner Miquel Strubell has been developing a circular model to describe social processes of language shift, which he calls the 'Catherine wheel', 'to convey the objective of a self-perpetuating change'. There are six stages in the circle: the greater supply of goods and services in a particular language (1) leads to the greater consumption of goods and services in the language (2), which leads to the greater perception of the usefulness of the language (3), which leads to the greater motivation to learn and use the language (4), which leads to more learning of the language (5), which leads to more demand for goods and services in the language (6), which takes us back to yet greater supply of goods and services in the language, and so on, creating a dynamic 'virtuous circle' (Strubell 2001: 279–81; Strubell 1998). Strubell recognises that this chain of cause and effect can be subject to a blockage at any of the six steps, and this is where language planners need to concentrate their attention; they need to identify then develop strategies and specific measures for overcoming the causes of the blockage (Strubell 2001: 280).

Against the backdrop of Fishman's model, the Swiss economist François Grin has discussed the three conditions which need to be met to achieve greater societal use of the minority language (which he views as the ultimate goal to which Fishman's model is directed [Grin 2003: 40–8]). These are capacity to use the language (referring to competence, and implying at least oral fluency), opportunities to use the language (in which the state can play a key role, by offering minority language services, for example), and the desire or willingness to use the language. Language planning for the minority language involves initiatives to strengthen all three.

Fishman, Strubell and Grin, among others, have all made an important contribution to the way in which language planners, and minority language communities themselves, understand how the process of RLS may work. However, even Fishman's model does not express immutable 'laws' in a scientific or a social scientific sense. They are useful guides to policy, but the field of enquiry is still a young one, and much more empirical testing of particular language revitalisation hypotheses, including Fishman's, must still be done.

LANGUAGE POLICY AND PLANNING FOR GAELIC

The state has seldom explicitly enunciated a language policy for Gaelic, but an implicit policy has been evident in the actual measures taken towards the language. Until fairly recently, this policy has been unsupportive, but over the last thirty or so years, state policy has changed, and both explicit and implicit language policy have become more supportive. By the time of the launch in October 2003 of the Bill which became the Gaelic Language (Scotland) Act 2005[9] (the 'Gaelic Act'), the government's policy was described in these terms by the then-First Minister, Jack McConnell:

> our challenge is to secure the future of Gaelic as a language of Scotland ... We need to see a confident bi-lingual community as part of the modern Scotland. We want to see a growing Gaelic education sector and an expanding Gaelic economy. This will help create the sustainable future for Gaelic in Scotland that I want to see.[10]

This has not, however, meant that the new policy orientation has always been clearly thought through, or translated into systematic and coordinated language planning. The lack of coordinated policy and planning was recognised almost thirty years ago in a groundbreaking report, 'Cor na Gàidhlig', commissioned by the Highlands and Islands Development Board ('HIDB', now Highlands and Islands Enterprise, or 'HIE'), the public body responsible for promoting economic and social development in the Highlands and Islands (HIDB 1982). To address this, the report recommended a new body to bring coherence, and in 1984 such a body, Comunn na Gàidhlig ('CNAG'), was created. While the pace of activity in support of Gaelic has increased considerably since then – the so-called 'Gaelic renaissance' – a similar lack of coordinated policy and planning (partly due to CNAG's limited powers and funding) was detected almost twenty years after the 'Cor na Gàidhlig' report:

relatively little consideration has been given to matters of language development in a more formal sense, to language planning, or to language policy. There has been a serious lack of strategy to this 'renaissance', and fundamental questions have been sidestepped. Initiatives have tended to be uncoordinated and haphazard, driven without the guidance of theory or the control of planning. Resources have been allocated unevenly, with some fields receiving disproportionate funding and others being severely neglected. (McLeod 2002b: 279)

This assessment was largely justified at that time, and to some extent remains valid today, although as we shall see, the Gaelic Act has the potential to address this. The situation giving rise to the assessment can be explained by two things which often characterise minority language policy and planning, particularly in its early stages. The first is that many initiatives which formed part of the 'renaissance' were the results of grassroots activism, the work of 'inspired amateurs', individuals and groups inspired by a commitment to the language but often with a limited technical understanding of language planning. The second is that, while the state has in recent years become more supportive of Gaelic, its measures of support have generally been reactive to this grassroots activism and therefore piecemeal.

Two particularly important recent milestones for language policy and planning for Gaelic should, however, be highlighted here, as they give expression to the broad outlines of a language policy and should help to fill the planning vacuum that has typified much Gaelic development. The first was the ratification on 27 March 2001 by the UK of the *European Charter for Regional or Minority Languages* (the 'Languages Charter'), an important Council of Europe treaty under which the state is required to take a range of measures in support of Gaelic. Importantly, in terms of language policy, this treaty requires the UK to base its policies, legislation and practice on a number of objectives and principles, including the following: the recognition of Gaelic as an expression of cultural wealth; the need for resolute action to promote Gaelic in order to safeguard it; the facilitation and/or encouragement of the use of Gaelic, in speech and writing, in public and private life; the provision of appropriate forms and means for the teaching and study of Gaelic at all appropriate stages; and, the provision of facilities enabling non-speakers of Gaelic to learn it (Article 7, subparagraphs 1 a, c, d, f and g).

The second is the Gaelic Act, which was passed without opposition in the Scottish Parliament in May 2005. In language policy and planning terms, it is the single most important development in the history of the language. It created Bòrd na Gàidhlig, a language planning body which is required to exercise its functions with a view to 'securing the status of the Gaelic language as *an official language* of Scotland commanding *equal respect to the English language*' (emphasis added) through increasing the number of persons able to use and understand Gaelic, encouraging the use and understanding of Gaelic and requiring the preparation of a national language plan for Gaelic, and facilitating access to the Gaelic language and culture (subsection 1(3)). Thus, in addition to articulating a policy which is in principle clearly supportive of Gaelic, the Act specifies a number of language planning priorities, and puts in somewhat more precise terms the implications of the rather vague expressions of goodwill towards Gaelic that have characterised more recent political discourse on the language.

In the remainder of this section, recent language planning initiatives in support of Gaelic outside the context of the Gaelic Act will be considered. Given the particular importance of the Gaelic Act and the Bòrd, special attention will be given to them in the last section of this chapter.

(a)   Acquisition Planning

Most efforts at acquisition planning for Gaelic have focused on the school system. In many respects, this is unsurprising, given the negative impact that past education policies have had on minority languages such as Gaelic. Indeed, most Gaelic acquisition planning has been directed at redressing the effects of the Education Act 1872, which introduced state-supported public education to Scotland, but made no provision for the teaching of Gaelic as a subject or its use as the medium of instruction. The development of Gaelic education in the school system has been ably described elsewhere (see Macleod's contribution to this collection, and the references therein), but the following features are particularly relevant to this discussion. First, until the 1970s, the presence of Gaelic in the school was limited to the teaching of Gaelic as a subject, usually through the medium of English, primarily at secondary school level, and largely in the Highlands and Islands (Thomson 1994: 261). Second, although education through the medium of Gaelic ('GME') has been made available since 1985, it has overwhelmingly been through Gaelic-medium classes (or 'units') in English-medium schools, and has been driven primarily by parental demand and the responsiveness of education authorities of local councils to such demand, not by any broader strategy.

From the perspective of language planning for a minority language, a number of problems are evident. First, given that the schools have been the main tool for producing Gaelic speakers (acquisition outside of the school system will be discussed below), present numbers are far too small to replace the loss of Gaelic speakers due to factors such as emigration and death (see MacKinnon's contribution to this collection).[11] Second, enrolment in majority Gaelic-speaking areas such as the Western Isles is far too low to maintain Gaelic as a language spoken by the majority in such areas.[12] Third, there is considerable concern about the actual linguistic competence in Gaelic of many students in GME, a situation that is greatly compromised by the very limited development of GME at the secondary school level,[13] and by the fact that virtually all GME is delivered through classes in English-medium schools, greatly limiting the creation of a Gaelic-speaking environment in the school as a whole. As a result, in terms of ability and therefore likely long-term use and ultimate transmission of Gaelic to the next generation, very many students in GME cannot reasonably be viewed as 'replacing' the loss of older Gaelic speakers for many of whom Gaelic was their first language and their language of choice or, perhaps, to contributing in a significant way either to use or transmission (McLeod 2002b: 283, although we do not yet have enough information based on research to confirm definitely such assumptions). Acquisition policy in the school system must therefore be aimed at increasing significantly overall numbers in GME, ensuring expansion of GME at secondary level to maximise continuity in provision, achieving much higher enrolment in GME in areas in which Gaelic is still spoken by a majority, and generally enriching language competence of pupils coming through the system.

Beyond the primary and secondary school sector, acquisition planning initiatives have been limited and uncoordinated. Gaelic at the tertiary level is discussed by Macleod in this collection. Outside this sector, there is a range of provision, primarily for learners, such as night-school classes, often supported by local councils, summer short courses, distance learning courses offered by Sabhal Mòr Ostaig, and immersion courses run by further extension colleges; however, this provision is uncoordinated, underfunded and generally insufficiently developed, and cannot be expected in its present forms to contribute significantly to Gaelic acquisition amongst adults, particularly young adults, a group which, according to Fishman, is of particular importance in any effort to address language shift (see, generally, MacCaluim 2007). Additionally, there is virtually no dedicated provision aimed specifically at the large number of 'semi-speakers' identified in the 2001 census (see MacKinnon's contribution to this collection).

Perhaps the most glaring weakness in Gaelic acquisition planning efforts to date, however, has been the almost total lack of initiatives to support Gaelic transmission in the home. This is particularly worrisome, as transmission of Gaelic in the home is very weak, as is its use in the family (see MacKinnon's contribution to this collection). As noted above, Fishman places central importance on transmission in the home, and although he notes that the school is important in reinforcing language competence first acquired in the home, he warns against over-reliance on the school and in particular the expectation that the school can effectively replace the home in the process of effective and sustainable language acquisition (Fishman 1991: 368–81).

(b)   Status (and Use) Planning

Until fairly recently, Gaelic has had virtually no presence in national, regional or local government or in the broader public sector, and has generally had little presence in voluntary or private sector organisations except small, community-based ones operating in the few remaining predominantly Gaelic-speaking communities. Furthermore, Gaelic has generally had a very limited presence in print and broadcast media at the national, regional and local level. As a result, both status and use planning must be major priorities for Gaelic language planning in the twenty-first century.

With regard to the use of Gaelic in high-status public institutions, the Scotland Act 1998, the legislation which created the Scottish Parliament and other devolved institutions, made no reference to Gaelic, but the Standing Orders of the Scottish Parliament permit the use of Gaelic in parliamentary debates and before committees. Given that only a small handful of Members of the Scottish Parliament speak any Gaelic, the opportunity to use it is rarely taken. Even before the Gaelic Act, however, both the Parliament and Executive (now the Scottish Government) made provision for some Gaelic signage, the publication of some material in Gaelic, and will respond to written correspondence in Gaelic (see, generally, Dunbar 2006). Gaelic is, however, almost totally absent from the Scottish court and broader legal system (Dunbar 2006; Dunbar 2007).

With regard to local government, prior to the Gaelic Act, only two of Scotland's thirty-two local authorities had developed Gaelic policies allowing for the use of the language in the conduct of council business. From its creation in 1975, the Western Isles Council (now Comhairle nan Eilean Siar) introduced a Gaelic policy. Occasionally revised, the most recent version of the policy (which has recently been superseded by a Gaelic language plan under the Gaelic Act) provided that the

Comhairle was 'committed to safeguarding and promoting the Gaelic Language and its use', and the Comhairle made the commitment that in its dealings with the public and in the exercise of the democratic process, Gaelic and English would be treated 'on the basis of equality'. The policy suffered from two significant limitations. First, its more detailed provisions tended to be filled with hortatory language, imprecise obligations, or exculpatory conditions (commitments to do something 'where possible' or to use Gaelic 'as appropriate'). Second, the policy was often interpreted (in part thanks to these drafting weaknesses) in a minimalist way, and was never fully implemented.[14] A manifestation of this is evident in the Comhairle's hiring policies. In particular, a policy which aims at delivering fully bilingual services could be expected to have a significant number of front-line jobs in which Gaelic was an essential job skill; yet, outside teaching jobs in GME, the Comhairle almost never requires that job applicants have Gaelic language skills.[15] It is difficult to argue with this overall assessment of the Comhairle's policy: 'Gaelic clearly does not serve as a normal language for [the Comhairle's] internal operations or the delivery of their services' (McLeod 2001b: 19–20).

On the whole, the Comhairle's Gaelic policy has been a lost opportunity for significantly expanding the status and use of Gaelic at the local level in its most sizeable remaining 'heartland'. While more robust implementation (together with a much more aggressive approach to Gaelic education) may not by itself have completely altered the current bleak sociolinguistic picture in the Western Isles, it could have contributed to a much more supportive environment for the language and to other development initiatives. The ability of the Comhairle's Gaelic language plan prepared under the Gaelic Act to effect significant and rapid change will be a major test of the capacity of that legislation to address such status planning failures.

To conclude on status planning initiatives in the public sector prior to the Gaelic Act, any recognition of Gaelic has been relatively recent, and has tended to be more symbolic than substantive. While this could be considered to be an improvement on the historical position, in status planning terms such initiatives have done little to fundamentally address, and indeed may simply reinforce, existing language beliefs and hierarchies. In use planning terms, they cannot be expected to change existing unstable diglossic patterns.

With regard to the private and voluntary sector, the community and the home, in the absence of a national Gaelic language use survey it is difficult to say with certainty how the language is being used in these domains (see, however, MacKinnon's contribution to this collection, which shows a limited and weakening presence in most domains, and relatively recent research which suggests that use of Gaelic in the workplace in the Western Isles is very weak: McLeod 2001b; McLeod 2002a). Some voluntary organisations – notably, the churches, and particularly the Free Church of Scotland – have consistently sought to use Gaelic in their operations, thereby engaging in status planning, and there have been some useful community-based initiatives – notably, the Western Isles Language Plan (NicAoidh 2006). Too frequently, however, both ideas and best-laid local plans have not been fully turned into practical measures, partly due to insufficient institutional support. The result is that little strategic and sustained language planning has taken place with regard to status planning in these various domains. This must be considered one of the major weaknesses of recent revival efforts, and the ability of the Bòrd to rectify this will be another of the most important tests of the new policy and planning structures ushered in by the Gaelic Act.

By contrast, much effort has been invested in status planning in the area of the broadcast media. Once again, most of these developments have taken place only in the last twenty years or so (see Macleod in this collection). At present, however, Gaelic enjoys a radio service, BBC's Radio nan Gàidheal, which is available in most parts of Scotland and which broadcasts about 92 hours per week. The presence of Gaelic on television was considerably expanded on Friday, 19 September 2008, when BBC Alba (www.bbc.co.uk/alba), the Gaelic digital television service formed by a partnership between the BBC and MG Alba (the body created under the Communications Act 2003 to replace Comataidh Craolaidh Gàidhlig [CCG], previously Comataidh Telebhisein Gàidhlig [CTG], the organisation created by earlier broadcasting legislation to fund the expansion of Gaelic television [and radio] programming) was launched. It broadcasts approximately six and a half hours of programming a day between 5:00 and 11:30 p.m., although it is still only available to a minority of the viewing public in Scotland, as the BBC Trust, the organisation which oversees the BBC's operations, has not yet agreed to allow the service on Freeview (a final decision is expected in March 2010).

Status planning with respect to print media has not, however, been nearly as successful; there is now no Gaelic-medium newspaper of any description, and the presence of the language in periodical publishing is limited to columns and articles in English-medium newspapers (see Macleod's contribution to this collection for a review of relevant developments). A considerable barrier has been a small potential readership, due in part to the ongoing decline in numbers of speakers but also to relatively low levels of literacy in the language amongst Gaelic speakers, thanks to the generally limited presence of Gaelic in the educational system.

Nevertheless, the media has undoubtedly been the most successful area of Gaelic status planning activity, and unlike most of the other initiatives considered in this section, developments have gone well beyond the tokenistic. In addition to greatly increasing the visibility and audibility – and thereby the profile – of the language, significant numbers of jobs have been created in the media sector. It will be important now to monitor the sociolinguistic and other effects of these developments: what are the attitudinal effects of these developments for both Gaelic speakers and non-speakers; what impact, if any, have these developments had on actual language use; how have they contributed to Gaelic language acquisition; have they, for example, demonstrated Strubell's 'Catherine Wheel' effects?

As important as these developments are, it is also important to recognise that, in language planning terms, questions remain. The investment in broadcasting has been very significant, and outpaces all other areas of Gaelic development expenditure combined, and this raises the question of whether, from a minority language planning perspective, this is an appropriate allocation of resources, particularly given the serious needs in other areas, already highlighted in this chapter. While significant numbers of jobs are being created in the media sector, not all of these are for Gaelic speakers, and while the language 'on screen' is Gaelic, the language of the workplace still often tends to be English. Given the small Gaelic-speaking labour market, there is the danger that attractive jobs in the media sector may deprive other important sectors, such as education, community development and so on, of potential employees. Finally, the heavy emphasis on media, particularly television, appears to be inconsistent with the approach recommended by Fishman, for whom television is a 'higher level prop' which should only be tackled once measures have been taken to strengthen the transmission of the language in the home, the presence of the language in schools, the use of the language in the community and in workplaces, and so forth. To avoid the pitfalls implied here, there is a clear need for media to form part of a wider strategic approach to language planning for Gaelic.

(c)   Corpus Planning

Arguably, corpus planning initiatives have constituted some of the earliest forms of language planning for Gaelic, with important developments traceable to the eighteenth century (if not earlier), such as *Leabhar a Theagasc Ainminnin*, an early proto-dictionary published in 1741 by the SSPCK and compiled by Alexander MacDonald, 'Alasdair mac Mhaighstir Alasdair', and the publication in Gaelic of the New Testament in 1767 and the Old Testament from 1802, which contributed profoundly to the standardisation of modern Gaelic orthography. In spite of this long history, though, corpus planning is arguably the least developed area of contemporary Gaelic language planning, and the one in which a lack of coordination and strategic and authoritative leadership is most apparent. Efforts in this area have generally been undertaken by inspired individuals, by non-Gaelic institutions for particular purposes not necessarily related to Gaelic development, and by specialist Gaelic organisations for specialist purposes.

There is, for example, still no generally agreed orthography for Gaelic. The single most important development in this respect is the 'Gaelic Orthographic Conventions' ('GOC'), first issued in 1981 and revised in 2005 (SQA, 2005). These were initially developed by the predecessor organisation to the Scottish Qualifications Authority for the very limited purpose of addressing inconsistencies in the standard of written Gaelic that had been identified by examiners, with a view to providing a single standard to teachers and state secondary school examination candidates. They were never intended to be the definitive guide to Gaelic orthography. In the absence of any authoritative alternatives, though, they have become fairly widely accepted in Gaelic writing and publishing circles. As is typical of much Gaelic corpus planning, standard-setting has occurred on an *ad hoc* basis, driven by the particular difficulties facing an organisation whose primary concern is not Gaelic corpus planning, or indeed the broader needs of the language. (See also Black in this volume.)

Much the same story can be told in respect of the creation of dictionaries and grammars. The single most important development in Gaelic lexicography, for example, was the publication at the start of the twentieth century of Edward Dwelly's *Illustrated Gaelic Dictionary*, a Gaelic-to-English dictionary which was the work of a single amateur lexicographer. While a number of dictionaries have been published since (see, for example, Mark 2004, and Robertson and MacDonald 2004, Watson 2007, and generally Thomson 1994: 61–3), the fact that Dwelly's has never truly been superseded is indicative of the rather poorly developed state of this aspect of Gaelic corpus planning. While Faclair na Gàidhlig, a major inter-university project, will ultimately produce for Gaelic an authoritative historical dictionary comparable to the Oxford English Dictionary for English, it is unlikely that the first significant fruits will be borne in the near future (http://www.faclair.ac.uk/english/index.html). Meanwhile, the introduction (or reintroduction) of

Gaelic into new domains, such as public administration, politics and economics by virtue of status developments mentioned in the previous section, has exposed the need for considerable lexical development. The main response has been the publication by the Scottish Parliament of a dictionary of terms relevant to public business (McNeir 2001); however, this dictionary has a number of gaps, and must be considered to be a work in progress (McLeod 2001a; McLeod 2004). Similarly, there is still no single definitive prescriptive grammar of the Gaelic language (see Lamb 2008, which contains a very useful descriptive grammar), and use is still made of George Calder's 1923 grammar (Calder 1923) and a grammar produced in both Gaelic and in English for use in schools (but which again is not intended to be an all-purpose definitive grammar) (Byrne 2002).

One final area of corpus planning in which there has been some considerable activity is in the production of literary texts, other works of literature, and materials for Gaelic education (see Macleod in this collection). However, in spite of these developments, many gaps remain – there is, for example, still no definitive modern edition of the complete works of 'Mac Mhaighstir Alasdair', referred to earlier, arguably Gaeldom's greatest poet, and in spite of recent developments, the range of subject matter and volume of publication of Gaelic books is still very constrained.

Thus, while there has been considerable activity in the area of Gaelic corpus planning, like other areas of Gaelic development, much of this activity has been *ad hoc*, frequently conducted by inspired individuals, usually insufficiently funded, and almost always lacking in a broader strategy – particularly one which is more closely integrated with other aspects of Gaelic language planning.

RECENT DEVELOPMENTS: THE GAELIC ACT AND BÒRD NA GÀIDHLIG

As already noted, as well as giving expression to the general contours of a language *policy* for Gaelic, the Gaelic Act also represents a potentially revolutionary step forward with respect to language planning for the language. In particular, it creates a public body, the Bòrd, which is specifically tasked with engaging in language planning for Gaelic: it requires the Bòrd to promote Gaelic language acquisition and use (clause 1(2)(a)(i) and paragraphs 1(3)(a) and (b)), and by referring to Gaelic as 'an official language' of Scotland and by tasking the Bòrd with 'securing the status' of the language as such, 'commanding equal respect to the English language', the Gaelic Act makes clear the importance of promoting the status of the language (subsection 1(3)). It also creates important mechanisms which, if used effectively by the Bòrd (and the Scottish Government), should ensure that such language planning has some effect.

First, the Gaelic Act requires that the Bòrd must within a year of the coming into force of the act and at least every five years thereafter prepare a National Gaelic language plan (section 2), which must include 'a strategy' for promoting the use and understanding of Gaelic, and for promoting Gaelic education[16] and Gaelic culture (subsection 2(2)). Thus, the act requires that the Bòrd engage in strategic and holistic language planning. While the act is less clear on how the national plan will be put into effect, it requires that each national plan receives Scottish Government approval, thereby arguably implying acceptance by the government of the funding and other policy implications of them. Also, the act requires that the national plan be considered in the preparation of other language plans (see below), and this should also contribute to national plan implementation. Furthermore, the Scottish Government has turned over to the Bòrd the funding of a range of Gaelic development organisations, in the hope that this will promote participation of those organisations in the implementation of the national plan.

The Bòrd's first national plan, approved by the then-Scottish Executive in 2007, identified four main challenges which need to be addressed: an overall loss in numbers of speakers; the weakening of the remaining 'heartlands' (districts in which Gaelic is spoken by a majority), in terms of contracting numbers, domains, and use in such domains; the increasing percentage of Gaelic users living in areas where they are a tiny minority, thereby limiting the opportunities for use in most domains; and, a general weakness in intergenerational transmission in the home (Bòrd na Gàidhlig 2007a: 10). The Bòrd set out a range of general objectives and then more detailed initiatives, organised by reference to the categories acquisition, usage, status and corpus planning, and it placed particular emphasis on the acquisition of the language in the home and on expanding the domains in which it can be used. The plan also noted the need for corpus planning measures, in particular improvements in the relevance and consistency of the language to its anticipated expansion in domains (and to this end pledged to work towards the establishment of a corpus planning body, a 'language academy'), and in the quality and accessibility of translation and interpretation, as well as the need for research to underpin policy development and implementation (Bòrd na Gàidhlig 2007a: 12–13).

Usefully, in the discussion of particular initiatives, the Bòrd identified partners, including existing Gaelic organisations and public authorities, thereby highlighting the linkages between the national plan and the plans and activities of these other important organisations. This is beginning to manifest itself in potentially productive ways. As noted earlier, the neighbourhood-community context which forms part of Fishman's crucial stage 6 generally has not received much strategic and sustained planning in the Gaelic context. Influenced by the experience in Wales in this area, and notably its 'Mentrau Iaith' community language planning initiative, the Bòrd has made this context a priority: in conjunction with Comhairle nan Eilean Siar, it held an important conference on community language planning in Breasclete, Lewis, in September 2008, and in 2009 CNAG, with Bòrd support, launched seven 'Iomairtean Cànain' (Language Initiatives), community language planning pilot projects in four majority Gaelic-speaking areas, in one formerly strongly Gaelic-speaking area in the Highlands, and in two urban areas where there are significant numbers of Gaelic speakers (www.cnag.org.uk/iomairtean/). Finally, the plan set out a number of targets, for both the immediate future and the longer term (the years 2021, 2031 and 2041), although these were almost exclusively directed at acquisition planning targets, and are in some cases possibly overly optimistic (Bòrd na Gàidhlig 2007a: 14–15).

The second mechanism created under the Act is the power given to the Bòrd to require public authorities in Scotland to prepare a Gaelic language plan in which the public authorities must set out the measures they will take in relation to the use of Gaelic both in the provision by them of any services to the public and also in their internal operations (subsections 3(1) and (4)). In preparing its plan, a public authority must consider the most recent National Gaelic language plan (and, presumably, how it might assist in its implementation), the extent to which the public it serves uses Gaelic, the potential for developing the use of Gaelic in its services and internal operations, any guidance given by the Bòrd or the Scottish Government, and any representations made to the authority by the public (subsection 3(5)).

In addition to requiring each public authority to set out how it will implement relevant priority areas in the National Gaelic language plan, the guidance prepared by the Bòrd requires the public authority to set out its core commitments as to how it will use Gaelic in its internal processes and in dealing with the public, in areas such as identity (e.g. in corporate identity and on signage), communications (e.g. the use of Gaelic at reception areas and service desks, on telephones, in mail and e-mail, and in public meetings), publications (e.g. in printed material, on websites and in exhibitions), and staffing (e.g. in training, language learning, and recruitment of Gaelic-speaking staff) (Bòrd na Gàidhlig 2007b: sections 5 and 6). The guidance anticipates that higher and broader levels of commitments will be made by public bodies operating in areas in which users of Gaelic form a majority of the population. Given the very weak presence of Gaelic in the public sector at present, the Scottish Government has established a Gaelic Language Act Implementation Fund ('GLAIF'), worth £1.4 million annually, administered by the Bòrd, to assist with some of the costs of implementing public authority Gaelic language plans.

As well as being the Bòrd's single most important policy tool, these Gaelic language plans have the potential to have a significant language planning impact. In particular by increasing the visible and audible profile of the language (through public signage, use in forms, brochures, leaflets and on websites, and so forth), they can contribute to the status of the language. By expanding the range of services that can be provided through the language, they can contribute to the use of the language. Rigorous plans would imply the expansion of Gaelic-speaking staff, creating demand for Gaelic as an essential or desirable job qualification, and thereby potentially contributing to Strubell's 'Catherine Wheel' effects. And although these plans only apply to the public sector, they can have an impact on other sectors, indirectly, by contributing to a culture of bilingualism and a broader awareness of good practice in relation to the use of Gaelic, and directly, by, for example, making purchasing by public authorities conditional on contractors having a policy to use and promote Gaelic. It is crucial, however, that the Gaelic language plans create real, substantive changes, rather than simply tokenistic measures which have the danger of actually reinforcing existing language hierarchies and beliefs, and with them negative diglossic patterns (see, for example, Walsh and McLeod 2008). It is also essential that the plans actually be implemented, and this will require serious ongoing scrutiny by the public authorities themselves, the Gaelic users they serve, and the Bòrd.

Thus far, the Bòrd has approved only six public authority language plans: Highland Council, Comhairle nan Eilean Siar, Argyll and Bute Council, Highlands and Islands Enterprise, the Scottish Parliament Corporate Body, and the Scottish Government (available at the website www.bord-na-gaidhlig.org.uk). Several more public authorities have been notified by the Bòrd to prepare such plans. An analysis of these first plans is beyond the scope of this contribution; however, while the plans of those public authorities which already had some form of Gaelic policy in place have gone beyond their earlier commitments, it is not clear that the new Gaelic language plans represent the step-change in provision for Gaelic services and for the use of Gaelic in their operations that the present state of the language requires.

Finally the Gaelic Act contains mechanisms which allow the Bòrd to take action with respect to Gaelic education. First, the National Gaelic language plan must include a strategy for promoting Gaelic education, and the Bòrd's first national plan does include a National Gaelic Education Strategy. Second, the Bòrd can require councils and their education authorities (which have significant control over pre-school, primary and secondary education) to make commitments in their Gaelic language plans with respect to the enhancement of Gaelic education. Third, the Bòrd has the power under the Gaelic Act to prepare and submit to the Scottish Government for approval guidance in relation to the provision of Gaelic education and the development of such provision (section 8), to which local authorities would be required to have regard in the provision by them of educational services. The Bòrd has not yet produced such guidance, and so it is not yet possible to say what the impact of this power may be.

To conclude, while some have been critical of aspects of the Gaelic Act – for example, the absence of any clear language 'rights', the ambiguous description of the precise legal status of the language, the lack of clear enforcement mechanisms, and the failure to include stronger measures with respect to education – it nonetheless represents a major step forward, for it does create real and potentially far-reaching language planning and language policy development mechanisms. The question now is how the Bòrd will use its powers, how the Scottish Government will continue to support the work of the Bòrd, and how Gaelic organisations, public authorities potentially subject to the act, and the broader public respond. It is hoped that the Bòrd's work will be researched-based (see Dunbar forthcoming) and will be informed by the emerging theoretical and practical approaches to minority language planning discussed above.

BIBLIOGRAPHY

Bòrd na Gàidhlig (2007a), *Plana Nàiseanta na Gàidhlig 2007–2012/ The National Plan for Gaelic 2007–2012*, Inverness: Bòrd na Gàidhlig.

Bòrd na Gàidhlig (2007b), *Stiùireadh air Deasachadh Phlanaichean Gàidhlig/Guidance on the Development of Gaelic Language Plans*, Inverness: Bòrd na Gàidhlig.

Byrne, Michel (2002), *Gràmar na Gàidhlig*, Cearsiadar: Stòrlann-Acair.

Calder, George [1923] (1990), *A Gaelic Grammar, Including a Chapter on Personal and Place Names*, Glasgow: Gairm.

Comhairle nan Eilean Siar (n.d.), *Gaelic Policy/Poileasaidh Gàidhlig*, Stornoway: Comhairle nan Eilean Siar.

Comunn na Gàidhlig (1988), *Towards a Gaelic Television Service*, Inverness: Comunn na Gàidhlig.

Comunn na Gàidhlig (1989), *The Case for a Gaelic Broadcasting Service: Response to the White Paper 'Broadcasting in the 90s'*, Inverness: Comunn na Gàidhlig.

Comunn na Gàidhlig (1997), *Inbhe Thèarainte dhan Ghaidhlig/Secure Status for Gaelic*, Inverness: Comunn na Gàidhlig.

Comunn na Gàidhlig (1999), *Dreach iùl airson Achd Gàidhlig/Draft Brief for a Gaelic Language Act*, Inverness: Comunn na Gàidhlig.

Cooper, Robert L. (1989), *Language Planning and Social Change*, Cambridge: Cambridge University Press.

Cormack, Mike (2004), 'Gaelic in the Media', *Scottish Affairs* 46, pp. 23–43.

Davies, Alan and Elder, Catherine (eds) (2006), *The Handbook of Applied Linguistics*, Oxford: Blackwell.

Dunbar, Robert (2006), 'Gaelic in Scotland: the Legal and Institutional Framework', in McLeod (2006: 1–23).

Dunbar, Robert (2007), 'Scotland: Language Legislation for Gaelic', *Cambrian Law Review* 38, pp. 39–82.

Dunbar, Robert (forthcoming), 'A Research Agenda to Support Gaelic Language Policy in Scotland', in Munro (forthcoming).

Evans, A. C. (1982), 'The Use of Gaelic in Court Proceedings', *1982 Scots Law Times*, pp. 286–7.

Fishman, Joshua A. (1991), *Reversing Language Shift: Theoretical and Empirical Foundations of Assistance to Threatened Languages*, Clevedon: Multilingual Matters.

Fishman, Joshua A. (2001), *Can Threatened Languages Be Saved? Reversing Language Shift, Revisited: A 21st Century Perspective*, Clevedon: Multilingual Matters.

Fishman, Joshua A., Cooper, Robert L. and Ma, Roxana (1971), *Bilingualism in the Barrio*, Bloomington, IN: Research Center for the Language Sciences, Indiana University.

Grin, François (2003), *Language Policy Evaluation and the European Charter for Regional or Minority Languages*, Basingstoke: Palgrave Macmillan.

Hale, Amy and Payton, Philip (eds) (2000), *New Directions in Celtic Studies*, Exeter: University of Exeter.

Highland Council (2005), *Plana Gàidhlig & Cultair/Gaelic Language and Culture Plan*, Inverness: Highland Council.

Highlands and Islands Development Board (HIDB) (1982), 'Cor na Gàidhlig, Language, Community and Development: The Gaelic Situation', A report prepared for the Highlands and Islands Development Board, with recommendations for action, November 1982.

Hinton, Leanne, and Hale, Ken (eds) (2001), *The Green Book of Language Revitalization in Practice*, San Diego: Academic Press.

Hornberger, Nancy H. (2006), 'Frameworks and Models in Language Policy and Planning', in Ricento (2006), pp. 24–41.

Johnstone, Richard (1994), *The Impact of Current Developments to Support the Gaelic Language: Review of Research*, Stirling: Scottish Centre for Information on Language Teaching and Research.

Johnstone, Richard, et al. (1999), *The Attainments of Pupils Receiving Gaelic-medium Primary Education in Scotland*, Stirling: Scottish Centre for Information on Language Teaching and Research.

Kaplan, Robert B., and Baldauf Jr., Richard B. (1997), *Language Planning: From Practice to Theory*, Clevedon: Multilingual Matters.

Kymlicka, Will, and Patten, Alan (eds) (2003), *Language Rights and Political Theory*, Oxford: Oxford University Press.

Lamb, William (2008), *Scottish Gaelic Speech and Writing: Register Variation in an Endangered Language*, Belfast: Cló Ollscoil na Banríona.

MacCaluim, Alasdair (2007), *Reversing Language Shift: The Social Identity and Role of Scottish Gaelic Learners*, Belfast: Cló Ollscoil na Banríona.

MacKinnon, Kenneth (1991), *Gaelic: A Past and Future Prospect*, Edinburgh: The Saltire Society.

McLeod, Wilson (2001a), *Faclair na Pàrlamaid: A Critical Evaluation*, Edinburgh: Department of Celtic and Scottish Studies, University of Edinburgh. Available on the internet at www.arts.ed.ac.uk/celtic/poileasaidh/FACLAIRREP.htm.

McLeod, Wilson (2001b), *The State of the 'Gaelic Economy': A Research Report*, Edinburgh: Department of Celtic and Scottish Studies, University of Edinburgh. Available on the internet at www.arts.ed.ac.uk/celtic/poileasaidh/GAELJOBSREP3.htm.

McLeod, Wilson (2002a), 'Language Planning as Regional Development: The Growth of the Gaelic Economy', *Scottish Affairs* 38, pp. 51–72.

McLeod, Wilson (2002b), 'Gaelic in Scotland: A "Renaissance" Without Planning', in *Hizkuntza Biziberritzeko Saoiak/Experiencias de Inversión del Cambio Lingüístico/Récupération de la Perte Linguistique/Reversing Language Shift*, pp. 279–95. Vitoria-Gasteiz: Eusko Jaurlaritzaren Argitalpen Zerbitzu Nagusia/Servicio Central de Publicaciones del Gobierno Vasco. Available on the internet at http://www.euskara.euskadi.net/r59738/es/contenidos/informacion/argitalpenak/es_6092/adjuntos/EREMU.PDF.

McLeod, Wilson (2004), 'The Challenge of Corpus Planning in Gaelic Development', *Scottish Language* 23, pp. 68–92.

McLeod, Wilson (ed.) (2006), *Revitalising Gaelic in Scotland: Policy, Planning and Public Discourse*, Edinburgh: Dunedin Academic Press.

McNeir, Clive Leo (ed.) (2001), *Faclair na Pàrlamaid: Dictionary of Terms*, Edinburgh: The Scottish Parliament.

Mark, Colin (2004), *The Gaelic–English Dictionary*, London: Routledge.

Marshall, David (1993/4), 'Language Maintenance and Revival', *Annual Review of Applied Linguistics* 14, pp. 20–33.

May, Stephen (2001), *Language and Minority Rights: Ethnicity, Nationalism and the Politics of Language*, Harlow: Pearson Education.

Munro, Gillian (ed.) (forthcoming), *Rannsachadh na Gàidhlig 4: Cànan & Cultar*, Edinburgh: Dunedin Academic Press.

NicAoidh, Magaidh (2006), 'Pròiseact Plana Cànain nan Eilean Siar: A' chiad ìre – rannsachadh air suidheachadh na Gàidhlig anns na h-Eileanan Siar', in McLeod (2006: 73–86).

Patten, Alan, and Kymlicka, Will (2003), 'Introduction: Language Rights and Political Theory: Context, Issues, and Approaches', in Kymlicka and Patten (2003: 1–51).

Pauwels, Anne (2006), 'Language Maintenance', in Davies and Elder (2006: 719–37).

Ricento, Thomas (2000), 'Historical and Theoretical Perspectives in Language Policy and Planning', *Journal of Sociolinguistics* 4, pp. 196–213.

Ricento, Thomas (ed.) (2006), *An Introduction to Language Policy: Theory and Method*, Oxford: Blackwell.

Robertson, Boyd and MacDonald, Ian (2004), *Teach Yourself Gaelic Dictionary*, London: Hodder Arnold.

Scottish Qualifications Authority (SQA) (2005), *Gaelic Orthographic Conventions 2005*, Glasgow: Scottish Qualifications Authority.

Shohamy, Elana (2006), *Language Policy: Hidden Agendas and New Approaches*, Abingdon: Routledge.

Spolsky, Bernard (2004), *Language Policy*, Cambridge: Cambridge University Press.

Spolsky, Bernard (2009), *Language Management*, Cambridge: Cambridge University Press.

Strubell, Miquel (1998), 'Can Sociolinguistic Change be Planned?' in *Proceedings of the 1st European Conference 'Private Foreign Language Education in Europe. Its contribution to the Multilingual and Multicultural Aspect of the European Union'. Thessaloniki, November 1997*, Thessaloniki: Palso, pp. 23–31.

Strubell, Miquel (2001), 'Catalan a decade later', in Fishman (2001: 260–83).

Thomson, Derick (ed.) (1994), *The Companion to Gaelic Scotland*, Glasgow: Gairm.

UNESCO Ad Hoc Expert Group on Endangered Languages (2003), *Language Vitality and Endangerment*. Document submitted to the International Expert Meeting on UNESCO Programme Safeguarding of Endangered Languages, Paris, 10–12 March 2003.

Walsh, John and McLeod, Wilson (2008), 'An Overcoat Wrapped Around an Invisible Man? Language Legislation and Language Revitalisation in Ireland and Scotland', *Language Policy* 7, pp. 21–46.

Watson, Angus (2007), *The Essential Gaelic-English Dictionary: a Dictionary for Students and Learners of Scottish Gaelic*, Edinburgh: Birlinn.

Welsh Language Board (n.d.), *The Welsh Language: A Vision and a Mission for 2000–2005*, Cardiff: Welsh Language Board.

Wright, Sue (2004), *Language Policy and Language Planning: From Nationalism to Globalisation*, Basingstoke: Palgrave Macmillan.

NOTES

1   Although he is Reader in Law and Celtic at the University of Aberdeen, and board member of Bòrd na Gàidhlig and MG Alba, the opinions expressed in this paper are solely those of the author.
2   Domains are the contexts in which language is used, and they are defined by three dimensions: the location in which discourse is taking place, the participants in the discourse, and the topic of the discourse. Examples would include the home, the church, the school and the workplace. See Fishman, Cooper and Ma (1971); Spolsky (2004: 39–56).
3   In his important recent contributions to the literature, Bernard Spolsky uses the term 'language management' rather than 'language planning': Spolsky (2004; 2009).
4   For a discussion of typologies of language policies, see those developed by Jacques Leclerc for the website L'aménagement linguistique dans le monde, available at http://www.tlfq.ulaval.ca/axl/. See also Patten and Kymlicka (2003: 26–31).
5   Sometimes referred to as 'graphization': Hornberger (2006: 29).
6   Sometimes referred to as 'renovation': ibid.
7   Sometimes referred to as 'modernisation': ibid.
8   UNESCO has also recently produced a very useful analytical framework for assessing the degree to which a language is threatened, based on the concept of language vitality: see UNESCO (2003).
9   Available on the internet at http://www.uk-legislation.hmso.gov.uk/legislation/scotland/acts2005/asp_20050007_en_1.
10 10 October 2003; available on the internet at http://www.scotland.gov.uk/Topics/ArtsCultureSport/gaelic/18299/13235.
11 In 2008/9, GME was available at sixty primary schools (2.8% of Scotland's 2153 publicly funded primary schools), with 2206 pupils enrolled (0.6% of the 370,839 pupils enrolled in Scotland's publicly funded primary schools).
12 In 2008/9, only twenty-three of the thirty-six primary schools operated by the local council, Comhairle nan Eilean Siar, offer GME, and the number of students getting such education – 505 – represented only 26.5% of primary students in the Comhairle's primary schools.
13 In 2008/9, only nineteen secondary schools (about 5% of Scotland's 376 publicly funded secondary schools) offered at least one course other than Gaelic through the medium of Gaelic, and only 397 pupils were enrolled on such courses (a little over 0.1% of the 303,978 pupils enrolled in Scotland's publicly funded secondary schools). With respect to courses in the language itself, courses for fluent speakers were offered at thirty-nine secondary schools (a little over 10% of all such schools), with 981 pupils in attendance (about 0.3% of all such pupils in Scotland), and courses for learners were offered at thirty-nine secondary schools (again, a little over 10%), with 2813 pupils in attendance (about 0.9% of all such pupils in Scotland).
14 The other local authority which had a Gaelic policy (now also superseded by a Gaelic language plan under the Gaelic Act) was Highland Council, which has a significant Gaelic-speaking population although, unlike the Western Isles, one which is spread much more thinly over a much larger area, and which constitutes a relatively small percentage of the total council area population. Not surprisingly, given these circumstances, the policy contained even fewer hard commitments than the Comhairle nan Eilean Siar policy (Highland Council 2005).

15 Over an eighteen-month period in 2000 and 2001, outside of jobs in the Gaelic education sector, only two of 194 jobs advertised, or 1%, were identified as 'Gaelic essential', and only six, or 3.1%, were 'Gaelic desirable' (McLeod 2001b: 19–20).

16 'Gaelic education' is defined broadly in subsection 10(1), and would include GME, the teaching of Gaelic as a subject, and even teaching about Gaelic.

CHAPTER 9

Sociolinguistic Ethnography of Gaelic Communities

Emily McEwan-Fujita

INTRODUCTION

The sociolinguistic ethnography of Gaelic speakers in various contexts, from crofting communities to language planning institutions, has contributed significantly to knowledge about the structures, uses and meanings of Gaelic in the twentieth and twenty-first centuries.[1] Such studies have also made contributions to the theoretical understanding of language shift and ethnolinguistic revitalisation processes. Sociolinguistic ethnography, which involves 'a close look at language practices in a specific setting' (Heller 2006: 13), has been conducted on Gaelic from a range of allied and overlapping disciplinary perspectives, including social and cultural anthropology, linguistic anthropology, education, linguistics, sociolinguistics, sociology and the sociology of language. The term 'sociolinguistic' indicates a basic research focus on language in its social context, while the term 'ethnography' refers to the methodological orientation of these studies towards largely qualitative field research on the linguistic, social and cultural aspects of people's lives.

The reliance of these studies on ethnographic fieldwork to collect data distinguishes them from historical and literary research on Gaelic, and from policy-oriented surveys. Surveys and questionnaires are essential research tools, but researchers who conduct both surveys and ethnographic observations of the same population report difficulties with administering the surveys and disparities between responses and observed behaviour (Coleman 1975: 184–205, Dorian 1981a: 157–78, Pollock 2006: 189).[2] The advantage of fieldwork is that it lets local interests and categories emerge from the data (e.g., MacKinnon 1977: 7); it also helps the analyst to understand and convey the feel of everyday life in a particular place. Ethnographic fieldwork in the anthropological tradition requires long-term residence in an area and is therefore time-consuming, demanding and potentially expensive: the informal standard is to spend at least one full year 'in the field', often with shorter follow-up visits. The most common methodologies of ethnographic fieldwork are participant observation and ethnographic interviewing. Participant observation involves active participation in local activities, while making fieldnotes with analytical observations about these activities, with the aim of combining both insider and outsider perspectives on the culture. Ethnographic interviewing is more loosely structured than other forms of interviewing, but aims to systematically elicit people's views and information on particular topics of cultural relevance. Other methodologies such as household censuses, language attitude and usage surveys, proficiency tests, elicitation, and matched-guise experiments may also be used, but they are administered by the researcher in the field, and participant-observation fieldwork informs their design and interpretation. The fieldwork also may inform various modes of discourse analysis on media and other texts gathered in the field and archives.

This chapter will consider the theoretical contributions that sociolinguistic ethnographies of Gaelic have made to the study of two main areas: processes of Gaelic language shift in traditional Gaelic communities, and Gaelic language revitalisation efforts in traditional and new Gaelic communities. The chapter then considers issues of representation, diversity of researchers and audiences, and continuity in research on Gaelic-speaking communities, before finally discussing future directions in the sociolinguistic ethnography of Gaelic speakers.

PROCESSES OF GAELIC LANGUAGE SHIFT IN TRADITIONAL GAELIC COMMUNITIES

National boundaries, disciplinary interests and institutional configurations have contributed to the temporal and conceptual gaps in academic approaches to Gaelic. Since the nineteenth century, Scottish folklore collecting (and later ethnology) has focused on documenting the oral traditions and other folkways of Gaelic speakers, while Celtic studies developed around history, literature and philology (MacKinnon 1977: 4). Although twentieth-century ethnologists, geographers and dialectologists conducted field research in the Highlands, ironically Scottish anthropologists preferred to focus on more 'exotic' peoples, and mostly non-Scottish anthropologists and linguists pioneered the study of Gaelic speakers in sociolinguistic context.

MacKinnon was the first to undertake a sociolinguistic ethnography of Gaelic speakers in the early 1970s, though he describes some sociologically aware approaches predating his own in Scotland (Campbell 1950) and Canada (Dunn 1953; Campbell and MacLean 1974), which have been followed by others in history and historical geography (Durkacz 1983; Withers 1984, 1988). MacKinnon also points out that polymath scholars in the field of Celtic have produced valuable work describing changes in structures, uses and ideologies of Gaelic in sociocultural context (including Black 1994; Gillies 1980, 1989; MacAulay 1976–8, 1978, 1979, 1982a, 1982b, 1986; Meek 1996, 2001; Thomson 1979, 1994; Thomson and Grimble 1968). In these cases, the authors' personal experiences of Gaelic-speaking communities, combined with their linguistic competence and interest in sociolinguistic matters allow them to closely approximate the combined outsider-insider perspective of the ethnographer.

Overall, ethnographies in the traditions of anthropology and sociology of language have described and analysed the cultural meanings and practices of Scottish Gaelic in the context of ongoing processes of language shift from Gaelic to English from the 1950s to the 2000s (with a gap in the 1960s). Most studies have focused on the meanings and uses of Gaelic in traditional geographically bounded community contexts: Hebridean crofting communities (Coleman 1975; Ducey 1956; Ennew 1980; Macdonald 1987, 1997b; MacKinnon 1977; Parman 1972, 2005; Vallee 1954), east Sutherland fishing communities (Dorian 1981a; Constantinidou 1994), and Canadian Cape Breton mining and fishing communities (Mertz 1982a). This focus is characteristic of the early orientation of the anthropology of Europe towards 'community studies' of traditional, bounded rural localities (Cole 1977).

However, in the 1970s anthropologists began to take a broader perspective, grounding their fieldwork in one or several crofting townships while insisting on analysing wider processes of sociocultural change. These studies have explored the relatively recent nineteenth- and twentieth-century historical construction of the 'crofting community' and its cultural and social legitimation by community residents through the ongoing construction of history and local identity (Ennew 1978, 1980; Macdonald 1987, 1997b; Parman 1972, 1990, 2005). Rather than seeing the situation as modernity overtaking static tradition, anthropologists have chosen to highlight the intensive and long-standing economic relationships of crofting communities with mainland Scotland, the United Kingdom, the European Union and the global capitalist economy. The most comprehensive ethnographies of this kind focused on the industries of Harris Tweed, fishing, and oil on the Isle of Lewis (Ennew 1980; Parman 1990, 1993).[3]

As Condry points out, however, the study of language in Scotland from a social perspective was severely lacking (Condry 1983: 89). Many of the ethnographic studies of Gaelic-speaking communities from the 1950s through the 1980s omit detailed information about the Gaelic linguistic practices and ideologies of their subjects, taking them for granted as a backdrop to the dramas of croft succession or underdevelopment. Nonetheless, such studies do provide a valuable and consistent picture of the local cultural, social and economic practices of kinship, childrearing, social hierarchies, land ownership, agriculture and religion that have formed the fabric of life in Hebridean crofting communities where Gaelic was or is still spoken by half or more of residents. The studies by and large focused on crofting and Calvinism on Lewis and Skye; with the exception of Vallee (1954), language use in Catholic Gaelic-speaking communities has not been studied from anthropological or sociolinguistic perspectives.

The sociolinguistic studies that treat Gaelic-speaking practices in detail have all found that most Gaelic speakers assign very *local* meanings to Gaelic in crofting communities. Participant observation of daily life on Barra in the 1950s (Vallee 1954), Lewis in the 1970s (Coleman 1975), Harris in the 1970s (MacKinnon 1977), Skye in the 1980s (Macdonald 1997b), and South Uist and Benbecula in 2000 (McEwan-Fujita 2003) all reveal remarkably consistent conceptions of Gaelic-speaking as a local practice in the nexus of home, family and crofting community. As a result of ongoing language shift, Gaelic has been conceptualised by these speakers as most suitable for interactions with kin and neighbours, and has been ideologised as egalitarian. For example, in the 1970s MacKinnon found in questionnaires with adults (1977: 167) and secondary pupils, and group interviews with secondary pupils (125) from Harris, that 'The significance of Gaelic within community life is seen essentially as being bound up with everyday behaviour patterns' (167) and not with, for example, political institutions.[4]

The local significance assigned to Gaelic is the result of speakers noticing and interpreting the replacement of Gaelic with English in non-domestic, non-locally-oriented domains. Domains may be defined as 'distinct spheres of activity' (Dorian 1981a: 75) or 'major clusters of interaction situations that occur in particular multilingual settings'; these tend to be organised around either 'institutional contexts' or 'socio-ecological co-occurrences' (Fishman 1965: 231). Identifying changes over time in the pattern of language usage in different domains is one way of conceptualising and measuring language shift. Two other complementary ways of assessing shift are measuring changes over time in the number of speakers in particular geographical areas, and testing for differences in linguistic proficiency between different generations of speakers at a particular point in time.[5]

Ethnographies of Gaelic-speaking communities describe similar patterns of distribution of Gaelic and English use across various domains in the latter half of the twentieth century. Domains are not universal, but specific to various cultural contexts and must be defined through the use of ethnographic observation (Dorian 1981a: 75). Some domains can be clearly associated with particular times, places and settings, while others are more dispersed (Coleman 1975: 171). Due to the relative cultural and geographical homogeneity of the Highlands and Islands, analysts have identified similar types of domains in various Gaelic-speaking communities. In early twentieth-century East Sutherland, for example, the domains of Gaelic use identified by Dorian were home, work (mainly fishing-related), and religion (Presbyterian), while the domains of English were the national secular institutions (school, political parties, military, police, the courts), local public life and print media (Dorian 1981a: 75). Dorian reported that in some domains Gaelic and English linguistic compartmentalisation was complete, while in others, such as the work domain, it was only partial. Factors such as setting and interlocutor could also determine or constrain language choice in various domains (76–7).

In the early 1970s on Harris, Gaelic represented solidarity and was used predominantly in the home and in local locations such as the post office, local shop, traveling grocery van, church, and village entertainment, while as in East Sutherland, 'The domains within which English predominates are those where a power dimension is conspicuously to the fore' (MacKinnon 1977: 28). However, MacKinnon (145–9) points out the weaknesses of the domain concept, which cannot adequately explain the nuances of such activities as counting in English in an otherwise Gaelic conversation with a friend, or 'the [recent] shift in favour of Gaelic in the usage with local councillors' (147). The relative nature of the domain concept is also apparent in the fact that Gaelic might be used at clubs or society meetings, 'where solidary group values are encouraged' (28) despite the expectation that English might be used in such a 'public' domain. Moreover, because Gaelic actually had a temporarily stable legitimate place in the community, with some locally prestigious uses such as the use of an elaborated code in religious worship (Dorian 1978e), MacKinnon proposed 'demesne extension' as a supplementary concept to Weinreich's 'dominance configuration,' in order to 'associate together the situations which predominantly call for one particular language and distinguish those other situations predominantly calling for the other language' (MacKinnon 1977: 148). His aim was to show how language use points up clusters of culturally-significant social behaviours, without focusing exclusively on the symbolic dominance of one language over another, which indeed cannot explain why Gaelic-speaking communities have continued to maintain and reproduce themselves for as long as they have.

Coleman's findings complement MacKinnon's critique of over-reliance on the analytical concept of domain to document or explain language shift. On the basis of participant observation and interviewing Coleman identified six domains for the 1970s crofting community of Carloway: household (both nuclear and extended), neighbourhood and peer group, religion, education, official and administrative, and speech to animals. He used these domains as the basis for a language usage survey conducted at the end of his fieldwork. On the basis of casual observation, Coleman had hypothesised that in his survey results these domains would be arrayed in sequence, such that 'household' would be the domain where the most Gaelic and least English was spoken in Carloway, while the 'official and administrative' domain would be the least Gaelic and most English, and that the older the respondent, the more domains in which they would report speaking Gaelic and the younger the respondent, the more domains in which they would report speaking English. However, the results of his survey did not completely or even strongly uphold this hypothesis (Coleman 1975: 189). He speculated inconclusively on the various reasons why, including the fact that other factors such as personal affect (positive personal relationship, hostility, fear), topic, style of speech, and setting could affect code choice, that the survey was flawed,[6] and that men aged twenty to twenty-nine who stayed in the village underwent a social transition from 'student' to 'adult worker' which may have caused them to over-estimate their usage of Gaelic at the time they were surveyed (189–201).

Mertz (1993) made a further critique of the application of domains, based on a retrospective critique of her research methodology in Cape Breton. In examining and attempting to code her data, she found that interviewees responded to questions from a very different perspective than her own. For them, Gaelic or English 'language preference is not an attribute of an individual approaching situations in the abstract, but is embedded in the complex social life of the community, a life that is not primarily understood as a series of segmented "domains"' (Mertz 1993:

168). She therefore recommended that researchers not lose sight of 'the unexpected, creative, contingent, and socially dependent character' of language choice in particular settings (170). Such an approach would stay centered, in anthropological fashion, on the concerns of the people themselves who are under scrutiny.

For the sake of convenience, both Gaelic-English bilinguals and researchers often refer to the verbal repertoire of Gaelic-English bilinguals as composed simply of 'Gaelic' and 'English'. However, analysts have identified multiple varieties of both Gaelic and English in twentieth-century Gaelic-speaking communities based on observation and subjects' metalinguistic descriptions (Dorian 1981a: 84). Coleman identified three main varieties of Gaelic in 1973 in Carloway, providing transcripts of examples in an appendix. The first is 'Casual Gaelic', sometimes called by the Carlowegians '*Gàidhlig taobh an teine*' ['fireside Gaelic'] or 'tinker Gaelic' due to 'the unusual intonational contours and stress patterns on the island ..., the ellipsis and often very fast and blurred pronunciation, and the very large amount of lexical borrowing from English that is found in rural Lewis' (Coleman 1975: 152). The second variety is 'Careful Gaelic', characterised by far fewer English borrowings, which was almost never spoken and not very often encountered in Carloway except in the media, and which was 'most closely associated with secular Gaelic literacy, language loyalism or public speech before socially heterogeneous audiences' (154).[7] The third was 'Church Gaelic', a formal variety used for prayer and Presbyterian worship, 'distinguishable by its archaic lexicon [drawn from the Bible], its often distinctive intonational contours, the formality of settings in which it is used, and the near total lack of English loan words' (158).[8] Coleman also identified two varieties of English: 'Island English' influenced by Gaelic syntax, semantics and the distinctive prosody of Lewis Gaelic (166); and a regional 'Standard English' which was spread by secondary education, the media, and English-speaking incomers (168).

Dorian likewise identified four varieties of Gaelic and at least four varieties of English spoken and heard in the east-coast fishing villages of Brora, Golspie and Embo. The varieties of Gaelic included: (1) the local East Sutherland Gaelic (ESG), (2) other regional dialects, (3) a standard she called 'textbook Gaelic' (analogous to Coleman's 'Careful Gaelic'), and (4) 'church Gaelic' which had a 'higher prestige among ESG speakers than other regional dialects or textbook Gaelic' (Dorian 1981a: 90).[9] Both Coleman and Dorian noted that the varieties can be described linguistically, but their relative prestige among speakers must also be considered from a sociolinguistic perspective.

Intra-situational codeswitching patterns, or patterns of switching between Gaelic and English in a single interaction, have also received consideration from Coleman (1975) and Dorian (1981a).[10] Coleman identified three types of switching, which he labeled instrumental, metaphorical and macaronic. Instrumental switching from English to Gaelic could be done to 'create temporary relations of solidarity for some specific purpose', particularly by a superordinate person to a subordinate person, while instrumental switching from Gaelic to English could be done to 'establish or maintain social distance between interlocutors' (Coleman 1975: 210). Metaphorical switching 'involves the use of a second code in the context of the first for purposes of emphasis, humor, exaggeration, ridicule, etc.', which, in Coleman's account, nearly always involved the incorporation of English phrases into Gaelic speech (211–12). Macaronic switching 'involves the apparently unconscious, sometimes very rapid, alternation between English and Gaelic within the context of a single speech event, act or utterance'. Coleman speculated that this seemed to be a partial blending of the codes of Gaelic and English into a single macaronic code. It was found when the interlocutors were 'coordinate bilinguals of similar social status and background, and are very well known to each other'; when 'participants in the speech situation are deeply engrossed in a task-oriented activity (as opposed to a speech-oriented activity)', 'most often when topics of conversation are highly concrete, local, with a minimum of abstraction or esoterica', and often in the speech of people who were aged twenty-five to fifty-five at the time of the study (in other words, in the speech of people born in 1918–48), but never, he noted, in the speech of people over fifty-five (born before 1918). Coleman also noted that certain individuals were known for macaronic switching, a point that Dorian also mentioned (1981a: 98–9). In fact, in East Sutherland, Dorian observed that codeswitching was mostly done by individuals who were known for the behaviour, rather than on a community-wide basis, and also that the majority of codeswitching behaviour in the community was precipitated by a change in interlocutor (99).

Mertz described different codeswitching patterns related to the more advanced state of language shift in late 1970s Cape Breton. After intergenerational transmission had largely ceased in the 1930s and 1940s, the status and popularity of Gaelic increased in Mabou and the North Shore, in part through the influence of urban revival efforts. Although English remained dominant, once again it became socially acceptable to use Gaelic in public domains; this took the form of a Gaelic 'greeting routine' followed by a shift to English, and a 'peppering' of Gaelic words, phrases and sentences in English conversations (Mertz

1982a: 245–59), which served the functions of marking boundaries (the beginnings and endings of conversations, or boundaries between insiders and outsiders) and expressing strong emotion or humour. Thus even though Gaelic was not being used in great quantity, its use was symbolically significant to the community (Mertz 1989: 113–14).

One notable aspect of both intra- and inter-situational codeswitching in Gaelic-speaking communities is a set of rules dictating the choice of Gaelic or English with particular interlocutors. This 'ethic of politeness' or 'etiquette of accommodation' is similar to that found in other European situations of minority language shift (Gal 1979: 165–6; Woolard 1989: 68–82; Trosset 1986: 169). This pattern of behaviour is both an indicator and perpetuating mechanism of language shift, since it works to reduce the number of situations in which Gaelic may be spoken. Coleman, who has described the phenomenon most thoroughly, terms it the 'Courtesy Rule' and sums it up as 'English to strangers, Gaelic to locals' (Coleman 1975: 74–94). 'English to strangers' means that 'To speak Gaelic in Carloway in the presence of a non-Gaelic-speaking stranger is widely and unequivocably considered to be extremely bad manners, even if the stranger is situationally peripheral' (80). The corollary to this is that for local Gaelic-English bilinguals, Gaelic must be used with other locals in informal situations; to use English would be negatively evaluated as 'snobbish' (see also Parman 1972: 136–7). Dorian also described such norms for East Sutherland (1981a: 79), and McEwan-Fujita identified them in Uist in 1999–2000 (2003, 2010). Coleman believed such behaviour to be a result of the defensive position of Gaelic speakers vis-à-vis English and English speakers in Scotland. He theorised that such behaviour helps Gaelic-English bilinguals to enact cultural norms of politeness and hospitality while simultaneously maintaining a sociolinguistic boundary between themselves and non-Gaelic speakers, whether consciously or unconsciously (Coleman 1975: 84).

Naming and kinship are areas of classic anthropological interest, and distinctive local Gaelic naming practices and orientations towards kinship, as well as the changes apparent in such practices with the process of language shift, are described in nearly every ethnography of a crofting community, sociolinguistic or otherwise.[11] The two main kinds of practices described are patronymics (*sloinnidhean*) and by-naming or nicknaming, which are generally used together (MacKinnon 1977: 23) to designate individuals in areas where many people have traditionally shared a relatively small number of surnames and given names. MacKinnon (22–4), who reports having documented naming practices and collected patronymics from three villages in Harris during his fieldwork, gives the example of a patronymic: '*Rachag Dhòmhnaill Iain Raghnaill* ('Little Rachel [daughter of] Donald [son] of John [son] of Ronald)', whose 'official' English name might be Rachel MacLennan (22–3). MacKinnon observed that 'Widespread knowledge of people's *sloinnidhean* acts as a constraint upon behaviour – and a form of social control. The *sloinneadh* places a person immediately upon a network of kin-relationships, as the form of the *sloinneadh* is a skeletal pedigree' (23). Ethnographic descriptions indicate that across the mid- to late-twentieth century the practice has been incorporated or modified into a more general cultural practice of nicknaming and by-naming in both Gaelic and English (Dorian 1970; Ennew 1980: 77–9; Mertz 1982b).

Such abbreviated usage is also apparent in Dorian's thorough and detailed description of the Gaelic by-naming system of the East Sutherland coastal villages of Brora, Golspie and Embo (Dorian 1970).[12] Dorian described five basic types of by-names in great detail: (1) basic genealogical, which were like traditional Gaelic patronymics, but only included two generations, ego and first ascending, which could refer to the father or the mother (but could be different in this respect even between siblings); (2) descriptive; (3) derisive; (4) nonsense; and (5) secondary genealogical patterns built on the second, third and fourth groups (Dorian 1970: 306). Ennew noted that in Lewis, nicknames of the second, third and fourth types could come from either family context in early childhood, or from the peer group (1980: 77–9).

The nicknames circumscribed and enacted kinship and friendship networks at the local level, even encompassing the 'exiles' who were away from the village or island (Mewett 1982b: 234–9). In day-to-day interaction, licence to use an offensive nickname to a person's face marked in-group status or intimacy (Dorian 1970; MacKinnon 1977). However, Dorian noted that there were social hazards for the outside researcher and even for residents of the community who did not speak Gaelic: the inability to determine which non-genealogical nicknames were offensive and which were not, and to determine to which kinship and friendship networks the nicknamed person belonged, meant that the outside researcher and even community residents who did not speak Gaelic ran the risk of inadvertently using a derogatory nickname to his or her face. In East Sutherland, this represented a hazard in varying degrees depending on English-speaking residents' kinship connections with the village and whether they were raised there or recent arrivals (Dorian 1970: 305–6, 315).[13]

Anthropologists have also noted the semantic re-calibration of Gaelic terms to English ones in the context of language shift. Ardener (1989: 134–54) presented an account of traditional Gaelic calendrical terms as non-linear and non-fixed: 'the Scottish Gaelic year consisted of overlapping categories of weather and agricultural epochs, into which three or four ancient ritual seasons intruded.' Such a system was incompatible with the modern Gregorian calendar. By tracing Gaelic-English dictionary definitions over time, Ardener demonstrates how dictionary makers created standardised meanings for the context-dependent Gaelic calendrical terms, with the result that now every 'English' month and season has its exact equivalent in modern Scottish Gaelic (142).[14] Macdonald also discussed how the semantic domain of colour terminology in Gaelic may be shifting from a different cultural system to a code for English-language categories (Macdonald 1997b: 249–50; Macdonald 1999). Using examples from her research in Skye, Macdonald noted how this phenomenon seemed to be accompanied, or perhaps caused, by a shift on the part of native Gaelic speakers towards viewing written sources as prior and superior to oral ones, and English as the yardstick against which Gaelic should be measured (Macdonald 1999: 187–8, 190–1).[15]

Academically, Scottish Gaelic is best known outwith Scotland as a relatively well-documented case study of Celtic and Western European language shift. Scholars have taken multiple approaches in their theoretical contributions to our understanding of the sociolinguistic processes of Scottish Gaelic language shift. Coleman (1975) focused on the way that rapid social change, speech networks and language acquisition patterns were contributing to the shift from Gaelic to English in 1970s Lewis. MacKinnon (1977) focused on the institution of the schools, and assessing changes in linguistic practices over time, in the context of local community life in 1970s Harris. Mertz (1982a; 1989) focused on how people's views about the social meaning of language use acted as a 'filter' through which they interpreted the significance of macro-level economic and social change, in the process of shift from Gaelic to English in 1970s Cape Breton Island, Nova Scotia. Dorian's work from the 1960s to the present has focused on structural, social and ideological aspects of shift from the isolated east-coast dialect of East Sutherland Gaelic to English among the formerly stigmatised fisherfolk and their descendants. Dorian has made substantial contributions to the theorisation of structural change in an obsolescing dialect (1972, 1973, 1978b, 1978c, 1978d, 1986, 1989), social, cultural and ideological aspects of language shift (1977, 1978a, 1980a, 1980b, 1981a, 1981b, 1982b, 1987, 1993a, 1994a, 1994b, 1998, forthcoming a),[16] and micro-level linguistic variation that cannot be explained by language shift or social class differences (1982a, 1993b, 1994c, 2001, forthcoming b).

Coleman (1975) describes how a variety of factors in 1970s Carloway contributed to the process of language shift from Gaelic to English. The most basic factor was rapid social and economic change in the village beginning around the time of the First World War, which had increased in pace since the Second World War, bringing radical changes in the standard of living in the 1950s and 1960s, greater integration into the rest of the UK and the corresponding self-consciousness of the villagers as marginal, isolated and backward (Coleman 1975: 69–70). After the Second World War, changes in subsistence and employment patterns contributed to the development of social networks along lines of sex, age and religion, with deep cleavages that severely reduced the amount of verbal interaction across network lines, including interaction in Gaelic. Men became isolated in their working lives (in croft work or weaving tweed), and women were even more isolated in their homes, since at that time women had few opportunities for employment or a social role outside the home (Ennew 1980: 80–1). According to Coleman's observations, relations between the sexes, between the generations (Coleman 1975: 65–7), and between the so-called 'Bible' and 'bottle' networks could be antagonistic, sometimes greatly so (also see Parman 1972, Ennew 1980). He visualised the village of Carloway as 'consisting of a number of partially discrete speech networks based upon age, sex and religion'. Although kin, neighbours and communal work groups could help overcome the boundaries between these networks, the kinds of social situations in which people would cross network boundaries to speak to one another were declining in number due to a variety of interrelated factors, including outmigration, the decline of the village center, television, patterns of solitary labour, and the disappearance of local weddings. Thus,

> speech has tended to run more and more into isolated pockets. Differences of age, sex and religion, which once might have been largely overlarded by the sheer quantity and intricacy of social interaction, have taken on the nature of barriers inhibiting communication. Behind these barriers, and particularly among the young, changes in the quantity and quality of Gaelic spoken are rapidly taking place. (Coleman 1975: 108)

Local cultural patterns of language acquisition in household, village and school settings also contributed to language shift: in the household with mockery and inconsistent treatment of children by adults (see also Parman 1990) and the devaluation of children's speech, in the village with peer group interactions in English, and in the school which was an 'essentially English domain'. All interacted to produce processes of language shift from Gaelic to English on the west side of Lewis. These changes were accompanied by an entrenched pattern of sociolinguistic boundary maintenance of locals versus strangers through the 'etiquette of accommodation' as previously described.

Kenneth MacKinnon's (1977) study focused on the schools as an institution, within the context of Gaelic-speaking crofting communities in Harris. His field research included extensive participant observation which informed his main focus on questionnaires, surveys, interviews, a matched guise test, and group interviews with children. MacKinnon found that language shift from Gaelic to English was ongoing, both in real diachronic comparison (re-administering a survey of Harris school children in 1972–3 which he directly compared with the results of a 1957–8 survey conducted by the Scottish Council for Research in Education), and in virtual diachronic comparison of different age groups in the adult population in a language attitudes and usage survey.

One of MacKinnon's most important conclusions was about the role of the secondary education system in the Western Isles in the process of language shift. Secondary education was structured so that the most academically able girls and boys (and the girls in greater proportion), who also tend to be the most loyal to Gaelic and the most literate in Gaelic (MacKinnon 1977: 134, 169), were selected to be sent away from Harris (either to Portree or Stornoway). This became an 'anticipatory socialisation' for them eventually migrating away altogether to seek work (104). In contrast, the young women who stayed in their Harris communities showed lower language loyalty to Gaelic on MacKinnon's survey (161). Thus, summing up, 'The individuals who might possibly change the situation are the ones most likely to leave the island' (169).[17]

Based on his community-level and island-level research, MacKinnon theorised about the macrosociological process of Gaelic language shift (MacKinnon 1977: 32–6). He proposed 'the "cultural retreat" or *Gàidhealtachd* model' of shift, which is not so much a model as a description of the process, represented by the 'ever-shrinking area' of the *Gàidhealtachd* in histories, maps and census reports. MacKinnon also pointed out that reality is not so neat, since Gaelic-English contact also occurs *within* Gaelic-speaking areas. To the extent that language shift is a function of language contact and culture clash, MacKinnon saw the 'cultural retreat' as a result of the combination of four different factors or mechanisms which have been 'differentially operative' in Gaelic-speaking areas: (1) 'Clearance': large numbers of the native population are removed from an area, leaving it relatively depopulated; (2) 'Economic Development': new forms of economic organisation bring about cultural changes requiring language-shift; (3) 'Changeover': new people migrate into an area while local people leave or die out; and (4) 'Social Morale': in which the power relationship changes between social groups identified with the local and the national language, such that 'the local community loses confidence in its system of values' through the local influence of national institutions such as education and the church (35). No single factor among these can completely account for Gaelic language shift, and different combinations may account for shift in different areas.

While MacKinnon's work on Gaelic language shift on Harris and in national perspective is best known among Gaelic scholars in Scotland, Nancy Dorian's work on the isolated east-coast dialect of East Sutherland Gaelic is best known among scholars working on issues of language shift, obsolescence and revitalisation outside of Scotland. Dorian conducted field research in Scotland periodically from 1963 to 1978; her research by telephone began in 1991 and continues today (personal communication). Her 1981 book *Language Death* describes the history of Gaelic in Sutherland, the sociolinguistic situation of ESG in the latter half of the twentieth century, and the linguistic changes to ESG in the final phases of obsolescence (Dorian 1981a: 4). Even in examining some of the most detailed and technical linguistic aspects of structural change and variation in an obsolescing variety of Gaelic, she has related these phenomena to the social conditions experienced by Gaelic-speaking individuals in communities undergoing language shift.

Dorian (1981a) details the historical formation of the east-coast fishing communities of Brora, Golspie and Embo, and the way in which their poverty, segregation in particular villages or neighbourhoods, occupational distinctiveness and 'linguistic lag' relative to the surrounding populations of agriculturalists and townspeople (Dorian 1980b: 38–9) led to their stigmatisation as a separate ethnic group from the early nineteenth to the mid-twentieth centuries. By the time Dorian worked with the population, her adult informants had been raised in fisherfolk households but had found other occupations, since the fishing declined around the turn of twentieth century and even more around the time of the First World War (Dorian 1981a: 46–7).

Dorian also explored and introduced respectively the sociolinguistic concepts of 'tip' and 'semi-speakers' in language shift. 'Tip', as Dorian described it (1981a: 51), was a 'possible [route] toward language death': 'it would seem that a language which has been demographically highly stable for several centuries may experience a sudden "tip," after which the demographic tide flows strongly in favor of some other language'. Although the tip might have actually been 'several centuries in the making', it would take a push in the form of a particular economic or social event to turn the tide. For example, Coleman (1975) identified a stable boundary between English-speaking Stornoway and the Gaelic-speaking rural crofting townships in Lewis in the description of Smith (1948) and located a 'tip' to English in the rural areas by the time of his own research in the early 1970s. Mertz (1989) located a 'tip' in Cape Breton, Nova Scotia during the 1930s–40s.

Semi-speakers are bilinguals who control the majority language well, and the minoritised language imperfectly, but who nonetheless choose to use the minoritised language frequently with others (Dorian 1980a). Dorian found that ESG semi-speakers were characterised by two or more of the following factors: late birth order in a family with many children, having been linguistically socialised by an older relative outside the nuclear family, having a strong sense of community identity, particularly if they had been in exile, and/or an inquisitive and gregarious personality (Dorian 1981a: 107; also see 1980a for further discussion of the last three factors). Dorian also noted that semi-speakers have no conversation partners with whom Gaelic is the preferred language (forthcoming a).

Elizabeth Mertz's 1982 dissertation makes a theoretical contribution to the study of language shift based on the case of Gaelic in Cape Breton Island, Nova Scotia, Canada. She conducted research in the late 1970s in the communities of Mabou and the North Shore, chosen for their contrasting characteristics: Mabou was more affluent, more diverse in religious backgrounds though with a strong Catholic presence, settled relatively early (beginning in the 1790s), and had easier access to the outside world; the North Shore was settled later (beginning in 1843) by poorer, predominantly Presbyterian emigrants, and was a more geographically isolated area with less access to natural resources.

These two communities, despite their contrasting situations, underwent a relatively rapid shift from Gaelic to English as the language of socialisation of their children at about the same time, in the 1930s and 1940s. Mertz concludes that since they both underwent the shift at about the same time, despite being so different, ideological factors common to both areas, which she terms 'metapragmatic views' (people's views about the social meaning of language use) must have been significant factors in parents' shift from Gaelic to English as the language of socialisation for their children. Mertz argues that although factors like migration to industrial centers, economic dominance of majority language speakers, state boundaries, political events and ecological and demographic factors have been significant in Cape Breton and other cases of language shift (1982a: 17–18), simply identifying various external 'factors' and imputing a direct causal relationship does not fully explain the relatively sudden tip from Gaelic to English in Cape Breton. Instead, speakers who observe and experience these 'external' factors interpret them through an 'internal' filter of cultural conceptions about the social nature of language, which Mertz terms a 'metapragmatic filter'. The particular filter that Mertz describes for Cape Breton consists of two main elements: (1) a view of Gaelic and English as incompatible (175–8) and (2) a dichotomy between English and Gaelic such that English is seen as the language of the mainstream, the new and progress, and Gaelic is seen as the language of rural areas, the old and backwardness (178–85). The former 'provided the link between parents' desire for their children to learn English and their move away from Gaelic' (178), while the latter took on 'an economic focus' with the arrival of the Great Depression in the 1930s (182). Specific evidence to support Mertz's hypothesis includes contemporary reports from the 1930s, oral histories, economic and general histories, archival records and data from age proficiency profiles based on Gaelic language proficiency tests which she conducted.

LANGUAGE REVITALISATION EFFORTS AND NEW GAELIC COMMUNITIES

Together with the focus on language shift, sociolinguistic researchers since the 1970s have increasingly turned their attention to Gaelic language revitalisation efforts. These efforts may create new kinds of social and linguistic identities, communities and institutions, which in turn help dialectically shape the efforts themselves. Research on revitalisation efforts focuses on the diversity and multiplicity of positions in, for and against the revitalisation of Gaelic, including conflict and accommodation between new and traditional cultural meanings of Gaelic, and new and emerging contexts and forms of use. Conflict arises because some people have difficulty accepting the legitimacy of new and diverse ways of conceptualising Gaelic as a language, culture, or community (Oliver forthcoming: 18), especially when they have been socialised into conceptions of Gaelic as a 'language of the local' in the crofting communities where concentrations of speakers are found (Oliver 2002: 160–1, McEwan-Fujita 2003).

The paradox is that Gaelic-speaking areas are experiencing ongoing shift, even as Gaelic has been undergoing revitalisation since the 1980s (or since the nineteenth century, if earlier efforts are included). How could Gaelic be experiencing a revitalisation and a decline at the same time (Oliver 2002: 176)? Oliver has called the current revitalisation efforts a 'culturally imagined revival' rather than a 'successful linguistic one' (4). Lack of a successful linguistic revival to date may be attributed to: (1) the fact that the macro-level conditions contributing to language shift are extremely difficult for small groups to alter (see the discussion of Mertz 1982a below); and (2) the fact that once a revitalisation effort is instituted, it generates a paradox of its own: in the process of garnering political support for a minoritised language and creating a standardised form to serve as the basis for education, such a movement further marginalises the people who live in economically marginal rural areas and speak dialectal forms (Eckert 1983).

One of the biggest problems of Gaelic revitalisation is why some native Gaelic speakers in Gaelic-speaking communities oppose or do not cooperate with revitalisation efforts in their own communities. Various researchers have located the problem in the conflicts in cultural and sociolinguistic values between rural, crofting native speakers and urban, middle-class, university educated activists. Coleman had noted of revitalisation attempts in the 1960s and 1970s that they were based on either scholarly and 'literary/antiquarian' orientations, or expatriate nostalgic romanticisation of traditional Highland and island life. Both sets of values were meaningless to most of the Carloway crofters with whom he worked (Coleman 1975: 226–7; see also Parman 1972: 130–1).

Social anthropologist Sharon Macdonald engaged with this problem by focusing in part on the diversity and contestation emerging from Gaelic revitalisation efforts on Skye. Her ethnography of a crofting community in Skye, based on PhD thesis research conducted 1983-6, is about the ways that people who lived in a Gaelic-speaking area constructed their local identities out of a 'repertoire' of available cultural meanings (Macdonald 1997b). Its major point is that identity, often conceptualised as fixed and inherent, is actually fluid and constructed or produced through ongoing social relationships, subject to ambivalence, diversity and contestation.

As a precursor to her analysis of local Gaelic revitalisation efforts, Macdonald presented ethnographic descriptions of everyday social relations and analyses of local cultural values in the crofting township. She looked at the economic and symbolic roles of crofting in defining members of the community as 'locals', and the way that crofters defined themselves as 'classless' in contrast with 'away' (1997b: 117) while still being keenly aware of local differences in social status and power. She explored how nostalgia, exile and emigration fed back into locals' understandings of place, and incomers' and locals' conflicting understandings of their own identity, belonging and what it meant to be local.

Finally, Macdonald analysed local-level disagreements and controversies over community-oriented Gaelic-related developments in the early to mid-1980s, including the village hall and the community cooperative (*co-chomunn*), which the Highlands and Islands Development Board intended to strengthen Gaelic as well as economic development in communities. Macdonald also described the competing English and Gaelic playgroups, and local parents' doubt and ambivalence over the Bilingual Education Project which was introduced on Skye in 1978. Macdonald showed how people constructed their opposing positions on these developments with reference to local cultural values and social relations (1997b: 220). For example, in 1986 there was an existing playgroup in the crofting township. Two women helped to start a new *cròileagan* with newly available HIDB funding, to provide a more intentionally Gaelic-medium and structured learning environment for their own children and others in the community. The women, who were both native Gaelic speakers (one raised in the township and the other elsewhere on Skye) articulated a number of reasons for wanting the playgroup. One criticised other local parents for 'not bothering' with Gaelic (228). The other, concerned that her three-year-old refused to speak Gaelic to her, worried that as a Gaelic teacher she would be judged negatively for trying to be 'fancy' and teaching her son English (1997b: 230). Local mothers who opposed the new playgroup (whose children could not speak Gaelic for the most part) criticised it on the grounds that they should not be made to feel excluded from the playgroup just because their children did not speak Gaelic and that language should not be used to divide people into different categories, and felt that the *cròileagan* would force the children to speak Gaelic (231). Macdonald identified a cultural repertoire of shared ideas among mothers on both sides about egalitarianism in local social relations (the avoidance of seeming 'fancy'), the autonomy of children (in which education would provide the chance for their natural abilities to emerge), and disapproval of 'pushing' and 'forcing' children or adults to do anything (223–5, 232). Later, some mothers who initially opposed it ended up joining the Gaelic playgroup (243).[18]

There is also apparent conflict between attitudes and actions in support of Gaelic. Public support for Gaelic is now seen as a positive thing, and many people will make verbal expressions of support for Gaelic – but decline to speak it regularly themselves. Some will teach it to others, or conduct other paid employment through the medium of Gaelic, while not speaking it regularly to their children or sending them to a Gaelic-medium playgroup or school (Coleman 1975: 229–30; McEwan-Fujita 2003: 116–18). As already discussed in the previous section, Mertz explains this conflict through the concept of 'metapragmatic beliefs'. Using theories about the differing levels of awareness that speakers have about the various structures and sociolinguistic functions of the languages they speak, Mertz theorises that some beliefs about language are so deeply ingrained that speakers simply do not have conscious access to them (1982a: 261–272). They may deny holding such beliefs even if they are explicitly confronted with them. Local cultural concerns may also simply not include a need to explain language shift in the community, or culturally relevant explanations may have been developed that do not match the ethnographic observations – for example, attributing to children themselves the choice not to speak Gaelic (Macdonald 1997: 223–5), even though children are linguistically socialised by their caregivers (Kulick 1992). Therefore, although Fishman (1991) included 'prior ideological clarification' as a precursor to undertaking ethnolingusitic revitalisation efforts, paradoxes and ideological conflict are in fact endemic to the process and it seems likely that such clarification may not be possible (Dauenhauer and Dauenhauer 1998).

Another problem of Gaelic revitalisation efforts noted in sociolinguistic ethnographies is a lack of coordination between various efforts across geographical space and across time (Coleman 1975: 225; Mertz 1982a). This fragmentation and lack of coordination may be a function of several issues, including the fact that due to historical prejudices and the unwillingness to commit financial resources, few regional or national-level governments give full funding, legal and logistical support to minority language movements (for the example of education, see critiques in Pollock 2006). The diversity in attitudes and experiences among Gaelic speakers also contributes to the fragmentation, as Coleman noted (1975: 225); in both Scotland and Nova Scotia, there has tended to be an ideological gap between urban and rural priorities, approaches and concepts. Mertz's study of Gaelic-speaking communities in Cape Breton documented the scattered and uncoordinated local-level revitalisation efforts in Nova Scotia from the nineteenth century to the late 1970s (1982a: 187–227). An additional factor in Cape Breton was a split between the Catholic west and south areas of Cape Breton, oriented towards Gaelic media from Antigonish, and the Protestant North Shore oriented towards the Sydney and Baddeck media and the Gaelic College (Mertz 1982a: 210; Campbell and MacLean 1974: 222).

The role of 'outsiders' of various kinds in ethnolinguistic revitalisation presents us with another layer of complexity. Non-Gaelic speakers may be the ones to have denigrated the language in the first place, but other outsiders can help to restore social (and economic) value to the language, both to the outside world and in the eyes of speakers themselves. Mertz noted the contribution to the Cape Breton Gaelic revival of the urban and even international 'outsiders', including hippies, 'U.S.ers', and folklorists who visited and moved to Cape Breton, learned Gaelic and collected folklore, and demonstrated that some people outside of Cape Breton saw Gaelic as worthwhile (Mertz 1982a: 199). However, research in anthropology and ethnomusicology (Dembling 2005; Sparling 2003) reveals that the cultural orientations and priorities of native Gaelic speakers can be quite different from those of non-native speakers and non-Gaelic speakers. The latter groups, who are usually stronger in numbers or influence, may ironically end up imposing their own conceptions of 'authentic' Gaelic culture onto the native Gaelic speakers, despite holding them up as paragons of authenticity, for example in regard to what constitutes the best or most authentic traditional Gaelic music and song. This is the paradox of minority language revitalisation efforts: the more they proceed, the more they run the risk of marginalising the cultural practices, views and experiences of the very people whose language and culture they are meant to help (Eckert 1983).

According to a Corsican saying, saving the minoritised Corsican language is 'as difficult as castrating a grasshopper' (Jaffe 1996: 824). Nonetheless, based on the cases of Scottish and Irish Gaelic, Dorian (1987) takes the view that language revitalisation efforts are culturally useful, valuable and laudable, even if they are not succeeding in reversing language shift. She has even advocated in the face of some opposition within her discipline that linguists who study minority languages and language shift could usefully take a position of advocacy, following the lead of speakers themselves, because when a researcher is working directly with speakers (or indeed collaborating with governments), there is no such thing as a neutral position (Dorian 1993a; Dorian 1994a).

On the whole, sociolinguistic ethnographies of Gaelic are descriptive of speakers, practices and contexts, rather than normative or prescriptive (though some make recommendations for best practice in revitalisation). But the disagreement in Gaelic-speaking communities that is documented by academics is sometimes interpreted by the national media, other outsiders, or community members themselves as pathological, rather than as a sign of a healthy, vigorous diversity (Macdonald 1997b).[19] Sometimes, 'the Gaelic community' is held to an unrealistic standard, expected to show a united public face to the rest of the world (Macdonald 1997a). However, as Macdonald points out, it would only be logical for all Gaelic speakers to support all revitalisation efforts if one assumes that Gaelic determines one's identity to the exclusion of everything else – a nineteenth-century romantic nationalist model of ethnolinguistic identity (Macdonald 1997b: 50–1, 219–20, 240–2).

In addition to studying the reception of revitalisation efforts in traditional communities, sociolinguistic ethnographies of Gaelic revitalisation have explored the new and changing contexts of use for Gaelic in institutions of education, the media, development and language planning, with a focus on workplaces, classrooms and the new and changing ideologies of participants. This represents a shift away from the traditional village study paradigm, to the study of new and emerging Gaelic 'communities of practice' (Eckert and McConnell-Ginet 1992; Wenger 1998; Oliver forthcoming) bound together by a shared workplace, a shared status as students on a course, or shared interests, values, or goals defined around the Gaelic language, and not necessarily by co-residence in a geographically bounded community – or even a shared level of Gaelic language proficiency.

Several recent studies of Gaelic-language and Gaelic-medium educational practices, which are by definition oriented towards revitalisation of the language, have focused on institutions, classroom practices and students using a sociolinguistic ethnographic approach or survey informed by field experience (Gossen 2001; Oliver 2002; Pollock 2006). Other studies have focused on the attributes and experiences of adult Gaelic learners outside of institutional contexts (MacCaluim 2007; McEwan-Fujita forthcoming).

Pollock (2006) conducted ethnographic research on the acquisition of Gaelic literacy in seven Gaelic-medium classrooms ranging from Primary 1 to 3 located in six local authority areas, together with interviews and questionnaires of parents, teachers and education authorities.[20] She described and analysed the available resources, the teaching techniques used to teach literacy, the behaviour of pupils, and the physical and sociolinguistic environment of the classrooms and the schools. While the Gaelic-medium education (GME) system appeared to be 'largely successful' in its goals stated in the National Guidelines for Gaelic 5–14 (Pollock 2006: 218), and literacy teaching in GME had made 'significant progress', Pollock concluded that there were still a number of issues for concern. The first was uneven teacher training, which resulted in a wide range of teacher practices and competencies in the classroom. The second was a shortage of classroom resources, including Gaelic storybooks and reference books such as dictionaries

(240). The third was not enough reading aloud in Gaelic taking place outside the school environment (243). Pollock cautioned that due to the limitations of her study, it was not possible to determine more than tentatively whether GME was successful in revitalising Gaelic, but due to a range of factors and since the P1–P3 students were not reading Gaelic independently outside the school, 'The children's academic success cannot ... be equated with the level of language use needed for Gaelic to be reinstated as a community language' (239).

The research of James Oliver has focused on the contextual and contingent nature of identities and the Gaelic language and culture (Oliver 2002, 2005, 2006, forthcoming).[21] His work aims to challenge the traditional bounded ideas about Gaelic and identity, showing instead how 'multiple communities of practice ... overlap with and extend beyond any bounded notion of Gaelic (as language, culture or community)' (Oliver forthcoming). In other words, there is not a single Gaelic community, but Gaelic communi*ties*, and even the most structured language planning efforts must take account of the multiplicity and constant change (Oliver forthcoming).

Oliver's dissertation research on Gaelic and young people's negotiations of identity was based on qualitative interviews and focus groups in the field with secondary pupils in Skye and Glasgow in 2000 (Oliver 2002). He found that the young people he interviewed felt themselves to be Scottish, and thought of Gaelic as Scottish, but this in itself did not motivate them to learn Gaelic or actually speak it outside of school. The Glasgow interviewees were more likely to identify themselves or others as 'Gaels' purely on the basis of linguistic proficiency, while Skye interviewees were more likely to take family heritage and place into account, but again, this did not imply any increase in Gaelic usage. Gaelic-medium education had not made these young people fluent in Gaelic, which supports Pollock's conclusions above, and the learners were not really keen to become Gaelic speakers in the future. There were differences between how young people in Skye and Glasgow viewed Gaelic, but overall, for the fluent speakers, Gaelic was 'not used greatly' at home, and 'sparsely used', if at all, at school (Oliver 2002: 164).[22] In Skye, the local community networks of Gaelic and the social meaning of place were important in the definition of a 'Gaelic identity'. By contrast, in Glasgow, 'a supra-community of dispersed Gaelic speakers and Gaelic learners' (167) rather than a traditional crofting community, linguistic ability was most important in the definition of a 'Gaelic identity', with a distinct focus on the Gaelic media (and the possibility of getting a job).

The sociolinguistic bottom line, and 'the dilemma for assessing Gaelic revival, then, is this: increasing the number of young people able to speak Gaelic does not directly equate with the reversal of language shift' (Oliver 2002: 169). Oliver concludes that while GME can be highly supportive of Gaelic in families, nevertheless a Gaelic-speaking family unit and a Gaelic-speaking geographically bounded local community giving a 'local sense of relevance' are essential to intergenerational transmission of the language (171).

Andrew Gossen's (2001) PhD dissertation in anthropology was an ethnography of Sabhal Mòr Ostaig, the Gaelic college on the Isle of Skye (hereafter SMO), based on archival research, interviews and nine months of participant observation on the *Cùrsa Comais* in 1998–9. This was also the first year of the new Gaelic and Related Studies Scheme BA degree courses[23] of which the Cùrsa Comais had newly become a part. Gossen's study focused on 'student response to the new degree courses and the problems that surfaced at the college during a period of dramatic institutional change', setting students' experiences in the context of the history of the 'maverick' institution and its relatively recent and ongoing integration into the University of the Highlands and Islands Millennium Project as it was known at the time of his fieldwork (Gossen 2001: iii). Gossen concluded that SMO as an institution was so internally diverse that it could not be approached and analysed through a single theoretical approach (290).

Gossen described the structure of the new four-year degree courses, the first ever to be offered entirely through the medium of Gaelic, and their role in the larger curriculum of an institution 'devoted to revitalisation'. The aim of the degree course was to 'cultivate a particular worldview that is centered on the Highlands and Islands instead of the traditional foci of Edinburgh or London', and to train future leaders of the Highlands and Islands 'to define and address local problems' in order to 'bring about the social, cultural, and economic revival of the area' (Gossen 2001: 296). On the basis of his study of this strategy, Gossen pointed out that although revitalisation is a social movement, analysts must focus not only on mass participation, but also on 'strategic positioning' (and, I would add, on the efforts of key individuals doing the positioning) in order to understand how Gaelic language revitalisation efforts work (298).

Gossen's ethnography described the staff, faculty and students of that academic year, a group that shared a commitment to Gaelic language and culture and to SMO, but who also held quite different understandings of what the mission and goals of SMO were. The views varied from rigid and essentialising to open and constructivist, and caused interpersonal conflict to erupt at times over contradictions between SMO's various missions and constituencies.

Gossen also explored the dilemmas of tertiary-level education through the medium of a minority language, which included in this case problems with using Gaelic in tertiary-education courses in which the bulk of course readings were in English, issues of coining new academic terminology for areas like social science, students' difficulty writing research papers in Gaelic based on reading materials in English, and the difficulty of finding instructors with both the necessary academic background and linguistic skills to teach university-level courses in Gaelic (Gossen 2001: 128–9). Students were also not happy about being used as test subjects for the new degree course, as they felt was the case.

All of these ethnographies of Gaelic education note one crucial point: that pupils and students for the most part were not speaking Gaelic outside of the school, and at the school for the most part were only speaking Gaelic to the teacher in the classroom. Gossen (2001: 149) describes how the patterns of language choice among students at SMO were impacted by the presence or absence of the 'institutional gaze' – in other words, when college staff were within earshot, Cùrsa Comais students tended to converse in Gaelic, but in private, all but a few habitually spoke English with one another (149). These findings underline a number of points about language revitalisation: (1) how difficult it is to engineer an all-encompassing sociolinguistic environment, even in the 'bubble' of a residential college, when surrounded by a dominant language and culture; (2) how difficult it is to linguistically socialise, or re-socialise, people when there is no single compelling ideological motivation to unify them; and (3) the fact that one cannot rely on a single institution or 'fix' to 'save' a language.

Alasdair MacCaluim's (2007) study of adults learning Gaelic generates a detailed demographic description of Gaelic learners inside and outside Scotland, with the large number of open-ended comments by respondents providing a particularly interesting window on the learners' experiences.[24] MacCaluim analysed the social identity of Gaelic learners as such, describing how the categories of 'learner' and 'native speaker' are culturally constructed (2007: 102). He explored the difficulty of acquiring Gaelic as an adult; this is due to several factors, among them fragmented provision in Scotland, the challenges of acquiring a language after the 'critical period' of childhood, and a lack of interaction between learners and native speakers. A number of open-ended survey responses mentioned tension between learners and native speakers, which manifests in learners' complaints that native speakers do not always support their efforts. Indeed, learners challenge popular and traditional views of the contexts where Gaelic is appropriate (89), namely the home-family-crofting community nexus and the Hebridean islands. MacCaluim discusses how learners could contribute to reversal of language shift and act as 'consciousness raisers' for the language (93), in the process finding their own social identities evolving as their linguistic proficiency increases (97). While MacCaluim treats adult Gaelic learners as a national and even international group, those who live in traditional crofting communities seem to face greater barriers in their efforts to construct their own meanings for Gaelic. McEwan-Fujita (2010) identifies emotional stances of wariness, blame and shame in adult learners' descriptions of their community-based Gaelic learning experiences in the Western Isles. These adult learners are socialised by Gaelic-speaking family members and community members into the etiquette of accommodation, in ways that make it difficult for them to speak Gaelic regularly and thus contribute to language revitalisation in traditional Gaelic-speaking communities.

Konstanze Glaser's (2007) comparison of Gaelic and Sorbian minority language revitalisation efforts takes a broad ideological perspective on issues of cultural and linguistic distinctiveness as perceived by members of linguistic minorities. The Gaelic portion of her study was based on interviews with fifty-three Gaelic 'elites' (defined as members of Gaelic-oriented societies, journalists, academics, artists, teachers, school and nursery staff, parents, and students of the language) across Scotland, together with a survey of teachers and parents involved in Gaelic-medium education, collection of relevant media materials, and non-systematic participant observation, with similar research performed on Sorbian in the former East Germany (Glaser 2007: 7–10). Glaser collated and presented the views of minority cultural 'elites' on the relationship of the minority language to thought, culture and self, the relative importance of linguistic and cultural continuity, and the role of language as a source of social and cultural boundaries. Echoing the insights of Macdonald (1997a) and Oliver (2002), Glaser concluded that two conflicting paradigms, (1) essentialising and (2) dynamic/situationalist, characterise minority language community leaders' views about the role of language in identity. The former requires a cultural purism and 'heartlandism' (Glaser 2007: 305–6) that focus on 'Gaelic or Sorbian culture as clearly delineated sets of traditional practices' (6), while the latter encourages hybridity, openness and language-focused views that may be less respectful of ethnocultural unity, but may be of more help in ensuring that 'some kind of 'Gaelic' and 'Sorbian' will still be spoken several generations down the line' (6). Despite the continued popularity of essentialism, Glaser identifies a move towards the latter paradigm among minority language 'campaigners and agencies', which she says they view as a 'pragmatic compromise' (308); this is the difficult tightrope that minority language advocates must walk in the twenty-first century.

Based on field research in Uist crofting communities and a language planning organisation in the Western Isles, Inverness and Glasgow, McEwan-Fujita (2003; 2005) explored the impact of neoliberalism on Gaelic language revitalisation in connection with local and regional economic development. Neoliberalism, broadly defined, is a mode of governance that 'involves extending and disseminating market values to all institutions and social action' (Brown 2003). McEwan-Fujita traced the incorporation of Gaelic as a priority into the Highlands and Islands Development Board's mission of economic development, the founding of Comunn na Gàidhlig, and the roles of CNAG and HIDB (later Highlands and Islands Enterprise) in conceptualising the 'Gaelic economy' according to the quantifiable measures of neoliberalism promoted under Thatcher, Major and Blair, such as the number of full-time equivalent jobs created (2003; 2005). Since the 1980s language planners have commonly promoted Gaelic as a skill, asset, or commodity that can aid in the economic development of Scotland (and conversely detractors have portrayed it as a waste of public money). Oliver found that secondary pupils in Glasgow perceived Gaelic 'largely … as a skill and an opportunity provider' (2002: 172), and this is consonant with changes in the approach to minority languages elsewhere (Heller 2006). Unfortunately, the neoliberal approach has resulted in revitalisation efforts that are successful in obtaining EU funding, but due to restrictions on the lengths and types of funding given (which in the case of Objective One 1994–1999 included infrastructure, but never specific minority language support), they are not always able to take into account sociolinguistic aspects of actual Gaelic use. Consequently, some programmes can contribute little to the reversal of language shift. Oliver concurs, concluding that revitalisation is not 'dependent on a technical or structural intervention' (forthcoming: 18–19).

McEwan-Fujita set her study against the backdrop of public media discourse about Gaelic in Scotland, finding that negative stereotypes of Gaelic, some of which originated as early as the sixteenth century, continued to circulate in the Scottish media even into the twenty-first century (McEwan-Fujita 2003: 159–231). For example, journalists have taken linguists' well-meaning warnings about the loss of endangered languages and transformed them into spurious 'scientific' evidence of the death of Gaelic (McEwan-Fujita 2006). Revitalisation efforts have portrayed Gaelic in rejoinder as natural, ancient, more expressive than English, Scotland's national language, and more recently as a precious natural resource akin to an endangered species (McEwan-Fujita 2003). This discourse analysis of the media representations of Gaelic follows in the tradition of textual analyses by Malcolm Chapman (1978, 1993), Parman (1990, 2005: 32–47), and Macdonald (1997a: 33–66) which have explored the historical and cultural construction of the Gael and the Celt as symbols of otherness and romantic but tokenistic national essence in Scotland.

Within the revitalisation-focused institutions of the media, education and development, new linguistic forms and new contexts of use emerge, which may coalesce into new registers of Gaelic. A register may be defined as 'a variety of a language associated with situation and purpose' (Lamb 1999). Using interviews, recordings and original news scripts, Lamb (1999) traced the historical development of the register of Gaelic radio 'news-speak' and the relationship between its changing institutional context and content, including professionalisation, the strong influence of the BBC, and changes in linguistic forms including the lexicon, the genitive case, syntax, dialect and accent, and prosodic features. McEwan-Fujita (2008) described the speakers, context and ideology of the register of white-collar workplace Gaelic as it was emerging through the daily experiences of workers in the offices of a Gaelic language planning organisation. The workers had developed a variety of strategies for negotiating between constructing a new 'professional Gaelic' and remaining true to their own linguistic socialisation, which for many of them was in Hebridean island-based domains of family and village-level community (McEwan-Fujita 2008: 86–7).

More recently, Lamb conducted a comprehensive study of late twentieth-century register variation in spoken and written Gaelic, based on the collection of examples of naturally occurring discourse in the field (Lamb 2008). Lamb identified spoken registers of conversation, radio interviews, radio sports reporting and traditional narrative, and written registers of fiction, formal prose, radio news scripts and popular writing, and described these based on a quantitative tabulation of linguistic features such as clause types and information structure, morphosyntax, lexicon, and noun phrase grammar and complexity. Lamb's study found that despite the endangerment of Gaelic, its register variation was comparable in level to major languages such as English, and it shared with English universal patterns of variation. These findings contribute to linguistic knowledge and also serve the social purpose of countering denigrating views of Gaelic.

REPRESENTATION, DIVERSITY OF RESEARCH AUDIENCE, AND CONTINUITY

Issues of power and representation are key in the sociolinguistic ethnography of Gaelic communities. Research always creates an unequal power relationship between the researcher and his or her 'subjects' or 'informants', because the researcher holds the power to represent the community and its members to a wider audience (Clifford and Marcus 1986). Contemporary social scientists tend to focus on the diversity of opinions and practices in a community, and the processes of contestation (that is, power struggles) through which language and culture are enacted. Subjects of a study may disagree with the author's analysis and/or be unhappy with the portrayal of themselves, others, or their community or institution (for example, see Black 1998, MacCaluim 1998, Macleod 2004).

Dishearteningly, the researcher's promise to protect subjects through anonymity may be almost meaningless in such a densely interconnected social network of institutions and rural communities that are also well-informed by the media and connected to the internet. Even when the author gives pseudonyms and changes identifying details, readers familiar with *saoghal na Gàidhlig* will probably scan the text closely for clues to the true identity of subjects. Some researchers delay or abandon the effort to write up their research on Gaelic language shift partially out of reluctance to offend their subjects or a fear of compromising the goals of Gaelic revitalisation. They so do in the awareness that delay or failure to complete the thesis or publish a book can spell the end of their academic career.[25]

Research techniques are ubiquitous in twenty-first century Gaelic-speaking communities, and community members may also feel 'research fatigue'. Research is carried out not only by academics, but also by journalists, management consultants, and even by school pupils doing local investigation projects (McEwan-Fujita 2003: 59). Ordinary people are increasingly using research as a tool to constitute their own understanding of themselves as Gaelic speakers, and as members of a community, whether they want to or not. But outside researchers are still the focus of grievances over the unequal power relationship of research.[26]

The diversity of audiences for research on Gaelic, and the diversity of disciplinary perspectives from which is it conducted, also constitute major challenges for researchers. Sociolinguistic perspectives have been increasingly acknowledged and included in Celtic studies departments over the past two decades, and the biannual Rannsachadh na Gàidhlig conference has been making increasing contributions in this area since its inception in 2000.[27] However, the difficulty of cross-disciplinary communication remains, made all the more difficult by the obligation of social science researchers to use specialised terminology, engage with the latest theories, publish in the journals of their own field, and contribute to general theoretical knowledge in their discipline, knowledge that may be of little interest or practical use to Gaelic speakers in general, or language planners in particular.

Finally, continuity has been a major problem in studies of Gaelic communities. Although Dorian and MacKinnon have each sustained their focus on Gaelic-related research for decades, they are the exception rather than the rule (and MacKinnon turned to the statistical analysis of survey and census data). Several individuals have changed career paths before or after completing a PhD thesis, many have stayed within academia but substantially changed their research focus, and most have never published a great deal beyond the dissertation or thesis and perhaps an article or two. Some of the reasons why may be apparent in the topics already discussed. Fraser MacDonald, a geographer whose fieldwork in North Uist went unpublished, maintains that 'Ethnography is surely one of the most personally difficult, as well as one of the most ambitious, forms of intellectual enquiry ...' (MacDonald 2004: 159). Whatever the reasons, this lack of continuity represents a shortcoming in the sociolinguistic ethnography of Gaelic communities that remains to be overcome.

CONCLUSIONS AND FUTURE DIRECTIONS

A number of recommendations can be made for future studies. More research is needed on the actual proficiencies, usage patterns and ideologies of Gaelic speakers in residential community contexts, since language shift is so much further underway than in the early 1980s when the last 'community studies' were conducted. Overall, more of the ethnography of communication in everyday life is needed for the twenty-first century. For example, how do people use Gaelic on the job, in both Gaelic-essential and Gaelic non-essential occupations?[28] How are children linguistically socialised and educated in Gaelic?[29] For that matter, how are adults (McEwan-Fujita forthcoming)? Following Pollock's (2006) line of inquiry, how is Gaelic literacy taught, learned, used and conceptualised? Gaelic language standardisation, an ideological as well as technological process (Milroy and Milroy 1999), should be explored ethnographically as well as from historical and language planning perspectives.

We should also be examining interconnections between and differences within Gaelic communities. Lines of division such as rural and urban, Presbyterian and Catholic, 'learner' and 'native speaker', Old World and New World, should be acknowledged, questioned and analysed, for we may find that the flows of people, ideas and practices *across* these historically and socially constructed boundaries make them as interesting and illuminating to study as the boundary construction process itself. In order to understand the complex, simultaneous processes of language shift and revitalisation, we must maintain and refine the classic methodologies, concepts and concerns of sociolinguistic ethnography, while incorporating rigorous contemporary social theory from a range of disciplines concerned with language in sociocultural context. For example, care should be taken not to utilise 'identity' as a unit of analysis or an explanatory concept; if people are making language-based claims and ascriptions of identity, then that is an ethnographic fact that must be analysed, not used in circular fashion as an explanation for linguistic behaviour (see Bucholtz and Hall 2006; Kiesling 2006).

Greater coordination and language-training support is also needed for researchers to attain higher levels of proficiency in spoken Gaelic prior to undertaking field research. The fragmented provision for adult learners described by MacCaluim (2007) impacts would-be researchers from the US and elsewhere, as does the difficulty and expense of obtaining funding for Celtic language training outside of university Celtic and Gaelic departments. Support for language training of sociolinguistic researchers would not only enhance the quality of research, but also help to normalise the idea that in order to do research on Gaelic speakers, one should acquire linguistic proficiency in Gaelic – an idea that has been marginalised in Scottish popular opinion and academia, but seems only logical to sociolinguistic researchers.[30]

This chapter can be no more than a snapshot in time of studies of Gaelic speakers and communities. It is hoped that ten or twenty years after its publication, such studies will be even more abundant, even better integrated into Gaelic and Celtic studies, and given even stronger consideration in language planning efforts. At the same time, researchers also need to maintain a place in the academy outside the realm of policy making, so that they may provide an independent perspective on Gaelic revitalisation efforts. Sociolinguistic ethnography is challenging to research and write, and the participants do not always agree with its findings. But the value of ethnographic field research on

Gaelic speakers has been well established and should have a secure place in twenty-first century Gaelic studies. Students and scholars of Celtic and the social sciences have much to offer one another through mutual understanding, cooperation and collaboration.

BIBLIOGRAPHY

Ardener, Edwin (1989), 'The Voice of Prophecy: Further Problems in the Analysis of Events', in Edwin Ardener, *The Voice of Prophecy and Other Essays*, Malcolm Chapman (ed.), Oxford: Blackwell, pp. 134–54.

Ardener, Edwin (2007), *The Voice of Prophecy and Other Essays*, 2nd edn, Malcolm Chapman (ed.), Oxford: Berghahn Books.

Black, Ronald (1994), 'Bog, Loch and River: The Nature of Reform in Scottish Gaelic', in István Fodor and Claude Hagège (eds), *Language Reform: History and Future*, Vol. 6, Hamburg: Helmut Buske Verlag, pp. 123–48.

Black, Ronnie (1998), 'Tàmailt air' [Review of *Reimagining Culture* by Sharon Macdonald], *Scotsman*, 15 April, p. 14.

Brown, Wendy (2003), 'Neoliberalism and the End of Liberal Democracy', *Theory and Event* 7(1), Electronic document, http://muse.jhu.edu/login?uri/=journals/theory_and_event/v007/7.1brown.html (accessed 17 July 2009).

Bucholtz, Mary and Hall, Kira (2006), 'Identity and Interaction: A Sociocultural Linguistic Approach', *Discourse Studies* 7:4–5, pp. 585–614.

Callan, Hilary (2004), 'Ardener, Edwin William', in H. C. G. Matthew and Brian Harrison (eds), *Oxford Dictionary of National Biography*, New York: Oxford University Press, pp. 365–6.

Campbell, D. and MacLean, R. A. (1974), *Beyond the Atlantic Roar: A Study of the Nova Scotia Scots,* Toronto: McClelland & Stewart.

Campbell, John Lorne (1950), *Gaelic in Scottish Education and Life: Past, Present and Future,* Edinburgh: W. & A. K. Johnston Ltd.

Chapman, Malcolm (1978), *The Gaelic Vision in Scottish Culture*, Montreal: McGill-Queen's University Press.

Chapman, Malcolm (1989), 'Introduction', in Edwin Ardener, *The Voice of Prophecy and Other Essays*, Malcolm Chapman (ed.), Oxford: Blackwell, pp. vii–xxviii.

Chapman, Malcolm (1993), *The Celts: The Construction of a Myth*, New York: St. Martin's Press.

Clifford, James and Marcus, George E. (eds) (1986), *Writing Culture: The Poetics and Politics of Ethnography,* Berkeley: University of California Press.

Cole, John W. (1977), 'Anthropology Comes Part-Way Home: Community Studies in Europe', *Annual Review of Anthropology* 6, pp. 349–78.

Coleman, Jack David Bo (1975), 'Language Shift in a Bilingual Hebridean Crofting Community', PhD dissertation, University of Massachusetts.

Condry, Edward (1983), *Scottish Ethnography*, Association for Scottish Ethnography Monographs, no. 1, Edinburgh: Social Science Research Council.

Constantinidou, Evi (1994), 'The "Death" of East Sutherland Gaelic: Death by Women?', in Pauline Burton, Ketaki Kushari Dyson and Shirley Ardener (eds), *Bilingual Women: Anthropological Approaches to Second Language Use*, Providence: Berg, pp. 111–27.

Dauenhauer, Nora Marks and Dauenhauer, Richard (1998), 'Technical, Emotional, and Ideological Issues in Reversing Language Shift: Examples from Southeast Alaska', in Lenore A. Grenoble and Lindsey J. Whaley (eds), *Endangered Languages: Current Issues and Future Prospects*, Cambridge: Cambridge University Press, pp. 57–116.

Dembling, Jonathan (2005), 'You Play It As You Would Sing It: Cape Breton, Scottishness and the Means of Cultural Production', in Celeste Ray (ed.), *Transatlantic Scots*, Tuscaloosa: University of Alabama Press, pp. 180–97.

Dorian, Nancy C. (1970), 'A Substitute Name System in the Scottish Highlands', *American Anthropologist* 72, pp. 303–19.

Dorian, Nancy C. (1972), 'A Hierarchy of Morphophonemic Decay in Scottish Gaelic Language Death: The Differential Failure of Lenition', *Word: Journal of the International Linguistic Association* 28, pp. 96–109.

Dorian, Nancy C. (1973), 'Grammatical Change in a Dying Dialect', *Language* 49, pp. 413–38.

Dorian, Nancy C. (1977), 'The Problem of the Semi-speaker in Language Death', *International Journal of the Sociology of Language* 12, pp. 23–32.

Dorian, Nancy C. (1978a), 'The Dying Dialect and the Role of the Schools: East Sutherland Gaelic and Pennsylvania Dutch', in J. E. Alatis (ed.), *International Dimensions of Bilingual Education. Georgetown University Round Table on Languages and Linguistics (Washington, D.C., 1978)*, Washington, DC: Georgetown University Press, pp. 646–56.

Dorian, Nancy C. (1978b), *East Sutherland Gaelic*, Dublin: Dublin Institute for Advanced Studies.

Dorian, Nancy C. (1978c), 'The Fate of Morphological Complexity in Language Death', *Language* 54:3, pp. 590–609.

Dorian, Nancy C. (1978d), 'The Preservation of the Vocative in a Dying Gaelic Dialect', *Scottish Gaelic Studies* 13 (Part 1), pp. 98–102.

Dorian, Nancy C. (1978e), Review of Kenneth MacKinnon, 'Language, Education and Social Processes in a Gaelic Community', *Language in Society* 7, pp. 137–40.

Dorian, Nancy C. (1980a), 'Language Shift in Community and Individual: The Phenomenon of the Laggard Semi-Speaker', *International Journal of the Sociology of Language* 25, pp. 85–94.

Dorian, Nancy C. (1980b), 'Linguistic Lag as an Ethnic Marker', *Language in Society* 9, pp. 33–41.

Dorian, Nancy C. (1981a), *Language Death: The Life Cycle of a Scottish Gaelic Dialect,* Philadelphia: University of Pennsylvania Press.

Dorian, Nancy C. (1981b), 'The Valuation of Gaelic by Different Mother-Tongue Groups Resident in the Highlands', *Scottish Gaelic Studies* 8, pp. 169–82.

Dorian, Nancy C. (1982a), 'Defining the Speech Community to Include Its Working Margins', in Suzanne Romaine (ed.), *Sociolinguistic Variation in Speech Communities*, London: E. Arnold, pp. 25–33.

Dorian, Nancy C. (1982b), 'Language Loss and Maintenance in Language Contact Situations', in Richard D. Lambert and Barbara F. Freed (eds), *The Loss of Language Skills*, Rowley, MA: Newbury House Publishers, pp. 44–59.

Dorian, Nancy C. (1985), *The Tyranny of Tide,* Ann Arbor: Karoma Publishers, Inc.

Dorian, Nancy C. (1986), 'Making Do with Less: Some Surprises Along the Language Death Proficiency Continuum', *Applied Psycholinguistics* 7, pp. 257–76.

Dorian, Nancy C. (1987), 'The Value of Language-Maintenance Efforts Which Are Unlikely to Succeed', *International Journal of the Sociology of Language* 68, pp. 57–67.

Dorian, Nancy C. (ed.) (1989), *Investigating Obsolescence: Studies in Language Contraction and Death,* New York: Cambridge University Press.

Dorian, Nancy C. (1990), 'Writing without Reading: An Illiterate Imperfect Speaker's Adventures in Writing Gaelic', in A. T. E. Matonis and Daniel F. Melia (eds), *Celtic Language, Celtic Culture: A Festschrift for Eric P. Hamp*, Van Nuys, CA: Ford & Bailie, pp. 218–44.

Dorian, Nancy C. (1993a), 'A Response to Ladefoged's Other View of Endangered Languages', *Language* 69, pp. 575–9.

Dorian, Nancy C. (1993b), 'Stylistic Variation in a Language Restricted to Private-Sphere Use', in Douglas Biber and Edward Finegan (eds), *Sociolinguistic Perspectives on Register*, Oxford: Oxford University Press, pp. 217–32.

Dorian, Nancy C. (1994a), 'Comment: Choices and Values in Language Shift and Its Study', *International Journal of the Sociology of Language* 110, pp. 113–24.

Dorian, Nancy C. (1994b), 'Varieties of Variation in a Very Small Place: Social Homogeneity, Prestige Norms, and Linguistic Variation', *Language* 70, pp. 631–96.

Dorian, Nancy C. (1997), 'Telling the Monolinguals from the Bilinguals: Unrealistic Code Choices in Direct Quotations within Scottish Gaelic Narratives', *International Journal of Bilingualism* 1, pp. 41–54.

Dorian, Nancy C. (1998), 'Western Language Ideologies and Small-Language Prospects', in Lenore A. Grenoble and Lindsey J. Whaley (eds), *Endangered Languages: Current Issues and Future Prospects*, Cambridge: Cambridge University Press, pp. 3–21.

Dorian, Nancy C. (2001), 'Surprises in Sutherland: Linguistic Variability amidst Social Uniformity', in Paul Newman and Martha Ratliff (eds), *Linguistic Fieldwork*, Cambridge: Cambridge University Press, pp. 133–51.

Dorian, Nancy C. (2009), Personal communication (e-mail correspondence), 12 January and 30 July.

Dorian, Nancy C. (forthcoming a), 'Age and Speaker Skills in Receding Languages: How Far Do Community Evaluations and Linguists' Evaluations Agree?', *International Journal of the Sociology of Language*.

Dorian, Nancy C. (forthcoming b), *Investigating Variation: The Effects of Social Organization and Social Setting*, Oxford: Oxford University Press.

Ducey, Paul (1956), 'Cultural Continuity and Population Change on the Isle of Skye', PhD dissertation, New York: Columbia University.

Dunn, Charles W. (1953), *Highland Settler: A Portrait of the Scottish Gael in Nova Scotia,* Toronto: University of Toronto Press.

Durkacz, Victor (1983), *The Decline of the Celtic Languages: A Study of Linguistic and Cultural Conflict in Scotland, Wales and Ireland from the Reformation to the Twentieth Century,* Edinburgh: John Donald Publishers Ltd.

Eckert, Penelope (1983), 'The Paradox of National Language Movements', *Journal of Multilingual and Multicultural Development* 4, pp. 289–300.

Eckert, Penelope and McConnell-Ginet, Sally (1992), 'Think Practically and Look Locally: Language and Gender as Community-Based Practice', *Annual Review of Anthropology* 21, pp. 461–90.

Ennew, Judith (1978), 'The Impact of Oil-Related Industry on the Outer Hebrides, with particular reference to Stornoway, Isle of Lewis', PhD dissertation, Cambridge University.

Ennew, Judith (1980), *The Western Isles Today,* Cambridge: Cambridge University Press.

Fishman, Joshua A. (1965), 'Bilingualism, Intelligence and Language Learning', *The Modern Language Journal,* 49:4, pp. 227–37.

Fishman, Joshua A. (1991), *Reversing Language Shift: Theoretical and Empirical Foundations of Assistance to Threatened Languages,* Clevedon: Multilingual Matters.

Gal, Susan (1978), 'Peasant Men Can't Get Wives: Language Change and Sex Roles in a Bilingual Community', *Language in Society* 7:1, pp. 1–16.

Gal, Susan (1979), *Language Shift: Social Determinants of Linguistic Change in Bilingual Austria.* New York: Academic Press.

Gillies, William (1980), 'English Influences on Contemporary Scottish Gaelic', *Scottish Literary Journal: A Review of Studies in Scottish Language and Literature,* Supplement 12 (Language), pp. 1–12.

Gillies, William (ed.) (1989), *Gaelic and Scotland/Alba agus a' Ghàidhlig,* Edinburgh: Edinburgh University Press.

Glaser, Konstanze (2007), *Minority Languages and Cultural Diversity in Europe: Gaelic and Sorbian Perspectives,* Clevedon: Multilingual Matters.

Gossen, Andrew (2001), 'Agents of a Modern Gaelic Scotland: Curriculum, Change, and Challenge at Sabhal Mòr Ostaig, the Gaelic College of Scotland', PhD dissertation, Harvard University.

Heller, Monica (2006), *Linguistic Minorities and Modernity: A Sociolinguistic Ethnography,* 2nd edn, London: Continuum Books.

Jaffe, Alexandra (1996), 'The Second Annual Corsican Spelling Contest: Orthography and Ideology', *American Ethnologist* 23, pp. 816–35.

Kiesling, Scott (2006), 'Language and Identity in Sociocultural Anthropology', in Keith Brown (ed.), *Encyclopedia of Language and Linguistics,* 2nd edn, Vol. 5, Oxford: Elsevier, pp. 495–502.

Kulick, Don (1992), *Language Shift and Cultural Reproduction: Socialization, Self, and Syncretism in a Papua New Guinean Village,* London: Cambridge University Press.

Lamb, William (1999), 'A Diachronic Account of Gaelic News-speak: The Development and Expansion of a Register', *Scottish Gaelic Studies* 19, pp. 141–71.

Lamb, William (2008), *Scottish Gaelic Speech and Writing: Register Variation in an Endangered Language,* Belfast: Cló Ollscoil na Banríona.

Labov, William (1972), *Sociolinguistic Patterns*, Philadelphia: University of Pennsylvania Press.

MacAulay, Donald (1976–8), 'The Writing of Scottish Gaelic: Uses of Convention and Innovation', *Transactions of the Gaelic Society of Inverness* 50, pp. 81–96.

MacAulay, Donald (1978), 'Intra-Dialectal Variation as an Area of Gaelic Linguistic Research', *Scottish Gaelic Studies* 13 (Part 1), pp. 81–97.

MacAulay, Donald (1979), 'The State of Gaelic Language Studies', in A. J. Aitken and Tom McArthur (eds), *Languages of Scotland*, Edinburgh: W. & R. Chambers, pp. 120–36.

MacAulay, Donald (1982a), 'Borrow, Calque and Switch: The Law of the English Frontier', in John Anderson (ed.), *Language Form and Linguistic Variation. Papers dedicated to Angus Macintosh*, Amsterdam: John Benjamins B. V., pp. 203–37.

MacAulay, Donald (1982b), 'Register Range and Choice in Scottish Gaelic', *International Journal of the Sociology of Language* 35, pp. 25–48.

MacAulay, Donald (1986), 'New Gaelic?' *Scottish Language* 5, pp. 120–5.

MacCaluim, Alasdair (1998), 'A'Cur Clach Chlaon air a'Chàrnan/Adding an Oblique Stone to the Cairn' [Review of *Reimagining Culture* by Sharon Macdonald], *Cothrom* 16, pp. 52–4.

MacCaluim, Alasdair (2007), *Reversing Language Shift: The Social Identity and Role of Scottish Gaelic Learners*, Belfast: Cló Ollscoil na Banríona.

McCoy, Gordon and Scott, Maolcholaim (eds) (2000), *Gaelic Identities/ Aithne na nGael*, Belfast: Institute of Irish Studies, Queen's University Belfast and Ultach Trust/Iontaobhas Ultach.

MacDonald, Fraser (ed.) (2004), 'Colloquium: Susan Parman's *Scottish Crofters: A Historical Ethnography of a Celtic Village*', *Journal of Scottish Historical Studies* 24:2, pp. 159–81.

Macdonald, Sharon (1987), 'Social and Linguistic Identity in the Scottish Gàidhealtachd', PhD dissertation, Oxford University.

Macdonald, Sharon (1997a), 'A People's Story: Heritage, Identity and Authenticity', in Chris Rojek and John Urry (eds), *Touring Cultures: Transformations of Travel and Theory,* New York: Routledge, pp. 155–75.

Macdonald, Sharon (1997b), *Reimagining Culture: Histories, Identities and the Gaelic Renaissance*, Oxford: Berg.

Macdonald, Sharon (1999), '"*A bheil am feur gorm fhathast?*"': Some Problems Concerning Language and Cultural Shift', *Scottish Studies* 33, pp. 186–97.

McEwan-Fujita, Emily (2003), 'Gaelic in Scotland, Scotland in Europe: Minority Language Revitalization in the Age of Neoliberalism', PhD dissertation, University of Chicago.

McEwan-Fujita, Emily (2005), 'Neoliberalism and Minority Language Planning in the Highlands and Islands of Scotland', *International Journal of the Sociology of Language* 171, pp. 155–71.

McEwan-Fujita, Emily (2006), '"Gaelic Doomed as Speakers Die Out"?: The Public Discourse of Gaelic Language Death in Scotland', in Wilson McLeod (ed.), *Revitalising Gaelic in Scotland: Policy, Planning and Public Discourse*, Edinburgh: Dunedin Academic Press, pp. 279–93.

McEwan-Fujita, Emily (2008), '"9 to 5" Gaelic: Speakers, Context, and Ideology of an Emerging Minority Language Register', in Kendall A. King, Natalie Schilling-Estes, Lyn Fogle, Jia Jackie Lou and Barbara Soukup (eds), *Sustaining Linguistic Diversity: Endangered and Minority Languages and Language Varieties*, Washington, DC: Georgetown University Press, pp. 81–93.

McEwan-Fujita, Emily (2010), 'Ideology, Affect and Socialization in Language Shift and Revitalization: The Experiences of Adults Learning Gaelic in the Western Isles of Scotland', *Language in Society* 39:1.

MacGaffey, Wyatt (1991), Review of Malcolm Chapman, Edwin Ardener: *The Voice of Prophecy and Other Essays*, *American Anthropologist* 93:4, pp. 972–73.

MacKinnon, Kenneth (1977), *Language, Education and Social Processes in a Gaelic Community*, London: Routledge and Kegan Paul.

Macleod, Donald (2004), 'Ciall and its Calvinists', in Fraser MacDonald (ed.), 'Colloquium: Susan Parman's *Scottish Crofters: A Historical Ethnography of a Celtic Village*', *Journal of Scottish Historical Studies* 24:2, pp. 172–5.

Meek, Donald E. (1996), 'Saints and Scarecrows: The Churches and Gaelic Culture in the Highlands since 1560', *Scottish Bulletin of Evangelical Theology* 14, pp. 3–22.

Meek, Donald E. (2001), 'The Language of Heaven? The Highland Churches, Culture Shift and the Erosion of Gaelic Identity in the Twentieth Century', in Robert Pope (ed.), *Religion and National Identity: Wales and Scotland c. 1700–2000,* Cardiff: University of Wales Press.

Mertz, Elizabeth (1982a), '"No Burden to Carry": Cape Breton Pragmatics and Metapragmatics (Nova Scotia)', PhD dissertation, Duke University.

Mertz, Elizabeth (1982b), 'Pragmatic and Semantic Change: A Cape Breton System of Personal Names', *Semiotica* 44:1/2, pp. 55–74.

Mertz, Elizabeth (1989), 'Sociolinguistic Creativity: Cape Breton Gaelic's Linguistic "Tip"', in Nancy C. Dorian (ed.), *Investigating Obsolescence: Studies In Language Contraction and Death,* Cambridge: Cambridge University Press, pp. 103–16.

Mertz, Elizabeth (1993), 'Learning What to Ask: Metapragmatic Factors and Methodological Reification', in John Lucy (ed.), *Reflexive Language: Reported Speech and Metapragmatics,* Cambridge: Cambridge University Press, pp. 159–74.

Mewett, Peter G. (1982a), 'Associational Categories and the Social Location of Relationships in a Lewis Crofting Community', in Anthony P. Cohen (ed.), *Belonging: Identity and Social Organisation in British Rural Cultures,* Manchester: Manchester University Press, pp. 101–30.

Mewett, Peter G. (1982b), 'Exiles, Nicknames, Social Identities and the Production of Local Consciousness in a Lewis Crofting Community', in Anthony P. Cohen (ed.), *Belonging: Identity and Social Organisation in British Rural Cultures,* Manchester: Manchester University Press, pp. 222–46.

Milroy, James and Milroy, Lesley (1999), *Authority in Language: Investigating Standard English,* 3rd edn, New York: Routledge.

Morrison, Marion F. (2006), 'A' Chiad Ghinealach – the First Generation: A Survey of Gaelic-medium Education in the Western Isles', in Wilson McLeod (ed.), *Revitalising Gaelic in Scotland: Policy, Planning and Public Discourse,* Edinburgh: Dunedin Academic Press, pp. 139–54.

Müller, Martina (2006), 'Language Use, Language Attitudes and Gaelic Writing Ability Among Secondary Pupils in the Isle of Skye', in Wilson McLeod (ed.), *Revitalising Gaelic in Scotland: Policy, Planning and Public Discourse,* Edinburgh: Dunedin Academic Press, pp. 119–38.

Munro, Gillian (ed.) (forthcoming), *Coimhearsnachd na Gàidhlig An-Diugh/Gaelic Communities Today*, Edinburgh: Dunedin Academic Press.

Oliver, James (2002), 'Young People and Gaelic in Scotland: Identity Dynamics in a European Region', PhD dissertation, University of Sheffield.

Oliver, James (2005), 'Scottish Gaelic Identities: Contexts and Contingencies', *Scottish Affairs* 51, pp. 1–24.

Oliver, James (2006), 'Where Is Gaelic? Revitalisation, Language, Culture and Identity', in Wilson McLeod (ed.), *Revitalising Gaelic in Scotland: Policy, Planning and Public Discourse*, Edinburgh: Dunedin Academic Press, pp. 155–68.

Oliver, James (forthcoming), 'The Predicament? Planning for Culture, Communities and Identities', in Munro (forthcoming).

Parman, Susan (1972), 'Sociocultural Change in a Scottish Crofting Township', PhD dissertation, Rice University.

Parman, Susan (1976), 'General Properties of Naming, and a Specific Case of Nicknaming in the Scottish Outer Hebrides', *Ethnos* 41, pp. 99–115.

Parman, Susan (1990), *Scottish Crofters: A Historical Ethnography of a Celtic Village*, Fort Worth: Holt, Rinehart and Winston, Inc.

Parman, Susan (1993), 'The Future of European Boundaries: A Case Study', in Thomas M. Wilson and M. Estellie Smith (eds), *Cultural Change and the New Europe: Perspectives on the European Community*, Boulder: Westview Press, pp. 189–202.

Parman, Susan (2005), *Scottish Crofters: A Historical Ethnography of a Celtic Village*, 2nd edn, Fort Worth: Holt, Rinehart and Winston, Inc.

Pollock, Irene (2006), 'The Acquisition of Literacy in Gaelic-medium Primary Classrooms in Scotland', PhD dissertation, University of Edinburgh.

Sasse, Hans-Jürgen (1992), 'Theory of Language Death', in Matthias Brenzinger (ed.), *Language Death: Factual and Theoretical Explorations with Special Reference to East Africa*, Berlin: Mouton de Gruyter, pp. 7–30.

Shaw, John (1997), 'The Ethnography of Speaking and Verbal Taxonomies: Some Applications to Gaelic', in Ronald Black, William Gillies and Roibeard Ó Maolalaigh (eds), *Celtic Connections. Proceedings of the 10th International Congress of Celtic Studies*, East Linton: Tuckwell Press, pp. 308–23.

Shaw, John (2003), 'Gaelic Cultural Maintenance and the Contribution of Ethnography', *Scotia: Interdisciplinary Journal of Scottish Studies* 27, pp. 34–48.

Smakman, Dick and Smith-Christmas, Cassandra (2008), 'Gaelic Language Erosion and Revitalization on the Isle of Skye, Scotland', in Tjeerd de Graaf, Nicholas Ostler and Reinier Salverda (eds), *Proceedings XIIth conference of the Foundation for Endangered Languages*, Leeuwarden: Fryske Akademy, pp. 115–22.

Smakman, Dick and Smith-Christmas, Cassandra (forthcoming), 'Gaelic on Skye: Older speakers' identity in a language-shift situation', *International Journal of the Sociology of Language* 200.

Smith, Christina A. (1948), *Mental Testing of Hebridean Children in Gaelic and English*, London: University of London Press, Ltd.

Sparling, Heather (2003), '"Music is Language and Language is Music": Language Attitudes and Musical Choices in Cape Breton, Nova Scotia', *Ethnologies* 25:2. Electronic document, http://www.erudit.org/revue/ethno/2003/v25/n2/008052ar.html (accessed 25 February 2008).

Thomson, Derick S. (1964–1966), 'The Role of the Writer in a Minority Culture', *Transactions of the Gaelic Society of Inverness* 44, pp. 246–71.

Thomson, Derick S. (1979), 'Gaelic: Its Range of Uses', in A. J. Aitken and Tom McArthur (eds), *Languages of Scotland*, Edinburgh: W. & R. Chambers, pp. 14–25.

Thomson, Derick S. (1994), 'Attitudes to Linguistic Change in Gaelic Scotland', in M. Mair Parry, Winifred V. Davies and Rosalind A. M. Temple (eds), *The Changing Voices of Europe: Social and Political Changes and Their Linguistic Repercussions, Past, Present and Future*, Cardiff: University of Wales Press, with Modern Humanities Research Association, pp. 227–35.

Thomson, Derick S. and Grimble, Ian (eds) (1968), *The Future of the Highlands*, London: Routledge & Kegan Paul.

Trosset, Carol S. (1986), 'The Social Identity of Welsh Learners', *Language in Society* 15, pp. 165–92.

Vallee, F. G. (1954), 'Social Structure and Organisation in a Hebridean Community. A Study of Social Change', PhD dissertation, London School of Economics.

Walker, Maud (1973), 'Social Constraints, Individuals, and Social Decisions in a Scottish Rural Community', PhD dissertation, University of Illinois at Urbana-Champaign.

Wenger, Etienne (1998), *Communities of Practice*, Cambridge: Cambridge University Press.

Withers, Charles (1984), *Gaelic in Scotland 1698–1981: The Geographical History of a Language*, Edinburgh: John Donald.

Withers, Charles (1988), *Gaelic Scotland: The Transformation of a Culture Region,* New York: Routledge.

Woolard, Kathryn A. (1989), *Double Talk: Bilingualism and the Politics of Ethnicity in Catalonia,* Stanford: Stanford University Press.

NOTES

1 Acknowledgements. Many thanks to the editors and to Andrew Carnie, Jonathan Dembling, Nancy Dorian, Fraser MacDonald, Nicholas Malaspina and James Oliver for critical readings of the manuscript. Any remaining mistakes or omissions are entirely the responsibility of the author. Thank you also to the people who facilitated and agreed to participate in my own and others' research on Gaelic language revitalisation and development; without their patience and generosity there would be no sociolinguistic ethnography of Gaelic. Finally, I wish to thank Meg Bateman, Colm Ó Baoill, Seumas Grannd and Janet Hunter, who were the first to formally teach me about Gaelic language and culture at Aberdeen University.

   Dedication. This chapter is dedicated to the memory of Angus Spence (2006–2009).

2 Dorian felt that responses to her survey were so problematic, she relegated them to an appendix in her book, together with a discussion of the methodological difficulties of administering the survey and interpreting the results (1981a: 157–160). In a classic article focusing on language shift from Hungarian to German in an Austrian village, Susan Gal (1978: 6) achieved 86% agreement for men and 90% agreement for women between observed behaviour and survey responses of the situations in which people habitually spoke German or Hungarian – and she considered this to be a very high level of agreement.

3 The influence of Edwin Ardener (1927–1987) is key to understanding how UK social anthropologists finally began to study Gaelic-speaking communities and other areas of the 'Celtic fringe.' Ardener had carried out studies in Nigeria and Cameroon, in British West Africa, from 1949 to 1969 (MacGaffey 1991). From 1963 until his death in 1987, he was a lecturer in social anthropology at the University of Oxford. Later in his career at Oxford, he developed an interest in minority language issues in Europe, specifically in the United Kingdom. While spending summers in the Cameroons, he studied modern Welsh with a native Welsh-speaking colonial officer, and by the early 1980s, Ardener had started making regular trips to the Outer Hebrides and making a comparative study of Gaelic dialects (Chapman 1989: xii). However, the work was still incomplete when he died (Callan 2004: 366). Ardener's published work on Gaelic speakers is brief, ethnographically and linguistically informed, and theoretical in nature. His most lasting contribution in this area was to train a generation of British social anthropologists of Europe, many of whom did their PhD dissertation research on the so-called 'Celtic fringe': Malcom Chapman (Breton in Brittany), Edward Condry (Arnol, Isle of Lewis), Evi Constantinidou (East Sutherland), Tamara Kohn (Inner Hebrides), Sharon Macdonald (Isle of Skye and Gaelic), and Maryon McDonald (Breton-medium education and cultural revival in Brittany). Ardener also trained Robert Storey in social anthropology at the undergraduate level at Oxford. Storey remained a keen proponent of cultural approaches to the

Highlands and Islands in his work with the Highlands and Islands Development Board, and with his wife Lisa encouraged and significantly assisted a number of anthropologists working in the region (including Susan Parman, Andrew Gossen, Gillian Munro, and the author).

4 Macdonald described her older interviewees as 'rather amused that I should ask them about what language they used at home, so inevitable did it seem' (1997b: 219). This local, taken-for-granted meaning for Gaelic was also found by Dorian in former fishing villages in East Sutherland, in their case made even stronger by speakers' awareness that their dialect was divergent from dominant west coast forms (1981a: 75).

5 Dorian (1981a: 114–56) was the first to conduct these for Scottish Gaelic speakers. See Mertz (1982a: 85–144) for analysis of Cape Breton Gaelic combining proficiency and domain-based data; the appendices in Mertz (Mertz 1982a: 362–70) reproduce the proficiency tests administered by Mertz and Dorian. See Smakman and Smith-Christmas (2008) and Smakman and Smith-Christmas (forthcoming) for analysis of proficiency tests conducted by Smith-Christmas on three generations of a single family in Skye in 2007.

6 Coleman describes how the survey design forced respondents to respond to a highly unlikely hypothetical situation in which they would speak first to a higher-ranking person who represented a particular domain.

7 Coleman borrowed the terms 'Casual' and 'Careful' from the sociolinguist William Labov (1972); they were not native terms (Coleman 1975: 151).

8 Ennew (1980: 107) corroborated Coleman's observations in the later 1970s for Lewis, noting a difference between the dialects in everyday use in the villages, the Gaelic used in broadcasting, and the Gaelic of the church.

9 Dorian also identified four varieties of English spoken in East Sutherland: RP or received pronunciation English, standard Highland English, Scots-influenced East Sutherland English, and Gaelic-influenced Highland English and East Sutherland English (Dorian 1981a: 84–5).

10 As of 2009, Cassandra Smith-Christmas is conducting a new study of Gaelic-English codeswitching by speakers in an extended family on Skye for her doctoral dissertation research, jointly supervised by the Departments of Celtic and English, University of Glasgow.

11 Perhaps due to the intellectual division of labour between anthropologists and folklorists, oral traditions are barely mentioned at all in the ethnographic literature, except to say that they have vanished due to the influence of the Presbyterian church and changes to the way of life brought by modernisation. However, the former role of the *taigh-cèilidh* is described from memories of informants (Coleman 1975: 97; Ennew 1980: 86). Coleman describes the traditional *cèilidh* going extinct in Carloway in the early 1960s and discusses the reasons why (Coleman 1975: 97–8).

12 The by-naming system arose in concert with traditional Gaelic patronymic practices and the fact that there was a great deal of endogamy (in-group marriage) in the area, resulting in only three surnames accounting for the vast majority of surnames in each village (Dorian 1970: 304). There were also a relatively small number of Christian names used frequently (Dorian 1970: 305), and people had large families, so every family had children with at least one popular boy's and girl's name; this is likely related to the Hebridean practice in which people were obligated to name children after grandparents (Walker 1973: Chapter 4; Parman 1976: 103), thereby perpetuating a relatively small number of names. Dorian makes a distinction between by-names (as they are called in East

Sutherland) and nicknames, because in East Sutherland the by-names have only been used to refer to people, never to address them directly as nicknames often are (Dorian, personal communication).

13 Several crofting township ethnographies include brief descriptions of Gaelic kinship terminology, which is 'descriptive' rather than 'classificatory', meaning that collateral 'blood' relations are described by an augmentation or combination of the primary terms of relationship (for example, 'mother's brother' and 'father's brother' instead of the more general classificatory term 'uncle') (Ducey 1956: 259–61). Walker lists Gaelic kinship terms she collected from elderly informants (1973: 233–8), which she claims give an account of late nineteenth-century usage but were not in daily use by the early 1970s. Otherwise, however, most of Walker's descriptions of kinship are in English, with use of the term *teaghlach* (family) throughout her thesis being the only tantalising hint of the Gaelic linguistic practices she must have observed.

14 Ardener believed that the original cultural meanings and references of the Gaelic terms were only preserved in older Gaelic dictionaries and texts (1989: 142). However, I speculate that the ongoing preference for the English month names in daily Gaelic conversation by older speakers may actually indicate avoidance of or resistance to repurposing the Gaelic lexicon.

15 Ennew speculated (but offered no evidence) about the cognitive and behavioral implications of the 'disappearance of the conceptual distinction between maternal and paternal kin' in Gaelic culture 'as children reared in an increasingly English environment now translate the English "my uncle" back into Gaelic as '*m'uncaill*,' rather than *brathair mo mhathair* (my mother's brother) or *brathair m'athair* (my father's brother), which 'corresponds to a difference in attitude to maternal and paternal kin' [*sic*] (Ennew 1980: 76).

16 Sasse (1992) constructed his 'Gaelic-Arvanítika Model' of language death partially upon Dorian's (1981a) description and analysis of East Sutherland Gaelic.

17 MacKinnon's insight provides a nuanced explanation of one way in which gender might play a factor in Gaelic language shift. Constantinidou (1994) argued that women played a significant role in Gaelic language shift in East Sutherland. However, Dorian (forthcoming b) contests this interpretation, finding that among the Gaelic speakers of Brora and Embo, more women than men continued to use Gaelic 'despite imperfect speaker skill'. For a classic and detailed discussion of how gender and social networks may influence language shift see Gal (1978). Research on this topic is ongoing in US linguistic anthropology.

18 Coleman had also noted that in Carloway, Lewis, a 'Gaelic Infants Play School [*sic*]' set up in 1973 with external funding was subject to differing interpretations: 'the function of the school, as envisaged by the financial backer and by the people whose children used it, was apparently rather different' (1975: 228). Unfortunately he did not go into any further detail about the situation.

19 Ironically, Macdonald's book itself was criticised in this very way. These ethnographies have also been criticised for portraying Presbyterian Gaelic-speaking communities in a negative light by frankly describing the alcohol-drinking habits of some of their members (Black 1998). Reviews of Macdonald's book tended to fixate on her brief, contextualised descriptions of local people drinking on Sunday morning and at the fank. Parman also received criticism for her analysis of 'the Bible and the Bottle' social networks on the west side of Lewis.

20 The pupils in the observed classrooms totaled 104, or about 11% of the total

number of P1–P3 Gaelic-medium pupils in Scotland for that year (Pollock 2006: 122).

21 Oliver is Sharon Macdonald's former student and thus constitutes a third intellectual generation in the British sociolinguistic ethnography of Gaelic speakers, since Edwin Ardener supervised Macdonald's research.

22 The fluent speakers in Skye reported that they spoke Gaelic in the home, with family members, and with older people, and very rarely used Gaelic with their peers, either in school or out (Oliver 2002: 159). The young people who had no opportunity to speak Gaelic in the home did not speak it at all (163–4). Fluent Gaelic speakers in Glasgow also just 'sometimes' used it with parents or other older family members, never with friends, and would not even think to initiate a conversation in Gaelic (165–6).

23 BA in Gaelic Language and Culture (BA *Cànan is Cultar*), and BA in Gaelic and North Atlantic Studies (BA *Gàidhlig is Iomall a' Chuain Shiar*).

24 Although MacCaluim's work is based on a survey and does not contain a fieldwork component, it was conducted from the perspective of the sociology of language.

25 A long gap between fieldwork and publication of research results on Gaelic-speaking communities has also been noted. This can happen for a number of reasons besides the difficulty of writing up ethnographic research. The length of time it may take to secure a tenure-track academic position after obtaining the PhD, the relative demand of different institutions of higher education for one to publish a monograph, and the challenge of finding a publisher are all possible factors, as is the fact that for female academics, the childbearing years often coincide with the period intervening between fieldwork and publication of a monograph. The gap between fieldwork and book has been highlighted by the unfortunate tendency of anthropologists to write in the 'ethnographic present', phrasing in the present tense their descriptions of matters as they found them at the time of their fieldwork (e.g., Parman 1990, though this has been corrected to some extent in the 2005 edition). A book title like *The Western Isles Today* – which describes the world of Lewis in the 1970s – may give the misleading and unintended impression that Gaelic-speaking communities are frozen in time.

26 Ronnie Black quoted one resident of the crofting township where Macdonald (1997a) conducted her research: '*Daoine tighinn bhon taobh a-muigh 's a'sgrìobhadh leabhraichean mar gum biodh eòlas acasan air an àite! Bidh a'chaothaich air daoine gu bheil iad mar ann an test tube 's iad a'sealltainn orra.*' ['Folk coming from the outside and writing books as if they knew the place! People hate feeling they're in a test tube being looked at.'] (translation supplied in Black 1998).

27 The proceedings of Rannsachadh na Gàidhlig (RnaG) 2006 at Sabhal Mòr Ostaig (Munro forthcoming) contain Oliver (forthcoming). The proceedings of RnaG 2004 at University of Edinburgh contain McEwan-Fujita (2006), Morrison (2006), and Müller (2006). Also see McCoy and Scott (2000) and the Belfast Studies in Language, Culture and Politics series edited by John Kirk and Donall Ó Baoill for Cló Ollscoil na Banríona, based in Queen's University Belfast (which includes MacCaluim 2007 and Lamb 2008).

28 As of 2009, Ann Stewart is planning to conduct doctoral dissertation research on Gaelic television; she is based in the Department of Anthropology, Memorial University of Newfoundland.

29 As of 2009, Vanessa Will is writing up the results of her doctoral dissertation research on Gaelic language socialisation of children on Lewis; she is based in

the Department of Anthropology, University of Michigan.

30 Well does the author remember defending this position on the Highland Research Network email list some years ago against indignant historians of the Highlands, and being called a 'fanatic' by a Scottish sociologist studying Highland communities for trying to speak to him in Gaelic at the first Scottish Gaelic Studies conference in 2000.

CHAPTER 10

Gaelic Vocabulary

Andrew Breeze

INTRODUCTION

We may start with Dr Johnson. 'Of the Earse language, as I understand nothing, I cannot say more than I have been told. It is the rude speech of a barbarous people, who had few thoughts to express, and were content, as they conceived grossly, to be grossly understood.' Johnson contrasted Gaelic with Welsh and Irish, which were 'cultivated tongues' as Gaelic was not (Johnson 1924: 104–5).

When Johnson was wrong, he was wrong with a vengeance. We now know what he did not know, that Gaelic is an ancient language which became a vehicle for acute learning, vivid narration and powerful and memorable poetry. This is in part suggested by its vocabulary, casting light on its speakers through the ages. The lexis of Gaelic is purer than that of many languages (particularly English). The earliest records of Common Gaelic, from which (like Irish and Manx) it derives, offer almost no evidence of borrowing from any pre-Celtic tongue, and are hence thoroughly Indo-European in their nature. Many Gaelic words thus have cognates (= words of common ancestry) in Latin, Greek, Old Slavonic, Sanskrit, or other languages of Europe and Asia. These expressions can be traced back from Gaelic to the Indo-European spoken some 5,000 years ago in the region north of the Black Sea. Since then Gaelic has (effectively) borrowed words from five other sources: Latin, Pictish, Norse, French and English or Scots. It has also loaned many words to Scots, though this has been less noticed.

INDO-EUROPEAN

First, the Indo-European aspect of Gaelic, shown in basic and every-day words. These often concern natural phenomena: night, sea, snow, star, thunder, water; or animals: bird, fish, horse, hound; or parts of the body: ear, eye, foot, leg, nail; or numbers. But perhaps most signifi-cant are those for family relationships: father, mother, brother, sister. Gaelic words for all these, going back to speakers of the New Stone Age, are the bedrock of speech, referring to some very old concepts indeed. Here are a few of them.

Brà 'quern'. Cognates here include Welsh *breuan*, Cornish *brou*, Armenian *erkan*, Gothic *asilu-qairnus* 'donkey mill', English *quern*, and Tocharian B *kärwenne* (Vendryes 1981: 92). The drudgery of using a quern, the handmill now seen in the archaeological or folk museum, was the work of slaves (especially women slaves), whether they used the older saddle-quern (which wore down the user's finger-nails) or more advanced rotary quern. Querns (mentioned in Shakespeare's *Midsummer Night's Dream*) were used in the Western Isles into the twentieth century, and were (are?) still used in North Africa. Although a rotary quern can grind up to 10lb of grain in an hour, nobody ever used a quern for pleasure.

Cas 'leg'. Legs are universal, but cognates of *cas* occur in Italic, Germanic and Indo-Iranian with some shifts of meaning. The most obvious of these is Latin *coxa* 'hip-bone', giving French *cuisse* 'thigh'. Yet Old High German *hahsa* 'back or hollow of the knee', English *hock* 'backward-pointing joint on the leg of a horse, etc.', and Sanskrit *kákṣah* 'armpit' may likewise share ancestry with *cas* (Vendryes 1987: 214). We may also mention the Pictish leader Argentocoxos 'silver leg' (mentioned by the historian Dio Cassius, consul in 205), whose name helps prove that Pictish was Celtic (Jackson 1955: 129–60).

Cluas 'ear'. The original Common Gaelic form meant not merely the fleshy external organ of hearing, but also the act of hearing. Cognates include Welsh *clust* 'ear' and, with reduced vocalisation, Sanskrit *srustih* 'obedience' and Old English *hlyst* 'act of hearing', which gives modern *listen* (Vendryes 1987: 126–7).

Cóig 'five'. The digits on each hand make five an obvious concept. But amongst unobvious developments of the cognates are Welsh *pump*, Sanskrit *pansa*, Greek *pempe*, Latin *quinque*, Armenian *hing*, and Gothic *fimf*, all meaning 'five' (Vendryes 1987: 142–3).

Deanntag 'nettle'. Celtic cognates here are Middle Irish *nenaid*, with original initial *n* preserved, and Welsh *danadl*. The Gaelic and Welsh forms show marked development from a common root, better represented in Lithuanian *notryne*, Old High German *nezzila*, and English *nettle* (Vendryes 1960: N 9–10). The root means not 'sting', as one might imagine, but 'twist', nettles being used to make cloth from the Bronze Age onwards until in Scotland at least the eighteenth century (for bed-sheets and table-cloths) and the twentieth century in

Poland and the Tyrol. Nettles as a material for fabrics were sooner or later driven out by flax (Grigson 1958: 238–9).

Each 'horse'. This noble animal had been tamed by Indo-European times, so cognates of *each* are easy to find. Amongst them are Welsh *ebol* 'colt' and Sanskrit *ásva-h*, Greek *hippos*, and Latin *equus*, all meaning 'horse'. An early Celtic love of horses is shown by the Gaulish name *Eposognatus*, figuring in Polybius (second century BC) and Livy, and meaning '(he who is) knowledgable about horses' (Evans 1967: 197–9)

Iasg 'fish'. Though fish are not as noble as horses, they are better eating. Hence many cognates: Latin *piscis*, Gothic *fisks*, English *fish*. Gaelic *iasg* shows loss of original Indo-European *p*, occurring throughout Celtic (Calder 1923: 53; Lewis and Pedersen 1937: 26).

Màthair 'mother'. Another universal with many cognates: Sanskrit *mátar-*, Armenian *mayr*, Greek *meter*, Latin *mater*, Old High German *muotar*, Old Slavonic *mati*, all meaning 'mother'; and, unexpectedly, Lithuanian *móte* 'wife' (Vendryes 1960: M 25).

Sneachd 'snow'. This is from Common Celtic *snig-* 'to flow, fall, rain, snow', linked to a root widely represented in Indo-European, as in Greek *neiphei* 'it snows', Latin *nivis* 'of snow', Gothic *snaiws* 'snow', and Old English *snaw* 'snow' (Vendryes 1974: S 153).

Sùil 'eye'. A philological surprise. Cognates include Sanskrit *súrah*, Albanian *húl*, Welsh *haul*, and, with differences in detail, Greek *helios*, Latin *sol*, Gothic *sauil*, and Old English *sunna*. All these mean 'sun'. Only in Goedelic has the meaning shifted from 'sun', the eye of heaven, to 'eye', with *grian* now supplying the original sense (Vendryes 1974: S 201–2).

LATIN BORROWINGS

After the Indo-European element, the borrowings. The first real wave of these comes from Latin. Some must be early, dating from the time of the Roman Empire, thanks to trade or piracy on the part of the Gaels. Instances here are *fion* 'wine' and *òr* 'gold'. Others, relating mainly to religion, date from the time of St Patrick and the conversion of Ireland in the fifth century.

Beannachd 'blessing'. From Latin *benedictio* 'blessing' (Vendryes 1981: 36–7).

Càise 'cheese'. From Latin *caseus* 'cheese', like Welsh *caws* (Vendryes 1987: 22). If it seems surprising that so basic a product should have a name from Latin (and at an early date), the same is true as well for

English *cheese* and German *Käse*, both due to a borrowing from Latin by Germanic before the fifth century.

Càisg 'Easter'. From Latin *Pascha*, borrowed at a time when Goedelic lacked initial *p*, so that *c* was substituted (Calder 1923: 65; Jackson 1953: 126; Vendryes 1987: 46).

Clann 'children'. Again, another archaic borrowing, from Latin *planta* 'sprout, twig; young plant' (with what Vendryes called 'une curieuse évolution de sens'), made not later than the fifth century, and so probably before Common Gaelic reached North Britain. Latin *planta* also gave Welsh *plant* 'children' (Vendryes 1987: 112–13; Stalmaszczyk 2005: 27). English *clan* 'collection of families under chief, of common ancestry', taken from Gaelic, is (according to the *Oxford English Dictionary*) first recorded in about 1425, in Wyntoun's *Chronicle*.

Eaglais 'church, kirk'. This is not from standard Latin *ecclesia* but from Vulgar Latin *eclesia*, perhaps via (unattested) Primitive Welsh *egles* (with long *e*), itself giving Modern Welsh *eglwys* (Jackson 1953: 412). It is evidence for the conversion of the Gaels to Christianity by St Patrick and other Britons.

Fìon 'wine'. The archaism of the form points to a loan while the Roman Empire, from which wine was a desirable export, still existed (Jackson 1953: 90 n. 2). Welsh *gwin* also comes from Latin *vinum* 'wine', as does English *wine* itself, entering Germanic before the Anglo-Saxons settled in Britain (see the *Oxford English Dictionary*'s entry for *wine*).

Pòg 'kiss'. This charming word is, somewhat unexpectedly, from Church Latin, as in the phrase *osculum pacis* 'kiss of peace' in the liturgy. Survival of initial *p* shows it is not amongst the earliest loans (Jackson 1953: 130 n. 1; Vendryes 1960: P 11).

Sabhal 'barn', ultimately from Latin *stabulum*, a place where one stands or remains, and so 'stall, stable; abode' (Vendryes 1974: S 3).

Sgoil 'school', from Latin *schola* 'school' (Vendryes 1974: S 49–50).

Sguab 'broom'. From Latin *scopae* 'twigs; broom' (Greene 1968: 75–86; Vendryes 1974: S 56). The loan is perhaps due less to the superiority of Roman brooms than to the Celtic slaves who, in Roman society, used them.

Sorn 'furnace', which, like Welsh *ffwrn*, French *four*, and Spanish *horno*, is from Latin *furnus* 'oven, bakery', and is further evidence for 'cultural contacts' with the Roman world (Greene 1968: 75–86; Vendryes 1974: S 174). The Gaelic term leaves a mark on the map at Sorn, fourteen miles east of Ayr, with a name from the now extinct Gaelic speech of Kyle (Watson 1926: 200).

Srian 'bridle', from Latin *frenum* 'bridle, curb, bit', also giving modern Spanish *frenos* 'brakes (of a car)'. Welsh *ffrwyn* and Old Cornish *fruinn* are likewise from *frenum*, Roman bridles being of high quality, unlike those of the Celts, who often used a mere cord (Vendryes 1974: S 186).

The terms from Latin are a strange mix. There are expressions for technology and the like, proof of the practical nature of the Romans, but also many Christian expressions. Yet they may have more in common than appears, the Roman genius for organisation showing itself as much in running the Church (with literacy and book-learning as a powerful weapon) as in running an empire.

PICTISH, SCANDINAVIAN AND FRENCH

Now for the next group. Although in principle Gaelic should have taken expressions from Pictish (and from Cumbric, the ancient language of Strathclyde) on the occupation of Argyll and beyond in the fifth century, this is hard to demonstrate. It is true that the place-name element *pett* 'piece; parcel of land', cognate with Welsh *peth* 'thing', is common in toponyms, as with Pitgersie 'shoemaker's land' in Aberdeenshire, or Pitskelly 'storyteller's land' in Angus and elsewhere. But this is not a common noun. Gaelic *pòr* means 'seed, grain, crops'; it may be related to a Pictish cognate of Welsh *pori* 'to graze (of sheep)', despite phonological and semantic difficulties (Jackson 1972: 69; Nicolaisen 2001: 180). It is unfortunate that, when Pictish died out in the ninth century and Cumbric in the twelfth, they left no written texts, and we therefore know little of them.

On Scandinavian we are better informed. The Western Isles were part of a Norwegian empire until as late as 1266, when the King of Scots annexed them after winning the battle of Largs. There are thus far more Scandinavian loans in Gaelic (and Manx) than there are in Irish. Amongst those unknown to Irish are *dail* 'field', *faodhail* 'seaford', *gocoman* 'look-out man', *òb* 'creek' (hence the name of Oban 'little creek'), *sgol* 'rinse, wash', *stalla* 'precipice, ledge', *tàbh* 'hand-net', and *ùidh* 'ford' (O'Rahilly 1972: 125). Many of these terms relate to trading and the sea, as one would expect from sea-rovers like the Vikings (Cox 2008).

Other words include the following.

Acair 'anchor'. This is from Scandinavian *akkeri*, itself borrowed from Latin *ancora*, itself from Greek *ankura*, with a root meaning 'what is bent or hooked'. Goedelic had earlier forms *ancaire* (which survives in Irish) and, still older, *ingor*, both taken directly from Latin (Vendryes 1959: 74; Sommerfelt 1975: 75–7).

Margadh 'market place', from Old Norse *markathr*, itself from Vulgar Latin *marcatus* (also giving English *market*), from Classical Latin *mercatus* 'market'. The Northmen were great traders, in furs, textiles and (of course) slaves, the last being highly profitable (Vendryes 1960: M 20).

Mòd 'assembly, court', a word (from Norse *mót*, related to English *meet*) which is unknown in Irish, but has entered English as *Mod* (first recorded by *OED* from 1893), the annual gathering for literary and musical competition of An Comunn Gaidhealach, the Highland Association.

Rannsaich 'search'. The verb in Gaelic is milder than is English *ransack* 'rob, plunder, pillage', which is likewise from Norse *rannsaka* 'to search for stolen goods', where the first element is *rann* 'house' and the second is a cognate of English *seek*.

Stiùir 'helm, rudder', from Norse *styri*, a cognate of the English verb *steer* and proof of Viking skill at seafaring (Vendryes 1974: S 191).

Uinneag 'window'. Like Irish *fuinneog* and English *window*, this is from Norse *vindaugr* 'wind eye'. Early Viking windows, lacking glass, let in wind as well as light.

On a different social level from the Norse loans are those from French. These suggest organised government, social hierarchy, military power and some beneficial contacts with Continental civilisation (food, for example). Unfortunately it is not always possible to tell if any particular item was borrowed direct from French or via English. However, the following seem instances of the first.

Caisteal 'castle'. As with Middle Irish *caistél*, the second syllable suggests a direct loan from Anglo-Norman (Vendryes 1987: 23).

Coineanach 'rabbit'. The hare (*maigheach*) has lolloped across Scotland time out of mind: the rabbit is a Norman import. *Coineanach*, with a native suffix, is from Anglo-Norman *conin*, itself giving English *coney* (Vendryes 1987: 151).

Dìnnear 'dinner', from Anglo-Norman *diner* (Ó Murchú 1985: 22).

Ruisean 'afternoon meal', now obsolete, but derived from Old French *reciner* from Late Latin *recenare* 'to dine again' (Campbell and Thomson 1963: 158).

Siùcar 'sugar'. Like Irish *siúcra*, this is probably a borrowing from Anglo-Norman *sucre* and not from English (Ó Murchú 1985: 22). The French word goes back via medieval Latin *succarum* to Arabic *sukkar*. This sweet substance reached Britain in the twelfth century. Henry II bought thirty-four pounds of it in 1176 in the rate of ninepence a pound, so it is clear that only the rich could then afford it (Stenton 1965: 31).

ENGLISH AND SCOTS

Finally, English or Scots, where influence is obvious. What is less obvious is that it began early, even long before the Norman Conquest, as shown by some of the following.

Bàta 'boat', where Gaelic preserves the vowel of early English *bad* 'boat' (Vendryes 1981: 22).

Bòrd 'table'. Like Welsh *bwrdd* 'table', this is from Old English *bord* and not Old Norse *borth* (Vendryes 1981: 72).

Pàipear 'paper', from English, like Welsh *papur*, the latter first attested in a love-poem by Dafydd ap Gwilym in the fourteenth century (Vendryes 1960: P 2). Paper was invented by the Chinese in the sixth century; the Arabs learned how to make it from Chinese prisoners-of-war at Samarkand. Paper-making passed through Arab influence into twelfth-century Spain, but almost all paper in Britain was imported until the seventeenth century (Denholm-Young 1964: 61).

Seobhag 'hawk'. Like Irish *seabhac* and Welsh *hebog*, this is surely borrowed from Old English *heafoc* 'hawk'. (It is not likely that the Goedelic words are from Welsh.) Hunting hawks were prestige items in the middle ages, whether as objects of trade, tribute, or royal gifts. Hence this surprising aspect of English influence on the Gaelic world (Vendryes 1974: S 59–60).

Loan-words are an index of cultural contact and political and social power. Gaelic, on a fighting retreat since the eleventh century, has thus inevitably borrowed words from other languages. What is remarkable, however, is to find that Gaelic not only imported vocabulary, but exported it as well. Loans in Scots suggest the early numbers of Gaelic speakers and provide evidence of their lexis. Sometimes we find a word of Gaelic origin in a Scots text long before it is attested in Gaelic itself; occasionally it is unknown in Gaelic, so that we have to draw on Irish dictionaries to prove its origins. References to many terms coming from Gaelic figure in a book by Finnish scholars (Filppula, Klemola and Paulasto 2008: 215–16). More numerous than has been appreciated, they point to the variety and copiousness of this tongue. Here is a sample.

Basare 'hangman'. In his *Fables*, the Dunfermline poet Robert Henryson (of the late fifteenth century) tells how the animals try the fox for his crimes and condemn him to death. The wolf hears his last confession, and the monkey hangs him.

> The volff, that new-maid doctour, couth him schrif [absolved his sins];
> Syne [then] furth him led and to the gallous gais,
> And at the ledder fute his leif he tais [takes his leave].

The ape wes basare and bad him sone ascend,
And hangit him, and thus he maid his end. (Fox 1981: 45)

Here *basare* has been a puzzle, described as of obscure origin (Robinson 1985: 31). Yet *bás* is Common Gaelic for 'death' and *básaire* is Modern Irish for 'executioner'. Henryson employs a borrowing from Gaelic, suggesting the well-known use of a foreign term for something unpleasant or taboo, like *coup de grâce* for 'death-blow, finishing stroke'.

   Brylyoun. This comes in a satire by William Dunbar on two plebeian lovers. The man calls the woman 'My bony baib with the ruch [rough] brylyoun'. Some take it as probably a 'nonsense word', others as 'shoe of undressed hide' (Robinson 1985: 65; Bawcutt 1998: 346). Alas, it is neither. Early Irish *brell* means *glans penis*; *brillín* is the diminutive form, used of the female equivalent and the female organ in general. This foreign term is useful (for Dunbar rather than the seducer) when plain speaking would be inartistic.

   Dyvour. In Dunbar's *Tretis of the Twa Mariit Wemen and the Wedo*, a robust commentary on the relations of men and women, the Widow says of her late husband,

   Deid is now that dyvour and dollin [buried] in erd:
   With him deit all my dule [misery] and my drey [dreary] thoghtis
   (Kinghorn 1970: 150–1).

With husband in the grave, farewell to sorrow! Here *dyvour* means 'debtor'. It is still current in Scots in the sense 'rogue, good-for-nothing'. Its origin is called 'obscure' (Robinson 1985: 167). But there is reason to derive it from a Gaelic equivalent of earlier Irish *daibhir* 'poor person; poor, indigent', which has been displaced in both languages by *bochd* or *bocht*.

   Drumlie 'clouded, troubled'. In 'Highland Mary', Burns blesses the leafy riverside place where he first met his love:

   Green be your woods, and fair your flowers,
   Your waters never drumlie!

This *drumlie* is a development of the *drubly* used by Dunbar and Gavin Douglas, itself treated as from English or French (Robinson 1985: 163). However, *draoibeal* is Modern Irish for 'mud, mire', deriving from earlier *drobél* 'rough place or road, difficult ground'. *Drubly* and *drumlie* make better sense as derived from the corresponding form in Gaelic, with the English adjectival suffix -y.

   Gaberlunzie 'beggar, tramp' figures in legal records and the novels of Scott, and (unexpectedly) at the graveyard of the High Church, Bathgate, with an inscription 'in Memory of George Wilson Alias PUDDIN died 1853, the celebrated Gaberlunzie' (McWilliam 1978: 95–6). *Gaberlunzie* is again described as of obscure etymology (Robinson 1985: 221). But there is reason to relate it to Irish *ciobar* 'dirt, grime' and *ciobarlán* 'grimy person', with the English or Scots diminutive suffix *-ie* (as in Burns's 'beastie').

Tod 'fox', attested in place-names from the thirteenth century, is regarded as of 'unknown' origin (Robinson 1985: 726). But it can be derived from a Gaelic form corresponding to early Irish *táid* 'thief', suiting the creature that steals the shepherd's lambs and farmer's chickens. As with *basare*, a term from another language would be used of an animal which country people hate and despise.

On the later development of Gaelic vocabulary, to express the abstract terms of theological or philosophical reasoning in a community where knowledge of Scripture was extensive and exact, or of its later extension with the administrative, legal and political expressions of modern broadcasting, journalism and government, readers may be referred elsewhere (Lamb 1999; McLeod 2004). It may well be that the resilience of Gaelic in the past suggests it is a more viable means of communication today than many might think.

When Robert Kirk, minister of Aberfoyle (on the upper Forth), completed his translation of the Psalms in 1684, he described them in his preface as pleasing and profitable, *beag nach mionfhlaitheas lán d'ainglibh, cill fhonnmhar le ceol naomhtha* 'almost a little kingdom full of angels, a church melodious with holy music', and *mar abholghort Eden, líonta do chrannaibh bríoghmhoire na beatha & do luibhennibh íochshláintemhal* 'like the Garden of Eden, full of vigorous trees of life and health-giving herbs' (Williams 1986: 170). For many, the Gaelic language is music coming from a holy place; or a paradisal garden, full of beautiful trees and flowers; or, at the very least, an object that supplies endless material for enquiry and admiration.

BIBLIOGRAPHY

Bawcutt, Priscilla (ed.) (1998), *The Poems of William Dunbar*, Glasgow: Association for Scottish Literary Studies.

Calder, George (1923), *A Gaelic Grammar*, Glasgow: MacLaren.

Campbell, J. L. and Thomson, D. S. (1963), *Edward Lhuyd in the Scottish Highlands 1699–1700*, Oxford: Clarendon Press.

Cox, Richard A. V. (2008), 'Old Norse Words for "Boat" in Scottish Gaelic', *Scottish Gaelic Studies* XXIV, pp. 169–80.

Denholm-Young, Noël (1964), *Handwriting in England and Wales*, 2nd edn, Cardiff: University of Wales Press.

Evans, D. Ellis (1967), *Gaulish Personal Names*, Oxford: Clarendon Press.

Filppula, Markku, Klemola, Juhani and Paulasto, Heli (2008), *English and Celtic in Contact*, London: Routledge.

Fox, Denton (ed.) (1981), *The Poems of Robert Henryson*, Oxford: Clarendon Press.

Greene, David (1968), 'Some Linguistic Evidence Relating to the British Church', in M. W. Barley and R. P. C. Hanson (eds), *Christianity in Britain, 300–700*, Leicester: Leicester University Press, pp. 75–86.

Grigson, Geoffrey (1958), *The Englishman's Flora*, London: Phoenix House.

Jackson, Kenneth (1953), *Language and History in Early Britain*, Edinburgh: Edinburgh University Press.

Jackson, Kenneth (1955), 'The Pictish Language', in F. T. Wainwright (ed.), *The Problem of the Picts*, Edinburgh: Nelson, pp. 129–60.

Jackson, Kenneth (1972), *The Gaelic Notes in the Book of Deer*, Cambridge: Cambridge University Press.

Johnson, Samuel (1924), *Journey to the Western Islands of Scotland*, London: Oxford University Press.

Kinghorn, A. M. (ed.) (1970), *The Middle Scots Poets*, London: Arnold.

Lamb, William (1999), 'A Diachronic Account of Gaelic News-Speak', *Scottish Gaelic Studies*, XIX, pp. 141–71.

Lewis, Henry and Pedersen, Holger (1937), *A Concise Comparative Celtic Grammar*, Göttingen: Vandenhoeck & Ruprecht.

McLeod, Wilson (2004), 'The Challenge of Corpus Planning in Gaelic Development', *Scottish Language* XXIII, pp. 68–92.

McWilliam, Colin (1978), *The Buildings of Scotland: Lothian*, Harmondsworth: Penguin.

Nicolaisen, W. F. H. (2001), *Scottish Place-Names*, 2nd edn, Edinburgh: John Donald.

Ó Murchú, Máirtín (1985), *The Irish Language*, Dublin: Department of Foreign Affairs.

O'Rahilly, T. F. (1972), *Irish Dialects Past and Present*, 2nd edn, Dublin: Dublin Institute for Advanced Studies.

Robinson, Mairi (ed.) (1985), *The Concise Scots Dictionary*, Aberdeen: Aberdeen University Press.

Sommerfelt, Alf (1975), 'The Norse Influence on Irish and Scottish Gaelic', in Brian Ó Cuív (ed.), *The Impact of the Scandinavian Invasions on the Celtic-Speaking Peoples*, Dublin: Dublin Institute for Advanced Studies, pp. 73–7.

Stalmaszczyk, Piotr (2005), *Celtic Presence*, Lódz: Lódz University Press.

Stenton, Doris (1965), *English Society in the Early Middle Ages*, 4th edn, Harmondsworth: Penguin.

Vendryes, Joseph (1959), *Lexique étymologique de l'irlandais ancien: Lettre A*, Paris: CNRS.

Vendryes, Joseph (1960), *Lexique étymologique de l'irlandais ancien: Lettres MNOP*, Paris: CNRS.

Vendryes, Joseph (1974), *Lexique étymologique de l'irlandais ancien: Lettres RS*, Paris: CNRS.

Vendryes, Joseph (1981), *Lexique étymologique de l'irlandais ancien: Lettre B*, Paris: CNRS.

Vendryes, Joseph (1987), *Lexique étymologique de l'irlandais ancien: Lettre C*, Paris: CNRS.

Watson, W. J. (1926), *The History of the Celtic Place-Names of Scotland*, Edinburgh: Blackwood.

Williams, N. J. A. (1986), *I bPrionta i Leabhar*, Baile Átha Cliath: Clóchomhar.

CHAPTER 11

Gaelic Orthography: The Drunk Man's Broad Road

Ronald Black

Spelling is art. As a boy growing up in Glasgow I was irresistibly attracted to the local library, a shining palace of polished wood and glass-topped tables. They had books in many languages, including French and Italian which were familiar to me at home from my mother's side of the family. What I loved to look at above all was Gaelic, a tongue whose sounds I only ever heard being spoken (mostly by young nurses who worked at the Victoria Infirmary) when travelling on trams or trolleybuses. It had a beautiful alternation of curvaceous vowels and consonants, decorated like tiles with equal numbers of acute and grave accents. These supplied the diagonals missing due to the absence of k, v, w, x, y and z – ugly letters anyway, I thought. I hated the appearance of languages that had too many of them, like Welsh or Polish.

Entranced by its spelling, I set about learning Gaelic, and discovered that the fluid quality which appealed to me so much had to do with a rule called *leathann ri leathann* (broad to broad). Recently I found that Professor Mackinnon would have agreed with me. He called Gaelic spelling 'picturesque' (1909–10: 193).

It could easily have been otherwise. In the late middle ages and for long after, Scottish Gaelic possessed two orthographies, one modelled on Irish and one on English. The Irish model brought with it centuries-old norms of script, grammar and morphology, and above all the sense that Irish, with its deep-rooted literary traditions, was the correct written register of Scottish Gaelic. The English model was used by the Dean of Lismore in his manuscript (written 1512–42) as well as by countless others, and remains familiar today from the spelling of Highland place- and personal names, not to mention the Manx language (Meek 1989; Black 1994: 127–31; Higgitt 2000: 336–8).

The Irish model became the accepted standard of Scottish Gaelic spelling, thanks to the fact that the first book printed in any kind of

Gaelic, John Carswell's liturgy *Foirm na n-Urrnuidheadh* (published in Edinburgh in 1567), employed Roman script but Irish orthography, the Reformed Church's intention being to have it used in both Scotland and Ireland. In a recent article, Aonghas MacCoinnich asks why the writing of Gaelic in English ('Scots') orthography was 'abandoned at much the same time as the last Classical Gaelic was being written in Scotland', then answers the question conclusively (MacCoinnich 2008: 329–30): the principal agent for orthographic development was the Synod of Argyll, operating in the firm political embrace of the Campbells, whose sphere of influence was that part of Scotland in which Irish orthography was practised, and who hoped to proselytise Ireland. To this I would only add that the use of Roman script represented a brilliantly simple compromise between Scotland's two systems; it was also adopted in Ireland, but not until the twentieth century. No Gaelic book has ever been published in Scotland using Irish script or English spelling.

The orthography of *Foirm na n-Urrnuidheadh* and of successive seventeenth-century religious texts has been described in detail by Thomson (1970: xi–xxi; 1971: 34–7; 1976: 143–8). From 1567 onwards he notes examples of *-eu-* (*beul, coimheud, soisceul, suibhisceul*) and the occasional loss of quiescent consonants, such as *beandaidhe* for *beandaighthe* (modern *beannachaidh*), *cánoin* or *canóin* for *canamhain* (modern *cànain*). Much of the dynamic represented by these changes was also present in Irish, but they became iconic in due course to Scottish Gaelic writers. He points out (Thomson 1970: xviii–xxi) that although seven grave accents may be found in *Foirm na n-Urrnuidheadh*, they do not seem to have any value different from that of Carswell's normal lengthmark, the acute. Perhaps the printer used them because they came to hand and, like p's and q's, were easily confused.

The Shorter Catechism of 1651 was translated by the Rev. Ewen Cameron of Dunoon, among others, and survives only in a second edition (1659). Thomson describes it (1962: xxxv) as 'definitely Scottish Gaelic'. This must be understood in a relative sense. Like the other prose texts of its era, it resembles an iceberg in which a minuscule Scottish superstructure stands atop a massive Irish infrastructure. The process of change quickened in 1659, however, with the publication (between the same covers as the Catechism) of the so-called *Ciad Chaogad* or 'First Fifty' metrical psalms. As these were in rhyme and meant to be sung, the vernacular sound system was to the fore, and the editors' introduction includes the following remarks on orthography (Cameron 1659: 5–6):

> Achd fos tuig gu bfedar ar uairaibh focaìl do dhearradh, cuid as
> an tosach, cuid as an deiradh agus cuid as a meadhon: deagla

gnbiodh [*sic*] an lin na bfhaid no thigeadh dhì bith. Achd chum
gu deanadh tu so aithniughadh, a nuair ata focal ar a dhearradh
as a thosach tuig gu bfuil an comharthasa (') ar a chur re tosach
an fhocail, *Salm 3. 8. lin. 1. 'Sle* arson *Is le*, *'Smairg* arson *Is mairg*,
&c. Marsin a nuair ata focal ar a dhearradh as a dheiradh ata an
comhartha sin fein ar a chur gu hard re deireadh an fhocail. *Sal.
1. 1. lin. 2. Comhairl'* arson *Comhairle*, *Tighearn'* arson *Tighearna*,
&c. Agus an tan ata focal ar a dhearradh as a mheadhon ata an
comharthasa (~) ar uairaibh gu hard eadar na siolaidh ata ar
an tarruing re cheile. *Sal. 39. 6.* lin. 1. *Samhlug~hadh*, is coir an
focal sin do sheinm mar fhocal da shìolaidh, mar gu nabradh tu
Samhluadh. Achd ar uairaibh eile rinn sinn cuid don fhocal fhagail
a muigh ar fad, *Sal. 39. 4. lin. 1. Toir* arson *Tabhair*. Agus ar uairaibh
ni bfuil comhartha sambith ar an fhocal is coir a dhearradh, is ni
mo ata cuid ar fhagail a muigh, achd fedfuidh tu sin aithniughadh
ar fuaim na liné, ma bheir tu fa near gu bfuil ochd siolaidh ann san
cheud lin, agus sé san dara lin.

('Please also note that words can sometimes be shortened initially,
medially or finally to prevent a line being longer than necessary.
To alert you to this, when a word is shortened initially the mark
' is placed before it, e.g. Psalm 3: 8, line 1 *'Sle* for *Is le*, *'Smairg* for
Is mairg, etc. When a word is shortened finally the same mark is
placed after it, e.g. Ps. 1: 1, line 2 *Comhairl'* for *Comhairle*, *Tighearn'*
for *Tighearna*, etc. When a word is shortened medially the mark ~
is sometimes placed between the juxtaposed syllables, e.g. Ps. 39:
6, line 1 *Samhlug~hadh*, which should be sung as a disyllable and
might be represented *Samhluadh*. On other occasions, however,
a part of the word may have been omitted silently, e.g. Ps. 39: 4,
line 1 *Toir* for *Tabhair*. And sometimes words that should be cut
are unmarked and unshortened; these can be recognised by the
sound of the line, provided it is noted that there are eight syllables
in the first line and six in the second.')

Thomson points out (1962: xxxviii) that in arranging for the composition of these metrical psalms, the Synod exhibited a great deal of
concern about 'syllabication'. He took this to mean simply 'spelling',
but it would probably be nearer the mark to say that it means 'spelling
as adjusted to metrical requirements'. The work had been done by a
committee which included Ewen Cameron along with the Revs Dugald
Campbell of North Knapdale, John Stewart of Kingarth and Alexander
MacLaine of Strachur & Strathlachlan (MacTavish 1934: viii–ix). The

Synod ordained that the 'syllabication' be corrected by the Rev. David Simpson of Killean (a scholarly Lowlander who had learned Gaelic) and John MacMarquis (an elderly member of the Gaelic learned orders). It looks as if the brethren felt that the committee's orthography had strayed too far from accepted standards. And when Thomson traced the development of the *Caogad* between the editions of 1659 and 1694, he found that linguistic change was both towards Irish and away from it, while orthographic change was towards it (Thomson 1976: 177–82).

There ensued a race to produce a Gaelic metrical version of all 150 psalms. It was won by the Synod's eager Episcopalian competitor, the Rev. Robert Kirk of Aberfoyle, who published the fruit of his labours with the following comment (Kirk 1684: iii–iv):

> I endeavour'd here what was native and proper, but clean and plain for all capacities, shunning as much as I could, tedious, tumultuous and disjoynted phrases. And tho I have also stript some words of their superfluous and ambulatory letters, reserving the possessive, as the several Irish Grammers come to my hands, do allow; Yet no humane work can pretend to be so absolute as to be beyond all Correction.

What Kirk seems to mean is that where Irish grammars offer a choice he has opted for shorter nominal forms, but not at the expense of the genitive case. *Dealughadh*, for example, declined in the Scottish way, would become *dealughaidh*, pronounced *dealachaidh*, but Kirk retains the 'correct' genitive form *dealuighthe*. He was no innovator. A semi-learner, poet and mystic, he was more interested in groping into the language's past and present existence than its future. Knowing the spoken Gaelic of Balquhidder and Aberfoyle and the written Gaelic of Uilliam Ó Domhnaill (whose New Testament was first published in 1603), he tried to find the common ground between them in his Psalms. Words which he knew in writing generally went unaltered; he was willing to reflect demotic speech in the ways of joining them up, but for dramatic change, such as plurals in -*n*, we must look to the occult expressions in his 'Secret Commonwealth of Elves, Fauns and Fairies': *hubhrisgeidh, caibe,n, lusbarta,n, siotbrudh*, or as we would probably understand them, *ùraisge* 'urisks, elves', *caibean* 'spades, curative stones', *luspardain* 'pigmies, fauns', *sìthbhreadha* 'fairies' (Black 2008a: 296–7, 306, 364).

Dugald Campbell is believed to have translated the Old Testament, but his manuscript disappeared from sight during the time (1660–89) when Episcopalianism remained supreme. It was last heard of in Australia (Mackinnon 1930: 44). In 1686 an Irish translation of the OT by Bishop William Bedell (1570–1642) was printed in Dublin, and in 1690 Kirk published his transliteration of the entire Bible into Roman characters, a work which he had accomplished with extraordinary care. His NT also appeared separately in the same year. These books contain some original material in Gaelic, in which distinct Scottish forms may be found: in the OT, lists of tribes, relationships, weights, measures and seasons, and in both books, Kirk's vocabulary, preceded by an introduction and followed by errata with comments. In 1694 it was the Synod's turn to publish their complete Psalms, the work of Campbell and others; these fared better than Kirk's, and successive editions contain an introduction devoted mainly to questions of language. A revised version of the introduction quoted above, it was reprinted by MacTavish (1934: xxvii–xxx). The point about words like *tabhair* is expressed a little less clumsily this time (Campbell 1694: v): 'Air uairaibh tàid air a ngearradh gun chomartha idir orra, mar atà *Toir* nó *Tabhr* air son *Tabhair*.' ('Sometimes they are cut without additional symbols, e.g. *Toir* or *Tabhr* for *Tabhair*.')

By 1699, then, the well-educated visitor to the Highlands, such as Edward Lhuyd, could regard the Irish orthographic model as 'usual', the English one 'different'. As a Welshman he found the dichotomy quite puzzling, and reported in that year (Lhuyd 1713: 97–8):

> We met with several Inscriptions, but none of them *Roman*, nor indeed ancient: However, we copied all we met of Two hundred Years standing, &c. for the sake of the Orthography of the *Irish* Names, which are writ differently from what is now usual.

He went on to publish four original Gaelic odes by Scottish poets (Robert Campbell, Andrew MacLean, the Revs John MacLean and James Currie) in his *Archaeologia Britannica* (1707). They are in what has been called 'a broken-down form of Classical Gaelic' (Ó Baoill 1979: 244). It is curious how script and orthography (the arts of written as opposed to oral composition) pulled the vernacular poets of that era in a linguistically classical direction. All other traceable verse by Currie (who, as a MacMhuirich, belonged to the hereditary learned orders) is in his own hand and in the classical language and script (Ó Cuív 1958–61: 173; Ó Baoill 2007: 65); all other traceable verse by the other three (who did not so belong) was recovered later from oral tradition and is entirely vernacular (Ó Baoill 1979: 60–81, 90–121; Ó Baoill 2007). In particular, close examination of the much-anthologised 'Rainn' by the Rev. John MacLean of Kilninian (*c.*1680–1756), which a non-Gaelic-speaking Muileach has described to me as one of the best Gaelic poems of its century, shows it to be a macaronic. Having chosen his metre,

MacLean makes it easy for himself by cherry-picking classical and vernacular forms and linking them with grand-looking nonsense like *le tuigse ghéir ler dtug le'n ceims a teid*. The line *'S gach droing don dúth an chánaimhn úd mar chaint* ('And all who speak that language as their own') depends for rhyme on vernacular *chànain* and classical *úd*. In the same way he rhymes *Gaoidheilg* with *cuimhne, ccríochsa* with *Gaoidhil, sgriobhth'* with *chroidh* (Ó Baoill 1979: 100–103). This is bad poetry, but it deserves to be set out in the same way as Alexander MacDonald's 'Moladh don t-Seann Chànain Ghàidhlig' (which it influenced) and examined in the context of the other odes to Lhuyd and of the Psalms. Thomas Pattison produced a vernacularised version in which he repaired the worst of the bad lines but not the metre (Pattison 1866: 199–200).

The Confession of Faith of 1725 is a valuable document for the simple reason that it fills a gap in our record of Gaelic orthographic development, little other new work having been published between 1707 and 1741. In fact all the copies of it which I have seen consist of three works, the Confession itself printed by Lumisden and Robertson in 1725, the Longer Catechism printed by the heirs of Andrew Anderson in 1714, and the Shorter Catechism printed by the heirs of Andrew Anderson in 1725, all continuously paginated from 1 to 276. In strong contrast with MacLean's poem, there is little or nothing in the Confession that would have been unacceptable in Ireland: it shows the forms of Irish orthography that became productive in Scottish Gaelic, especially the use of *-eu-*. The catechisms are more demotic – we find infinitive *do* becoming *a*, for example, and a very Scottish-looking nasalisation *chum a Nsláinte* (p. 108).

Alexander MacDonald's *Vocabulary* was published in 1741 by the Society in Scotland for the Propagation of Christian Knowledge (SSPCK), who wished to further their policy of 'extirpating the Irish language' by providing their schools with a key to the meaning of English texts (Campbell 2000: 170). Not being intended by the publisher as a contribution to Gaelic learning (quite the opposite, in fact), its orthography represents a break with the past, an attempt to spell words as they were spoken without undue respect to traditional rules, notably with regard to plurals. At that time MacDonald was working for the SSPCK as schoolmaster and catechist in Ardnamurchan. In preparing the *Vocabulary*, I think it likely that he would have conferred with those members of the Argyllshire clergy most interested in such matters, including John MacLean and Alexander MacFarlane (*c.*1712–63), yet another poet (Gillies 1786: 132–3). I have been able to document some of MacDonald's points of contact with MacLean (Black 1986b: 11, 16,

22, 25, 27); I wish I could say the same for MacFarlane, because in terms of orthography his story is curiously intertwined with MacDonald's.

What can be said is this. MacFarlane was minister of Kilninver from 1740, the year before the *Vocabulary* was published, to 1754, the year after his own edition of the Psalms came out; then he moved to Arrochar (Scott 1915–50: 3: 325–6, 4: 97). MacDonald secretly turned Catholic, and served Prince Charles's army as a captain in 1745–6. Afterwards he found employment on the Clanranald estates as ground officer or factor (Black 2001: 467–9). In 1750 MacFarlane published a pious Presbyterian tract called *Gairm an De Mhoir do 'n t Sluagh Neimh-Iompoichte* (a translation of Richard Baxter's *Call to the Unconverted*), which in terms of orthography was perhaps the most ground-breaking Gaelic work ever printed. In 1751 MacDonald, then working as baillie of Canna, published *Ais-Eiridh na Sean Chánoin Albannaich; no, An nuadh Oranaiche Gaidhealach* ('The Resurrection of the Ancient Scottish Tongue; or, The New Highland Songster'). Its orthography is less radical, less consistent, but in many ways more sensible than that of *Gairm an De Mhoir*, and clearly has a great deal in common with it; the two orthographies were certainly not conceived independently of each other. MacDonald dedicates his book in Gaelic to the other man's chief, the equally scholarly Walter MacFarlane. Unlike Alexander MacFarlane, who offers no preface at all, MacDonald provides one of six pages, of which two are devoted to orthography, including the following (Mac-Dhonuill 1751: x):

> No pains have been spared to render the language as plain and intelligible as reasonably can be expected. And in order to make the force and sound of the syllables approach as near as possible to that of the English, and to the more usual pronunciation of the generality of the highlanders, some quiescent letters formerly used in the Galic are thrown out; letters are frequently transposed; and some are changed, especially in words whose terminations are *bh*, instead of which, *n* and *on* are commonly used. As these innovations are intended for obtaining the ends above mentioned, it is hoped none will take them to be any trespass upon grammatical rules.

His 'quiescent letters' are consonants, *fágbhail* becoming *fágail*, *maoth-bhláths mao-bhlás*, etc. By 'words whose terminations are *bh*' he means the dative plural in *-ibh*, but his remark about *n* and *on* modestly disguises the fact that he is revolutionising the way in which all plurals are expressed, not merely the dative. *Na tagruighthe* was now *na tagraichion*, *gan ghníomh claidhmhe* was now *gun ghníomh chláidhin*, *le claidhmhibh* was now *le cláidhin*. By 'letters frequently transposed' I do not think he means 'letters put in place of each other' but 'letters brought across', e.g. in eclipsis *air am bualadh* for *air a mbualadh*.

Gairm an De Mhoir was printed in Glasgow in 1748–50 by Robert and Andrew Foulis at the expense of an Irish gentleman, Joseph Damer (Masson 1878–9a: 216). MacFarlane's Psalms of 1753 were printed in Glasgow by John Orr, a native of Bute. MacDonald's *Ais-Eiridh* is believed also to have been printed by Orr in Glasgow, albeit surreptitiously (MacLean 1915: 189; Black 2007b: 28), in which case the claim *nach b' aithne do na cloi-fheara aon fhacall do an chánoin* 'that the printers did not know one word of the language' (Mac-Dhonuill 1751: 212) is a blind. In the circumstances, it seems highly unlikely that MacDonald's manuscript was written, or even revised, after the publication of *Gairm an De Mhoir*. It is possible that MacFarlane and MacDonald were in contact between 1746 and 1750, and in fact we know that the latter was in Glencoe or Glen Etive in July 1749 (Paton 1895: 337), but it seems more likely that their substantive discussions on orthography took place before the '45. Indeed, had MacDonald based his spelling on MacFarlane's publication, he could not have referred to his own handling of quiescents and eclipsis as 'innovations'.

In 1749 the Synod of Argyll had discussed the preparation of a new edition of the Psalms, to be edited by MacFarlane and the Rev. Alexander Campbell of Inveraray and printed by Orr. On 27 July that year MacFarlane submitted his proposals for revising the orthography of the work. The Synod's decision was minuted (MacTavish 1934: xix):

> The Committee of Overtures, having perused the Act of last Synod concerning the new edition of the Psalms in Irish metre, together with the specimen thereof lately printed and the reasons given them by Mr Alexr. McFarlan for the alterations in the orthography from the edition of One thousand six hundred and ninety four, Did Overture that it be recommended to Mr McFarlan to cause reprint the said specimen on the paper and in the type proper for the new edition, and subjoin thereto the reasons for making the alterations.

In August 1751 they asked MacFarlane for a progress report. On receiving his response that he had 'corresponded and conversed with some brethren of neighbouring Synods and persons well skilled in Irish', they decided to delay printing any further specimens until it 'appeared how his translation of Baxter was relished' (MacTavish 1934: xx). Whether the 'persons well skilled in Irish' included MacDonald we have no way of knowing, but I believe that we should see MacDonald and MacFarlane, jointly and inseparably, as the founding fathers of Gaelic orthography.

The Synod were right to be concerned. With his Baxter translation MacFarlane had brought our spelling into a new era. Most of his innovations were sound, but a couple must have looked like steps too far. One was his use of double letters – he wrote not only *ll, nn* and *rr* in historically impossible contexts (*cheanna, cuirr, deallaich, fa dearr, gairrid, a leannas, uirrid*) but also *bb, dd* and *ss* (*obbair, obbann, creiddeamh, cuidd, cuiddeachadh, staidd, fioss, leassacha, mheass mì*). The other was his treatment of palatal *s*, which he made *sh* as in English: *foish, gluaish, a ghraish, laigsh', leish, rish, sheadh, sheirbhisheach, sho, shin, toishich, toisheachadh.* There are two objections to this. One is that, in all of these examples except *sho*, palatalisation is already shown by the presence of a slender vowel. The other is that MacFarlane made no attempt to alter the spelling of lenited *s*, writing for example *shaoilinn, a shaoil thu, a cheist shoillear sho, air a shuaimhneas, air a shon sho uille.* For no clear purpose other than with regard to the little words *so* and *sud*, he had created orthographic ambiguity on a huge scale.

More has already been written on MacDonald's orthography than on that of all his successors put together (Mackinnon 1907–8: 291–2; Campbell 1984: 42–7; Thomson 1996: 20–1). We know nothing of MacFarlane's character but a great deal about MacDonald's, and it is of a piece with his spelling. He perceived the way ahead more clearly than MacFarlane but moved too inconsistently along it. If MacFarlane was a sober man striking off boldly on the wrong road, MacDonald was a drunk man swaying about on the right one. Rough and erratic though it is, the spelling of the *Ais-Eiridh* is today's. It is the first Gaelic book of which this can be said.

The question of 'influence' must be faced, as some may think that one or other of these two books of 1750–1 was seldom read. In the eighteenth century there was an insatiable demand for works of popular pietism, and that there was a market for MacFarlane's book is undoubted. It was used in the SSPCK's schools. And it appeared again in 1755, 1811, 1822, 1845, 1866, 1877, 1884 and 1894. MacDonald's was an 'under the counter' publication; many of his songs were clever or beautiful, some were also seditious or obscene, but his power and originality made him the Gaelic poet emulated by his peers (Black 2007a). In 1764 Orr openly reprinted a cross-section of the songs (including seditious and obscene ones), and further editions or reprints followed in 1802, 1834, 1835, 1839, 1851, 1874, 1892, 1924 and 1996.

At last a sensible route had been pegged out for Gaelic spelling. In MacFarlane's new edition of the Psalms (along with the first edition of the Gaelic Paraphrases), which duly appeared in 1753, his earlier eccentricities were nowhere to be seen.

In 1754 Orr published a new edition of Kirk's NT, making one major orthographic change: whereas Kirk's work was comprehensively accented with acutes, the odd grave creeping in apparently by accident, Orr's was sparingly accented with graves. In Matt. 2: 1–3, for example, I count twenty-eight acutes and one grave in Kirk, seven graves and no acutes in Orr. I also notice Kirk's handling of proclitics causing a headache: in attempting to adapt the norms of Gaelic script to those of Roman, Kirk had written *a Mbetleem, go Híarusalem, na Niúduigheadh, agus Iárusaleim*; Orr 'corrected' these to *a Mbetleem, go Hierusalem, na Niuduigheadh, agus Hierusalem*!

He also replaced Kirk's vocabulary with a new one and appended two pages of advice, in Gaelic, on reading Gaelic. This consisted of an explanation of the *leathann ri leathann* rule, with some remarks on the pronunciation of certain consonants, on diphthongs, triphthongs and the function of the accent. Curiously, Orr allows for three lengthmarks, the *Sineadh-garbh* 'grave', *Sineadh-caol* 'acute' and *Sineadh-crom* 'circumflex', then proceeds to give examples of the contrast between short and long syllables using the grave only, e.g. *re* 'to', *rè* 'the moon', *le* 'with', *lè* 'with her', *mo* 'mine', *mò* 'more'. He ends by advertising some of his books and expressing, again in Gaelic, his intention of reprinting Kirk's OT (if demand for it is made known to him quickly) and *Gairm an De Mhoir* (Black 2007b: 30). This suggests that the Foulis brothers' edition was sold out and that they had decided not to reprint it. Orr was as good as his word, reprinting it in 1755. No changes were made to the spelling until 1811, when Patrick MacFarlane, an Appin schoolmaster (Mackinnon 1930: 57), published an orthographically revised edition described on its title-page as *air a ghlanadh o mhearachdaibh lionmhor eugsamhuil*, 'purged of numerous extraordinary errors' (Macpharlain 1811). Such is the fate of innovative ideas which are not adopted.

The precise route of MacDonald's broad road had been properly staked out in MacFarlane's Psalms and Paraphrases. What was now needed was consolidation, firm answers to a number of outstanding questions, leading to consistency of usage. What, for example, was to be the role of the acute accent, thus mentioned by Orr but not defined?

By the 1760s, with a nudge from Dr Johnson, the SSPCK had decided that they could no longer defend their policy in Highland schools of 'locking up the Scriptures in an unknown tongue' (Campbell 2000: 170). As Alexander MacFarlane preferred the work of writing a grammar, the task of translating the NT afresh into what was at last being recognised as a language in its own right – 'Gaelic' or 'the Highland language' rather than 'Irish' or 'Erse' – had fallen to the Rev. James Stuart of Killin (1700–89), a native of Glenfinlas in the Trossachs. It is curious to reflect that the *Ais-Eiridh* must have lain on his desk as one of his most most important sources, ready to be popped into a drawer whenever an elder came to call. The result of his labours was published in 1767. The fact that the work was a treasure-house of the new orthography is emphasised by the presence at the end of 'RULES for Reading the GALIC LANGUAGE', nine pages numbered 1–9 (the pages of the NT being unnumbered).

Stuart, a good Gaelic scholar, had wrestled manfully with the task of reconciling 'correct spelling' with 'correct pronunciation'. His 'Rules' were both a firm guide to the general usages found in the NT and a set of interim conclusions anticipating further orthographic change in matters of detail. Typical of the latter is his statement that '*chuaidh* went, *nuaidheachd* news, are commonly pronounced as if written *chaidh, noimheachd*' (Stuart 1767: 6). Looking further ahead, when he states that *na h innse, an t ainm, 'n a bheachd* and *le d' dheoir* are 'to be pronounced *na hinnse, an tainm, na bheachd, led dheoir*' (6–7), it strikes us that two of these four forms are approved by *GOC* (*Gaelic Orthographic Conventions*) today.

Typical of the 'Rules' as a firm guide, on the other hand, are Stuart's comments on the doubling of consonants other than *l, n* and *r*, which show him driving the orthographic carriage along the well-made road of long-established conventions while avoiding the unmentionable words 'Irish', 'Kirk' and 'MacDonald'. He cleverly turns the debate on its head, accepting that in certain cases consonants written single were 'generally pronounced as when written double in English' and listing examples: *bradan*, he points out, should be pronounced *braddan*, but that does not mean that it should be spelt that way.

With regard to lenition, however, Stuart's desire to adhere to fundamental Irish orthographic principles was strained to breaking point. 'The orthography of the Scotch Galic wants nothing so much', he says, 'as some proper marks or characters for distinguishing these different sounds of the consonants l, n, r.' This time the current of his mind is flowing towards, rather than away from, the examples which he cites in the form of pronunciation-spellings (Stuart 1767: 9):

as *lann* a sword, *lìth* colour, *sleadh* a spear, *nimh* venom, *ràmh* an oar; to be pronounced *llann, llìth, slleadh, nnimh, rràmh* . . . as *reubainn* I would have wounded, *o neart an teine loisgich* from the force of the consuming fire; to be pronounced *rheubainn, nheart, lhoisgich* . . .

He then shows how this would work in practice: '*eilid luath* (*lhuath*) a swift hind', '*cù luath* (*lluath*) a swift dog', '*a neart* (*nheart*) his strength', '*a neart* (*nneart*) her strength', '*ròn* (*rròn*) a sea-calf, *ròn* (*rhòn*) of sea-calves', '*leum* (*lheum*) *mi* I jumped, *leum* (*lleum*) *thusa* jump thou'. Thus was he beginning to pass on his thoughts to his son John (1743–1821). In fact he left a marked-up copy of the NT from which John edited a second edition. Following scrutiny by others, this was published in 1796 (Mackinnon 1930: 56); it was, however, still very 'Irish' (Masson 1878–9a: 102).

One of the correctors to the press of the NT in 1767 was the poet-catechist Dugald Buchanan (1716–68). He seized the opportunity to have his own hymns printed; it is no surprise that their orthography follows that of the NT, while using accents very sparingly (for reasons of economy, perhaps?) and charting some of the ways forward which were already in James Stuart's mind. Indeed, noting that SSPCK minutes show that Buchanan was the first person to turn any portion of the NT into Gaelic, Donald Meek (2009: 101) has speculated that Buchanan may have had a hand in the actual translation.

Work was proceeding on the OT throughout the last three decades of the century. It was divided into four equal parts, the Pentateuch (Genesis to Deuteronomy), Joshua to 1st Chronicles, 2nd Chronicles to the Song of Solomon, and the Prophets (Isaiah to Malachi). The first three parts were done (or at least supervised) by John Stuart, from 1777 minister of Luss, the fourth by Dr John Smith (1747–1807), a native of Glenorchy who became minister of Campbeltown. They were foils to each other. John Stuart was a modest, kindly man with a passion for botany who meekly carried out the tasks assigned him by his father and the Church (Mackinnon 1930: 76; MacKenzie 1992: 25). Before going to Luss he was minister of Arrochar, where tradition remembered him as possessing supernatural powers (Winchester 1916: 27), a fate shared by quiet men of mighty intellectual achievements – Kirk had been another. Smith was an extrovert who was proactive in everything he undertook. Psalms, hymns, paraphrases and exegetics poured from his pen (Masson 1878–9a: 191; Mackinnon 1930: 15–17, 34–9), while to make money on the side he fabricated Ossianic verse in the style of James Macpherson, and was bitterly disappointed when his *Galic Antiquities* (1780) and *Sean Dàna* (1787) met with a poor reception (Black 1986a: 12, 15, 17). He was a more intrepid poet and Biblical scholar than Stuart, but twice faced charges of heresy (Mackinnon 1930: 16, 17, 62; Thomson 1994: 23–4). His Prophets were so well researched that they differed alarmingly from King James's Bible (Masson 1878–9a: 191); in his Paraphrases, on the other hand, 'sound doctrine was weakened and emasculated for the sake of literary grace and rhythm' (Mackinnon 1930: 38).

The younger Stuart was assisted in his work by John and James MacNaughton (Masson 1878–9a: 142). Proofs of the Pentateuch were read by a committee including the Rev. Donald MacQueen of Kilmuir, Skye, whose learning had impressed Dr Johnson (Mackinnon 1930: 59–60; Black 2007c: 153). MacQueen's comments survive, revealing that Gaelic spelling was to him *terra incognita* (NLS Adv. MS 73.2.21; MacLeod 1931–3): he writes neither *ar* nor *air*, but *er*.

The Pentateuch appeared in 1783. Valuably, it contains footnotes which incorporate not only many of MacQueen's suggestions (Masson 1878–9a: 303–5) but also alternative and Irish spellings. Here for example is Gen. 1: 1–8, 14; I have brought the alternative and Irish spellings into square brackets to demonstrate how Stuart was creating a new orthodoxy in full awareness of the past and potential future.

> 'San toiseach chruthaich Dia na neamhan agus an talamh. Agus bha'n talamh gun dealbh agus falamh [folamh. *Eir.*]; agus bha dorchadas air [er] aghaidh na doimhne: agus bha Spiorad Dé a' gluasad air aghaidh nan uisgeacha. Agus thubhairt [thuirt; a dubhairt. *Eir.*] Dia, Biodh solus ann: agus bha solus ann. Agus chunnaic [chonnairc. *Eir.*] Dia an solus, gu [go. *Eir.*]'n robh [ro; raibh. *Eir.*] e math [maith]: agus chuir Dia dealachadh eadar an solus agus an dorchadas. Agus dh'ainmich Dia an solus Là [Latha], agus an dorchadas dh'ainmich e Oidhche: agus b'iad am feasgar agus a'mhadainn an ceud là. Agus thubhairt Dia, Biodh athar [aidhear] 'am meadhon nan uisgeacha, agus cuireadh e dealachadh eadar uisgeachan agus uisgeacha. Agus rinn Dia an t-athar, agus chuir e dealachadh eadar na h-uisgeachan a bha fuidh'n athar, agus na h-uisgeachan a bha os cionn [ceann] an athair: agus bha e mar sin. Agus dh'ainmich Dia an t-athar Nèamh: agus b'iad am feasgar agus a'mhadainn [do budh e an nòin agus an mhaidean. *Eir.*] an dara [darna] là ... Agus thubhairt Dia, Biodh soluis ann an speuraibh nèimh a chur dealachaidh eadar an là agus an oidhche, agus bitheadh iad air son chomharan [mar chomharthan], agus air son aimsirean, agus air son lài [làethe], agus bhliadhnacha.

The work thus conveys an impression of poetic sensibility and demotic change, underpinned by humility. Stuart had opened the flood-gates to plurals in *-an* in the nominative and genitive cases, but only before a following vowel – as Alexander Stewart (1801: 54) later remarked, 'other masculine nouns, and all feminine nouns, have their Nom. Plur. in *a*, to which *n* is added, *euphoniae causa*, before an initial vowel'. At the end of Stuart's volume are a five-page glossary and three pages of 'General Rules for Reading the Gaelic Language' (the pages are unnumbered, but I will refer to them as [1]–[8]). The reason why this is shorter than James Stuart's 'Rules for Reading the Galic Language' is that there were fewer loose ends. One remains, however – John points out that *l*, *n* and *r* may be 'aspirated', i.e. 'pronounced nearly as in English'. But he cites only one 'revolutionary' spelling, *lluath*, this time merely by way of explanation (Stuart 1783: [8]), as if he is weary of the discussion, and indeed these are the last words of the Pentateuch: 'With masculine substantives they retain their primitive sound, as *fear mòr* a great man, *cù luath* (*lluath*) a swift dog. When the consonants *l*, *n*, *r*, have their double sound in the middle or end of words, they are written double, as in *Gall* a foreigner, *fearr* better.'

In one fundamental respect, nasalisation, the Stuarts pulled our orthography in the direction of their own southern dialect. They wrote *am feasgar*, *am fearann*, *an sluagh*, *an so*, *an sin*, *an sud*, presumably on the grounds that the nasal was present in their Gaelic in all such cases – MacDonald had written all of these without -*m* or -*n*. It is ironic that in this most fundamental of orthographic features, a system representing a dialect effectively dead since 1900 was imposed upon the Gaelic language in perpetuity. Speaking of Badenoch, Braemar and Perthshire, Dr John MacInnes has expressed the same point more kindly (MacAonghais 1990: 25, cf. Newton 2006: 128): 'Tha sgrìobhadh an *m* romh *f* na riaghailte dhaingeann a' toirt far comhair gur h-ann anns na cèarnan sin, on ear gu deas, agus gu sònraichte an Arra Ghàidheal, a bha neart agus ùghdarras na Gàidhlig san ochdamh ceud deug nuair a thàinig leabhraichean Gàidhlig am follais.' ('The writing of *m* before *f* as a fixed rule brings home to us that when Gaelic books came to the fore in the eighteenth century, Gaelic power and authority lay in those districts – along a line from east to south, and especially in Argyll.')

In 1775 Dr Johnson wrote of Gaelic that 'whoever . . . now writes in this language, spells according to his own perception of the sound, and his own idea of the power of the letters' (Black 2007c: 207). As his principal informants were the Rev. Donald MacQueen and the clever but harum-scarum young son of the laird of Coll, it is not difficult to see where he was coming from. His comments roused the ire of the Rev. Donald McNicol, who pointed out (1779: 309) that 'nothing can be more false than what is here said of the uncertainty of Gaelic orthography', and that 'it has a regular and established standard, as is well known to many gentlemen of taste, candour, and curiosity'. But the sentiments picked up by Dr Johnson remain familiar today, and serve as a reminder that a spelling system can only be as good as the education system that underpins it. As long as English education penetrates further than Gaelic into Gaelic speakers' minds, Dr Johnson will be correct.

Smith's controversial Prophets came out in 1786. Stuart had allowed him his head with regard to the translation and scrutinised the spelling instead. Smith's revised edition of the Metrical Psalms, from which, in John Reid's opinion, 'all the North country words and Irishisms are thrown out' (Reid 1832: 27), followed in 1787. I have discussed the mystery of the 'North country words' elsewhere (Black 2008b: 79); there is no doubt that Smith's Psalms and Paraphrases were preferred in Argyll, MacFarlane's in the north, and that the divide was deepened when the Rev. Thomas Ross of Lochbroom (1768–1843) published a revised but unmodernised edition of MacFarlane's work in 1807 (Mackinnon 1930: 19–20, 24, 38). Smith had certainly not thrown out all the Irishisms either, however, for in Psalms 1 and 23 alone I find *lò* (fixed by rhyme), *d'an gluaisinn*, *dheasuigh's*, *comhnuigheam*, and *a t'ann* and *Ata'd* as well as *tha*. In 1820 there was to be virtual war between north and south over Ross's proposed new translation of the entire Scriptures; it was won by the south, and Ross's manuscript has since disappeared (Ross 1820; Masson 1878–9a: 347–50; Mackinnon 1930: 66–71).

The years 1786 and 1787 were busy ones for Smith, his Ossianic *Dan an Deirg* and *Sean Dàna* and his Psalms appearing hard on the heels of his Prophets; 1787 was also the year of Stuart's second volume, Joshua to 1st Chronicles, which marked not advance but consolidation. A few years later, having referred in a Gaelic preface to the boost which the translation of the Scriptures had given to the language's chances of survival, the schoolmaster Robert Macfarlan remarked (1795: iii–iv):

> Tha na Sailm eadar-theangaichte ann Dànachd, agus cuid eile do leabhraiche crabhach; Thuille air a so, tha moran Oran, rannachd agus sean-fhocail air an cur ann clar anois leis an deagh run cheadna, cia fhad a bhios iad sin foghainteach chum a chainnt aosda agus shnasmhor so a dheanamh measail si uine amhain a dh'fheadas innseadh, ach tha aon ni cinnteach, gu'm bheil an riaghail air an sgriobhar i gu mor air a leasacha', mar 'eil i gu h iomlan air a socrucha, agus feadar a radh gur buanachd mhor so.

This he expressed in his English preface (Macfarlan 1795: vi):

> To this we may add a metrical Translation of the Psalms, with other Religious Tracts, Ancient Songs, Poems and Proverbs, which have been collected and published for the same purpose. How far these well intended labours may contribute to the revival, or

preservation of this Venerable Language, time only can determine. One thing is certain, and a point of no small importance, that the Orthography has been much improved, if not completely fixed.

Clearly the orthography had not been fixed in Macfarlan's brain, however, since his own spelling habits suggest that it had passed him by completely.

As the curtain went down on the century Smith's brother Donald, an army surgeon with an interest in medieval manuscripts (Black 1986a: 11–12, 15), published an essay on Gaelic orthography in which he suggested four principal changes (Smith 1799). Firstly, to remove the ambiguity of our/your, which 'according to the caprice of writers, we find differently written *ar, nar, 'ur, bhur*', he says, 'let *nar*, in every case answer to *our*, and *bhur* to *your*'. Secondly he suggests simplifying the writing of plurals in *-an*, irrespective of how they are spoken: *cathraichean* he would make into *cathairan*, *litrichean* into *litiran*, and so on, thus making clear his disdain for both *leathann ri leathann* and the realities of everyday speech. Thirdly, by using *-th-* he seeks to distinguish, e.g. '*Mharbhadh*, he would kill; *mharbhthadh*, he was killed . . . *Marbhar*, he will be killed; *marbhthar*, let him be killed'. Fourthly he returns to the topic of the lenited and unlenited sounds of *l, n* and *r* which John Stuart had kicked into the long grass. He considers two principal cases, first verbs: '*Las*, kindle thou; *Lhas (mi)*, I kindled: *Leon*, do thou wound; *Lheon (mi)*, I wounded. *Nith*, clean thou; *Nhith (mi)*, I cleaned; *Ruaig*, pursue thou; *Rhuaig (mi)*, I pursued . . . *Lhasin*, I would kindle; mu *lhasas (mi)*, if I kindle. Tha an teine air a *lhasadh*, the fire is kindled. *Lhasthadh* an teine, the fire was kindled.' Then possessives: '*Thog bean a LAMH . . . Thog am fear a LHAMH . . . Mhugh eisan a NHOS*, He changed his usual practice. *Mhugh ise a NOS*, She changed her usual practice.' Similarly, with regard to the dual and the copula, he suggests *da nhathair, da lhaoch, bu lhuaithe*.

In 1801 the SSPCK published John Stuart's third volume, from 2nd Chronicles to the Song of Solomon. The Bible was now complete. Stuart had driven the orthographic stagecoach steadily throughout the project, and it was difficult to claim that Gaelic spelling was not fixed. However, it was underpinned by a syntax which was going to look increasingly old-fashioned as the new century advanced. *Dh'ardaich se e, do na ceannardaibh* and *cinn nan aithriche* strike the eye immediately, for example, in 2nd Chronicles 1: 1–2. But this was not a matter of concern when a highly respected evangelical, the Rev. Alexander Stewart of Dingwall, returned to the aspect of lenition which had so troubled Donald Smith (Stewart 1801: 30–1):

Is there room to hope that it is not yet too late to recommend a method of remedying this defect? The method I would suggest is the most simple and obvious of any. It is to annex to the initial *l, n,* and *r,* in their aspirated state, the letter *h,* just as has been done to all the other consonants . . . There is hardly any writer, who has even cursorily mentioned the sound of these letters in Galic, that has not hinted at this method of correcting the error now mentioned. Is there not reason then to expect, if any Galic author or editor shall introduce the amendment here proposed, that he will meet with the approbation of his literary countrymen, and that his example will be followed by succeeding writers?

By 1807, however, when the SSPCK published Stuart's new two-volume edition of the complete OT, things had changed. Smith's 'heretical' Prophets had been rejected, and Alexander Stewart himself had been paid 100 guineas for a new translation to slot in with the parts done by Stuart (Masson 1878–9a: 191–2). In the same year, the British and Foreign Bible Society published a Bible consisting basically of John Stuart's three parts of the OT from 1783, 1787 and 1801, a version of Smith's Prophets from 1786 edited by the Rev. Dr Daniel Dewar, and the two Stuarts' NT from 1796 (Masson 1878–9a: 192–4; Mackinnon 1930: 61–4). The chance to innovate seemed to have been lost, and Stewart changed his mind (1812: 31):

> Another mode, proposed by a learned correspondent, of marking the distinction in the sound of the initial Linguals, is by writing the letter double, thus ll, nn, rr, when its sound is the same with that which is represented by those double letters in the end of a syllable; and when the sound is otherwise, to write the letter single; as, 'llamh' *hand,* 'llion' *fill,* 'mo lamh' *my hand,* 'lion mi' *I filled.* It is perhaps too late, however, to urge now even so slight an alteration as this in the Orthography of the Gaelic, which ought rather to be held as fixed beyond the reach of innovation, by the happy diffusion of the Gaelic Scriptures over the Highlands.

Despite this, something *was* done, but the chosen method was revolutionary. In the 'Quarto Bible' of 1826 – an edition of Stuart and Stewart revised by the Rev. John Macdonald of Comrie – lenited *l, n* and *r* were shown as *ḷ, ṅ* and *ṙ.* This device kept the preacher right, but was unlikely to be widely imitated; indeed, the special letters cost the SSPCK more than £40 (Masson 1878–9a: 352, 390; Mackinnon 1930: 74). To my knowledge, the only other work ever to use them was the Highland Society's *Dictionary of the Gaelic Language* (1828), where they can be found in the section 'Elements of Gaelic Grammar' and the entries *Ŧe*, *Ṙi*, etc.

Macdonald's edition, which remained the pulpit Bible for a hundred years in most places where Gaelic was preached, thus has a unique appearance, but on opening it one's immediate impression is of modernity. It was Macdonald who introduced *á* 'out of', turned *fòs* into *fathast*, employed the apostrophe for the zero possessive *('athair* 'his father'), and ended the practice of deconstructing prepositional pronouns, a 'big idea' of Alexander MacFarlane's which the Stuarts had followed. The great dictionary-makers of the 1820s duly cited *di'*, *dh'ibh*, etc., as they were obliged to do, but their own views are revealed in their 'grammar' sections, where the apostrophised forms are conspicuous by their absence.

On general principles the lexicographers were in agreement. The first to publish, Armstrong, declared (1825: ix):

> Throughout this work, I have followed the orthography of two writers, who are relied on as guides by their countrymen;—the one, Dr. Stewart of Luss, the translator of the Holy Scriptures into Gaelic; the other, Dr. Smith of Campbelton, the author of a Gaelic metrical version of the Psalms, and other creditable works. These writers spent much of their time in settling the orthography of our language; and, as they have a just and acknowledged claim to be considered authorities, it is much to be desired that they should, henceforth, be regarded in that light. Fluctuations in the Gaelic language are perilous at this stage of its existence; for, if it be not transmitted to posterity in a regular, settled form, it is to be feared, that it must soon share the fate of the forgotten Cornish.

They were not, however, entirely at one with Scripture. In the Irish period *bhith* had been *bheith*, but every Protestant writer since Alexander MacFarlane had written *bhi*, only the Catholic catechism (1781) and *Imitatio Christi* (1785) using *bhith*; now the dictionaries unanimously recommended *bhith*. Nevertheless, MacLeod and Dewar felt able to write of their own publication (1831: vi):

> We consider that one of the excellencies of this Dictionary is an uniform adherence to the justly recognised standard of Gaelic orthography, the Gaelic Bible. The venerable translators of the Scriptures, who were so competent to form an accurate judgment on this subject, gave it the most serious consideration during the many years they were engaged in their beneficent labours: and feeling as we do, the propriety of entirely acquiescing in

their decision [*sic*], as well as the advantages which result from uniformity in orthography, we have invariably conformed to the rules which they have prescribed. 'Every language,' says the great lexicographer, Dr. Johnson, 'has its anomalies, which, though inconvenient, and in themselves once unnecessary, must be tolerated among the imperfections of human things, and which require only to be registered that they may not be increased, and ascertained that they may not be confounded.'

While MacLeod and Dewar's was grinding its way through the presses of W. R. McPhun & Co. in Glasgow's Trongate, the issue of Gaelic orthography came to popular attention as never before or since (with the possible exception of a spat between Alexander Cameron and Archibald Clerk in the *Edinburgh Courant* of May–October 1870). As thousands of children were now being taught through the medium of Gaelic in a network of charity schools (Masson 1878–9a: 263–5), the resolution of this controversy was important. The principal antagonists were a failed learner who called himself 'Gathelus' and John Mackenzie from Gairloch (1806–48), who later achieved fame as the compiler of *Sar-Obair nam Bard Gaelach* (1841) and *An English-Gaelic Dictionary* (1847). Gathelus made the case for a 'new' English-based orthography which 'would throw out about a fifth of the letters now employed in every Gaelic publication, and consequently lessen the cost; and thus by saving time and expense, and facilitating the acquirement of the English language, would render Gaelic schools much more acceptable to the Highlanders'. Mackenzie expressed concern about what the directors of the SSPCK and Gaelic School Society would think, described the proposals as 'macadamizing as it were, the Gaelic language', and argued that such reforms would consign every existing Gaelic book to oblivion: 'All violent changes are dangerous.'

The controversy can be followed through the columns of *The Scots Times* (a Glasgow newspaper) from 20 February to 23 November 1830; additionally, after reading the issue of 24 August, Mackenzie (then living in Wick) penned a reasoned 6000-word reply which, although not published at the time, saw the light of day in the *Celtic Magazine* long after his death (Mackenzie 1876–7). Gathelus was given a platform by the Glasgow Celtic Society, and his proposals gained a head of steam. To the publisher of MacLeod and Dewar's it was alarming, and on 28 August McPhun placed an advertisement for his books in the *Scots Times* headed: 'GAELIC LITERATURE. *Printed according to the established, and only correct rule of Orthography.* Mun d'thoir thu air falbh na th'againn, thoir d'huinn beagan *nis fearr.*' ('Before you take away what we have, give us something better.')

In the end the Celtic Society neutralised Gathelus's campaign, which was essentially subversive, by launching a competition for essays on 'The Best Method of Improving the Orthography of the Gaelic Language', deadlined 1 January 1831. Eight were received, and the prizes went to the Rev. Dr Thomas Ross of Lochbroom, James Macintyre from Balquhidder (Black 1996: 36), James Munro from Fort William, who later published a Gaelic grammar containing a fifteen-page section on orthography (Munro 1835), and Alexander Munro, Glasgow. The essays were made available to Mackenzie, who remarked in 1847 (McAlpine 1852: ix): 'I have derived no small advantage from their perusal.'

Gathelus's assault on the broad road had been a cannonade from over the hedge, but as the nineteenth century wore on, more and more pot-holes appeared through the inadequacy of its foundations. From being the solution, the Scriptures were becoming the problem. Their orthography was based on southern Gaelic; now southern dialects were dying, and writers and editors were coming from the west. MacDonald's *Ais-Eiridh* had begun an unstoppable trend, and the quantity of secular verse on the market – demotic in nature, locked in by rhyme, almost entirely western or northern in origin – was beginning to exceed even that of translated religious prose. The dictionaries were mainly based on the Scriptures; no new ones appeared between Mackenzie's in 1847 and Macbain's in 1896. In his influential *Sar-Obair* Mackenzie launched a number of innovations: *ás* 'out of', *a's* or *as* for *is* 'and', *sid* for *sud*. He also substituted a hyphen for the apostrophe in *dh'* and *t'*, e.g. *dh-ith, dh-fhuilig, t-iomhaidh, 'ga t-iarraidh*, on what seems to me, *pace* Professor Mackinnon (1909–10: 206–7), the logical basis that the apostrophe indicates an omission, and that nothing was here omitted.

In the climate of the day, an assault on the orthography of the Scriptures was likely to be misconstrued as an assault on the Scriptures themselves. Fr Ewen MacEachen from Arisaig (1769–1849) suffered few such inhibitions. Pointing out that the Gaelic Bible contained 'many errors', he demonstrated with almost incoherent delight that this Protestant emperor had no clothes (Mac Eachainn 1842: iii–iv):

> 1. It has many Irishisms; as eadhon, to wit: gidheadh, nevertheless; feadh, as long as; àithne, commandment, (it should be fàithne;) cuthach, madness, (i.e. caothach.) 2. It has a number of provincial impure and improper words in it: as amhluadh, confusion; (i.e. aimhreit,) oilean, an island, education; (eilean,) ocar, interest; (riadh.) 3. It spells the same word various ways, as bleodhainn, bleoghainn, milk; daingionn, dainnionn, daingeann, daingean; giuthas is five ways, spelled, &c.

It was some time before a Protestant writer took up the cry. In their 'Revised Bible' of 1860, which falsely claimed on its title-page to have the 'Authority of the General Assembly of the Church of Scotland', the Revs Dr Archibald Clerk and Dr Thomas Maclauchlan quietly corrected many of the errors and inconsistencies of Macdonald's Quarto Bible (Mackinnon 1930: 84). Standardisation of orthography, grammar and syntax was to these men an obsession, and when taken to task, Clerk launched an attack on the Quarto Bible whose venom left Fr MacEachen in the shade. 'The irregularity of the orthography from beginning to end', he splutters, 'is such as to defy description.' He instances *comhar*, *comhara*, *comharra*, *comharadh*, and complains that 'a very unscholarly system prevails throughout of running short words together', e.g. *anns an* almost always becomes *san*, *anns a* becomes *'na* or *na*, and *an uair* becomes *'nuair*. In Rom. 7: 15–20 he finds *tha mi a' deanamh* four times and *tha mi deanamh* five times; elsewhere he finds *tha mi 'deanamh* (Clerk 1879–80a: 27–9; Mackinnon 1930: 93–5). Personally I regard syntactic variations of this kind as matters of style, perfectly appropriate to the Bible as a work of literature; as Gaelic editor of *The Scotsman* I use them as subbing devices to reduce wordage or fill unsightly gaps in lines.

Gaelic orthography was becoming as cluttered as a Victorian drawing-room. In the 1860s the meetings of an inter-church committee on the Gaelic scriptures were disrupted by two of its Free Church members, Maclauchlan himself and the Rev. Alexander Cameron, who wrangled endlessly over 'the insertion or non insertion of a hyphen or an inverted comma' (Mackinnon 1930: 81); it was the beginning of a 'fierce controversy' (Grant 2006: 206) which lasted twenty years. Donald Mackinnon even claims (1930: 26) that Clerk and Maclauchlan 'introduced hyphens and apostrophes, hitherto unknown to Gaelic orthography' to their 1860 and 1880 revisions of the Bible, Psalms and Paraphrases. Unless we remove Mackinnon's comma (!) this is untrue as to fact, but forgiveable as to perception. Believing with Mackenzie that omissions should be marked with an apostrophe, and that if an apostrophe had hitherto been employed where nothing was omitted it should be changed to a hyphen, Clerk and Maclauchlan went seeking omissions, producing *'an* (for *an* 'in'), *a' m' ionnsuidh*, *gu 'bhi* (why not *gu 'bhi'*?), *cha-n*, *mu-n* (Cameron 1878–79b: 463). Comparison of the Quarto Bible with their 'Reference Bible' of 1880 shows that they made *san t-slochd a's ìsle t'ann* into *'s an t-slochd a's ìsle 't'ann* (Ps. 88: 6) and *le luibhibh gorm is craobhaibh meas* into *le lùibhean gorm' 'us craobhan meas* (Par. 1: 5, cf. Mackinnon 1930: 27, 40). Carswell's solid cannonballs of 1567 had turned into shrapnel; we have been trying to put our words back together again ever since.

The most pernicious of all Clerk and Maclauchlan's reforms was the preposition *de*. It had never previously been a feature of our orthography, although its separate existence from *do* was implicit in there being two sets of prepositional pronouns (Masson 1878–79a: 352). It could do no great harm in 1860, but is destroying the language today, every second 'of' being made *de* by younger speakers as if they were French. Cameron points (1878–79a: 385) to Judges 21: 22, Ruth 1: 1 and 2nd Kings 18: 1 as particularly bad examples; of these the first (and worst) has since been fixed, but the others survive in Meek's Bible of 1992. Cameron remarked (1878–79b: 465) that another, *Rinn Iehosaphat longan de Tharsis* (1st Kings 22: 48), would make congregations think the ships were made of some material called tharshish – thus demonstrating, *pace* Masson (1878–79b: 418), that he had a keen sense of humour. This error survives in the 1939 reprint which I purchased new in 1977, but has been corrected by Meek. By way of response, Clerk retorted (1879–80b: 115) that *de* in its north-country form *dhe* was frequent in the 'extremely filthy' poems of Rob Donn as edited in 1829 by Cameron's late Free Church colleague, Dr Macintosh Mackay.

Put simply, Cameron's argument was that the Bible must be numinous; Clerk's and Maclauchlan's was that secular publications were now in the orthographic driving seat, and that if the Scriptures were to be relevant to ordinary people's lives they must keep up with the times. In 1860–2 J. F. Campbell's influential *Popular Tales of the West Highlands* had repositioned our orthography closer to the spoken language of the west (*fhéin, fhathast, a rithis, se* for *is e*, etc.) and solved the old problem of *so* and *sud* by spelling them *seo* and *siud*. Mackenzie's *á* and *ás* had been picked up by D. C. Macpherson and appear consistently in his *Duanaire* of 1868. In due course this led to another innovation, *ám* 'time' (for John Stuart's *àm*), which I have noticed in *Oiteagan á Tìr nan Òg* (Mac Dhughaill 1938), though no doubt it can be found earlier. Similarly, Clerk and Maclauchlan strove to eliminate surviving 'Irishisms' like *fuidh* (Irish *faoi*) for *fo* (Mackinnon 1930: 94), but their replacement of surviving instances of *ta* with *tha* provoked a complaint from Cameron (1878–9a: 384) that 'an interesting and expressive verbal form which still exists in the spoken language has been removed from the Scriptures'. They also standardised vocalic plural endings to *-ean, -an* (nominative) and *-ibh, -aibh* (dative), to which Cameron said, with reference to forms like *nithe* and *briathra* (1878–9a: 384): 'Thus, the regular nominative plural is banished from written Gaelic, while it is still in use in spoken Gaelic.'

The Education (Scotland) Act swept away the institution which could have held our orthography together – the Gaelic schools – in 1872, and Fr MacEachen's translation of the NT from the Vulgate, revised by Fr Colin Grant (Roberts 2006: 381–2), was published posthumously in 1875. It was full of dialect-based innovation: *ciad, ciadna, fiach,* etc., for *ceud, ceudna, feuch, nichean* for *nithean, mua* for *motha, saghach* for *soitheach, gheobh* for *gheibh, a g-radh* or *a gh-radh* for *ag ràdh* (Mackinnon 1930: 87). Grant's orthographic models were secular, not sacred. He wrote *fhein, fhathast, 'sann* and *coig,* not *cùig*; typically, his was the first religious work to abandon *focal,* even though *facal* had been in secular books since 1751. Like all other writers he used medial and final *sd* in some words and *st* in others, but he was the first since Alexander MacFarlane, I believe, to use *st* in the name of Christ, calling him *Iosa Criosta* – in this respect, as in so many others, the Stuarts had quietly followed the Episcopalian Robert Kirk.

Of all the Gaelic books I have ever seen, Fr Grant's NT is the 'cleanest', with accents, apostrophes, hyphens all kept to a minimum. This was the opposite of prevailing trends. No wonder the Rev. Robert Blair, a future co-editor of the OT, spoke of 'the unsettled state of Gaelic orthography' (Blair 1882: v; Mackinnon 1930: 102, 105, 117–18).

Our spelling was rescued in the new century by Edward Dwelly, who established a fresh orthodoxy to rival that of the Scriptures. His hugely influential *Illustrated Gaelic-English Dictionary* (1901–11), the sum of all previous word-books, contained carefully edited literary quotations and headword spellings which sometimes differed from the bulk of his sources (*á, ás, seo, siod, taigh, a staigh*). On the other hand, he gives our *gun* 'that' as *gu'n* and our *chan eil* as *cha'n 'eil,* leaving it to Professor Mackinnon to propose *chan iarr, gun iarr* (1909–10: 206).

Mackinnon noted of usages like *le h-eagal, ri h-Abraham* (1909–10: 205) that 'the latest Revisers of the Gaelic Scriptures felt themselves justified in discarding the *h* in such cases'. This was the 'Pulpit Bible', also known from the name of its principal editor – the Rev. John Maclean, a Hebraist from Tiree – as 'Dr Maclean's Bible' (Mackinnon 1930: 105–17). It was not popular, but the other Donald Mackinnon remarked (1930: 114): 'Throughout the whole work we have a uniform system of orthography.'

The drunk man's broad road remains our metaphor, but it merely defines the 'variations' in the expression 'Pentateuch with variations', or perhaps we should now say 'Bible with variations'. Alexander Carmichael, for example, used hardly any accents at all in volumes 1 and 2 of *Carmina Gadelica*. Fr Allan McDonald used an orthography as full of apostrophes as a shower of rain, but with only one accent, the grave; following MacEachen and Grant, he always wrote *ia* for 'broken' *eu* or *èa*, e.g. *fiar*, *dian*. In January 1923 An Comunn Gaidhealach, looking for a simpler name for its magazine *An Deo-Greine*, changed it to *Gailig*; this sensible little innovation fell foul of Professor Watson, who objected to 'the mis-spelling, most glaring when the word mis-spelled is the name of our language' (Thompson 1992: 52). In *Na Baird Thirisdeach* (1932) the Rev. Hector Cameron used no accents at all. In *Highland Songs of the Forty-Five* (1933) John Lorne Campbell used *us* for *is* 'and'. In *Fuaran Sléibh* (1947) and *O na Ceithir Airdean* (1952) George Campbell Hay approached the same problem by distinguishing between *s* ('and') and *'s* (the copula), though he was also willing to use *is* for both when necessary. And in *Òrain Luaidh Màiri Nighean Alasdair* (1949) and *Leigheas Cas O Céin* (1950) K. C. Craig used *mm* in *amm*, *dramm*, and *chunnaig* for *chunnaic*.

As found in the classic publications of the Scottish Gaelic Texts Society, notably perhaps those of the Rev. William Matheson (1938 and 1970), Gaelic orthography came close to perfection as a sharp but flexible tool for the consistent rendering of sound and meaning. Nothing was needed now except the codification of best practice, a process which would have led by itself to the most necessary of the *GOC* reforms, the standardisation of unstressed schwa as *a*. It is a great pity that, following his triumphant completion of *Carmina Gadelica* in 1971, Matheson was not asked by the Society to launch such a process.

What happened instead was that in 1976 Scottish Certificate of Education examiners in Gaelic reported an alarming decline in candidates' orthographic competence, and the Gaelic panel of the examination board appointed a sub-committee to look into the matter. Chaired by Donald MacAulay of the University of Aberdeen, in 1978 it produced a report entitled *Gaelic Orthographic Conventions* (*GOC*). Following consultation, the report was adopted in full by the board – a rare occurrence in public life. It was published in August 1981 with the rubric: 'To be used in the board's question papers in and after 1985. To be used by candidates in and after 1988.'

GOC was the most stimulating treatise ever written on Gaelic spelling. The thinking, like Alexander MacFarlane's, was off the road. One simple but brilliant example was the distinction proposed between *ceud* 'a hundred' and *ciad* 'first'. To me, having been brought up to believe that the weaknesses of our orthography were carved in stone along with its strengths, it was a revelation. Among other things, I was appalled to find that learners of Gaelic, such as myself, had been deceived by orthography into thinking that *sd* and *st* were different sounds. I took immediately to the principles set out in the report and the diffident and consensual way in which they were expressed – this, I thought, was the perfect springboard for development.

Alexander Cameron had believed that an accurate orthography was an 'organic' one which correctly represented the sounds of words using letters which served to indicate their origin and history (Cameron 1894: 578). *GOC* radically adjusted these principles. There now appeared to be a consensus that our orthography should show in writing both the sound and the meaning of Gaelic words, doing so as briefly, consistently and unambiguously as possible, keeping the number of exceptions to a minimum, differentiating homophones like *ceud* and *ciad*, and representing each sound by a single letter or combination of letters. Roots were no longer to be a primary consideration. The road ahead was open to *nàdar, coileanadh, comann* and a thousand other forms fixed not by history but by phonetics.

By 1988 it had emerged that one of the *GOC* reforms, the jettisoning of apostrophes, was working well in most respects, but not all. For example, if *gillean 'nam brògan* 'boys in their shoes' is written *gillean nam brògan*, its primary meaning becomes 'the boys of the shoes'. In a recent Gaelic-medium geography examination, 'slatted sides' (a piece of text in a diagram showing a Stevenson screen) was translated *taobhan 'nan slatan*, but the orthographic scrutineer removed the apostrophe, thus making the meaning ambiguous, and more likely read as 'the sides of the slats'. Such difficulties are faced by professionals on a daily basis. Where a text is difficult or not quite right and an editor, examiner, reader or translator is struggling to interpret or clarify the writer's meaning, little signals can be vital. Having made the experiment, the editor of *Gairm*, a member of the *GOC* committee, went back to placing an apostrophe on *'nam, 'nad, 'na, 'nar, 'nur* and *'nan*, but the Examination Board carried on regardless. As Professor Mackinnon, who favoured the elimination of apostrophes, wrote (1909–10: 202): 'In these, and indeed in all cases, clearness is the first consideration, and where the insertion of an Apostrophe or other mark helps to remove possible uncertainty, let it be used freely.'

The reforms were brought forward by the work of two further sub-committees in 1990–1 and 2000–5. They permeated the schools and were adopted for children's literature, then spread to the universities, to adult literature, to dictionaries, and ultimately to the internet. They also came to be underpinned by money in a way that was new. The Gaelic Books Council has made its grants to authors and publishers conditional upon adherence to the letter of *GOC* (the word-list) rather than to its spirit (the narrative). Gaelic spelling is a simple, logical system, of which only the narrative needs to be taught; once it is grasped, the specifics will fall into place automatically. This of course assumes some knowledge of the rules of grammar which underpin European languages in general, and it has to be said that the decline in pupils' Gaelic spelling was probably due to the decline in the teaching of English grammar during the 1960s and 1970s. It increasingly became clear that many teachers had no interest in the narrative and merely wished to be provided with a word-list. As *GOC*'s original narrative was actually at odds with its word-list, there emerged two remarkably different understandings of it. Regretfully I have come to the conclusion that the reforms have not been beneficial, because the tiny proportion – two or three per cent – of the original report which was incautious has been allowed to do a great deal of damage. *GOC* as it has been applied will not prevent a committed person learning Gaelic, but will retard progress. As for the uncommitted, at the point in history where intergenerational transmission ceased and orthography became crucial to the acquisition of the language, more and not fewer visual aids were required, but *GOC* reduced the number of characters from twenty (eighteen letters, two accents) to nineteen (eighteen letters, one accent).

Mackenzie's warning to Gathelus in 1830 that his proposals would consign existing Gaelic books to oblivion is becoming a reality. As the first sub-committee was warned in 1979, many in the younger generation now regard books containing acute accents as 'old-fashioned'. There is also a trend towards a single sound for *ò, è* and even *à*; one young speaker has described this trend to me as 'inevitable', while an exasperated publisher's view of spelling reformers is: 'Why do they want to change the sound of the language?'

The blame does not lie with the authors of the original report. The deficiencies have been structural. Reliance on occasional reports from a body concerned with school examinations has been inappropriate, and inadequate consideration has been given to other sectors, such as typography, literature (including poetry), scholarship and the translation industry. When I was compiling *An Tuil* (Black 1999), a poet whose day-job involved the removal of apostrophes from *'nam*, etc., in other people's work asked me to take care that they were included in his poems so that they would be understood. And the Gaelic dialects survey editors based their spellings on Dwelly, not *GOC* (Ó Dochartaigh 1997: 59), because the latter had ironed out – macadamised, to use Mackenzie's word – the kind of distinctions that they sought to illustrate, such as Dwelly's *lòn* 'food', *lón* 'meadow'.

This historical survey shows that no matter how 'fixed' an orthography may seem to be after some major step forward, be it Carswell's prayer-book in 1567, Kirk's Bible in 1690, the translation of the Scriptures in 1767–1801, Dwelly's dictionary in 1901–11, or *GOC* in 1981, it gradually unravels. Like Alexander Stewart, Michel Byrne has written that 'the modernisation of spelling in Gaelic is universally accepted in principle though still a matter for debate in its details' (Byrne 2000: xii). Unfortunately we still have our Robert Macfarlans, who blithely continue to write what they learned fifty years before while claiming to support reform, and our Gatheli, who believe that Gaelic spelling is unphonetic because it differs from English. Both are a lot of trouble. History also shows us that predictions of the imminent death of Gaelic can distract us from the necessary task of planning for the future. Orthography must be made a broad road once again, inclusive and with room for U-turns, but with speed limits. Reports should focus on specific orthographic questions, such as accenting, and on fields of application, such as translation. Follow-up reports should provide full information on feedback and dissent. Above all we must recognise that the following words of Clerk's remain as true today as when they were written (1878–9: 422):

> If . . . there be any language on which a person should write with moderation, and tolerance of the opinions of those who differ from him it is Scottish Gaelic; for its orthography is still so very unsettled that no two writers in it can be found who entirely agree as to its minuter points. Nay, I have never yet seen five pages by the same author free from variations and discrepancies, and in the various districts of the country there are wide diversities as to words and inflections, especially as to pronunciation. If people would allow each other to write after his own fashion, the better expressions would in course of time commend themselves to general acceptance. There would be 'a selection of the fittest,' as in all other cultivated languages, and a uniform style would establish itself in peace and goodwill; but if I must judge of the future by the past and the present, I see no hope of so happy a prospect for Gaelic.

ACKNOWLEDGEMENTS

I am grateful for assistance to Roibeard Ó Maolalaigh, Katrin Thier, Marilyn Waters, and the staffs of Edinburgh Central Library, Edinburgh University Library, the Mitchell Library (Glasgow) and the National Library of Scotland. All errors are my own.

BIBLIOGRAPHY

Armstrong, R. A. (1825), *A Gaelic Dictionary*, London: James Duncan.

Black, Ronald (1986a), 'The Gaelic Academy: The Cultural Commitment of the Highland Society of Scotland', part 1, *Scottish Gaelic Studies* 14:2, pp. 1–38.

Black, Ronald (1986b), *Mac Mhaighstir Alasdair: The Ardnamurchan Years*, Isle of Coll: Society of West Highland & Island Historical Research.

Black, Ronald (1994), 'Bog, Loch and River: The Nature of Reform in Scottish Gaelic', in István Fodor and Claude Hagège (eds), *Language Reform: History and Future/La Réforme des Langues: Histoire et Avenir/Sprachreform: Geschichte und Zukunft*, Vol. 6, Hamburg: Helmut Buske, pp. 123–48.

Black, Ronald (1996), 'James Macintyre's Calendar', *Scottish Gaelic Studies* 17, pp. 36–60.

Black, Ronald (ed.) (1999), *An Tuil: Anthology of 20th Century Scottish Gaelic Verse*, Edinburgh: Polygon.

Black, Ronald (ed.) (2001), *An Lasair: Anthology of 18th Century Scottish Gaelic Verse*, Edinburgh: Birlinn.

Black, Ronald (2007a), 'Alasdair mac Mhaighstir Alasdair and the New Gaelic Poetry', in Susan Manning (ed.), *The Edinburgh History of Scottish Literature*, Vol. 2, Edinburgh: Edinburgh University Press, pp. 110–24.

Black, Ronald (2007b), 'Some Notes from my Glasgow Scrapbook, 1500–1800', in Sheila M. Kidd (ed.), *Glasgow: Baile Mòr nan Gàidheal, City of the Gaels*, Glasgow: Department of Celtic, University of Glasgow, pp. 20–54.

Black, Ronald (ed.) (2007c), *To the Hebrides: Samuel Johnson's Journey to the Western Islands of Scotland and James Boswell's Journal of a Tour to the Hebrides*, Edinburgh: Birlinn.

Black, Ronald (ed.) [2005] (2008a), *The Gaelic Otherworld: John Gregorson Campbell's Superstitions of the Highlands & Islands of Scotland and Witchcraft & Second Sight in the Highlands & Islands*, 2nd edn, Edinburgh: Birlinn.

Black, Ronald (2008b), 'Gaelic Religious Publishing 1567–1800', *Scottish Gaelic Studies* 24, pp. 73–85.

Blair, Robert (ed.) (1882), *Duain agus Orain le Uilleam Mac Dhunleibhe, am Bard Ileach*, Glasgow: A. Sinclair.

Byrne, Michel (ed.) (2000), *Collected Poems and Songs of George Campbell Hay*, Vol. 2, Edinburgh: University Press.

Cameron, Rev. Alexander (1878–9a), 'The Scottish Bible Society's 8vo. dn of the Gaelic Scriptures', *The Celtic Magazine* 4, pp. 381–6.

Cameron, Rev. Alexander (1878–9b), 'Reply to Dr Maclauchlan', *The Celtic Magazine* 4, pp. 462–5.

Cameron, Rev. Alexander (1894), *Reliquiæ Celticæ*, Vol. 2, Inverness: Northern Counties.

[Cameron, Rev. Ewen, et al. (eds)] (1659), *An Ceud Chaogad do Shalmaibh, Dhaibhidh*, Glasgow: printed for Synod of Argyll by Andrew Anderson.

[Campbell, Rev. Dugald, et al.] (1694), *Sailm Dhaibhidh A Meadar Dhàna Gaoidheilg*, Edinburgh: printed for Synod of Argyll by heirs of Andrew Anderson.

[Campbell, Duncan, and Macbain, Alexander] (1890–1), 'The Spelling of Gaelic', *The Highland Monthly*, p. 762.

Campbell, John Lorne (ed.) [1933] (1984), *Highland Songs of the Forty-Five*, Edinburgh: Scottish Gaelic Texts Society.

Campbell, John Lorne (2000), *A Very Civil People: Hebridean Folk, History and Tradition*, Hugh Cheape (ed.), Edinburgh: Birlinn.

Clerk, Rev. Dr Archibald (1878–9), 'The Scottish Bible Society's 8vo. Edn of the Gaelic Scriptures', *The Celtic Magazine* 4, pp. 418–24.

Clerk, Rev. Dr Archibald (1879–80a), 'Gaelic Scriptures – Editions of 1826 and 1860', *The Celtic Magazine* 5, pp. 26–31.

Clerk, Rev. Dr Archibald (1879–80b), 'The Gaelic Scriptures – Further Answer to Mr Cameron's Charges', *The Celtic Magazine* 5, pp. 112–16.

[Gillies, John (ed.)] (1786), *A Collection of Ancient and Modern Gaelic Poems and Songs*, Perth: John Gillies.

Grant, William (2006), 'Alexander Cameron and *Reliquiae Celticae*', in M. Byrne, T. O. Clancy and S. Kidd (eds), *Litreachas & Eachdraidh, Rannsachadh na Gàidhlig 2: Literature & History, Papers from the Second Conference of Scottish Gaelic Studies*, Glasgow: University of Glasgow, Department of Celtic, pp. 200–13.

Higgitt, John (2000), *The Murthly Hours: Devotion, Literacy and Luxury in Paris, England and the Gaelic West*, London: British Library.

Kirk, Raibeard (ed.) (1684), *Psalma Dhaibhidh a nMeadrachd*, 'Ar a ngcur a ngcló a nDún-Edin le M. Sémus Kniblo, Iosua van Solingen agus Seón Colmar'.

Lhuyd, Edward (1707), *Archæologia Britannica*, Vol. 1, Oxford: printed for the author.

Lhuyd, Edward (1713), 'Observations in Natural History and Antiquities', *Philosophical Transactions* 28, pp. 93–101.

McAlpine, Neil (1852), *Rudiments of Gaelic Grammar*, 3rd edn, Edinburgh: Maclachlan and Stewart.

MacAonghais, Iain (1990), 'Cainnt is Canan', *An Tarbh* 1, Sabhal Mor Ostaig, pp. 23–5.

MacAulay, Donald (1976–8), 'The Writing of Scottish Gaelic: Uses of Convention and Innovation', *Transactions of the Gaelic Society of Inverness* 50, pp. 81–96.

MacCoinnich, Aonghas (2008), 'Where and How Was Gaelic Written in Late Medieval and Early Modern Scotland? Orthographic Practices and Cultural Identities', *Scottish Gaelic Studies* 24, pp. 309–56.

Mac-Dhonuill, Alastair (1751), *Ais-Eiridh na Sean Chánoin Albannaich; no, An Nuadh Oranaiche Gaidhealach*, 'Clo-bhuailt' ann Duneidiunn, Go feim an Ughdair'.

Mac Dhughaill, Eachann (deas.) (1938), *Oiteagan á Tìr nan Òg: Orain agus Dain le Ruairidh Mac Aoidh, Loch-nam-Madadh*, Glascho: A. MacLabhruinn.

Mac Eachainn, Eobhan (1842), *Faclair, Gailig us Beurla*, Perth: R. Morison. [MDCCCLXII on title-page should read MDCCCXLII, see preface to later editions.]

Macfarlan, Robert (1795), *A New Alphabetical Vocabulary, Gailic and English*, Edinburgh: printed for the author by John Moir.

[MacFarlane, Rev. Alexander (trans.)] (1750), *Gairm an De Mhoir do 'n t Sluagh Neimh-Iompoichte . . . le Richard Baxter*, Glasgow: Robert and Andrew Foulis.

[MacFarlane, Rev. Alexander (ed.)] (1753), *Sailm Dhaibhidh ann Dan Gaoidhealach*, Glasgow: John Orr.

MacKenzie, Donald W. (1992), *The Worthy Translator: How the Scottish Gaels Got the Scriptures in their Own Tongue*, Killin: Society of Friends of Killin and Ardeonaig Parish Church.

Mackenzie, John (1876–7), 'Defence of the Orthography of the Gaelic Language', *The Celtic Magazine* 2, pp. 312–16, 332–6.

Mackinnon, Prof. Donald (1907–8), 'Unpublished Poems by Alexander Macdonald (Mac Mhaighstir Alastair)', part 1, *The Celtic Review* 4, pp. 289–305.

Mackinnon, Prof. Donald (1909–10), 'Accents, Apostrophes, and Hyphens in Scottish Gaelic', *The Celtic Review* 6, pp. 193–207.

Mackinnon, Rev. Donald (1930), *The Gaelic Bible and Psalter*, Dingwall: Ross-shire Printing and Publishing Co.

MacLean, Rev. Donald (1915), *Typographia Scoto-Gadelica*, Edinburgh: John Grant.

MacLeod, Fred. T. (1931–3), 'Observations on the Gaelic Translation of the Pentateuch, by Rev. Donald Macqueen, Skye, 1777–83', *Transactions of the Gaelic Society of Inverness* 36, pp. 346–407.

Macleod, Rev. Dr Norman, and Dewar, Rev. Dr Daniel (1831), *A Dictionary of the Gaelic Language*, Glasgow: W. R. McPhun.

McNicol, Rev. Donald (1779), *Remarks on Dr. Samuel Johnson's Journey to the Hebrides*, London: Cadell.

Macpharlain, P. (ed.) (1811), *Gairm an De Mhoir do'n t-Sluagh Neo-Iompaichte*, Edinburgh: 'Clo-bhuailte le I. Clèireach, 'an Sràid a Chruidh'.

MacTavish, Duncan C. (ed.) (1934), *The Gaelic Psalms 1694*, Lochgilphead: James Annan.

Masson, Rev. Donald (1878–9a), 'Our Gaelic Bible', *The Celtic Magazine*, vol. 4, pp. 99–102, 141–5, 190–5, 210–17, 259–65, 302–6, 347–54, 390.

Masson, Rev. Donald (1878–9b), 'The Scottish Bible Society's 8vo. Edn of the Gaelic Scriptures', *The Celtic Magazine* 4, pp. 417–18.

Matheson, Rev. William (ed.) (1938), *The Songs of John MacCodrum*, Edinburgh: Scottish Gaelic Texts Society.

Matheson, Rev. William (ed.) (1970), *The Blind Harper: The Songs of Roderick Morison and his Music*, Edinburgh: Scottish Gaelic Texts Society.

Meek, Donald (1989), 'The Scots-Gaelic Scribes of Late Medieval Perthshire: An Overview of the Orthography and Contents of the Book of the Dean of Lismore', in J. D. McClure and M. R. G. Spiller (eds), *Bryght Lanternis: Essays on the Language and Literature of Medieval and Renaissance Scotland*, Aberdeen: University Press, pp. 387–404.

Meek, Donald (2009), 'Evangelicalism, Ossianism and the Enlightenment: The Many Masks of Dugald Buchanan', in Christopher MacLachlan (ed.), *Crossing the Highland Line: Cross-Currents in Eighteenth-Century Scottish Writing*, Glasgow: Association for Scottish Literary Studies, pp. 97–112.

Munro, James (1835), *A Practical Grammar of the Scottish Gaelic*, Edinburgh: Maclachlan and Stewart.

Newton, Michael (ed.) (2006), *Dùthchas nan Gàidheal: Selected Essays of John MacInnes*, Edinburgh: Birlinn.

Ó Baoill, Colm (ed.) (1979), *Eachann Bacach and Other Maclean Poets*, Edinburgh: Scottish Gaelic Texts Society.

Ó Baoill, Colm (2007), 'Robert Campbell, Forsair Choire an t-Sìth', *Scottish Gaelic Studies* 23, pp. 57–84.

Ó Cuív, Brian (1958–61), 'A Seventeenth-Century Manuscript in Brussels', *Éigse* 9, pp. 173–80.

Ó Dochartaigh, Cathair (ed.) (1997), *Survey of the Gaelic Dialects of Scotland* 1, Dublin: Dublin Institute for Advanced Studies.

Paton, Henry (ed.) (1895), *The Lyon in Mourning* 2, Edinburgh: Scottish History Society.

Pattison, Thomas (1866), *Selections from the Gaelic Bards*, Glasgow: Archibald Sinclair.

Reid, John (1832), *Bibliotheca Scoto-Celtica*, Glasgow: John Reid.

Roberts, Alasdair (2006), 'Maighstir Eobhann Mac Eachainn and the Orthography of Scots Gaelic', *Transactions of the Gaelic Society of Inverness* 63, pp. 358–405.

Ross, Thomas (1820), *Quarto Gaelic Bible. There is to be published by subscription, an elegant and improved edition of The Sacred Scriptures, in the Gaelic Language: with notes, critical, explanatory and practical*, Lochbroom.

Scott, Hew (1915–50), *Fasti Ecclesiæ Scoticanæ*, new edn, 8 vols, Edinburgh: Oliver & Boyd.

Smith, Capt. Donald (1799), 'Remarks on Some Corruptions which have been Introduced into the Orthography, and Pronunciation, of the Gaelic; with Proposals for Removing them, and Restoring the Purity of the Language', *Transactions of the Highland Society of Scotland* 1, pp. 324–43.

Stewart, Alexander (1801), *Elements of Galic Grammar*, Edinburgh: C. Stewart.

Stewart, Alexander (1812), *Elements of Gaelic Grammar*, 2nd edn, Edinburgh: C. Stewart.

[Stuart, Rev. James (trans.)] (1767), *Tiomnadh Nuadh ar Tighearna agus ar Slanuigh-Fhir Iosa Criosd*, Edinburgh: printed for SSPCK by Balfour, Auld and Smellie.

[Stuart, Rev. John (trans.)] (1783), *Leabhraiche an t-Seann Tiomnaidh, air an Tarruing o'n Cheud Chanain chum Gaelic Albannaich. Ann an Ceithir Earrannaibh. Earrann I*, Edinburgh: printed for SSPCK by William Smellie.

Thompson, Frank (1992), *History of An Comunn Gaidhealach: The First Hundred (1891–1991)*, Inverness: An Comunn Gaidhealach.

Thomson, Derick S. (ed.) [1983] (1994), *The Companion to Gaelic Scotland*, 2nd edn, Glasgow: Gairm.

Thomson, Derick S. (1996), *Alasdair Mac Mhaighstir Alasdair: Selected Poems*, Edinburgh: Scottish Gaelic Texts Society.

Thomson, R. L. (ed.) (1962), *Adtimchiol an Chreidimh: The Gaelic Version of John Calvin's Catechismus Ecclesiae Genevensis*, Edinburgh: Scottish Gaelic Texts Society.

Thomson, R. L. (1970), *Foirm na h-Urrnuidheadh: John Carswell's Gaelic Translation of the Book of Common Order*, Edinburgh: Scottish Gaelic Texts Society.

Thomson, R. L. (1971), 'The Language of the Shorter Catechism (1659)', *Scottish Gaelic Studies* 12, part 1, pp. 34–51.

Thomson, R. L. (1976), 'The Language of the *Caogad* (1659)', *Scottish Gaelic Studies* 12, part 2, pp. 143–82.

Winchester, Rev. Hugh (*c.*1916), *Traditions of Arrochar and Tarbet and the MacFarlanes*, n.p., n.pub.

CHAPTER 12

Phonology in Modern Gaelic

Anna R. K. Bosch

INTRODUCTION

Students of the phonology of Scottish Gaelic are fortunate in the array of excellent descriptive studies of Gaelic available today, spanning a good part of the twentieth century, from the early impressionistic sketches of Robertson (1899–1901, 1900) and Dieckhoff (1926); through the detailed descriptions of regional varieties exemplified by Borgstrøm's several studies (Borgstrøm 1937, 1940, 1941); to the more recent comprehensive five-volume project *The Survey of the Gaelic Dialects of Scotland* (Ó Dochartaigh 1994–7; henceforth SGDS). [1] Despite the range of descriptive material available, however, Scottish Gaelic has been largely ignored by theoretical phonologists, with some few exceptions. This chapter aims to sketch out the basic phonological structure of Scottish Gaelic, to indicate where theoretical and experimental work has contributed to our understanding of Gaelic phonetics and phonology, and to point up where significant gaps remain yet to be filled. Drawing on evidence from SGDS, and with particular emphasis on the Gaelic of Barra as described by Borgstrøm (1937) and confirmed by the present author's own fieldwork on Barra, we present an outline of the phonological organisation of Gaelic, highlighting principal questions of interest to phonologists. In addition, this chapter illustrates certain of the advantages and difficulties of working with the SGDS: a resource which offers laser-like detail in phonetic transcription and yet on occasion fails to provide the simple phonological contrasts that one might desire.

SGDS AND TWENTIETH-CENTURY RESEARCH INTO GAELIC PHONOLOGY

Several decades in the middle of the twentieth century saw a flourishing of research into the dialects of Scottish Gaelic, beginning with Borgstrøm's several volumes on Barra, the Outer Hebrides, and Skye and Ross-shire, and including the later work of Ternes (1973), Dorian (1978), and Ó Murchú (published in 1989, but based on fieldwork from the 1960s). In Scotland as elsewhere in Europe and North America we have today the tangible results of this period of concentrated interest directed towards the spoken language of local communities. Indeed, the origins of the Linguistic Survey of Scotland, culminating in the eventual publication of the SGDS, also drew from this well of interest in dialect geography. As Hamp outlines in a detailed chapter in volume one of the SGDS, work on the Survey was initiated in the late 1940s and early 1950s in the context of a lively and active European research programme on folk speech and folk-ways generally. The Gaelic Survey project was roughly contemporaneous with the various dialect projects of North America, especially the *Linguistic Atlas of New England* (already then published in three volumes as Kurath et al. 1939–43). Fieldwork for the *Linguistic Atlas and Survey of Irish Dialects* (Wagner and Ó Baoill 1958–69; 4 vols) had already begun, as had work for the *Survey of English Dialects* (Orton et al. 1962–71; 4 vols). As the Gaelic Survey project developed under the direction of Kenneth Jackson, however, it was envisaged as a dialect study with purely philological – that is, historical phonetic – interest (Jackson 1958; see also Gillies 1988). The 48-page word-list questionnaire was administered by seven trained fieldworkers and noted in a narrow transcription which was adapted from the International Phonetic Alphabet as influenced by Celticist practice. The survey itself focused entirely on phonetic detail, and included virtually no questions on lexical difference or syntax. Thus as a record the published SGDS and its associated archives present an enormous wealth of geographically structured data, in the form of narrow transcriptions of the Survey word-list, accompanied by the marginal notations of Jackson and the individual fieldworkers.[2]

While there is no recognised standard variety of Gaelic, Gillies (1993) refers to an informal standard, that employed by speakers from the 'core' region of the Gaidhealtachd. This area, from the west central Highlands to the Western Isles 'combines many of the best known Scottish Gaelic phonological innovations with a conservative inflectional system' (Gillies 1993: 146), and is often held up as an informal standard; this chapter will make occasional note of regional differences in Gaelic phonology while otherwise describing the phonology of this 'core' or central variety.

We begin with a discussion of the Gaelic vowel system, presenting a phonological inventory of oral and nasal vowels, vowels in stressed and unstressed position, and the distribution of diphthongs. The sections on Gaelic consonants address contrastive palatalisation, the voiced/ voiceless or aspirated/unaspirated contrast in stops, and the problem of preaspiration, including a brief presentation of experimental phonetic studies on Gaelic preaspiration. A description of the complex system of sonorants follows. We make only brief parenthetical remarks about the initial mutations here, as the mutations are addressed more fully elsewhere in this volume. The prosodic phonology of Gaelic is detailed in the final sections, comprising discussions of stress, word-level intonation, and syllable structure, particularly as these interact with the phenomena of hiatus and svarabhakti.

THE VOWEL SYSTEM

Short vowels

What we may call central Gaelic (see Gillies 1993) employs a straight-forwardly symmetrical nine-vowel system; all vowels can be distinctively long or short when stressed, although unstressed vowels are only short. The system below corresponds to Borgstrøm's discussion of Barra, Oftedal's (1956) description of Leurbost, and most contemporary pedagogical material (e.g. Byrne 2002).

Table 1 The short vowel system (stressed)

	Front unrounded	Back unrounded	Back rounded
High	i	ɯ	u
Mid	e	ɤ	o
Lower-mid	ɛ	ɑ	ɔ

There has been some discussion as to whether the mid and high back unrounded vowels are distinct; certainly some dialects collapse the distinction. Short [ɯ] is found only in a limited number of words (e.g. *uisge* 'water' [ɯʃgʲə]), while the long [ɤː] is itself infrequent.

In unstressed position, a subset of vowels is found, with schwa certainly prevalent.[3] In unstressed syllables the mid vowels [e, o] and back unrounded vowels [ɤ, ɯ] are absent.

Table 2 The short vowel system (unstressed)

	Front unrounded	Central/back unrounded	Back rounded
High	i		u
Mid		ə	
Lower-mid	ɛ	ɑ	ɔ

Long vowels and most diphthongs[4] appear only in a stressed syllable, of which there is exactly one per word, regularly the first syllable of the word. Borgstrøm cites one instance of non-initial stress accompanied by a long vowel in Barra: *buntàta* 'potato(es)' [məᴺdaːhtə]; the woman's name Catróna or Catrìona typically demonstrates a stressed long vowel in the second syllable;[5] other examples of non-initial stress derive from compounds. No irregularly-stressed target words are included in the Survey questionnaire, with the exception of a handful of hyphenated prepositions (34 *a-mach* 'out(wards)' [ə ˈmax], 38 *a-muigh* 'out(side)' [ə ˈmuj]).

Table 3 The vowel length contrast (examples primarily drawn from SGDS points 28–30: these points represent speakers from Barra)[6]

Short vowels: SGDS #, transcription, gloss	Long vowels: SGDS #, transcription, gloss
617 [miɲ] 'meal'	618 [miːɲ] 'soft'
84 [bek] 'small'	476 [ɡ̊leː] 'very'
172 [kʲɛrxk] 'hen'	474 [kʲɛːsdɤx] 'smithy'
261 [krʲɯi̯] 'cattle (g.sg.)'	247 [krɯːv] 'tree'
225 [kɤlʲə] 'forest'	46 [ɤːprʲən] 'ankle'
541 [lˠag] 'weak'	558 [lˠaːn] 'full'
138 [bun] 'base'	139 [buː] 'shop'
689 [dolˠ] 'go (pres.prt.)'	219 [koːɡʲ] 'five'
236 [kɔrʲə] 'kettle'	232 [kɔːrʲ] 'honest'

Diphthongs

Diphthongs can be identified as either rising or falling; rising diphthongs terminate with the high vowel, while falling diphthongs begin with the high vowel. Borgstrøm notes that 'in diphthongs the stress is almost equal on both components' (1937: 90). True diphthongs are prosodically distinct from sequences of vowels in hiatus, which bear the stress and pitch patterns of disyllables (see section on prosody, below). Typically a high front vowel in a diphthong is contiguous with a palatalised consonant; the section on the consonant system (below) presents a more complete discussion of the palatal contrast. In the case of labial consonants the high vowel may itself be the sole phonetic realisation of palatalisation.

Table 4 Diphthongs: oral and nasal (examples primarily from Borgstrøm 1937)

Rising: V2 = [i, u]	Falling: V1 = [i, e, u]
[saiʌtʃə] 'salted' [Lãĩv] 'hand (dat.s)'	[bialʸ] 'mouth' [gʲrʲĩãv] 'deed'
[Rui] 'king' [mrũĩ] 'wife (dat.s)'	[piu-ər] 'sister' [ĩũːʃəxəɣ] 'to learn'
[eilʲeɣ] 'kilt'	[ʃeɔːlʸ] 'sail'
[bẽĩʃəɣ] 'wedding (gen)'	[feoːmalʲ] 'useful'
[fʀiɲəxk] 'to ask'	[fiəxkilʲ] 'tooth'
[aum] 'time' [dãũsə] 'to dance'	[kuan] 'ocean' [ũã-a] 'cave'
[kʲɛunʸ] 'head' [gʲẽũrəɣ] 'winter'	[klʸuəs] 'ear'
[dɔunʸ] 'brown'	

Nasalisation

A stressed vowel may be phonetically nasalised by assimilation when preceding or following a nasal consonant; however, nasality may also be contrastive in stressed position, for long and short vowels and for diphthongs, as illustrated in Tables 4 and 5. Mid vowels are never contrastively nasalised. As demonstrated by traditional orthography, nasal vowels derive primarily from instances where historical nasal consonants are deleted or lenited: for example, in Barra Gaelic as in other regions, consonant + nasal clusters are regularly [Cr-] followed by nasalised vowel (see *tnùth* 'envy' or *cnap* 'lump'). The lenited 'm', spelled –mh– but pronounced [v] (or deleted) is typically preceded or followed by a nasalised vowel, as in *caomh* 'kind' or *tomhas* 'measure'.

Table 5 Examples of short and long nasalised versus oral vowels (SGDS)[7]

i	521 dh'innis 'tell (pret)' [jĩːʃ][7]	532 iosal 'low' [iːʃalʸ]
	592 a mhic 'son (voc)'[vĩxʲkʲ]	122 bric 'trout (g.sg.)' [brʲixʲkʲ]
ɛ	483 gnè 'kind' [grẽ̃ː]	476 glé 'very' [glʲeː]
	162 ceangail 'tie (v)' [kʲẽ̃-ɛlʲ]	174 ceart 'correct' [kʲɛst]
ɯ	148 caomh 'kind (adj)' [kũ̃ːv]	247 craobh 'tree' [krɯːv]
a	550 làmh 'hand' [lʸã̃ːv]	548 làir 'mare' [lʸaːðʲ]
	211 cnap 'lump' [krahp]	158 cat 'cat' [kaht]
u	850 tnùth 'envy' [trʲũ̃ː]	139 bùth 'shop' [buː]
ɔ	860 tomhas 'measure' [tõ̃-əs]	667 ogha 'grandchild'[o-ə]

The front/back contrast in vowels, and 'slenderisation'

The systematicity of the vowel inventory may be relevant when we turn to examine the result of 'final mutation', or mutation 'of quality' as it is described by Borgstrøm (1937: 154 ff), by which the final vowel-consonant sequence of a word may be palatalised. Also termed 'slenderising' in the pedagogical literature, this morphophonological alternation is commonly described in terms of its effect on orthography, but typically results in the palatalisation of the final consonant and may include the fronting and/or raising of the vowel preceding that consonant. Changes in vowel quality are not entirely regular enough to be described by phonological rule, and must be lexically determined: compare for example the following singular/plural pairs: [kʰaht], [kʰahtʲ] 'cat' , but [maxk], [miçkʲ], 'son'; or [ɛx], [eç] 'horse' but [fɛr], [firʲ] 'man'. However, there are general tendencies throughout the paradigms: in unstressed syllables, for example, [ɑ] regularly is fronted to [ɛ], while [ə] is raised to [i] (see Borgstrøm 1937: 161). In long vowels or diphthongs, slenderisation generally creates a high front offglide. The Survey questionnaire did not directly request the paradigmatic information that would be relevant here, but some evidence is provided by nominative/genitive word pairs included in the Survey material, as shown in Table 6.

Table 6 Representative effects of slenderisation on vowel quality (examples from SGDS, points 28–30)

Nominative singular	Genitive or dative singular
478 gleann 'glen' [glʲɛʊnˠ]	479 glinne (gsg) [glʲiɲə]
550 làmh 'hand' [lˠãː v]	552 làimh (dat.sg) [lˠãĩv]
560 laogh 'calf' [lˠɯːɣ]	561 laoigh (gsg) [lˠʊiː]
807 sùgh 'juice' [sʊː]	808 sùigh (gsg) [suːiʲ]
857 toll 'hole' [toʊlˠ]	858 tuill (gsg) [tʊiʎ]
885 uinneag 'window' [ʊɲɑk]	886 uinneige (gsg) [ʊɲɛkʲ]
260 crodh 'cattle' [krʲoʰ]	261 cruidh (g.sg.) [krʲɯi]

THE CONSONANT SYSTEM: OBSTRUENTS

The obstruent inventory

An abstract phonological analysis of the Gaelic obstruent system would take the bilabial, dental and velar stops to be basic: /p t k/. Over this we can lay the distinction of aspiration, which produces /pʰ tʰ kʰ/ word-initially, and results in preaspiration [ʰp ʰt ʰk] following a stressed vowel. Palatalisation is also contrastive for Gaelic obstruents: /pʲ tʲ kʲ pʲʰ tʲʰ kʲʰ/. Finally, with the exception of the dentals, we also find a corresponding series of [+ continuant] obstruents, which roughly also show a [+/- voice] contrast (in lieu of aspiration): /v - ɣ f – x/ and palatalised /vʲ - ɣʲ fʲ - xʲ/. The alveolar /s sʲ/ and glottal /h hʲ/ sibilants complete the inventory of obstruents. It is worth noting, however, that it is rare to find a descriptive text maintaining this level of abstraction through-out the phonological discussion; the layers of diacritics, together with the perceived distance between the abstract representation and the surface pronunciation, often argue for a more user-friendly level of phonetic detail in transcription. For example, palatalisation of the labial consonants is generally represented either by means of a full rather than superscript [j], or as part of the following vowel or diphthong, as in headword 96 *beó* 'alive' [bɛɔ]. The palatalised dentals are often tran-scribed as voiced or voiceless alveo-palatal affricates or similar [dʒ tʃ]. In addition, the articulatory phonetic and phonological nature of the contrast in voicing and/or aspiration requires a greater detail of expla-nation, explored below.

Table 7 Obstruent inventory

	[-cont] [-asp]	[-cont] [+asp]	[+cont] [+voice]	[+cont] [-voice]
[-pal]	/p t k/	/pʰ tʰ kʰ/	/v ɣ/	/f x s h/
[+pal]	/pʲ tʲ kʲ/	/pʰʲ tʰʲ kʰʲ/	/vʲ ɣʲ /	/fʲ xʲ sʲ hʲ/

The aspiration contrast in stops

It is generally recognised that the voiced/voiceless opposition in Scottish Gaelic stops is more accurately described as a distinction between unaspirated and aspirated, but in all cases voiceless. In word-initial position, aspirated stops are heavily post-aspirated, whereas following a stressed vowel they are preaspirated, a feature which is noteworthy of Scottish Gaelic, and typologically unusual (see for exam-ple Silverman 2003). Preaspiration, described as a breathy interval between the voicing of the vowel and the consonant closure, typically occurs after the first vowel, which is the locus of regular stress; although we lay out the surface variants of preaspiration here, we maintain that phonologically these are all variants of the aspiration distinction across the stop system.

Preaspiration is variously described as [ʰp ʰt ʰk] as in Lewis (compare Oftedal 1956), or as [hp ht xk] as in Barra (Borgstrøm 1937). A third more heavily fricated preaspiration series is found in the central mainland area: [xp xt xk]. In the Lewis system, preaspiration shows up consistently as [h] across all places of articulation, although Survey data show it can be either a full or a superscript [h]; this system is also found across the Minch in the westernmost regions of Wester Ross. The Barra system turns out to be the most widespread geographically, according to SGDS evidence: from Harris to Barra in the Outer Isles; from Skye to Islay across the Inner Isles; from the western mainland closest to Skye, and here and there dispersed through much of Inverness-shire and Perthshire. The 'Western Perthshire' system (see Ó Murchú 1985), which expresses preaspiration primarily as a velar fricative across the board, covers much of the same area of the mainland, centred diagonally along the Great Glen. Survey data show that Sutherland, Arran and Kintyre, and the easternmost points of East Perthshire are consistent in representing no preaspiration – for these speakers the post-vocalic aspiration contrast has been fully neutralised.

Rather than foregrounding the particular articulatory realisation of preaspiration, however, from a phonological perspective we would do well to distinguish between those systems that regularly demonstrate a contrast in aspiration – of any kind – from those that do not. As Gillies (1993) notes, phonologically we can interpret all three fully contrastive systems (Lewis, Barra, West Perthshire) to represent the same systematic contrast in aspiration, and we argue here that this is indeed the most economical approach to the phonology of the Gaelic stop system. We take the aspiration contrast to be distinctive throughout central Gaelic, despite the phonetic variation described by the Survey material. The aspiration contrast is maintained only word-initially and following a stressed vowel. In addition, although Hebridean speakers typically maintain the aspiration contrast following a long vowel or diphthong, many dialects fail to show preaspiration in these environments, neutralising the distinction in these instances. The North Sutherland speaker in (1) below neutralises the aspiration contrast after a long vowel, while the Barra speaker maintains the distinction.

(1) 678 *Pàpa* 'Pope' Barra: [pʰɑːʰpə]   N. Sutherland: [pʰɑːp]
    681 *pòca* 'pocket' Barra: [pʰɔːxkə]   N. Sutherland: [pʰoːkɑtʃ]

However, here again, while Gaelic may present a regular contrast between aspiration and non-aspirated stops across most of the Gaidhealtachd, the actual transcription of this contrast throughout the Survey material is surprisingly variable (see Bosch forthcoming).

Variation in transcription practice

Unfortunately, the transcription practices of most descriptive studies, including SGDS, also show variation in the representation of the word-initial contrast, /p t k/ versus /pʰ tʰ kʰ/, often transcribing the contrast as one of voicing rather than aspiration – employing some version of [b d g] versus [p t k], especially word-initially. This transcription practice is prevalent despite the fact that word-initially the lenes or unaspirated stops are clearly not voiced. Ladefoged (2006) contends that 'voiced' /b/ in the Gaelic of the Outer Hebrides shows a voice onset time of around 20ms, approximately equivalent to the French voiceless /p/, while the voiceless Gaelic /p/ demonstrates a VOT around 65ms, longer than that for English aspirated /p/. Further, the generally voiceless quality of Gaelic orthographic *BDG* is recognised as a shibboleth which carries over into Hebridean English, demonstrated to comic effect, for example, in Compton Mackenzie's *Whisky Galore* (Cram 1981). Nonetheless – perhaps to maintain consistency with orthographic representation – most descriptions of Gaelic persist in transcribing the word-initial unaspirated consonants as [b d g], occasionally employing the under-circle as a devoicing diacritic (see also Gillies 1993: 150), especially in word-initial position; the aspirated stop series is commonly transcribed [p t k], without aspiration, word-initially. Phonologists employing the Survey material are advised to use caution when working with the narrow transcriptions in the published volumes, since neither initial aspiration of voiceless stops, nor initial devoicing of 'voiced' stops, are consistently marked by fieldworkers. As Ó Dochartaigh first remarks concerning the aspirated consonants, 'voiceless stops in word-initial position are probably postaspirated in all dialects of Scottish Gaelic ... {however} ... initially KHJ {Kenneth H. Jackson} appears not to have considered this a notable feature ... and postaspiration is not normally recorded by him or by FM {fieldworker}' (SGDS Vol. 1: 134), and word-initial aspiration may not be systematically noted by other fieldworkers, either. Ó Dochartaigh warns later, regarding the BDG series, 'given that voiceless lenes are a normal feature of the Scottish Gaelic dialects, it is likely that in a number of instances fieldworkers have omitted to mark voicelessness' (SGDS Vol. 1: 135). Thus, a reader can mistakenly infer that the usual pattern of obstruent contrast is one of voicing.

Experimental studies of preaspiration

A handful of experimental studies shed some light on the nature of preaspiration in Gaelic (including Ladefoged et al. 1998, Rogers 1995, Shuken 1979, 1984, and Ní Chasaide and Ó Dochartaigh 1984), although much remains to be done in this area, particularly given the cross-linguistic rarity of this feature. Ladefoged et al. reiterate that 'there is no doubt that the phonological contrast between the two sets of Gaelic stops always depends on differences in aspiration and never on differences in voicing' (Ladefoged et al. 1998: 5). Shuken's earlier instrumental study of Gaelic, however, makes the claim that preaspiration 'though usually described as voiceless, is often voiced in the Gaelic of Lewis, although usually voiceless in some other Gaelic dialects' (Shuken 1984: 127), and suggests preaspiration can be described as a feature of breathy voice. She presents kymographic tracings of *poca* 'bag' and *bàta* 'boat', showing the words to have 'the high airflow and reduction of amplitude characteristic of breathy voice' (127); furthermore, low amplitude friction is visible in the preaspiration before [k] in *poca*.

The articulatory evidence for the regressive spread of preaspiration in sonorant-stop clusters also remains to be examined in more detail; SGDS evidence from lexemes such as 233 *coirce* 'oats', or 392 *falt* 'hair' show that phonetic devoicing of the sonorant is common.

Hiatus and the glottal stop or empty C-position

Although descriptive studies of Gaelic do not commonly posit a glottal stop as part of the consonant inventory, many studies do dispense a fair amount of ink describing hiatus: the meaningful and perceptible distinction between contiguous vowels that compose a diphthong in a single syllable (represented [VV]), versus contiguous vowels in hiatus, resulting in two syllables, often represented as [V-V]. Historically, as is evident from the traditional orthography, the contemporary disyllabic sequences derive from original disyllables in which the intervocalic consonant has elided; the monosyllabic [VV] sequences were original monosyllables. In dialects which maintain this distinction, this 'hiatus' is represented phonetically by means of various strategies, depending on the salience of the 'break': the hyphen [V-V] is the most common symbol, but other representations are also employed in SGDS and in descriptive texts: a glottal stop [VʔV], a pipe [V|V], an abruptly falling pitch contour (see Ó Dochartaigh 1994–7, Vol. 1: 119 ff). Occasionally the vocalic interval is in fact described as a glottal stop; whatever the case, in most dialects the difference between a diphthong and a two-syllable sequence of vowels in hiatus is clearly distinctive, both to native speakers and to fieldworkers. Ladefoged et al. (1998) find clear differences in pitch patterns between the long vowel or diphthong [VV] with steady or rising F0, as in *bò* 'cow' /poː/ or *duan* 'song' /tuɑn/, and the two-vowel, disyllabic sequence in *bogha* 'underwater rock' /po-ə/ or *dubhan* 'hook' /tu-ɑn/, with a rise-fall F0 curve. Given that the distinction between the two sets of forms remains contrastive in the central dialects, rather than proposing 'hyphen' as a phonological segment, we propose to add the glottal stop to the phonological inventory of Gaelic. Depending on dialect, this glottal stop surfaces as a 'glottal catch' or 'break in glottal tension' (Oftedal 1956) or indeed in some cases as a full glottal stop – ensuring that the stress and pitch patterns of original diphthongs and original disyllables remain distinct.

THE NASALS AND SONORANTS

Although the survey instrument included sections investigating 'slender m' in various word-positions,[8] SGDS data do not provide any evidence for a palatalised [mʲ]. The vowel preceding or following the bilabial nasal may be high or front, but the articulation of the nasal is invariable. The velar nasal, however, does show contrastive palatalisation.

(2) Sonorants: Non-coronal nasals: /m ŋ ŋʲ/

The sonorants. The coronal nasals, like the laterals and rhotics, are distinguished by a three-way contrast which we can refer to as velarised, palatalised, and plain.

(3) Sonorants: Coronal nasals: /nˠ nʲ n/
                 Laterals: /lˠ lʲ l/
                 Rhotics: /Rˠ rʲ r/

The velarised /nˠ lˠ/ are strongly dental or even interdental as well as velarised, in contrast with the plain /n l/, which are alveolar and perceptibly 'light', often transcribed with the 'underbar' diacritic to indicate specifically alveolar place of articulation (as in Pullum and Ladusaw 1986: 205). Many descriptive or historical studies make reference to an original four-way contrast among sonorants, by which a strong/weak opposition intersects with a [+/– palatal] opposition. Nonetheless, the three-way opposition presented here is the most common contemporary Gaelic inventory.[9] In the context of initial lenition, the palatalised /lʲ/ alternates with the plain /l/, while the velarised /lˠ/ remains unchanged; both velarised and palatalised /nˠ nʲ/ lenite to plain /n/.

The rhotics, too, demonstrate a three-way phonological contrast, including a heavily trilled, velarised /Rˠ/, a plain tap /r/, and finally a palatalised /rʲ/ which appears to have quite a variable range of surface phonetic expressions. This palatalised rhotic is variously described as a grooved or spirant retroflex; throughout the outer isles it is commonly articulated as an interdental voiced fricative, approximating [ð] (compare Ladefoged et al. 1998). The strong /Rʸ/ is a trill word-initially, or a retroflex fricative medially; -rt clusters may surface as the retroflex cluster [-ʂt]. In lenited contexts the trilled initial /Rʸ/ alternates with [r].

PROSODIC PHONOLOGY: STRESS, SYLLABLE STRUCTURE AND PITCH

Stress

Primary stress in Gaelic falls on the initial syllable, with a very few though noteworthy lexical exceptions; for this reason stress is rarely indicated in descriptive or pedagogical studies except when hiatus or svarabhakti are under discussion. As mentioned above, stress is largely omitted from the transcribed survey material. Within the phonological word, there is no evidence for secondary stress (again, leaving aside the question of the svarabhakti vowels). While some languages demonstrate a recurring pattern of binary metrical feet in addition to primary stress, Gaelic is not one of these. Although the great majority of lexemes included in the Survey are mono- or disyllabic, polysyllabic words (529 ionnsachadh, 596 màirnealach, 812 suidheachadh, etc.) demonstrate a single primary stress word-initially, with no secondary stresses.

The syllable and evidence from svarabhakti

Dialects of Gaelic provide an interesting case study for examining syllable structure and constituency, especially as we turn to examine the phenomenon traditionally known as svarabhakti. Most Hebridean dialects demonstrate the epenthesis of a vowel between a sonorant and obstruent which do not share place of articulation, following a short stressed vowel; in descriptive literature this epenthesis is commonly known as svarabhakti. Due to the regular environment of epenthesis, the epenthetic vowel is invariably the second vowel in the word. Traditional orthography does not recognise the epenthetic vowel; L2 learners of Gaelic require instruction on this pronunciation feature. Both the presence and the quality of the epenthetic vowel are generally predictable: examples from SGDS are given below.

For certain dialects the inserted vowel is regularly a schwa; nothing more need be noted in such instances (compare SGDS points 31–8, Arran and Kintyre). However, for the majority of speakers of the central

Gaelic regions, taking Barra as a particular example, we find that the epenthetic vowel is regularly a copy of the previous vowel; if the sonorant and/or final consonant is palatalised, the epenthetic vowel will be fronted, as in 'feast' (see also the implications for this claim on theories of feature geometry and feature spreading in Ní Chiosáin 1994, Halle 1995).

(4) Svarabhakti (examples from SGDS)

orthography	gloss	transcription
dearbh	'certain'	[dʲ̪araᵥv]
dealg	'thorn'	[dʲ̪alᵛa̪gan]
cuirm	'feast'	[kʰ̪ʇurʲiɪ̯m]
gainmheach	'sand'	[g̪ãnã̪ᵥvhɔx]
fairrge	'sea'	[f̪aRa̪gʲə]
earball	'tail'	[̪ɯrɯ̪pəlᵛ]
gorm	'blue'	[g̪ɔrɔ̪m]
gairm	'call'	[g̪ɤrʲɤ̪m]
meirg	'rust'	[m̪erʲe̪kʲ]
marbh	'dead'	[m̪ara̪v]

Also of special interest are the stress and intonation patterns associated with the epenthetic vowel for these speakers. The reader will have noted immediately that the [vowel-sonorant-vowel] sequences above are represented in SGDS by a rather peculiar transcription practice of 'internal bracketing'; as discussed in Ó Dochartaigh (1994–7, Vol. 1), this takes the place of Jackson's practice of a subscript ligature linking the two vowels. Jackson describes the phenomenon:

> Many dialects have ... a treatment [of svarabhakti] where the second vowel is a full vowel, generally repeating the first, and both syllables seem to be of equal *prominence* ... In these the question of *stress* seems difficult; the stress may seem to be on the first syllable ... or on both ...; in this last case the second vowel may be more or less long as well as stressed ... The intonation seems to be level or rising all through. (Jackson 1963, in Ó Dochartaigh 1994–7, Vol. 1: 120)

In his description of Leurbost Gaelic, Oftedal (1956) indicates the epenthetic vowel specifically by emphasising the unusual stress pattern, regularly employing a secondary stress-mark ['] on the inserted vowel. This is the practice that Hamp (1988) also recommends in his detailed discussion of Gaelic transcription practice. Borgstrøm, however, drew particular attention to what he perceived to be a distinction in syllabification of the sonorant between the initial (stressed) vowel and the epenthetic second vowel. As Borgstrøm describes the phenomenon, in ordinary disyllables 'a single consonant after a short vowel belongs to the preceding syllable, e.g. [bɔt-ɔx] "old man" bodach ...', whereas in the epenthetic environment, 'a single [sonorant] after a short vowel may belong to the following syllable, e.g. [ma-rav] "dead" (marbh). This syllabic division is peculiar to the words which have developed a svarabhakti-vowel in certain original groups of consonants.' He continues: 'In the type ma-rav the stress is more equal on both syllables of the word than in the type ar-an; but this difference of stress is only an accessory part of the phenomenon, and the chief accent is on the first syllable in both types.' Borgstrøm goes on to cite one of his local language consultants claiming that the words with epenthetic vowels are 'nearly monosyllabic' (Borgstrøm 1937: 76–8).

This passage by Borgstrøm has been taken up by a number of phonologists, including Kenstowicz and Kisseberth (1979), Clements (1986) and Smith (1999) as one of the few known language descriptions positing a distinction in syllabification: 'ordinary' disyllables, according to Borgstrøm, are CVC-VC, whereas disyllables created by the insertion of a svarabhakti vowel are said to be typically CV-CVC. Two parts of this claim are noteworthy: most studies have focused on the unusual claim that there must be a contrast between different types of syllabification, 'forward' CV-CV versus 'backward' CVC-V. However, it is worth emphasising that Borgstrøm's claim of a usual VC syllable is in itself atypical; there is a widely held assumption that CV-CV syllabification is universal (see for example Roca 1994: 145). Nonetheless, most descriptive studies of Gaelic dialects repeat Borgstrøm's claim that the VC syllable is usual, including Gillies (1993), Ladefoged et al. (1998) and Hamp (1989: 206), who mentions almost as an aside, 'it may be of interest in passing to note that non-initial consonants always belong syllabically with the vowel that precedes them and not with the following vowel'.[10]

While many experimental studies attempt to unravel the phonetic correlates of syllabification, current phonetic research still does not provide a clear articulatory or acoustic definition of the syllable. Maddieson (1985) suggests that syllable constituency is reflected in the presence or absence of compensatory shortening of the vowel in closed syllables; he claims that shortening only occurs within a syllable constituent. This claim can be understood in concert with Laver's (1994) suggestion that syllables are coordinated complexes of actions among which many accommodations have been made. Two experimental studies by Bosch and de Jong (1997, 1998) confirm that for Barra speakers, epenthetic vowels are systematically longer than non-epenthetic vowels; that F0 peaks appear later when there is an epenthetic vowel; and that coarticulatory effects are found across [-VCV-] in epenthetic sequences, but only across [-VC-] in non-epenthetic sequences. Another instrumental study focusing on the question of syllable structure in Gaelic similarly supports Borgstrøm's account of Gaelic syllable structure, arguing from F0 traces of sonorants in epenthetic and non-epenthetic environments (Ellison 1999).

For those dialects that maintain a distinction between ordinary polysyllabic words and those demonstrating svarabhakti, we can outline three possible analyses, all three of which have been suggested by authors of descriptive studies. The first analysis, drawing on Borgstrøm (1937) and others, locates the primary distinction in terms of syllable structure: ordinary disyllables show [VC.V] syllabification as in [ɑɾ.ɑn] 'bread', while svarabhakti-forms show an epenthetic vowel and a [V.CV] syllabification pattern, as in [ɑ.ɾɑm] 'army'. Differences in stress and pitch patterns must be shown to result from the primary difference in syllabification, under this analysis (compare Fraser 1914).

The other two analyses essentially offer lexical rather than phonological solutions: Ternes (1973) explicitly contrasts his analysis with Borgstrøm's, claiming that the svarabhakti words in Applecross demonstrate distinctive vowel-length in the second syllable. According to his analysis, there is no syllabification distinction; the intervocalic sonorant always forms the onset of the second syllable. Likewise, there is no difference here noted in pitch patterns or stress: stress regularly falls on the word-initial syllable (despite contrastive vowel-length in the second syllable).

MacAulay (1992) suggests essentially that Gaelic demonstrates a phonological contrast in tone patterns (see also Ternes 1980). According to this analysis, Gaelic, like Swedish perhaps, simply offers two sets of tonal patterns; one, the basic or default pattern, is simply a H-L or falling pattern, as we find in ordinary disyllables, where the first syllable demonstrates high pitch and regular primary stress. The second pattern, restricted specifically to words exhibiting svarabhakti, is a level tone pattern over two syllables, falling thereafter if the word is more than two syllables in length. This lexical solution relies on speakers (and learners) correctly classifying lexical items into one or the other tone pattern.

Each of these analyses has its strong and weak points; they each represent different emphases of phonetic and phonological properties of stress, pitch and syllabification that are inevitably inter-related. It is possible that different analyses may be better suited to different dialects, depending on the salience of stress versus pitch, for example. Certainly additional instrumental studies – acoustic, articulatory, or perceptual – would provide useful information about how speakers produce and attend to these distinctions. We can say a few things for certain here: speakers of the central or 'core' dialects of Gaelic make a salient distinction between 'ordinary' polysyllables and those exhibiting svarabhakti, whether through stress, pitch, or some underlying properties of syllabification. Words with the epenthetic vowel – although they are common – remain 'marked' phonetically and phonologically. This is unlike Irish, for example, where cognates of the Gaelic svarabhakti generally demonstrate an epenthetic schwa without otherwise altering stress or pitch patterns, and without otherwise diverging from Irish phonotactics. In sum, literate learners of Gaelic must learn both the appropriate vowel epenthesis and the particular stress and pitch pattern of svarabhakti words; even non-literate learners (or native speakers) must recognise the distinctive stress and pitch patterns associated with this particular set of lexical items.

CONCLUSION

Although Scottish Gaelic shares with its Irish cousin evidence of contrastive palatalisation and the use of palatalisation as a morphoph-onological property, and shares with the other Celtic languages the complex systems of initial mutation, certain phonological phenom-ena set Gaelic apart as worthy of further investigation. The phonetic and phonological properties of preaspiration; the phonological role of intervocalic hiatus; and the prosodic effects of svarabhakti all present intriguing questions to the phonologist interested in the varied prop-erties of sound systems, and to the phonetician wishing to learn more about cross-linguistic articulatory and acoustic properties.

Detailed dialect descriptions spanning the twentieth century, as well as the magnum opus represented by the five volumes of the *Survey of the Gaelic Dialects of Scotland*, present a wealth of data on Gaelic dialects, particularly at the lexical level. However, virtually nothing has been published on prosodic structure at the sentence-level or above, with the exception of MacAulay's (1979 and 1992) studies; here additional work, both data collection and analysis, is clearly required. Finally, additional work is desperately needed on current factors of language contact, language change, and indeed code-switching during this contemporary period of demographic change, and the retrenchment and readjustment of Gaelic speakers throughout the *Gàidhealtachd*.

BIBLIOGRAPHY

Ball, Martin and Fife, James (eds) (1993), *The Celtic Languages*, London: Routledge.

Borgstrøm, C. Hj. (1937), 'The Dialect of Barra in the Outer Hebrides', *Norsk Tidsskrift for Sprogvidenskap* 8, pp. 71–242.

Borgstrøm, C. Hj. (1940), *A Linguistic Survey of the Gaelic Dialects of Scotland I: The Dialects of the Outer Hebrides*, Oslo: H. Aschehoug and Co.

Borgstrøm, C. Hj. (1941), *A Linguistic Survey of the Gaelic Dialects of Scotland II: The Dialects of Skye and Ross-shire.* Oslo: H. Aschehoug and Co.

Borgstrøm, C. Hj. (1974), 'On the Influence of Norse on Scottish Gaelic: Preaspiration of Stops and Pitch Patterns', *Lochlann* 6, pp. 91–103.

Bosch, A. (1998), 'The Syllable in Scottish Gaelic Dialect Studies', *Scottish Gaelic Studies* 18, pp. 1–22.

Bosch, A. (forthcoming), 'Revisiting Preaspiration: Evidence from the Survey of the Gaelic Dialects of Scotland', *Proceedings of the Harvard Celtic Colloquium* 27.

Bosch, Anna and De Jong, Kenneth (1997), 'The Prosody of Barra Gaelic Epenthetic Vowels', *Studies in the Linguistic Sciences* 27, pp. 1–16.

Bosch, Anna and Kenneth De Jong (1998), 'Syllables and Supersyllables: Evidence for Low-level Phonological Domains', in *Texas Linguistic Forum 41: Exploring the Boundaries Between Phonetics and Phonology*, pp. 1–14.

Byrne, Michel (2002), *Gràmar na Gàidhlig*, Isle of Lewis: Stòrlann-Acair.

Clements, G. N. (1986), 'Syllabification and Epenthesis in the Barra Dialect of Gaelic', in Bogers et al. (eds), *The Phonological Representation of Suprasegmentals*, Dordrecht: Foris.

Cram, David F. (1981), 'Code-switching, Pidgin Gaelic and *Whisky Galore*', *Scottish Gaelic Studies* 13, pp. 241–62.

Dieckhoff, H. C. (1926), 'Notes on Scottish Gaelic dialects', *Scottish Gaelic Studies* 1, pp. 188–94.

Dorian, Nancy (1978), *East Southerland Gaelic: The dialect of the Brora, Golspie and Embo Fishing Communities*, Dublin: Dublin Institute for Advanced Studies.

Dorian, Nancy (1989), *Investigating Obsolescence: Studies in Language Contraction and Death,* Cambridge: Cambridge University Press.

Ellison, T. Mark (1999), 'An Instrumental Study of Syllable Structure in Scottish Gaelic', unpublished ESRC grant report R000 22 2146.

Fraser, J. (1914), 'Accent and Svarabhakti in a Dialect of Scotch Gaelic', *Revue Celtique* 35, pp. 401–9.

Gillies, William (1988), 'The Atlas of Gaelic Dialects: An Interim Report', *Scottish Gaelic Studies* 15, pp. 1–5.

Gillies, William (1993), 'Scottish Gaelic', in Martin Ball and James Fife (eds), *The Celtic Languages*, London: Routledge, pp. 145–227.

Halle, M. (1995), 'Feature Geometry and Feature Spreading', *Linguistic Inquiry* 26, pp. 1–46.

Hamp, E. P. (1988), 'On the Representation of Scottish Gaelic Dialect Phonetics', *Scottish Gaelic Studies* 15, pp. 6–19.

Hamp, E. P. (1989), 'On Signs of Health and Death', in N. Dorian (ed.), *Investigating Obsolescence: Studies in Language Contraction and Death*, Cambridge: Cambridge University Press, pp. 197–210.

Jackson, Kenneth H. (1958), 'The Situation of the Scottish Gaelic Language, and the Work of the Linguistic Survey of Scotland', *Lochlann* 1, pp. 229–34.

Kenstowicz, Michael and Kisseberth, Charles (1979), *Generative Phonology*, New York: Academic Press.

Kurath, Hans, Hanley, Miles, Bloch, Bernard, Lowman, Guy S. and Hansen, Marcus L. (1939–43), *Linguistic Atlas of New England*, 3 vols, Providence, RI: Brown University Press.

Ladefoged, Peter (2006), *A Course in Phonetics*. Thomson-Wadsworth.

Ladefoged, Peter, Ladefoged, Jenny, Turk, Alice, Hind, Kevin and Skilton, St. John (1998), 'The Phonetic Structures of Scottish Gaelic', *Journal of the International Phonetic Association* 28, pp. 1–41.

Laver, John (1994), *Principles of Phonetics*, Cambridge: Cambridge University Press.

MacAulay, D. (1979), 'Some Functional and Distributional Aspects of Intonation in Scottish Gaelic: A Preliminary Study of Tones', in Donall Ó Baoill (ed.), *Papers in Celtic Phonology. Occasional Papers in Linguistics and Language Learning* 6, Coleraine: the New University of Ulster, pp. 27–38.

MacAulay, D. (1992), 'The Scottish Gaelic Language', in MacAulay (ed.), *The Celtic Languages*, Cambridge: Cambridge University Press, pp. 137–248.

Maddieson, Ian (1985), 'Phonetic Cues to Syllabification', in V. Fromkin (ed.), *Phonetic Linguistics: Essays in Honor of Peter Ladefoged*, New York: Academic Press.

Ní Chasaide, Ailbhe and Ó Dochartaigh, C. (1984), 'Some Durational Aspects of Preaspiration', in J. Higgs and R. Thelwall (eds), *Topics in Linguistic Phonetics in Honor of E. Uldall. Occasional Papers in Linguistics and Language Learning* 9, Coleraine: New University of Ulster, pp. 141–57.

Ní Chiosáin, Máire (1994), 'Barra Gaelic Vowel Copy and (non)-Constituent Spreading', *Proceedings of the West Coast Conference on Formal Linguistics* 13, Stanford: CSLI Publications.

Ó Dochartaigh, C. (ed.), (1994–7), *Survey of the Gaelic Dialects of Scotland* [SGDS], 5 vols, Dublin: Dublin Institute for Advanced Studies.

Ó Murchú, Máirtín (1985), 'Devoicing and Pre-aspiration in Varieties of Scots Gaelic', *Ériu* 36, pp. 195–8.

Ó Murchú, Máirtín (1989), *East Perthshire Gaelic: Social History, Phonology, Texts and Lexicon*, Dublin: Dublin Institute for Advanced Studies.

Oftedal, Magne (1956), *A Linguistic Survey of Gaelic Dialects of Scotland III: The Gaelic of Leurbost, Isle of Lewis*, Oslo: H. Aschehoug and Co. (*Norsk Tidsskrift for Sprogvidenskap* Supp. Vol. 4).

Orton, Harold et al. (1962–71), *Survey of English Dialects*, Leeds: E. J. Arnold.

Pullum, Geoffrey and William Ladusaw (1986), *Phonetic Symbol Guide*, Chicago: University of Chicago Press.

Robertson, C. M. (1899–1901), 'The Gaelic of the West of Ross-shire', *Transactions of the Gaelic Society of Inverness* 24, pp. 321–69.

Robertson, C. M. (1900), 'Perthshire Gaelic', *Transactions of the Gaelic Society of Inverness* 22, pp. 4–42.

Roca, Iggy (1994), *Generative Phonology*, London and New York: Routledge.

Rogers, Henry (1995), 'Aspirated Stops in Scots Gaelic', *International Congress of Phonetic Science* 3, pp. 448–51.

Shuken, C. (1979), 'Aspiration in Scottish Gaelic Stop Consonants', in H. Hollien and P. Hollien (eds), *Current Issues in the Phonetic Sciences*, Amsterdam: John Benjamin, pp. 451–58.

Shuken, C. (1984), '[?], [h], and Parametric Phonetics', in J. Higgs and R. Thelwall (eds), *Topics in Linguistic Phonetics in Honor of E. Uldall, Occasional Papers in Linguistics and Language Learning* 9, Coleraine: New University of Ulster, pp. 111–39.

Silverman, Daniel (2003), 'On the Rarity of Pre-aspirated Stops', *Journal of Linguistics* 39, pp. 575–98.

Smith, Norval (1999), 'Leurbost Gaelic Syllable Structure', in H. van der Hulst and N. Ritter (eds), *The Syllable: Views and Facts*. Berlin: Mouton de Gruyter, pp. 577–630.

Ternes, Elmar (1973), *The Phonemic Analysis of Scottish Gaelic*, Dublin: Dublin Institute for Advanced Studies.

Ternes, Elmar (1980), 'Scottish Gaelic Phonemics Viewed in a Typological Perspective', *Lingua* 52, pp. 73–88.

Wagner, Heinrich and Ó Baoill, C. (1958–69), *Linguistic Atlas and Survey of Irish Dialects* [LASID], Dublin: Dublin Institute for Advanced Studies.

NOTES

1 I wish to express my thanks to the department of Celtic and Scottish Studies, Edinburgh University, for access to the archives of the Linguistic Survey of Scotland. This research was supported in part by sabbatical fellowships from the American Philosophical Society and the Institute for Advanced Study in the Humanities, Edinburgh University, and most gratefully acknowledged.

2 The published SGDS includes only minimal footnotes; the fair copies of the surveys, still held in the archives of Edinburgh University's Celtic and Scottish Studies, include numerous discursive comments mainly in Jackson's hand.

3 In Barra the word-final schwa is commonly rendered a lax [ɔ] – with breve diacritic – by Borgstrøm, highlighting a local shibboleth.

4 The diphthongs [ei], [ɑi] may be found in unstressed syllables, mainly in place-names, such as [bɑRɑi], 'Barra'.

5 Ó Murchú (1989: 67) presents a 'near-complete' list of irregularly stressed forms in East Perthshire Gaelic; aside from the words cited above, only *a' Mhoderàtar* [vɔdèrá:dər] 'the Moderator' shows a long stressed vowel in non-initial position.

6 Items from SGDS henceforth will by cited by headword number as well as transcription and gloss. Where relevant, point number – indicating SGDS native speaker consultant reference – will also be specified.

7 Jackson's transcription practice was modified, as described in Hamp (1988) and Ó Dochartaigh (1994–7), for the publication of the SGDS volumes; phonetic transcription in the present essay is additionally modified so as to conform as closely as possible to the current (2005) approved version of the International Phonetic Alphabet. Notably, therefore, palatalised consonants are written with the superscript [ʲ] in this text, rather than an apostrophe; velarised consonants are transcribed here with a superscript gamma [ˠ], rather than a bisecting tilde as was Jackson's practice. Most vowel diacritics other than nasalisation have been omitted (fronting, backing, etc.).

8 Survey headwords include 516 *imir* 'ridge', 635 *muime* 'godmother', 351 *druim* 'back', 13 *aimsir* 'weather', 517 *imlich* 'lick (v)', and others.

9 Compare Hamp's discussion of Muasdal (Kintyre) Gaelic, in which he claims a more complex system: 'there are six distinctive surface phonemes each for the laterals and the nasals, without counting [m]' (Hamp 1989: 207); according to his fieldwork in this region, laterals and nasals are cross-classified as [+/– fortis], [+/– palatal], and [+/– velarised]; the [+velarised] segments are also distinguished as [+/– protruded (lips)]. Understandably, this is a phonological system exemplifying what Hamp terms 'language death without capitulation', conserving as it does 'archaic distinctions and features not paralleled elsewhere' (207), even down to its final handful of fluent speakers.

10 See Bosch (1998) for a thorough discussion of descriptions of the syllable in Gaelic dialect study.

CHAPTER 13

Gaelic Morphology

David Adger

INTRODUCTION

The purpose of this chapter is to survey the morphological structures of Scottish Gaelic in a fairly systematic fashion in a way that will be useful to students of linguistics wishing to have a basic grasp of Gaelic morphology, and to students of Gaelic who are interested in a perspective on their language of study that comes from modern linguistics.[1] Excellent overviews of Gaelic morphology, and of Gaelic grammar in general, can be found in MacAulay (1992), Gillies (1993) and Lamb (2003, 2007), and for those who have a background in phonetics, Borgstrøm (1937) is an extremely useful resource. The present chapter differs from these in that it attempts to connect Gaelic morphology more tightly to the methods, questions and results of contemporary theoretical linguistics. For those interested in gaining a background in current morphological theory, Booij (2005), Haspelmath (2002) and Harley (2006) are recent introductions.

In any survey of morphology, an important limitation on the discussion comes from the type of data considered. All spoken languages are highly variable and dynamic, with many different ways of saying the 'same thing'; speakers make choices about what forms to use to express their thoughts and those choices are constrained by the grammatical and morphological resources available to the speaker and influenced by the speaker's dialect, their age, their identity and their beliefs about who they are talking to. Connected to this is the issue of register and style. Formal written styles of Gaelic differ markedly from spoken varieties (see Lamb 2007) and this impacts on speakers' judgements about morphological forms in complex ways.

BASIC CONCEPTS OF WORD STRUCTURE

Although the notion 'word' is commonplace in non-theoretical discussions of language, defining this idea in a clear and universal fashion is extremely difficult. Written languages, such as Gaelic, come to us with an orthographic tradition of what constitutes words. As noted by Borgstrøm (1968), Gaelic orthographic tradition bases its decisions about word boundaries on mainly phonological grounds. Stressed syllables mark off the beginning of many orthographic words, since most Gaelic words which bear a stress have that stress on their initial syllable. Of course, this does not help with the many orthographic words which do not bear a stress in Gaelic (in fact Borgstrøm proposes analysing these as part of an adjacent stress bearing word). For example, take (1):

(1)   Cha   do   dhìochuimhnich   mi   na   litrichean
       NEG   PAST   forget.PAST   I   the.P   letter.P
       'I forgot the letters.'

The verb *dhìochuimhnich*, 'forget' has four syllables and is stressed on the first ['jiːəxə̃niç]. Following the generalisation about stress and orthography just given, the word boundary preceding the verb is expected. However, there are two elements that precede this verb (*cha* and *do*), neither of which can bear stress. Traditional orthography (although, as Borgstrøm notes, not classical manuscript tradition) treats these elements as separate orthographic words. The verb is also followed by an unstressed pronoun, which is also treated as a separate word orthographically. Similarly, *litrichean*, 'letters' is a trisyllabic word stressed on the first syllable ['lʲiʰtriçən]. This word is inflected with a plural ending –*ichean*, which tradition treats as part of the same word as the root. *Litrichean* is preceded by an unstressed element (the definite article) which, like *cha* and *do*, is treated as a separate word.

The issue here is why we treat certain unstressed elements as inflections and others as separate words. One classical, structuralist approach is to say that we treat elements as separate words when other elements that are clearly words can separate them. So the fact that we can intercalate *còig*, 'five' between the definite article and the noun in (1) motivates giving each element separate word status (*na còig litrichean*, 'the five letters'). But it is impossible to intercalate any element between *cha* and *do* or *do* and the verb in (1), yet these are treated orthographically as words rather than inflectional prefixes.

This highlights the problems that arise in applying the common sense concept of 'word' to the theoretical analysis of a language.

One approach to classifying the problematic cases is to treat elements like *cha* and *do* as intermediate between full (phonologically defined) words and true inflections: such elements are called 'clitics', and they are phonologically part of another word, although grammatically separate. Clitics are always phonologically dependent on another word, either to their right (in which case they are 'proclitics') or to their left (in which case they are 'enclitics'). Gaelic possesses both: in (1), *cha*, *do* and *na* are proclitics, while *mi* is an enclitic. However, this classification of categories (word, clitic, inflection) still leaves the boundary between clitic and inflection unclear.

An alternative mode of analysis starts from the concept of 'morpheme': a morpheme is the smallest unit of the language that connects sound and meaning. For example, *cha* is a morpheme linking the notion of grammatical negation with a particular phonology. *–ichean*, expressing plurality, is another such morpheme. These are 'grammatical morphemes', and to be contrasted with so-called 'root morphemes', which contribute conceptual rather than grammatical information, like *litir*, the morpheme which expresses the concept 'letter'. This morpheme actually has two phonological forms: *litir* and *litr*, the latter appearing when the morpheme is followed by a plural morpheme, so we have the contrast *litir*, 'letter' vs. *litr-ichean*, 'letters'. These two versions of the morpheme meaning 'letter' are known as 'allomorphs' of the basic morpheme. The plural form just mentioned, *-ichean*, is itself just one allomorph of the plural, with *-an*, as in *caileagan* GIRL-PLURAL 'girls' being another.

This morphemic approach allows one to define words in a language by giving what one might think of as a grammar of morphemes, specifying how the various morphemes can be put together to make words.

Take the verb in (1), for example. It consists of three obvious parts: the morpheme *cuimhne*, 'memory', the morpheme *dì-*, signifying a particular type of negation that attaches to verbs, and the morpheme *(a)ich* which can be used to turn a nominal into a verb.[2] The motivation for each of these morphemes comes from the fact that they are all used elsewhere, with the same meaning-sound pairing: *dì-cheann*, 'behead'; *dì-làraich*, 'destroy' etc.; *cuimhne*, 'memory'; *iomp-aich*, 'convert', *miann-aich*, 'desire', *stèidh-ich*, 'establish'. Note that morphemes do not match up one to one with syllables – they are defined independently of phonology.

The advantage of the notion of morpheme is that its definition is fairly clear, and one can use morphemes to build up a 'syntax of words', where rules of combination specify which morphemes can combine with which others. Morphemes which combine with roots to build up complex word meanings are known as 'derivational' morphemes (e.g. the –(a)ich morpheme which converts nouns to verbs), while those that add grammatical information (e.g. the –(a)ichean plural morpheme) are known as 'inflectional' morphemes.

However, the notion of morpheme also raises problems, especially in a language like Gaelic. One of the important typological facts about Gaelic word structure is that it uses phonological changes at the beginning and end of words to mark grammatical inflections. For example, the verb in (1) is not only morphologically complex in the way just described, it also marks grammatical information, specifically past tense, via a change to the initial sound of the word. The future of this verb is dìochuimhnichidh, with an initial d- (phonetically [dʲ]) rather than the dh- ([j]) found in the past tense. This phonological change, termed 'lenition', is discussed in more detail in the chapter on phonology in this volume. Here, we are interested in its morphological implications, but it is important to notice that lenition affects different classes of sounds differently. Vowels undergo no change when lenited, and certain consonant clusters are also immune to the effects of lenition (for example, sg or st). Certain consonants show no signs of change under lenition in some dialects, while they do in others (r is a notorious example), and some consonants (such as l and n) change their sound while lenited, but the orthography does not mark this.

A different sound change, 'palatalisation', takes place at the end of words to signify certain grammatical meanings. For example, the noun cat, 'cat' changes its final sound from [t̪] (a dental stop) to a palatalised alveolar stop [tʲ], to signify plural (orthographically this is represented by prefixing the final consonant with the letter i giving cait). This palatalisation process is more than a simple phonological change, however, as it also impacts on the quality of the vowel, creating fairly drastic effects which can be idiosyncratic to the lexical item being pluralised.

The question for a theory of morphology which holds fast to the notion of morpheme is the following: what morpheme is associated with these changes? The answer to this is not obvious and a number of solutions have been proposed. One idea, prominent in the literature since Massam's (1983) analysis of lenition in Irish, has been to take the relevant morpheme to consist of a bare phonological feature linked with the relevant meaning. The idea is that this feature attaches to the first or last sound of the relevant word. Schematically:

(2)   [+lenition]   Dhìochuimhnich

      PAST   Verb

In the same way that the past tense grammatical feature combines with the other grammatical information of the verb, the lenition phonological feature combines with the phonology of the verb. This approach keeps the strict definition of morpheme we have been using at the expense of having a rather abstract notion of the sound part of the morpheme. In a sense, this approach treates lenition, and palatalisation, as very abstract clitics. The problem for this approach is characterising the nature of the phonological feature(s) concerned.

An alternative is to treat the lenited and palatalised forms as allomorphs which are selected by adjacent morphological and syntactic items, so that for the morpheme *cat*, we have allomorphs *cat, chat, cait* and *chait* (see, for example, Green 2006). The third allomorph in this list would then be selected in certain syntactically plural environments. The issues for this kind of approach are: (i) how to capture the phonological regularities that clearly do obtain between lenited and non-lenited (palatalised and non-palatalised) forms, (ii) how to link the particular allomorph to the appropriate syntactic function (that is, in this system it appears accidental that one chooses the palatalised allomorph for the plural for every word) and (iii) where to state the generalisation that it is the initial and final morphemes of the word that undergo the sound changes (rather than, say, the root morpheme). As the reader will appreciate, the system of lenition and palatalisation in Gaelic raises interesting and unsolved questions for the general theory of word structure.

With these basic concepts of the theory of word structure in hand, we can now proceed to briefly sketch the morphology of Gaelic

VERBAL MORPHOLOGY

The Gaelic verb inflects for tense: past, future and conditional.[3] Only one verb also has a present tense form, the auxiliary *bi*, 'be', which is used syntactically to create periphrastic tenses (see pp. 305–25 of the following chapter for discussion).

Past tense is marked on regular verbs by initial lenition, unless the verb begins with a vowel or an *f*. In such circumstances, the vowel is prefixed by [ɣ] (orthographically *dh'*, for example *dh'òl*, 'drank') while the *f* is lenited. Lenited *f* is phonologically zero, and so the word is then treated as though the *f* were absent, and undergoes past tense formation as just described. If the original *f* was followed immediately by a vowel, then it is prefixed by [ɣ] (orthographically *dh'fh*, for example *fàg*, [faːk] 'leave' but *dh'fhàg*, [ɣaːk] 'left'); the only other cases are when the *f* is followed by an *r* or an *l*, in which case the *r/l* is lenited (in those dialects that have a relevant distinction). For example *freagair*, [frɛkər], becomes *fhreagair*, phonetically [r̩ɛkər].

The marking of [ɣ] on vowels and before lenited *f* is not a general property of lenition (recall that vowels do not usually change when lenited, while lenited *f* before a vowel simply deletes), but is morphosyntactically restricted to past tense and a few other environments. One way of analysing this morphologically is to say that tense related lenition is associated with a leniting morpheme [ɣ] which has a zero allomorph before consonants (in fact, historically these forms were preceded by a leniting particle *do*, [də], which when itself lenited would be [ɣə]). We can see how this analysis might work by considering the verbs *buail*, 'hit' (phonetically [bual]), *òl*, ('drink' [ɔːlʲ]) and *fàg*, 'leave' ([faːk]):

(3) a. [ɣ] [bual] →$_{\text{Lenition}}$ [ɣ] [vual] →$_{\text{Deletion}}$ Ø [vual]

     b. [ɣ] [ɔːlʲ] →$_{\text{Lenition}}$ [ɣ] [ɔːlʲ]

     c. [ɣ] [faːk] →$_{\text{Lenition}}$ [ɣ] [aːk]

Future tense is marked by suffixation of *(a)idh* (phonologically, [i]). The conditional is marked by both initial lenition (following the same rules as for past) and suffixation by [əɣ], (*(e)adh*). This gives us:

(4) | **past** | **future** | **conditional** | |
| --- | --- | --- | --- |
| bhuail | buailidh | bhuaileadh | 'hit' |
| [vual] | [buali] | [vualəɣ] | |
| dh'fhàg | fàgaidh | dh'fhàgadh | 'leave' |
| [ɣaːk] | [faːki] | [ɣaːkəɣ] | |
| dh'òl | òlaidh | dh'òladh | 'drink' |
| [ɣɔːlʲ] | [ɔːlʲi] | [ɣɔːlʲəɣ] | |

This system of tense marking cross-cuts with a system which marks whether the verb is 'independent', 'dependent' or 'relative'. These are traditional terms for forms the verb takes when it immediately follows certain preverbal clitics. One class of clitics gives rise to the dependent forms, another to the relative forms, and the absence of such clitics gives rise to the independent forms. For example, the negative interrogative clitic *nach* is followed by the dependent form of the verb, while the relative particle *a* (also a proclitic) is followed by the relative forms. All forms of the relative particle cause lenition on the verb, following the same pattern as past marking (that is, *a* is followed by the [ɣ] morpheme, in terms of the analysis given in (3)). The dependent past form of the verb is prefixed by the clitic *do*, which itself causes the set of alternations discussed above. Like *a*, we can take *do* to be followed by the [ɣ] morpheme:

(5) a. Dhìochuimhnich/Dh'òl   (independent past)

     b. Nach do dhìochuimhnich/Nach do dh'òl   (dependent past)

     c. An duine a dhìochuimhnich/An duine a dh'òl (relative past)

(5) shows that the past always involves prefixal material structurally (either lenition or the particle *do* followed by lenition; as mentioned above, sometimes the lenition has no phonological effect, if, for example, the verb begins with *sg*. However, even in these cases we would like to maintain that the zero allomorph of the [ɣ] morpheme is present).

The future tense shows a mix of prefixal and suffixal morphology, with a total lack of inflection in its dependent forms:

(6) a. Dìochuimhnichidh   (independent future)

     b. Nach dìochuimhnich   (dependent future)

     c. An duine a dhìochuimhnicheas   (relative future)

Finally, the conditional is always suffixal, but lenites in the independent and relative forms:

(7) a. Dhìochuimhnicheadh   (independent conditional)

     b. Nach dìochuimhnicheadh   (dependent conditional)

     c. An duine a dhìochuimhnicheadh   (relative conditional)

Independently of this pattern, some proclitics can cause lenition (for example, *cha*, negation, almost always lenites, giving *cha bhuail mi*, 'I will not strike', although there is some phonological blocking of this when the following word begins with a dental, and some dialectal variation when the following word begins with a fricative). Furthermore, certain clitics change form depending on the following verb, so both the clitics and the verb display a complex pattern of allomorphy. For example, *cha*, negation, when followed by a vowel (or *f* which is itself prevocalic) becomes *chan*, giving *chan òl mi*, 'I will not drink', *chan fhàg mi e*, 'I will not leave him'.

There is one extra twist in the conditional: for most dialects, when the conditional is first person singular, the suffix is –*inn*, and in this case the suffix takes the place of the first person pronoun subject. For some dialects this same pattern holds in the first plural, where the relevant suffix is –*(e)amaid* (recall that a prefixed asterisk signifies ungrammaticality):

(8) a. Dhìochuimhnichinn   'I would forget'
     b. *Dhìochuimhnichinn mi

(9) a. Dhìochuimhnicheamaid   'We would forget'
     b. *Dhìochuimhnicheamaid sinn

We return to this pattern of complementary distribution between agreement suffixes and the pronoun below. Note that this pattern follows if the pronoun is essentially an enclitic which shows allomorphy when cliticised to a conditional verb form (this is the analysis proposed in Adger 2000).

Corresponding with each active form here is an impersonal form (for the syntax of which see pp. 314–17 of the next chapter). In the past, this is *(e)adh*, in the future it is *(e)ar* (used for relative as well as non-relative forms) and in the conditional –*te* (or –*ist*).

Gaelic has an imperative, of which only the second person forms are in common use. Intriguingly, the imperative is the only paradigm of the Gaelic verb which displays a full paradigm of forms corresponding to the person and number of properties of the subject.

(10) buaileam   'let me strike'   buaileamaid   'let us strike'
      buail   'strike!'   buailibh   'strike!'
      buaileadh e, i   'let him/her strike'   buaileadh iad 'let them strike'

The impersonal forms of the imperative are all formed with the suffix –*t(e)ar*: *buailtear thu* 'May you be hit'; *buailtear sinn*, 'May we be hit', etc. These forms are extremely rare in use.

The Gaelic verb has one productive non-finite form, traditionally called the verbal noun. The verbal noun is generally formed from the root by a variety of processes, most involving suffixation or stem change. Two of the most common suffixes are *(e)adh*, and *(a)il*. Sometimes the verbal noun is formed by palatalising or depalatalising the root and sometimes there is no obvious phonological relation between the two forms (what is termed 'suppletion'). In general, it is not possible to determine what the morphology of the verbal noun will be on the basis of the root. Some examples:

(11) root   verbal noun

    òl   òl   'drink'   zero morphology

    cuir   cur   'put'   depalatalisation

    buail bualadh   'hit'   suffixation

    rach   dol   'go'   suppletion

NOMINAL MORPHOLOGY

The noun in Gaelic inflects for number (singular and plural) and for case (to be discussed below). Nouns are categorised morphologically for gender (a binary distinction between masculine and feminine), a categorisation which influences the forms that the noun takes in different numbers and cases. The category gender is syntactically active in Gaelic, having an impact on the forms of various elements that co-occur with nouns (such as articles and adjectives; see below). The noun is also categorised for various declensional classes, which cross-cut with gender to affect the form the noun takes. These declensional classes are not, however, syntactically active.

We have already seen how the noun *litir*, 'letter', has a plural suffix *–ichean*, giving the plural form *litrichean*. We have also seen how the noun *cat*, 'cat', palatalises its final segment to mark plurality. We also find more or less radical changes in the stem (for example *bò*, 'cow', but *bà*, 'cows'). These are the main modes of plural inflection in Gaelic nominals: suffixation by a plural morpheme, palatalisation and stem alternation. The particular type of suffix, or the possibility of palatalisation/stem alternation, depend on the gender and noun class of the nominal (see Lamb 2003 for more detailed description).

Case in Gaelic is more unusual. From a linguistic point of view, Gaelic case can be seen simply as the form that the noun takes in particular grammatical environments. For example, after a certain class of prepositions, the noun appears in what is traditionally termed the 'dative' case, but, given its distribution, perhaps 'prepositional case', following MacAulay (1992), is a better term. In certain possessive constructions, certain prepositional constructions, as well as in certain non-finite constructions, the noun appears in the 'genitive' case. When the noun is being used to address some person or thing it is preceded by a particle *a* and this particle affects the form of the noun, giving what is termed the 'vocative' case. In other grammatical situations, the noun is in what is traditionally called the nominative, accusative or nominative-accusative case. I will use the term 'direct', following Ramchand (1996), for this case form. One typologically unusual thing about the Gaelic case system is that it makes no distinction between the case form of a subject and an object in a finite clause, using the direct case for both.

The particular morphological form of case, like that of number, depends on gender and declensional class. It may involve initial lenition, final palatalisation, stem modification or suffixation. For example, the masculine noun *cat* and the feminine noun *caileag*, 'girl' decline as follows:

(12)

	singular		plural	
	masc	fem	masc	fem
direct	cat	caileag	cait	caileagan
dative	cat	caileig	cait	caileagan
genitive	cait	caileig(e)	chat	chaileagan
vocative	a chait	a chaileag	a chataibh	a chaileagan

However, for indefinite nouns, many speakers nowadays assimilate the genitive case with the direct/dative cases and giving a basic two way distinction between *cat/cait* and *caileag/caileagan* (putting aside the vocative).

Abstractly, we can see this paradigm as involving the interplay of lenition, palatalisation and suffixation, as follows (I abstract away from the lenition caused by the vocative proclitic):

(13)

	singular		plural	
	masc	fem	masc	fem
direct	0	0	palatalisation	ən-suffixation
dative	0	palatalisation	palatalisation	ən-suffixation
genitive	palatalisation	palatalisation+ə-suffixation	lenition	ən-suffixation
vocative	palatalisation	0	u-suffixation	ən-suffixation

The interplay of gender and noun class gives rise to different patterns of lenition, palatalisation and suffixation.

Grammatically, the noun appears with various other elements: the definite article, numerals, quantifiers, adjectives and demonstratives (see pp. 336–49 of the next chapter). Some of these elements change form to agree with the noun in gender, number and case. For example, the definite article takes the following forms:

(14)

	singular		plural	
	masc	fem	masc	fem
direct	an cat	a' chaileag	na cait	na caileagan
dative	a' chat	a' chaileig	na cait	na caileagan
genitive	a' chait	na caileig(e)	nan cat	nan caileagan

The definite article itself changes form, but also exerts various pressures on the initial segment of the following noun, leniting in the masculine dative and genitive singular and in the direct and dative feminine singular and suppressing lenition in the genitive plural (or in some dialects, phonologically nasalising the following noun). These case distinctions are much more commonly expressed when the definite article is present, although many speakers have exactly the same form (the direct) throughout the masculine plural, so that the genitive plural for these speakers is *nan cait* (or sometimes just *na cait*). Other prenominal particles, such as the quantifier *gach*, or the possessive proclitics, can suppress case distinctions for many speakers, although not for all.

Adjectives also change their forms dependent on the case and number of the noun. The major changes that happen with indefinite nouns are (i) lenition of adjectives that modify feminine singular nouns; (ii) the addition of –*a* to plurals; (iii) lenition of adjectives which follow nouns which pluralise via palatalisation:

(15)

	singular		plural	
	masc	fem	masc	fem
direct	cat mòr	caileag mhòr	cait mhòra	caileagan mòra
dative	cat mòr	caileig mhòir	cait mhòra	caileagan mòra
genitive	cait mhòir	caileig(e) mòir(e)	chat mòra	chaileagan mòra

Again, this traditional pattern is undergoing a number of changes: feminine singular adjectives are, for many speakers, lenited throughout, and for some speakers palatalisation is only found in the genitive singular.

When a modified noun is definite, in general, the pattern of lenition on the noun is copied on the adjective in the singular, while still following the general rules just mentioned (so, for example, *mhòra* in the direct and dative plural following the rule that a noun which pluralises via palatalisation lenites the following adjective).

(16)

		singular		plural
	masc	fem	masc	fem
direct	an cat mòr	a' chaileag mhòr	na cait mhòra	na caileagan mòra
dative	a' chat mhòr	a' chaileig mhòir	na cait mhòra	na caileagan mòra
genitive	a' chait mhòir	na caileig(e) mòir(e)	nan cat mòra	nan caileagan mòra

Interestingly, the presence of the definite article impacts on the form of the adjective, following the generalisation about copying the patterns of lenition and palatalisation across from noun to adjective. An indefinite masculine dative is unlenited, while a definite masculine dative is lenited, giving the contrast *le cat mòr/leis a' chat mhòr* (the preposition here also changes form to mark the following definite article; see pp. 336–49). A theoretically interesting question arises here: do the adjectives bear the grammatical features case, number, gender and definiteness, by virtue of which they inflect, or do adjectives simply copy whatever morphological processes their noun undergoes. The evidence is clear for gender and number and case: these are independent features, since indefinite feminine nouns are not lenited but their adjectives are; since the *–a* inflection on the adjective is not found on the noun and since an indefinite genitive masculine plural is lenited but an accompanying adjective is not. However, this is not so clear for the impact of definiteness on singular dative adjectives.

One other noteworthy point is the absence of any phonological mark of an indefinite article, except for the lenition in the genitive masculine plural. Analytically, the question is whether this constitutes evidence for a null indefinite article (which surfaces as lenition in the genitive plural), or whether there is no indefinite article, and the lenition on the noun independently marks case and is suppressed by the plural definite article.

Gaelic pronouns inflect for number, person and gender, but not for case:

(17)

		singular	plural
First Person		mi	sinn
Second Person		thu/tu	sibh
Third Person	masculine	e	
	feminine	i	iad

The *thu/tu* distinction in the second person singular holds only for subjects of finite verbs: the *tu* form is found following the copula and finite active verbs whose inflection ends in *dh* or *s*, while the *thu* form is found elsewhere.

These pronouns are all enclitic to the verb when in subject position. In object position, they preferentially shift to the right of adverbials (see pp. 314–17 of the next chapter), a phenomenon which has been argued to be related to their phonological weakness (Adger 1997). Since these pronouns are phonologically weak, they usually are not stressed (although they can be in certain situations). For emphatic use, the pronouns are usually suffixed as follows:

(18)

		singular	plural
First Person		mise	sinne
Second Person		thusa/tusa	sibhse
Third Person	masculine	esan	
	feminine	ise	iadsan

There are no genitive forms of the pronouns. To express pronominal possession a separate series of proclitics is used:

(19)

		singular	plural
First Person		mo	ar
Second Person		do	ur
Third Person	masculine	a (+ lenition)	
	feminine	a	an

Evidence that these are not simply genitive forms of the simple pronouns comes from their emphatic versions. The emphatic form of 'my cat' is not **mosa cat* but rather *mo chat-sa*. If we take the emphatic clitics to attach to pronouns, as in (18), this suggests that there is a null variant of the pronoun after the noun, and the proclitic grammatically agrees with this:

(20)   mo chat Ø-sa

The pronouns also lack dative forms. Recall that dative case appears on noun phrases which follow a certain class of prepositions. One might then expect that pronouns after prepositions are marked dative. However, in Gaelic, pronouns cannot follow prepositions; rather the preposition and pronoun form a single morphological unit.[4] We address this in the next section.

Finally, there are a number of derivational suffixes which create nominals from other categories and convert nominals to other categories. For example, *(e)as* creates abstract nouns from adjectives (*luath*, 'fast', *luathas*, 'speed'), while *ach* creates adjectives from concrete nouns (*cànan*, 'language', *cànanach*, 'linguistic'). These suffixes can be combined to make more complex words (*cànanachas*, 'linguistics').

PREPOSITIONAL MORPHOLOGY

Unusually for an Indo-European language, Gaelic prepositions have a fairly complex morphology. Some mark definiteness of their following noun phrase, and most also display a certain kind of agreement in number, gender and person with a following element. The definiteness marking is more straightforward. Consider the contrast between *le cat*, 'with a cat', and *leis a' chat*, 'with the cat', where the form of the preposition changes. This change also happens in the plural, suggesting that it is not phonologically conditioned *leis na cait*, 'with the cats', and for many speakers it also takes place when the following noun begins with the quantifier *gach*, 'every', and the particle *cho*, 'so': *leis gach cat*, 'with every cat'; *leis cho mòr 's a bha e*, 'with how big it was'. Other prepositions that behave like *le* are *ri/ris* 'to', *ann/anns* 'in' and *gu/gus*, 'to'.

Other prepositions also change their form when preceding definite noun phrases. For example, the preposition *do*, 'to, for' in formal Gaelic is followed by an encliticised form of the singular article giving *don*, while in less formal speech, it is lenited to *dha*, which, when followed by a definite noun phrase becomes *dhan* and itself may or may not be followed by the article, giving rise to the following variants (as is common in situations where there are multiple variants, there is a complicated interaction between register and dialect in this domain):

(21) a.   don bhaile   'to the town'   don abhainn   'to the river'
      b.   dhan bhaile   dhan abhainn
      c.   dhan a' bhaile   dhan an abhainn

Not all prepositions are followed by the dative case. Some are followed by the direct case (e.g. *eadar*, 'between') and some by the genitive (e.g. *chun*, 'towards'). Gaelic also possesses a rich system of what are traditionally termed 'complex prepositions', where a preposition occurs with a nominal. These complex prepositions are followed by a noun phrase in the genitive. For example, *os cionn*, 'above', and *os cionn a' chait*, 'above the cat', *mu dheidhinn*, 'about', but *mu dheidhinn na caileige*, 'about the girl'. For many of these complex prepositions the constituent simple preposition and/or its associated nominal are unusable independently, suggesting that these are not simply prepositional phrases with an internal complex nominal phrase.

Most simple prepositions agree in person, number and gender when they are interpreted as taking a pronoun as their object. These agreeing prepositions cannot have an overt pronominal object and emphatic particles appear encliticised to the agreeing preposition:

(22) a.   leotha
           with.3P
           'with them'
      b.   *leotha iad
           with.3P them
      c.   leotha-san
           with.3P-EMPH
           'with THEM'

Furthermore, only the non-agreeing form is possible with noun phrase objects (*le cait*, 'with cats' vs. *leotha cait*). This is the same generalisation that we saw with conditional verbs on pp. 288 ff. We state it here as (23), as this generalisation will also be important in the next chapter:

(23)   Argument/Agreement Generalisation

(i) Overt nominal phrase arguments co-occur with zero agreement

(ii) Overt agreement marking co-occurs with silent nominal phrase arguments

This complementarity between agreement and the noun phrase which is being agreed with has received a fair amount of theoretical attention in the literature on Gaelic and other Celtic languages (for Gaelic see Adger 2000; for Irish, Hale and McCloskey 1984; for Welsh, Roberts and Shlonsky 1996 and, for Breton, Anderson 1982). There are two basic perspectives: (i) the apparently agreeing forms are actually just the pronunciation of the preposition plus a following enclitic; (ii) the prepositions grammatically bear the features of person, number and gender and they agree with an obligatorily null pronoun. It is not inconceivable that the verbal agreement discussed on pp. 287–91 and the prepositional agreement outlined here actually have different analysis, and this is what is suggested for Gaelic by Adger (2000), who takes the verbal agreement to arise from encliticisation, but the prepositional agreement to involve a null pronoun.

The complex prepositions also display agreement. In this case, the nominal part is preceded by the same proclitic forms that are used to mark possessive pronouns (19). For example, the proclitic *mo* marks first person possession, so *mo cheann*, 'my head'; *do cheann*, 'your head', etc. Following this pattern we have:

(24)   a.   mu   mo   dheidhinn   (*mi)

about   POSS.1.S   N   (*I)

'about me'

b.   os   an   cionn   (*iad)

P   POSS.3P   N   (*they)

'above them'

Again, it is impossible to have an overt pronoun, and the emphatic particles are once again placed to the right of the structure:

(25)   a.   mu   mo   dheidhinn   -sa

about   POSS.1.S   N   EMPH

'about ME'

b.   os   an   cionn   -san

      P   POSS.3P   N   EMPH

      'above THEM'

ADJECTIVAL MORPHOLOGY

We have already seen above how adjectives change their morphological form through lenition, palatalisation and suffixation to agree with their nominal in gender, case, number and definiteness. This change of form only takes place when the adjective is attributive (i.e. directly modifies a noun) and not when it is predicative (see pp. 317–23 of the next chapter for discussion of the grammar of (27)):

(26) a'   chaileag bheag

      the girl   small

      'the small girl'

but

(27) Tha   a' chaileag beag

      be.PRES the girl   small

      'The girl is small'

The other major morphological change that adjectives undergo marks 'comparative formation'. Scottish Gaelic distinguishes morphologically between positive and comparative forms of adjectives (there is no distinct superlative form). The regular morphological formation of comparatives involves palatalisation of the final consonant, and the addition of the schwa vowel [ə], but, as can be seen from the table below, we also have irregularities, such as vowel alternations (*trom* ~ *truime*) and suppletion (*math* ~ *feàrr*).

(28) a. òg   òige   young

      b. trom   truime   heavy

      c. math   feàrr   good

      d. slaodach   slaodaiche slow

These forms cannot be used directly, but have to be syntactically augmented, in the way described in pp. 323–5 in the next chapter. So we have the contrast:

(29)   Tha   an   gille   òg
        be.PRES   the   boy   young
        'the boy is young'

(30)   *Tha   an   gille   òige   (na thusa)
        be.PRES   the   boy   young.CMP (than you)
        for: 'The boy is younger (than you).'

SUMMARY AND SUGGESTIONS FOR FURTHER WORK

Overall, Gaelic uses a gamut of morphological techniques to express grammatical distinctions. In common with many other Indo-European languages, it uses suffixation, stem changes, phonologically dependent clitics and suppletion. In addition, the language uses lenition and palatalisation processes, which can be analysed as the selection of allomorphs by grammatical elements, or as phonologically abstract morphemes which attach to adjacent elements.

The implications of Gaelic morphology for morphological theory have not been studied in any great detail. Even the brief sketch here raises a number of questions: if the analysis of past tense lenition as involving a morpheme [ɣ] is on the right track, does this morpheme correspond to some grammatical category, or is it a purely morphological element? What is the correct analysis of Gaelic nominal inflection: does it involve allomorph selection or abstract morphemes? What connections can be drawn between the morphological and phonological aspects of lenition and palatalisation?

There are also interesting questions to be raised about the connection between the syntax of Gaelic and its morphology. For example, the following two examples are very close in meaning, but the first uses a syntactic construction involving a nominal and a prepositional phrase, while the second uses an adjectivally derived form of the same nominal:

(31)   Tha   drip   orm
        be.PRES   hurry   on.1s
        'I'm busy/in a hurry.'

(32) Tha   mi   drìpeil

      be.PRES   I   hurried

      'I'm busy/in a hurry.'

This alternation is fairly productive for certain semantic classes of nouns (those involving a mental state), and raises the question as to whether there is an underlying commonality that can be captured syntactically and, if so, what this tells us generally about how the relationship between morphology and syntax is configured.

In addition to these more theoretical questions, there is also a great deal of descriptive work to be done. I have barely touched on the rich system of derivational morphology in Gaelic which is used for converting categories from nouns to adjectives, from nouns to verbs, from adjectives to verbs, etc. Nothing is known at a systematic level about what the constraints on these conversions are, or how productive they are in the language. There is also important descriptive work to be done on Gaelic compounding, and on the range of dialectal and register variation in the system of inflection. Connected to this is how the inflectional systems of the language are being lost or maintained across generations of speakers of the language.

BIBLIOGRAPHY

Adger, David (1997), 'VSO Order and Weak Pronouns in Goidelic Celtic', *Canadian Journal of Linguistics* 42, pp. 9–29.

Adger, David (2000), 'VSO Clause Structure and Morphological Feature Checking', in Robert Borsley (ed.), *Syntactic Categories*, New York: Academic Press, pp. 79–100.

Anderson, Stephen (1982), 'Where's Morphology?' *Linguistic Inquiry* 13, pp. 571–612.

Booij, Geert (2005), *The Grammar of Words*, Oxford: Oxford University Press.

Borgstrøm, Carl (1937), 'The Dialect of Barra in the Outer Hebrides', *Norsk Tidsskrift for Sprogvidenskap* 8, pp. 71–242.

Borgstrøm, Carl (1968), 'Notes on Gaelic Grammar', in James Carney and David Greene (eds), *Celtic Studies. Essays in Memory of Angus Matheson, 1912–1962*, London: Routledge and K. Paul, pp. 12–21.

Gillies, William (1993), 'Scottish Gaelic', in Martin J. Ball and James Fife (eds), *The Celtic Languages*, New York: Routledge, pp. 145–227.

Green, Antony Dubach (2006), 'The Independence of Phonology and Morphology: The Celtic Mutations', *Lingua* 116, pp. 1946–85.

Hale, Ken and McCloskey, James (1984), 'On the Syntax of Person-number Inflection in Modern Irish', *Natural Language and Linguistic Theory* 1, pp. 487–533.

Harley, Heidi (2006), *English Words: A Linguistic Introduction*, Cambridge, MA: Blackwells.

Haspelmath, Martin (2002), *Understanding Morphology*, London: Arnold.

Lamb, William (2003), *Scottish Gaelic*, Munich: Lincoln Europa.

Lamb, William (2007), *Scottish Gaelic Speech and Writing: Register Variation in an Endangered Language*, Belfast: Cló Ollscoil na Banríona.

MacAulay, Donald (1992), 'The Scottish Gaelic Language', in Donald MacAulay (ed.), *The Celtic Languages*, Cambridge: Cambridge University Press, pp. 137–248.

Massam, Diane (1983), 'The Morphology of Irish Mutation', in Isabel Haïk and Diane Massam (eds), *MIT Working Papers in Linguistics 5: Papers in Grammatical Theory*, Cambridge: MIT, pp. 10–29.

Ramchand, Gillian (1996), 'Two Types of Predication in Scottish Gaelic', *Natural Language Semantics* 4, pp. 165–91.

Roberts, Ian and Shlonsky, Ur. (1996), 'Pronominal Enclisis in VSO Languages', in Robert Borsley and Ian Roberts (eds), *The Syntax of Celtic Languages: A Comparative Perspective*, Cambridge: Cambridge University Press, pp. 171–99.

NOTES

1 Many thanks to my consultants Murchadh MacLeòid, Marion NicAoidh, Beathag Mhoireasdan and especially Iseabail NicIlleathain, and to Jule Landgraf and Marc Wringe for much help along the way. Many thanks too to Will Lamb and to the editors for comments on an earlier draft. I am grateful to the Leverhulme Trust, who have supported this work via a Major Research Fellowship.

2 The parentheses around *a* here signify different orthographic forms of this morpheme which are used depending on whether the preceding consonant is itself preceded orthographically by the vowels *a, o* or *u* vs. *i, e*; the *a* is used when the preceding vowel is in the former group. The same applies to *(a)ichean*, PLURAL. This is the well-known Gaelic Spelling Rule. See the chapter on phonology in this volume.

3 These morphosyntactic categories are used, semantically, to convey a wide range of meanings; see especially MacAulay (1992) for discussion.

4 There are exceptions to this: for example, where a coordinated pronoun follows the preposition *eadar*, 'between', (which in any case takes a direct rather than a dative noun phrase):

(i) eadar   mise   agus   tusa

between   I-EMPH   and   you-EMPH

'between me and you'

CHAPTER 14

Gaelic Syntax

David Adger

INTRODUCTION

The purpose of this chapter is similar to that of the last: it surveys some basic syntactic structures in Scottish Gaelic in a systematic fashion from the perspective of contemporary theoretical linguistics.[1] The previous chapter points to literature relevant also to this chapter, and discusses some limitations on the nature of the study, which apply equally here.

A survey like the present one will always suffer from a number of limitations; one such is scope: this chapter covers what I take to be some interesting syntactic characteristics of Gaelic, but languages are vast oceans of complexity, and what is done here is a shore-bound skim across the surface.

A second limitation comes from the type of data considered. Just like morphology and phonology, syntactic structures can be highly variable across speakers and across speech situations. People choose to use certain structures in certain situations to express their thoughts, and these choices are influenced by a highly complex system of beliefs and intentions relevant to the utterance, as well as to the particularities of the speaker's age, gender, dialect, capacity to handle a range of registers, etc. It is almost impossible to steer clear of such issues, but I have attempted in my fieldwork to control for certain influences by using sentences embedded in discourse contexts, and I note dialectal or age-related variation where I have sufficient confidence in the aetiology of the variant forms.

Since I have let what I consider to be linguistically interesting or surprising guide the choice of what to include, this piece should not be taken as a snapshot of contemporary spoken Gaelic or as the description of the grammar of a particular community. It is a fairly superficial survey of some phenomena in the language which raise analytical issues for linguistic theory. I hope, even with these limitations, that it will be somewhat useful.

CLAUSE STRUCTURE

The simplest clause type in Gaelic consists of a finite element which marks tense followed by a subject, an object, and various clausal modifiers:

(1) Phòg   Seonag   Calum   gu   luath   an-dè.
     kiss.PAST Seonag   Calum   PRT   quick   yesterday
     'Seonag kissed Calum quickly yesterday.'

From a general linguistic perspective, this is an interesting order, as it breaks up the verb and object. In many other languages, there is good evidence that the verb and object form a syntactic group (a constituent), usually termed the verb phrase. The typologically common SVO and SOV languages group the verb and the object together as follows:

(2)   a.   S[VO]
      b.   S[OV]

Syntactic constituents must be contiguous, so the fact that the verb in Gaelic is separated from the object by the subject, at first sight, suggests that this language lacks a verb phrase:

(3)   V S O

The initial finite element need not be a verb; the auxiliary *bi*, 'be', can also serve this purpose:

(4) Bha   Seonag   a'   pògadh   Chaluim   gu   luath an-dè.
     be.PAST Seonag   SIMP   kiss.VN Calum.GEN   PRT quick yesterday
     'Seonag was kissing Calum quickly yesterday.'

In these constructions, the main verb *pògadh* and the object *Chaluim* are contiguous syntactically; the main verb is in a non-finite form (the verbal noun form – see pp. 287–91 in the previous chapter) and between the subject and the verb we find the proclitic particle *ag/a'*, which signifies what we might call 'simple' aspect (the time of the event denoted by the non-finite verb overlaps the time denoted by the auxiliary). In fact, there is good evidence that the (non-finite) verb and object form a constituent in such structures. A good test for constituency is whether the putative constituent is treated as a unit in various different constructions. In Gaelic one construction where this can be tested is the cleft construction (see pp. 330–3 for further discussion). In this construction, part of the sentence is emphasised by being brought to the start of the sentence. It is possible to treat the verb and object as a unit in a cleft construction like (5):

(5) 'S   ann   [a'   pògadh Chaluim] a   bha   Seonag.
     COP   in.3MS SIMP   kiss.VN Calum.GEN that be.PAST Seonag
     'What Seonag was doing was kissing Calum.'

Various authors have suggested that VSO sentences like (1) actually do have a contiguous verb phrase, but that this is broken up by an obligatory syntactic rule that places the verb in the initial position if that position is not filled by an auxiliary (McCloskey 1983). Schematically, this perspective takes the relevant structures for such sentences to have (at least) two components, related by an operation that 'displaces' the verb to the initial position:

(6) a.   S V O   V S <V> O

Here the angled brackets simply signify that the verb is not pronounced in that position. This approach entails that an apparently simple sentence like (1) is actually structurally complex:

(7) Phòg   Seonag [<phòg> Calum].
     kiss.PAST Seonag <kiss>   Calum
     'Seonag kissed Calum.'

The advantage of this approach is that it allows a unified perspective on the structures for main verb VSO and AuxiliarySVO orders.

Although Gaelic is typologically a VSO language, there are various elements that may precede the finite verb/auxiliary. One important element is negation:

(8) Cha do   phòg   Seonag Calum.
     NEG PAST kiss.PAST Seonag Calum
     'Seonag didn't kiss Calum.'

This example also shows another preverbal element, *do*, which appears between negation and a (regular) past verb-form (pp. 287–91 in the previous chapter).

As we saw in Chapter 13, a particle marking yes/no question semantics also appears to the left of the finite verb; I gloss this particle as Q, (for question):

(9) An   do   phòg   Seonag   Calum?

Q   PAST kiss.PAST Seonag   Calum

'Did Seonag kiss Calum?'

Morphologically, all of these preverbal particles procliticise to the finite verb or auxiliary. Negation and Q can be combined semantically:

(10) Nach   do   phòg   Seonag   Calum?

Q.NEG PAST kiss.PAST Seonag   Calum

'Didn't Seonag kiss Calum?'

The other important element that appears before the finite verb (or auxiliary) occurs in embedded clauses. Here we find *gu(n)* as an obligatory marker of a positive embedded statement:

(11) Thuirt   Iain   gun   do   phòg   Seonag   Calum.

say.PAST Iain   that PAST kiss.PAST Seonag   Calum

'Iain said that Seonag kissed Calum.'

The negative of *gun* is, once again, *nach*:

(12) Thuirt   Iain   nach   do   phòg   Seonag   Calum.

say.PAST Iain   that.NEG PAST kiss.PAST Seonag   Calum

'Iain said that Seonag didn't kiss Calum.'

In addition to embedded statements, we have embedded questions, where we once again find Q:

(13) Dh'fhaighnich Iain   an   do   phòg   Seonag   Calum.

ask.PAST   Iain   Q   PAST kiss   Seonag   Calum

'Iain asked whether Seonag kissed Calum.'

One can complete the paradigm with an embedded negative question using *nach*:

(14) Dh'fhaighnich e   nach   robh   thu   sgìth?
      ask.PAST   he   Q.NEG be.PAST you   tired
      'He asked if you weren't tired?'

One final important preverbal element we find is the relative particle, *a* with its negative form *nach*:

(15) An   leabhar a   leughas   mi
      The   book   REL   read.FUT.REL I
      'The book I will read.'

(16) An   leabhar nach   leugh   mi
      The   book   REL.NEG read.FUT   I
      'The book I won't read.'

This *a* particle appears with the special relative form of the finite verb discussed on pp. 287–91 in the previous chapter. I return to the syntax of this particle on pp. 327–30.

From a theoretical point of view, it appears we need to distinguish questions from non-questions, positives from negatives, embedded from non-embedded clauses and relatives from non-relatives. These distinctions are sufficient to classify all of the various preverbal particles found in Gaelic (see, e.g. Byrne 2002 section 6.3 for a comprehensive list).

There seems to be a single syntactic position for all of these various preverbal particles (excluding *do* mentioned above), since it is impossible to combine them. We call this position the 'complementiser' position, and we take these particles to be complementisers, equivalent in function to English *that*, although richer in the grammatical features that they bear. Gaelic, then, marks the semantics of negation, interrogation, embeddedness and relativisation all via complementisers.

With this in place, we can draw a rough diagram of the Gaelic clause as follows:

(17) a.   [$_c$ gun/an/cha/nach/a] [$_{Fin}$ (do) Verb] Subj <Verb> Obj
      b.   [$_c$ gun/an/cha/nach/a] [$_{Fin}$ Auxiliary] Subj [$_{VerbPhrase}$Aspect$_{simp}$
           Verb$_{NonFin}$ Obj]^2

Here, the subscripted C marks the position for the various complementisers while the subscripted Fin marks the position of the finite element, whether it is an auxiliary or a verb.

With this much in hand, we can now turn to the syntactic positions of subjects and objects.

The position of verbal arguments

Arguments in their canonical positions

In a VSO clause, the subject is required to be strictly adjacent to the verb. It does not appear possible to place an adverbial modifier between them:

(18) Dh'itealaicheadh   na   bana-bhuidsich gu tric air   sguaban.
      fly.COND   the   witches   often   on   broomsticks
      'The witches would often fly on broomsticks.'

(19) *Dh'itealaicheadh gu tric/gu slaodach   na   bana-bhuidsich
      fly.COND   often/slowly   the   witches

      air   sguaban.
      on   broomsticks
      'The witches would often fly on broomsticks.'

However, it is possible to place certain adverbials between the subject and object, such as the temporal adverbial *gu tric*:

(20) Bhriseadh   na   bana-bhuidsich gu tric na   sguaban   aca.
      break.COND   the   witches   often   the   broomsticks   at.3P
      'The witches would often break their broomsticks.'

Such adverbials also may appear after the object, and this is their preferred position:

(21) Bhriseadh   na   bana-bhuidsich na   sguaban   aca   gu tric.
      break.COND   the   witches   the   broomsticks   at.3P often
      'The witches would often break their broomsticks.'

Not all adverbials can occur between subject and object, however. For example, manner adverbials like *gu slaodach* 'slowly' are impossible:

(22) *Bhriseadh   na   bana-bhuidsich gu slaodach na   sguaban   aca.
      break.COND   the   witches   slowly   the   broomsticks at.3P
      'The witches would slowly break their broomsticks.'

These adverbials are most natural after the object:

(23) Bhriseadh   na   bana-bhuidsich na   sguaban   aca   gu slaodach.
      break.COND the witches   the broomsticks at.3P slowly
      'The witches would slowly break their broomsticks.'

However, when the object is a weak pronominal, the weak pronominal tends to appear to the right of any adverbial modifier:

(24) Bhriseadh   na   bana-bhuidsich gu slaodach iad.
      break.COND the witches   slowly   them
      'The witches would slowly break them.'

Subject pronominals do not undergo this displacement:

(25) *Bhriseadh na   sguaban   aca   gu slaodach iad.
      break.COND the broomsticks at.3P slowly   them
      'They would slowly break their broomsticks.'

Emphatic pronouns also resist this rightwards placement (the verb here is changed to 'kiss' as emphatic pronouns have to be interpreted as referring to humans):

(26) *Phògadh   na   bana-bhuidsich gu slaodach iadsan.
      kiss.COND the witches   slowly   them.EMPH
      'The witches would slowly kiss them.'

Clauses headed by auxiliaries are a little different in their structure. In such clauses, the temporal adverbial is permitted to appear between the finite auxiliary and the subject or between the subject and the aspectual particle that precedes the verb (note the meaning difference that arises). In all of these cases, for many speakers, the adverb is preferentially placed to the right, but some speakers also allow the order given here. I have been unable to determine whether this variation is dialect or age related:

(27) Bhiodh   gu tric bana-bhuidsich a'   briseadh nan sguaban
      be.COND often   witches   SIMP break.VN the broomsticks
      aca   aig   an àm   sin.
      at.3P   at   the time   that
      'There would often be witches breaking their broomsticks at that time.'

(28) Bhiodh   bana-bhuidsich gu tric a'   briseadh   nan

be.COND   witches   often   SIMP   break.VN   the

sguaban   aca.

broomsticks at.3P

'Witches would often break their broomsticks.'

Not only temporal adverbials can appear in this position. Manner adverbials are also possible (although they are more natural after the object):

(29) Bhiodh   bana-bhuidsich gu slaodach a'   briseadh   nan

be.COND   witches   slowly   SIMP   break.VN   the

sguaban   aca.

broomsticks at.3P

'Witches would slowly break their broomsticks.'

However, no adverbial can appear between the verb and the object:

(30) *Bhiodh bana-bhuidsich a'   briseadh gu tric/gu slaodach

be.COND witches   SIMP   break.VN often/slowly

nan   sguaban   aca.

the   broomsticks   at.3P

'Witches would often/slowly break their broomsticks.'

In clauses with a non-finite verb, the operation that allows object weak pronouns to appear at the end of the clause, after modifiers, is impossible in most dialects.

(31) *Bhiodh bana-bhuidsich a'   briseadh gu tric/gu slaodach iad.

be.COND witches   SIMP   break.VN often/slowly   them

'Witches would often/slowly break them.'

This is because, in most dialects, pronominal objects of non-finite verb forms surface as agreement on the aspectual marker:

(32) Bhiodh   bana-bhuidsich gam   briseadh gu tric/gu slaodach.

be.COND witches   SIMP.3P   break.VN often/slowly

'Witches would often/slowly break them.'

A type of auxiliary construction we have not yet met, the perfect construction, displays an OV order contrasting with the non-perfect auxiliary construction:

(33) Tha   Calum   air   na   leabhraichean a   reic.
      be.PRES Calum   PERF   the.DIR.P   book.DIR.P   PRT   sell.VN
      'Calum has sold the books.'

(34) Tha   Calum   a'   reic   nan   leabhraichean.
      be.PRES Calum   SIMP   sell.VN the.GEN.P   book.GEN.P
      'Calum is selling the books.'

In this construction, the object appears immediately after the aspectual particle, and the verb follows, preceded by a particle *a*. If the object is pronominal, the particle inflects to agree with the understood object:

(35) Tha   Calum   air   am   pògadh   -san.
      be.PRES Calum   PERF   3P   kiss.VN   -EMPH.3P
      'Calum has kissed THEM.'

The emphatic particle which is associated with the pronoun surfaces after rather than before the non-finite verb form, parallel to the cases we saw earlier with possessors (pp. 291–6 in the previous chapter). This fact has led some authors to suggest that there is a syntactic dependency between the post-verbal and preverbal positions (Hale and McCloskey 1984, Adger 1996), with some kind of null pronominal in the post-verbal position to which the emphatic particle attaches. The preverbal particle would then agree in person, number and gender with this null pronoun:

(36) PERF PRT VerbalNoun Ø-EMPH

Indeed, an alternative construction allows the emphatic pronoun to appear in the preverbal position, treating the emphasised pronominal just like a full noun phrase:

(37) Tha   Calum   air   iadsan   a   phògadh.
      be.PRES Calum   PERF   3PL.EMPH   PRT   kiss.VN
      'Calum has kissed THEM.'

In this construction the preverbal particle appears in the same form as if it were third masculine singular. Just as in the simple aspect construction, a post-posed pronoun is impossible here:

(38) *Tha   Calum   air   a   phògadh iad.
      be.PRES   Calum   PERF   PRT   kiss.VN them
      'Calum has kissed them.'

These perfect constructions also allow temporal adverbs to appear in the position immediately before the aspectual particle, or after the verb, but not between the perfect particle and the verb:

(39) Tha   oileanaich (gu tric) air   *(gu tric) na   leabhraichean
      be.PRES   students   (often)   PERF   (often)   Det.DIR.P   book.DIR.P
      sin   *(gu tric) a   reic   gu tric   ann a shin.
      those   (often)   PRT   sell.VN (often)   there
      'Students have often sold those books there.'

The perfect construction is paralleled by a prospective construction, which has the general meaning of 'about to':

(40) Tha   Calum   gus   na   leabhraichean a   reic.
      be.PRES Calum   PROS   Det.DIR.P   book.DIR.P   PRT   sell.VN
      'Calum is about to sell the books.'

The syntax of the prospective construction is identical to that of the perfect construction in all the respects just mentioned.

We can now add a third clause structure to the two we have already seen:

(41) a. $[_C][_{Fin}(\text{do})$ Verb] Subj Obj
      b. $[_C][_{Fin}$Auxiliary] Subj $[_{VerbPhrase}$Asp$_{simp}$ Verb$_{NonFin}$ Obj]
      c. $[_C][_{Fin}$Auxiliary] Subj $[_{VerbPhrase}$ Asp$_{perf/pros}$ Obj PRT Verb$_{NonFin}]$

Evidence for the constituency of (c) once again comes from clefting:

(42) An   ann   [air   an leabhar   a   reic]   a   tha   thu?
      Q   there PERF   the book   PRT   sell.VN   REL   be.PRES   you
      'Have you sold the book?'

Arguments in non-canonical positions

There are a number of ways, in Gaelic, to 'demote' the subject, so that the proposition expressed by the sentence is primarily one about the object of the clause. One very common structure utilises the auxiliary headed clauses we have already met. The subject is not expressed and the object appears immediately after the finite auxiliary; that is, in the position the subject would usually occupy:

(43)   Tha   an   doras   air   a   dhùnadh.
        be.PRES the   door   PERF   PRT   close.VN
        'The door has been shut/is shut.'

The particle immediately preceding the verb shows agreement for the moved object:

(44)   Tha   a'   chaileag   air   a   pògadh.
        be.PRES the   girl   PERF   3FS   kiss.VN
        'The girl has been kissed.'

(45)   Tha   mi   gam   shàrachadh.
        be.PRES I   SIMP.1S   harrass.VN
        'I am being harrassed.'

These are passive in meaning, but note that there is agreement with the (moved) object, so they are transitive in form. In fact, (44) has a perfectly legitimate active transitive meaning: 'The girl has kissed her.' On such a reading, the particle is understood as a pronoun (or perhaps agrees with an unpronounced pronoun in the structure, as discussed above).

In addition to the auxiliary passive, Gaelic also possesses an inflectional means of demoting the subject. I give examples from the simple past and future here, but see Lamb (2003) 2.2.1.1 for the full paradigm:

(46)   Dhùineadh   an   doras.
        shut.PAST.PASS   the   door
        'The door was shut.'

(47) Dùinear   an   doras.
      shut.FUT.PASS   the   door
      'The door will be shut.'

These constructions, however, are in fact a kind of impersonal, rather than a passive. Many intransitive verbs allow this impersonal inflection, including the auxiliary and modals:

(48) Thathar   a'   toirt   rabhadh   dhaibh.
      be.PRES.IMP SIMP   give.VN   warning   to.3P
      'They are being warned.'

(49) Feumar   am   bùth   a   dhùnadh.
      must.IMPERS   the   shop   PRT   close.VN
      'The shop must close.'

Recall that only object pronouns move rightwards across adverbs. We can use this as a test to see whether the postverbal noun phrase in these constructions is a subject or object. We replace *an doras* in (47) with a pronominal, and then test to see whether it can postpose. If it moves rightwards across an adverb, then this means that, even though it appears to be in the subject position (immediately after the verb), it is actually an object. The following example confirms this conclusion:

(50) Dùinear   a-màireach   e.
      shut.FUT.PASS   tomorrow   it
      'It will be shut tomorrow.'

Given this, a plausible analysis of the impersonal suffix is that it either is itself the subject, or that it licenses a zero subject. Under such an analysis, *an doras* in (47) will be in canonical object position, explaining the postposing in examples like (50).

There are a number of other cases where the verb lacks a subject. One of the most common is an alternative means of expressing passivisation involving the verb *rach*, 'go'.

(51) Chaidh   òrain   Ghàidhlig   a   sheinn   aig   a'   chèilidh.
      go.PAST   songs   Gaelic   PRT   sing   at   the   ceilidh
      'Gaelic songs were sung at the ceilidh.'

This construction also allows impersonal passives to be easily constructed (MacAulay 1992: 177, ex. 112, his translation).

(52) Chaidh   falbh
      go.PAST   leave.VN
      'A departing was effected(?).'

Here we see the non-finite verb phrase with OV order again. In this case, rather than appearing after a perfect particle, it appears as an apparent complement to a full verb. There is evidence that the object of the verbal noun is, in this case, really in the subject position. Recall that in the perfect construction it was impossible to interrupt the OV non-finite verb phrase with an adverbial (39); in contrast, in these *rach*-passives, a temporal adverb can appear between the object and the non-finite verb:

(53) Chaidh   òrain   Ghàidhlig gu tric   a   sheinn   aig   a'   chèilidh.
      go.PAST   songs   Gaelic   often   PRT   sing.VN   at   the   ceilidh
      'Gaelic songs were often sung at the ceilidh.'

In contrast to the inflected impersonal, and similar to the auxiliary passive, these constructions apparently involve the object appearing in the same structural position as the subject of an active clause.

Before we can leave the issue of subjects and objects, I would like to make one further observation. Gaelic has a great many expressions which apparently lack any nominal subject:

(54) Thèid   agam   air   a   dhèanamh.
      go.FUT   at.1s   on   PRT   do.VN
      'I'll manage to do it.'

(55) Shoirbhich   leam   a   dhèanamh.
      succeed.PAST   with.1s   PRT   do.VN
      'I succeeded in doing it.'

It seems unlikely that the prepositional phrases here are structurally subjects, since in non-finite clauses they appear in post-verbal rather than preverbal position:

(56) Tha   a'   dol   agam   air   a   dhèanamh.
      be.PRES   SIMP   go.VN   at.1s   on   PRT   do.VN
      'I'm managing to do it.'

(57) *Tha   agam   a'   dol   air   a   dhèanamh.
      be.PRES at.1s SIMP go.VN on   PRT   do.VN
      'I'm managing to do it.'

These structures raise another important theoretical issue. We saw above with the *rach*-passive, for example, that the object, in the absence of a subject, must take the structural subject position. One way of capturing this would be to say that the structural subject position is obligatory in Gaelic (as it is in English). However, the last four examples show that this cannot be correct: when there is no noun phrase which will act as a potential subject, no subject is required. However, if we say that filling the structural subject position is not obligatory, then why, in *rach*-passives, for example, must the object appear in the subject position? It appears we must say that if the structural subject position is not filled by a true subject, and there is another noun phrase in the sentence, then this other noun phrase must appear in the structural subject position. There have been a number of attempts to capture this dependency (McCloskey 1996, Adger 2000), but none particularly satisfying.

Predicational Structures

We now turn to sentence structures where the clause is built around categories other than the verb. In Gaelic these are of two types, which, following Adger and Ramchand (2003), I will call the Substantive Auxiliary Construction (SAC) and the Inverted Copular Construction (ICC). In both, a finite element comes first: the familiar auxiliary we met in the previous discussion for the SAC, and the copular verb *is/bu* for the ICC. In the SAC, the subject precedes the predicate, while in the ICC the order is reversed (hence the name). Thus we have:

(58) a.   Auxiliary Subject Predicate (SAC)
      b.   Copula Predicate Subject (ICC)

ICCs are not productive in the modern spoken language, except in consciously archaic discourse, but the syntax of ICCs is used to build many other constructions in the language, as we will see.

Adjectival and prepositional predication

The simplest cases of the SAC involve an adjectival phrase (59) or a prepositional phrase (60) following the subject:

(59) Tha   Calum   faiceallach.
      be.PRES   Calum   careful
      'Calum is (being) careful.'

(60) Tha   Calum   anns   a'   bhùth.
      be.PRES   Calum   in   the   shop
      'Calum is in the shop.'

The equivalent ICCs would look as follows:

(61) Is   mòr   an   duine   sin.
      COP.PRES   big   that man
      'That man is big.'

(62) Is   le   Calum   an   cù.
      COP.PRES   with   Calum   the   dog
      'The dog belongs to Calum.'

Both (61) and (62) are rather literary, and not commonly heard. Neither SACs nor ICCs accept verbs as their predicates:

(63) *Tha   Calum   èist   ris   an   rèidio.
      be.PRES   Calum   listen   to.DEF   the   radio

(64) *Is   èist   Calum   ris   an   rèidio.
      Cop   listen   Calum   to.DEF   the   radio

Nominal predication

Interestingly, the SAC also rejects a nominal predicate:

(65) *Tha   Calum   tidsear.
      be.PRES   Calum   teacher
      'Calum is a teacher.'

An alternative with an aspectual/prepositional particle *ann*, 'in', must be used. Like the aspectual particles found in the passive constructions discussed above, these obligatorily trigger agreement:

(66) Tha   mi   nam   thidsear.
      be.PRES   I   in.1s teacher
      'I am a teacher.'

I take the particle here to be aspectual rather than straightforwardly prepositional, following Cram (1983). Cram's argument for the particle being aspectual is that the same syntax is used for verbal predication, which involves the aspectual category of stativity:

(67) Tha   Iain   na   chadal.
      be.PRES Iain   in.3s sleep.VN
      'Iain is sleeping.'

The ICC, to the extent that it is productive, allows nominal predicates; however, both (68) and (69) are preferentially expressed using cleft structures (see below, pp. 330–3):

(68) Bu   thidsear   Calum.
      COP.PAST teacher   Calum
      'Calum was a teacher.'

(69) Is   eun   sgarbh.
      COP.PRES bird   cormorant
      'The cormorant is a bird.'

Unlike English, Gaelic does not allow definite noun phrases as predicates. Compare (70) and (71) with their putative English translations:

(70) *Tha   Iain   an   tidsear.
      be.PRES Iain   the   teacher
      'Iain is the teacher.'

(71) *Is   an   tidsear   Iain.
      COP.PRES the   teacher   Iain
      'Iain is the teacher.'

To express these concepts, Gaelic uses what Adger and Ramchand term the Augmented Copular Construction (ACC). In such constructions, a pronominal follows the copula, and in turn is followed by the two noun phrases:

(72) 'S   e   Iain an   tidsear.
      Cop.pres   he   Iain the teacher
      'Iain is the teacher.'

Even though the two nominal phrases are both definite expressions in (72), there is an asymmetry in interpretation, with the latter nominal acting semantically as the predicate. Compare:

(73) 'S   e   Iain Hamlet a-nochd.
      Cop.pres   he   Iain Hamlet tonight
      'Iain is (playing) Hamlet tonight.'

(74) 'S   e   Hamlet Iain a-nochd.
      Cop.pres   he   Hamlet Iain tonight
      'Hamlet is Iain tonight.'

(74) cannot have the pragmatically usual interpretation that Iain is playing Hamlet, unlike its English translation. This shows that there is still a predicational asymmetry in ACCs, with the notional subject preceding the notional predicate.

In summary, the SAC allows prepositional and adjectival predicates, while the ICC also allows nominal ones. Neither allow verbs nor definite noun phrases as their predicates. For a definite noun phrase predicate, the alternative ACC must be used.

Psychological and possessive predication

One striking fact about Gaelic predicational structures is the paucity of verbs expressing internal feelings – so called 'psychological predicates', like the English verbs *fear, love, dislike*, etc. Gaelic uses the grammar of adjectival and prepositional predication to express these concepts.

(75) Tha   mi   brònach.
      be.pres   I   sad
      'I am sad.'

(76) Tha   mi   fo   chùram.
     be.PRES   I   under   anxiety
     'I am anxious.'

Both of these examples have the semantic predicate expressing the emotion as the syntactic predicate in an SAC. More interestingly, Gaelic can also (and in fact usually does) express the semantic predicate as the syntactic subject as follows:

(77) Tha   cùram   orm.
     be.PRES   anxiety   on.1s
     'I am anxious.'

(78) Tha   eagal   orm.
     be.PRES   fear   on.1s
     'I am afraid.'

For transitive psychological predicates, like *love*, the two arguments of the predicate are expressed as prepositional phrases:

(79) Tha   gaol   agam   ort.
     be.PRES   love   at.1s   on.2s
     'I love you.'

Analytically, the question is how the predicate connects with its two arguments. The obvious option would take (79) to consist of three separate constituents:

(80) Auxiliary [love] [at-me] [on-you]

However, this appears to be incorrect. If we apply our clefting test, we have the following results (Adger and Ramchand 2006b):

(81) 'S   e   [gaol   air   Iain]   a   th'   agam.
     Cop he   love   on   Iain   REL   is   at.1s
     'I love Iain.'

(82) *'S e   gaol   aig   Iain   a   th'   ort.
     Cop he   love   at   Iain   REL   is   on.2s
     'Iain loves you.'

What this shows is that the apparent subject *gaol*, 'love', and the right-most prepositional phrase *ort*, 'on you', are a constituent, even though they are separated by the prepositional phrase *agam*, 'at me'. This is reminiscent of the issue we discussed in pp. 305 ff, where there was evidence that the verb and the object form a constituent, and we solved that problem by taking the structure of the sentence to be complex, involving movement of the verb. If we apply the same logic here, we are led to say that (79) also involves movement:

(83) Tha   gaol agam [<gaol> ort]
      be.PRES   love at.1s [<love> on.2s]
      'I love you.'

Interestingly, this is consistent with our generalisation about subject positions in Gaelic: if the structural subject position lacks a subject, and there is another noun phrase in the sentence, then that other noun phrase appears in the structural subject position. In this case, the other noun phrase is a semantic predicate, rather than the object, but the same processes appear to apply.

The ICC can also be used to express psychological predication, with the semantic predicate in this case being the syntactic one:

(84) Is   toil   leam   an   duine sin.
      COP.PRES   pleasant with.1s   the man   that
      'I like that man.'

(85) Is   coma   leam   dè   thachras.
      COP.PRES   indifferent with.1s what   happen.FUT.REL
      'I don't care what will happen.'

Once again, the entity who has the emotion or feeling is expressed as a prepositional phrase.

A second important fact about Gaelic predication is that it lacks any equivalent of the English verb *have*. To express the semantics of possession, Gaelic uses a prepositional strategy again. Compare (86) with (87):

(86) Tha   peann aig Daibhidh.
      be.PRES   pen   at   David
      'David has a pen.'

(87) Tha   am ministear aig an   doras.
     be.PRES the minister   at   the door
     'The minister is at the door.'

For permanent possession, Gaelic uses the preposition *le*, 'with', rather than *aig*, 'at':

(88) 'S   ann   le   Daibhidh a   tha   am peann.
     COP in.3MS with David   REL be.PRES the pen
     'The pen is David's.'

While for the part-whole relationships, the preposition *air*, 'on' is used:

(89) Tha   cas bhriste air a'   bhòrd.
     be.PRES leg broken   on   the table
     'The table has a broken leg.'

Comparative constructions

As mentioned on pp. 299–300 in the previous chapter, the comparative form of adjectives cannot be used in the same way as the positive form; rather, it must be syntactically augmented. There are two types of augmentation, which roughly correspond to whether the adjective is in a SAC or ICC construction.

The first type of augmentation is mainly used with the Substantive Auxiliary Construction outlined above (and with other predicative structures). It involves prefixing the comparative adjective with the particle *nas*:

(90) Tha   mi nas òige   (na   thusa).
     be.PRES I   PRT young.CMP   (than you)
     'I am younger (than you).'

The *–s* part of this particle is the copula, as can be seen from a past tense version of (90):

(91) Bha   mi na   b'   òige   (na   thusa).
     be.PAST I   PRT COP.PAST young.CMP   (than you)
     'I was younger (than you).'

This same type of augmentation is used in an adverbial comparative:

(92) Ruith   esan   [na bu   luaithe   na   ruith   mise].
      run.PAST he   PRT Cop.PAST quick.CMP than run.PAST I
      'He ran more quickly than I did.'

The second type of augmentation is used for attributive comparatives, and involves prefixation with the particle *as/a bu*:

(93) An   gille as   òige   na   mise
      The boy   PRT+COP.PRES   young.CMP   than I
      'The boy younger than me'

(94) Gach   gille a   b'   òige   na   mise
      Every boy   PRT Cop.PAST young.CMP   than I
      'Every boy younger than me'

It is not possible to use the *as*-comparative in the Substantive Auxiliary Construction:

(95) *Tha   mi   as   òige   na   thusa
       be.PRES I   PRT+COP.PRES   young.CMP   than you

Nor is it possible to use the *nas* comparative in attributive position when the whole DP is definite or quantified:

(96) *An gille nas   òige   na   mise
       the boy   PRT+COP.PRES   young.CMP   than I

(97) *Gach gille nas   òige   na   mise
       each   boy   PRT+COP.PRES   young.CMP   than I

However, it is possible, and for many speakers mandatory, to use a *nas*-comparative in an indefinite DP:

(98) Chunnaic mi   gille nas   òige
      see.PAST I   boy   PRT+COP.PRES   young.CMP
      'I saw a younger boy.'

See Adger (2005) for suggestions as to the analysis of these constructions.

CLAUSAL COMPLEMENTATION

We have seen already that VSO order is maintained after complementisers in embedded clauses (pp. 305–25). In fact, the internal syntax of complement clauses is much the same as the internal syntax of main clauses (modulo the dependent/independent/relative marking on the complementiser and verb).

Non-finite complementation, however, is interestingly different. There is just one major type of non-finite subordinate argument clause, which is headed by the verbal noun. At its simplest, this clause consists just of the verbal noun, where the subject of the verbal noun is understood to be some argument of the embedding predicate:

(99) a. Tha   mi   airson   ithe.
          be.PRES   I   for   eat.VN
          'I want to eat.'

      b. Dh'fheuch   sinn   ri   coiseachd.
          try.PAST   we   to   walk.VN
          'We tried to walk.'

      c. 'S fheàrr   le   Anna   seinn.
          is better   with   Anna   sing.VN
          'Anna prefers to sing.'

      d. Bu   toigh   leam   falbh.
          be.COND   liking with.1s leave.VN
          'I'd like to leave.'

      e. Dh'iarr   e   orm   leum.
          ask.PAST   he   on.1s   jump.VN
          'He asked me to jump.'

The (a) example shows a (complex) preposition taking a verbal noun complement. The examples in (b) and (e) show cases where finite verbs have a verbal noun complement. The (c) and (d) examples are cases of the kind of psychological predication discussed on pp. 320–3, where adjectival and nominal heads take verbal noun complements. The examples above are all interpreted in the following way: one of the nominal phrases in the higher clause is interpreted as the 'subject' of the verbal noun as well as being the subject of the higher predicate.

The syntax of these non-finite complement clauses is by now familiar: it is the same as the syntax of the verbal noun in perfect and prospective constructions. If the verbal noun is transitive, then its object appears in a position preceding the verbal noun and the verbal noun itself is preceded by a particle:

(100) a. Tha   mi   airson   cèic   agus   aran   a   dhèanamh.
           be.PRES I   for   cake   and   bread   PRT   make.VN
           'I want to make cake and bread.'

       b. 'S   fheàrr le   Anna   òran   Gàidhlig a   sheinn.
           is   better with   Anna   song   Gaelic   PRT   sing.VN
           'Anna prefers to sing a Gaelic song.'

If the object is pronominal, the particle which precedes the VN inflects for person, number and gender features, taking the form of the relevant possessive proclitic.

(101) 'S   fheàrr le   Anna   an   seinn.
       is   better with   Anna   PRT.3.P sing.VN
       'Anna prefers to sing them.'

LONG-DISTANCE DEPENDENCIES

So far, we have concentrated on simple clausal structures in Gaelic. In this section, we look at clausal constructions which can be used to modify, emphasise or question constituents. These constructions all involve what are termed 'long-distance dependencies' (LDD). The reason for the name can be seen if we look at some English examples:

(102)   The cat that Calum hit.

Intuitively, the noun phrase 'the cat' is interpreted as the object of 'hit', but usually the object of a verb like 'hit' immediately follows it, and, moreover, has to be present (cf. * Calum hit). It appears then that there is some kind of relationship, or dependency, between the noun phrase to the left of the complementiser 'that' and the position immediately after the verb. The noun phrase is, in a sense, displaced from its usual position. Moreover, this dependency still holds when the distance between the two positions is very long:

(103)   The cat that you said that Calum hit miaowed.

These long-distance dependencies are found in relative clauses of the type just seen, but also in certain emphasis constructions (such as clefts) and certain types of question, in both Gaelic and English. The next three sections examine the syntax of these long-distance dependencies in Gaelic.

Relative Clauses

The most basic LDD construction in Gaelic is the relative clause. Relative clauses are a grammatical way of creating a predicate out of a sentence. For example, take the sentence in (104):

(104)   Bhuail   Calum   an   cat.
   hit.PAST   Calum   the   cat
   'Calum hit the cat.'

This sentence expresses a complete thought. However, we can modify it so that its subject or object are 'removed' from the meaning of the sentence as follows (note that, structurally, these examples are ambiguous, allowing the alternative interpretations *that the cat will hit*, and *that will hit Calum*, respectively):

(105)   a.   a   bhuaileas   an   cat
     REL   hit.FUT.REL   the   cat
     'that will hit the cat'

   b.   a   bhuaileas   Calum
     REL   hit.FUT.REL   Calum
     'that Calum will hit'

Syntactically, the verb is prefixed by the proclitic *a*, and some element is 'missing' from the remainder of the sentence. In the future, an extra inflection is added to the verb (see pp. 287–91 in the previous chapter). The resulting relative clause can then be used, much like an adjective, as a modifier of nominals:

(106) a. An   duine a   bhuaileas   an   cat
          the   man   REL hit.FUT.REL the   cat
          'The man that will hit the cat'

b. An   cat   a   bhuaileas   Calum
    the   cat   REL hit.FUT.REL Calum
    'The cat that Calum will hit'

In Gaelic, just as in English, relatives can be long-distance, but with an interesting twist. Recall that the embedding finite complementiser is *gu(n)* (11). However, when a relative in Gaelic spans an embedded clause, the embedding complementiser cannot be *gu(n)*, but must be *a* (see Adger and Ramchand 2005 for discussion and analysis).

(107) An   cat   a   thuirt   Daibhidh a   bhuaileas   Calum
      the   cat   REL say.PAST David   REL hit.FUT.REL Calum
      'The cat that David said Calum will hit'

(108) An   duine a   thuirt   Daibhidh a   bhuaileas   an cat
      the   man   REL say.PAST David   REL hit.FUT.REL the cat
      'The person that David said will hit the cat'

Unlike the closely related language Modern Irish, Gaelic does not allow a pronoun to appear instead of a gap; that is, no 'resumptive pronoun' is possible in these relative clauses (Adger and Ramchand 2006a):

(109) An   ghirseach ar   ghoid   na   síogaí í
      the   girl   REL.PAST steal.PAST the fairies her
      'The girl who the fairies stole'   Modern Irish (McCloskey 2006)

(110) *A'   chaileag a   ghoid   na   sìdhichean i
      the   girl   REL steal.PAST the fairies   her
      'The girl who the fairies stole'   (Scottish Gaelic)

As well as relative clauses where the relativised element is the subject or object, we have relative clauses on prepositional phrases. Extending in (111) our original sentence by adding prepositional modifiers, we have the corresponding relatives in (112):

(111) Thug   Calum an   cat do   Mhàiri air a'   bhàta.
       give.PAST   Calum the cat to   Mary   on   the.DAT boat

       'Calum gave the cat to Mary on the boat.'

(112) a. A' chaileag dhan an   tug   Calum   an   cat
           the girl to.DEF   C   give.PAST.DEP   Calum   the   cat
           air a'   bhàta
           on the.DAT boat
           'The girl to whom Calum gave the cat on the boat'

       b. Am bàta air   an   tug   Calum an   cat do   Mhàiri
           the boat on   C   give.PAST.DEP   Calum the cat to   Mary
           'The boat on which Calum gave the cat to Mary'

In these structures, the preposition appears at the left of the relative clause, followed by the complementiser *an*, which itself is followed by a dependent, rather than relative, form of the verb. Just as in the previous relative clauses, there is a gap in the position of the prepositional phrase.

Interestingly, speakers do not accept long-distance versions of these prepositional relative clauses:

(113) *A' chaileag dhan   an   tuirt   thu   a   thug   Calum
        the girl   to.DEF   C   say.PAST.DEP   you   REL   give.PAST.DEP   Calum
        an   cat
        the   cat
        'The girl to whom you said that Calum gave the cat'

Two strategies are followed: either the preposition is left in its base position in its default masculine form/appropriate agreeing form (this varies depending on the type of prepositional modifier, the age of the speaker and the dialect), or the preposition is placed to the left of its own clause:

(114) a. A' chaileag a   thuirt   thu   a   thug   Calum
           the girl   REL   say.PAST.REL   you   REL   give.PAST.REL   Calum
           an   cat dha/dhi
           the   cat to.3MS/to.3FS
           'The girl to whom you said that Calum gave the cat'

b.	A' chaileag	a	thuirt	thu	dhan	an	tug	Calum
	the girl	REL	say.PAST.REL	you	to.DEF	C	give.PAST.DEP	Calum
	an		cat					
	the		cat					

'The girl to whom you said that Calum gave the cat'

There appears to be considerable variation in the domain of long-distance prepositional relatives (Adger and Ramchand 2006a).

Cleft Constructions

We have already come across cleft constructions as a test for constituency. Clefts in Gaelic appear to be built up out of an ICC and a relative clause. The simplest version involves clefting a subject or an object:

(115) a.	'S	e	Calum	a	thug	an	cat
	COP.PRES	it	Calum	REL	give.PAST.REL	the	cat
	do	Mhàiri.					
	to	Mary					

'It's Calum who gave the cat to Mary.'

b.	B'	e	an	cat	a	thug	Calum
	COP.PAST	it	the	cat	REL	give.PAST.REL	Calum
	do	Mhàiri.					
	to	Mary					

'It's the cat that Calum gave to Mary.'

There can be agreement in tense between the copula and the verb in the relative, but this is not obligatory, as can be seen from (115). Prescriptively, the pronoun immediately following the copula (*e* in [115]) can agree in gender and number with the subject, but this is neither obligatory nor common:

(116)	'S	e/iad	Calum	agus	Iain	a	thug	an	cat
	COP.PRES	it/they	Calum	and	Iain	REL	give.PAST.REL	the	cat
	do Mhàiri.								
	to Mary								

'It's Calum and Iain who gave the cat to Mary.'

Gaelic allows many types of constituent to be clefted, and the element immediately after the copula changes depending on the category of the clefted constituent. A simple nominal phrase triggers a pronominal, as we have just seen, while a prepositional phrase triggers the appearance of the element *ann*, literally 'in it'.

(117) 'S   **ann**   do   Mhàiri a   thug   Calum   an   cat.

COP.PRES   in.3MS   to   Mary   REL   give.PAST.REL   Calum   the   cat

'It's to Mary that Calum gave the cat.'

Adjectives, adverbs and aspectual phrases also trigger *ann* while clausal complements trigger a pronoun:

(118) a.   'S   ann   brèagha   a   tha   i.

COP.PRES   in.3MS   beautiful   REL   be.PRES   she

'She's beautiful.'

b.   'S   ann   gu   slaodach   a   tha   i   a' ruith.

COP.PRES   in.3MS   PRT   slow   REL   be.PRES   she   SIMP run.VN

'She is running slowly.'

c.   'S   ann   [a'   pògadh   Chaluim]   a   bha   Seonag.

COP.PRES   in.3MS   SIMP kiss.VN   Calum.GEN   that   be.PAST   Seonag

'What Seonag was doing was kissing Calum.'

(119) a.   'S   e   gun   robh   e   tinn   a   thuirt   mi.

COP.PRES   it   that   be.PAST.DEP   he   ill   REL   say.PAST.REL   I

'What I said was that he was ill.'

b.   'S   e   an   leabhar   ud   a   leughadh   a   dh'iarr

COP.PRES   it   the book   that PRT   read.VN   REL   ask.PAST.REL

e   orm.

he   on.1s

'What he asked me to do was to read that book.'

One might take the difference between *e* and *ann* to be one of sensitivity to whether the clefted constituent is a predicate or an argument. Adjectives, Verb Phrases, Adverbs and Prepositional Phrases are all prototypical predicates, while nominal phrases and clauses are arguments. However, when a noun phrase is used as a predicate, we find *e* rather than *ann*:

(120) 'S   e   tidsear   a   tha   ann an   Calum.
       Cop.pres it   teacher   REL   be.pres in   Calum
       'Calum is a teacher.'

A further curious fact about clefted nominal predicates is the apparent lack of a source for the cleft. Recall that the SAC version of (120) is (121):

(121) Tha   Calum   na   thidsear.
       be.pres   Calum   in.3s   teacher
       'Calum is a teacher.'

The order of the subject *Calum* and the (reduplicated) prepositional element *ann an* in (120) and *na* in (121) is not the same. The subject precedes the preposition in the non-cleft and follows it in the cleft construction. So the clefted predicate nominal is not straightforwardly derived from the non-clefted version of the predicate nominal construction. See pp. 318–20 for more discussion of nominal predication.

Just like relatives, clefts can be formed long-distance:

(122) 'S   e   Calum   a   thuirt   thu   a   bha   tinn.
       Cop.pres it   Calum   REL   say.past.rel   you   REL   be.past.rel   ill
       'It's Calum that you said was ill.'

Unlike long-distance prepositional relatives, long-distance prepositional clefts are well-formed:

(123) 'S   ann   leotha   a   thuirt   thu   a   bha
       Cop.pres in.3ms   with.3p   REL   say.past.rel   you   REL   be.past.rel

       Calum,   nach   ann?
       Calum   NEG.Q   in.3ms
       'It was with them that you said Calum was, right?'

There are numerous analytical questions about the structure of Gaelic clefts. If they are simply an ICC plus a relative clause, as they look on the surface, what exactly is the syntactic relation between the two constructions? Why can we cleft prepositional phrases using the relative proclitic *a*, but in a relative clause we find the dependent marking proclitic *an*? Why can we cleft aspectual phrases or finite clauses at all (recall [5]), since we don't appear to be able to construct corresponding relative clauses? What accounts for the different behaviour of prepositional relatives and clefts?

Constituent Questions

The last type of long-distance dependency we will consider here is the consituent question construction. This construction basically asks a question about some element of the sentence by placing a question version of the relevant constituent at the beginning of the sentence:[3]

(124) a. Òlaidh   Calum uisge?
           drink.FUT   Calum water
           'Calum will drink water?'

       b. Cò   (a)   dh'òlas   uisge?
           who   (REL) drink.FUT.REF   water
           'Who will drink water?'

       c. Dè   (a)   dh'òlas   Calum?
           what   (REL) drink.FUT.REF   Calum
           'What will Calum drink?'

In addition to simple question words as in (124), whole constituents can be questioned:

(125) a. Cò   an   duine   (a)   dh'òlas   uisge?
           who   the   man   (REL) drink.FUT.REF   water
           'Which man will drink water?'

       b. Dè   an   leabhar (a)   leughas   Calum?
           what the   book   (REL) read.FUT.REF   Calum
           'Which book will Calum read?'

Note that unlike in English, the phrase which the question word precedes must contain the definite article:

(126) *Dè   leabhar   (a)   leughas   Calum?

       what   book   (REL)   read.FUT.REF Calum

       for: 'Which book will Calum read?'

Constituent questions follow the same pattern as relatives when they span more than one clause, with *a* in place of *gu(n)* as the embedding complementiser:

(127) Dè   an   leabhar   (a)   thuirt   thu   a   leughas   Calum?

       what the   book   (REL) say.PAST.REL you   REL read.FUT.REF   Calum

       'Which book did you say that Calum will read?'

Various sentence modifiers also have question variants, all of which, except one, follow the same pattern:

(128) a.   Cuine   (a)   dh'òlas   Calum   uisge?

            when   (REL)   drink.FUT.REF Calum   water

            'When will Calum drink water?'

       b.   Ciamar   a   dh'òlas   Calum   uisge?

            how   (REL)   drink.FUT.REF Calum   water

            'How will Calum drink water?'

       c.   Carson   a   dh'òlas   Calum   uisge?

            why   (REL)   drink.FUT.REF Calum   water

            'Why will Calum drink water?'

       d.   Càit   an   òl   Calum   uisge?

            where   C   drink.FUT.DEP Calum   water

            'Where will Calum drink water?'

Càit, 'where' forms its constituent question along the lines of a prepositional relative.

Questions about the degree to which some property holds in Gaelic have yet another structure:

(129) Dè   cho   luath   agus   a   ruitheas   e?

       what   so   fast   and   REL   run.FUT.REL   he

       'How fast will he run?'

This structure uses a coordinating conjunction, which apparently coordinates a simple predicate question (what is the degree of speed) with a relative clause (that he ran). Whether this simple surface structure is actually the structure of these constructions will have to be left for future work.

Finally, we turn to prepositional questions. These appear to be formed along two different lines. When the question word is simple, they follow a prepositional cleft-like pattern as in (130), where we find the relative proclitic and the relative form of the verb. If, however, the wh-word is complex, the constituent question follows a prepositional relative pattern:

(130) | Cò | ris | a | bhios | Calum | a' | bruidhinn?
| who | to.3MS | REL | be.FUT.REL | Calum | SIMP | speak.VN

'Who will Calum be speaking to?'

(131) | Cò | am | boireannach | ris | am | bi | Calum | a' | bruidhinn?
| who | the | woman | to.DEF | C.DEP | be.FUT.DEP | Calum | SIMP | speak.VN

'Which woman will Calum be speaking to?'

It does seem to be possible to use the second pattern for simple wh-words, too, giving variation, but it is impossible to use the cleft-like pattern for complex prepositional constituent questions:

(132) | Cò | ris | am | bi | Calum | a' | bruidhinn?
| who | to.3MS | C | be.FUT.DEP | Calum | SIMP | speak.VN

'Who will Calum be speaking to?'

(133) | *Cò | am | boireannach | ris | a | bhios | Calum
| who | the | woman | to.DEF | REL | be.FUT.REL | Calum

| a' | bruidhinn?
| SIMP | speak.VN

for: 'Which woman will Calum be speaking to?'

The variation between (130) and (132) appears to be in most speakers' grammars, and is plausibly tied to the possibility of using both syntactic strategies with the simple question word.

As might be expected from our previous discussion, long-distance versions of simple prepositional questions, which use the cleft-like strategy, are possible, but long-distance versions of the complex ones, which use the prepositional relative strategy, are not:

(134) Cò   ris   a   thuirt   thu   a   bhios

who   to.3MS   REL   say.PAST.REL you   REL   be.FUT.REL

Calum   a'   bruidhinn?

Calum   SIMP   speak.VN

'Who did you say that Calum will be speaking to?'

(135) *Cò   am   boireannach ris   an   tuirt   thu   gum

who   the   woman   to.DEF   C   say.PAST.DEP   you   that

bi   Calum   a'   bruidhinn

be.FUT.DEP Calum SIMP speak.VN

for: 'Which woman did you say Calum will be speaking to?'

(135) does have a reading, but only as a question about who you were speaking to, not about who Calum was speaking to. Once again, we see that the long-distance dependency is not available with the prepositional strategy.

NOMINAL PHRASE STRUCTURE

We have focused so far on the syntactic properties of clauses. In this section, we turn to the properties of nominal phrases, which consist of a noun plus various determiners, quantifiers, adjectives and other modifiers.

The core order of the main elements in nominal phrases can be summarised as follows, where categories in the same column in the tables are in complementary distribution (that is, if one category is present, none of the others in the same column is possible). I give first the prenominal elements and then the postnominal ones:

(136)

1	2	3	4
Articles	Counting Quantifiers	Adjectives	Noun
Quantifiers	Numerals		
Possessive Pronouns			

(137) 4   5   6   7   8
       Noun   Adjectives   Demonstratives   PPs   RelClauses
                                     Genitive
                                     Possessors

Of course, it would be extremely unusual and rather clumsy to have a
nominal phrase containing all these elements, but the basic order can be
gleaned through pairwise comparisons. Concentrating on prenominal
order, we have examples like:

(138) Na   ceithir   deagh-bhàtaichean
       The   four   good-boats

(139) Gach   trì   làithean
       Every   three   days

(140) Mo   chiad   droch-cheann   goirt
       my   first   badhead   sore
       'My first bad head-ache'

While for postnominal orders we find:

(141) Dealbhan   mòra   Sheumais   de   Iain   a   rinn   Màiri
       pictures   big   Seumas.GEN   of   Iain   REL   do.PAST   Màiri
       'Seumas's big pictures of Iain that Mary did'

(142) Na   dealbhan   mòra   seo   aig   Seumas   a
       the   pictures   big   this at   Seumas   REL
       rinn   Màiri
       do.PAST   Màiri
       'These big pictures of Seumas's that Mary did'

These orders are very strict, and altering them tends to lead quickly to
unacceptability:

(143) *Na   dealbhan   mòra   aig   Seumas   seo   a   rinn   Màiri
       the   pictures   big   at   Seumas   this REL   do.PAST   Màiri
       'These big pictures of Seumas's that Mary did'

In addition to the complementary distribution found in the various 'slots' in the noun phrase, there are syntactic dependencies across the slots. The most striking is that the genitive possessor cannot co-occur with a definite determiner, even though the meaning of the whole nominal phrase is definite:

(144)   mac   Sheumais
   son   Seumas.GEN
   '*A/the son of Seumas'

(145)   *am   mac   Sheumais
   the   son   Seumas.GEN
   'Seumas's son'

There are also dependencies that go the other way: for example, prepositional possessors and demonstratives require a definite article:

(146)   a.   *mac   aig   Seumas
     son   at   Seumas
     'A son of Seumas'

   b.   am   mac   aig   Seumas
     the   son   at   Seumas
     'Seumas's son'

(147)   a.   *cù   seo
     dog   this

   b.   an   cù   seo
     the   dog   this
     'this dog'

In the next two subsections, I briefly review some properties of the various prenominal and postnominal elements.

Prenominal elements

There is no indefinite determiner in Gaelic. Bare nouns generally are interpreted as indefinites, while nouns with the proclitic definite article are interpreted as definite. Possessive pronouns appear to have the same syntactic and semantic properties as the definite article: they are impossible with genitive possessors (although this is perhaps for semantic rather than syntactic reasons) and satisfy the requirements of demonstratives:

(148) a.   *a   leabhar   Sheumais
             his   book   Seumas.GEN

       b.   mo   leabhar   sin
             my   book   that
             'that book of mine'

The quantifiers *gach*, 'each/every', and *a h-uile*, 'every', occur in the first position in a nominal phrase, require a singular noun, and are incompatible with the definite article and with possessive pronouns:

(149) a.   gach/a h-uile   leabhar/   *leabhraichean
             each/every   book/   *books

       b.   *an   gach   leabhar
             (*the)   every   book

       c.   *ur   gach   rùn
             your   every   wish

Interestingly, while *a h-uile* is completely incompatible with a genitive possessor, *gach* is somewhat more acceptable:

(150) a.   *a h-uile   corrag   Sheumais
             every   finger   Seumas.GEN

       b.   ?gach   corrag   Sheumais
             every   finger   Seumas.GEN

Similarly, while *a h-uile* satisfies a demonstrative's need for a definite article, *gach* is not quite as acceptable:

(151) a.   a h-uile   bàta   sin
             every   boat   that

b.	?gach	bàta	sin
	every	boat	that

These data suggest that *a h-uile* is itself complex, containing a full definite article, unlike *gach*. Further evidence for this is that, while the definite form of certain prepositions is always obligatory before *a h-uile*, it is rather more variable before *gach*:

(152)	ris	a h-uile	duine/	ri(s)	gach	duine
	to.DEF	every	person/	to.DEF	every	person

'to everyone'

There is one other quantifier that co-occurs with a singular nominal, *iomadh* (sometimes *iomadach*), 'many'. Like *gach* and *a h-uile*, this quantifier is 'distributive' semantically: that is, it can be seen as an instruction to check the various elements in the set of things referred to by the noun to see whether each one has the property denoted by the predicate. For *gach* and *a h-uile* it must be the case that each checked element indeed has the relevant property, while *iomadh* just insures that a sufficiently large number do. The archaic English expression 'many a' is a good rough translation:

(153)	Tha	iomadh	leabhar	air	a'	bhòrd
	be.PRES	many	book	on	the	table

'Many a book is on the table.'

Contrast this with a non-distributive like *tòrr*, 'a lot', or *mòran*, 'many'. These quantifiers do not semantically require a check of every element in the set of books, but rather just that there be a sufficiently large number of books on the table. These non-distributive quantifiers always take plural rather than singular (count) nouns:

(154)	Tha	tòrr/mòran	leabhraichean/*leabhar	air	a'	bhòrd
	be.PRES	many	books/book	on	the	table

'Many books are on the table.'

The distributive quantifiers can be further diagnosed in that they disallow a pronoun in a following sentence to link back to them. Take the following example, where *e*, 'it', is taken to refer to a book and not a table:

(155) Bha   gach/a h-uile/iomadh leabhar air a'   bhòrd.
      be.PAST each/every/many   book   on   the table.
      *Bha   e mòr.
      be.PAST it big
      'Each/every/many a book was on the table. *It was large.'

As can be seen, the two sentences do not make a coherent discourse. Contrast this with a singular definite or indefinite article:

(156) Bha   leabhar/ an leabhar air a'   bhòrd. Bha   e   mòr.
      be.PAST book/   the book   on   the table. be.PAST it big
      'A/The book was on the table. It was large.'

However, the distributive quantifiers do allow a linked singular pronoun to appear in their own clause:

(157) Thuirt   gach/a h-uile/iomadh balach gun   robh   e   tinn.
      say.PAST each/every/many   boy   that be.PAST.DEP   he ill
      'Each/every/many a boy said he was ill.'

Within the non-distributive quantifiers, some, like numerals or *grunn*, 'several', are restricted to count nouns, while others, like *tòrr* occur with plural count nouns or with mass nouns:

(158) a. trì/grunn   leabhraichean/*sgudail
          three/several   books/rubbish

      b. tòrr/mòran   leabhraichean/sgudail
          many/much   books/rubbish

Unsurprisingly, the distributive quantifiers are incompatible with mass nouns:

(159) *gach/a h-uile/iomadh   sgudail
      each/every/many   rubbish

Numeral expressions themselves have a number of quirks. The numeral *dà*, 'two', occurs with a singular nominal (a remnant of an old dual system), and with a singular determiner:

(160)   An   dà   leabhar/*leabhraichean
        the   two   book/books

However, unlike the other quantifiers that occur with singular nouns, *dà* does not have a distributive reading, and it cannot be semantically linked to a singular pronoun. In (161) the pronoun cannot semantically link back to the relevant boys, unlike the pronoun in (157):

(161)   *Thuirt   dà   bhalach   gun   robh   e   tinn.
        say.PAST   two   boy   that   be.PAST.DEP   he   ill
        'Two boys said that he was ill.'

Numerals above *deich*, 'ten' are built up syntactically using a series of special modifiers. The word *deug*, roughly 'teen', which behaves syntactically like an adjective, is attached to the right of the counted nominal phrase:

(162)   ceithir   leabhraichean   mòra   deug
        four   books   big   teen
        'fourteen big books'

Larger numbers can follow a similar pattern (163-a) or they may use a co-ordinate syntax (163-b):

(163)   a.   ceithir   leabhraichean   mòra   air   fhichead
             four   books   big   on   twenty
             'twenty-four big books'

        b.   fichead   leabhar   mòr   's   a   ceithir
             twenty   book   big   and   PRT   four
             'twenty-four big books'

Gaelic also possesses a series of numerical nouns which refer to numbers of people:

(164)   Bha   còignear   ghrannda   ann.
        be.PAST   fivesome   ugly   there
        'There were five ugly people there.'

These nouns can appear with genitives which specify the type of individual more clearly, and they cannot occur with non-human referring nouns:

(165) triùir   bhalach/*leabhraichean
       three.HUMAN   boy.GEN.PL/books.GEN.PL

The appearance of a genitive plural after the numeral suggests that these numerals are nouns in their own right.

Finally, ordinal numerals in Gaelic, like in English, must co-occur with a definite article and take a singular noun:

(166) a. . an   còigeamh   latha
             the   fifth   day

       b. *còigeamh   latha
            fifth   day

The last class of prenominal elements we will (briefly) consider is a small set of adjectives that occur immediately before the noun. This set includes *deagh*, 'good', *droch*, 'bad', *seann*, 'old', *ath*, 'next'. They always cause lenition of the following noun and they cannot be iterated or undergo comparative formation in their prenominal position. Given this behaviour, we will take these adjectives to be compounded with the noun, rather than having their own specialised syntactic position.

With this discussion in hand, we can now make the relevant positions in our table more informative, where possessive pronouns are a subtype of agreeing article and *a h-uile* is analysed as a complex element built up from a determiner and a distributive quantifier:

(167)
Det	DistQuant	CountQuant	Noun
Articles	gach/iomadh	tòrr/mòran	compounded Adjectives
PossessivePronouns		Numerals	
a	h-uile		

Postnominal elements

We noted in the previous section that Gaelic does not possess an overt indefinite determiner. However, there are various postnominal modifiers which change the exact expression of indefiniteness, such as *air choreigin*, 'some X or other' and *sam bith*, 'any':

(168) a. Phòg   balach   an   cat.
          kiss.PAST   boy   the   cat
          'A boy kissed the cat.'

      b. Phòg   balach   air choreigin   an cat.
          kiss.PAST   boy   on N   the cat
          'Some boy or other kissed the cat.'

      c. An   do   phòg   balach   sam   bith   an   cat?
          Q   PAST kiss.PAST boy   in.DEF   be.VN   the cat
          'Did any boy kiss the cat?'

These expressions are not postnominal determiners, but rather prepositional modifiers of indefinites (they cannot occur with definites: *am balach sam bith).

The first major class of elements that appears after the noun is the class of attributive adjectives. The discussion in the previous chapter on pp. 291–6 shows that such postnominal adjectives agree in gender, number and case (and possibly definiteness) with the noun. In terms of order, they tend to occur most naturally following certain semantic classes: SIZE precedes QUALITY, which precedes COLOUR, which precedes PROVENANCE:

(169) cù   mòr   brèagha   dubh   Albannach
       dog   big   beautiful   black   Scottish
       'a beautiful big black Scottish dog'

It is possible to alter the order of adjectives, but this usually leads to certain changes in emphasis and prosody, so that the following example needs special emphasis on the provenance adjective *Albannach*, 'Scottish', represented in (170) with small caps:

(170) cù   ALBANNACH   dubh   mòr   brèagha
       dog   Scottish   black   big   beautiful
       'A Scottish beautiful black dog'

Although the order of the adjectives is somewhat flexible when considered as a class, it is impossible to place an adjective after, for example, a genitive possessor:

(171) *cù   Sheumais   dubh

dog   Seumas.GEN   black

'Seumas's dog'

(171) is ungrammatical when *dubh*, 'black', is taken to modify *cù*, 'dog'.
The genitive nominal phrase cannot have an interpretation as a
complement of the noun, so in (172), Murchadh cannot be the person
depicted in the picture, but must rather be the owner of the picture:

(172) dealbh   Mhurchaidh   aig/le   Seumas

picture   Murdo.GEN   at/by   Seumas

'Murchadh's picture by Seumas' *not* 'Seumas's picture of Murchadh'

And two genitives are impossible in a nominal phrase in general:

(173) *dealbh   Mhurchaidh   Sheumais

picture   Murchadh.GEN   Seumas.GEN

The complement of a noun like *dealbh*, 'picture' (that is, the nominal
phrase argument that expresses what is depicted in the picture), and in
fact complements of nouns in general, are expressed by prepositional
phrases:

(174) an   dealbh   seo   de   dh'Iain

the   picture   this   of   Iain

'this picture of Iain'

(175) an   t-ùghdar   mìorbhaileach   den   leabhar   sin

the   author   wonderful   of-the   book   that

'the wonderful author of that book'

These complement prepositional phrases occur after adjectives and
demonstratives. It is possible to combine a genitive possessor with such
a depictive complement, in which case the possessor also obligatorily
precedes the complement:

(176) dealbh   Sheumais   de   dh'Iain

picture   Seumas.GEN   of   Iain

'Seumas's picture of Iain'

We have already seen that genitive possessors cannot occur with an overt article. This generalisation holds for all articles in the nominal phrase. Only the rightmost genitive possessor may have an article:

(177) a.   doras   an   taighe
             door   the.GEN   house.GEN
             'the door of the house'

       b.   doras   taigh   na   mnatha
             door   house.NOM   the.GEN   wife.GEN
             'the door of the house of the wife'

       c.   doras   taigh   bean   Sheumais
             door   house.NOM   wife.NOM   Seumas.GEN
             'the door of the house of the wife of Seumas'

In addition to the lack of an article in the other possessors in these examples, genitive case itself is also only marked on the rightmost possessor, as can be seen from the contrast in the last two examples, where *bean*, 'wife', has a suppletive genitive *mnatha*.

The alternative means of expressing possession in a Gaelic nominal phrase uses a prepositional phrase, just as we saw on pp. 320–3. The preposition used is *aig*, 'at', and it obligatorily occurs with the definite article:

(178) a.   an   cù   aig   Seumas
             the   dog   at   Seumas
             'Seumas's dog'

       b.   *cù   aig   Seumas
             dog   at   Seumas
             'Seumas's dog'

To express the meaning 'a dog of Seumas's', a relative clause construction is used instead:

(179) cù   a   th'   aig   Seumas
        dog   REL   be.PRES at   Seumas
        'a dog of Seumas's'

Unlike the genitive possessor, a prepositional possessor is well-formed with a demonstrative. The demonstrative precedes the possessor:

(180) a.   an   cù   seo   aig Seumas
            the   dog   this at Seumas
            'this dog of Seumas's'

       b.   *an   cù   aig   Seumas seo
            the   dog   at   Seumas this
            for 'this dog of Seumas's'

The ordering between possessor prepositional phrases and complement prepositional phrases is more flexible, although the preference seems to be for the possessor to come finally:

(181) a.   ?an   dealbh seo   aig   Seumas   de   dh'Iain
            the   picture this at   Seumas   of   Iain
            'this picture of Iain of Seumas's'

       b.   an   dealbh seo   de   dh'Iain aig Seumas
            the   picture this of   Iain   at   Seumas
            'this picture of Iain of Seumas's'

One final element in the system that has not yet been mentioned is the postnominal quantifier *uile*, 'all'. Unlike its prenominal counterpart *a h-uile*, *uile* can occur with a plural noun; it requires a definite article:

(182) na   leabhraichean   uile
       the.PL   books   all
       'all the books'

In terms of position, *uile* appears sandwiched between demonstratives and prepositional phrases:

(183) na   dealbhan   sin   uile   de   dh'Iain

     the.PL   pictures   that all   of   Iain

     'all those pictures of Iain'

(184) na   leabhraichean sin   uile   aig   Seumas

     the.PL   books   that all   at   Seumas

     'all those books of Seumas's'

Nominal phrases may also be modified by relative clauses, which invariably come rightmost, after even the prepositional possessors:

(185) na   leabhraichean sin   uile aig Seumas a   sgrìobh Màiri

     the.PL   books   that all   at   Seumas REL write.PAST Màiri

     'all those books of Seumas's that Màiri wrote'

These relative clauses can be 'stacked', and there appear to be no strict ordering conditions on such stacking, so that both versions of (186) are well-formed:

(186) a.   na   leabhraichean a   sgrìobh   Màiri as

        the.PL   books   REL   write.PAST Màiri REL-Cop.PRES

        toigh   leam   fhìn

        pleasant with.1SG   EMPH

        'the books that Màiri wrote that I like'

     b.   na   leabhraichean as   toigh   leam   fhìn

        the.PL   books   REL-Cop.PRES   pleasant with.1SG   EMPH

        a   sgrìobh   Màiri

        REL   write.PST   Màiri

        'the books that I like that Màiri wrote'

Our discussion of postnominal elements leads us back to our initial table, and we see that many of the 'slots' in the table actually have their own internal complexity. Adjectives come in various classes, which can co-occur but which have specific natural orderings; possessor prepositional phrases and complement prepositional phrases can also co-occur, again with some weak ordering restrictions while relative clauses do not seem to be constrained in their order in any obvious way. However, many of the postnominal elements enter into a dependency with the leftmost position in the nominal phrase, allowing, denying or requiring the presence of an overt article. Exactly how to construct the grammatical system so that this is the outcome is an interesting question.

SUGGESTIONS FOR FUTURE WORK

There is little work on the syntax of Scottish Gaelic beyond what has been referred to here, and in the previous chapter. One important body of work is that by Gillian Ramchand on aspect and predication in Gaelic (Ramchand 1996, 1997). This leaves a great deal to be done, both descriptively and theoretically. Little systematic is known about the details of comparative constructions, about adverbial placement, particle constructions, the syntax of adjuncts and modifiers, the grammatical behaviour of anaphoric and emphatic pronouns, topic, focus and other information packaging constructions, coordination, ellipsis, extraposition, etc. In addition, of that which is known (a portion of which is surveyed here), little is known in any depth. Adding to this questions about dialectal variation, syntactic change and the impact of register, a great deal is left to be done. This survey attempts to do no more than scratch the surface. The grammar of Gaelic is still an understudied area with much to offer general linguistic theory.

BIBLIOGRAPHY

Adger, David (1996), 'Agreement, Aspect and Measure Phrases in Scottish Gaelic', in Robert Borsley and Ian Roberts (eds), *The Syntax of the Celtic Languages*, Cambridge: Cambridge University Press, pp. 200–22.

Adger, David (2000), 'VSO Clause Structure and Morphological Feature Checking', in Robert Borsley (ed.), *Syntactic Categories*, New York: Academic Press, pp. 79–100.

Adger, David (2005), 'Fracturing the Adjective: Evidence from the Gaelic Comparative', http://ling.auf.net/lingBuzz/000256.

Adger, David and Ramchand, Gillian (2003), 'Predication and Equation', *Linguistic Inquiry* 34, pp. 325–59.

Adger, David and Ramchand, Gillian (2005), 'Move and Merge: *Wh*-dependencies Revisited', *Linguistic Inquiry* 36, pp. 161–94.

Adger, David and Ramchand, Gillian (2006a), 'Dialect Variation in Gaelic Relative Clauses', in Wilson McLeod, James Fraser and Anja Gunderloch (eds), *Cànan is Cultar: Rannsachadh na Gàidhlig 3*, Edinburgh: Dunedin Academic Press, pp. 179–92.

Adger, David and Ramchand, Gillian (2006b), 'Psych Nouns and Predication', in Chris Davis, Amy-Rose Deal and Youri Zabbal (eds), *Proceedings of NELS 36*, Amherst: GLSA, pp. 89–102.

Byrne, Michel (2002), *Gràmar na Gàidhlig*, Isle of Lewis: Stòrlann-Acair.

Cram, David (1983), 'Scottish Gaelic ANN as an Aspect Particle', *Studia Celtica* 19, pp. 311–26.

Hale, Ken and McCloskey, James (1984), 'On the Syntax of Person-number Inflection in Modern Irish', *Natural Language and Linguistic Theory* 1, pp. 487–533.

Lamb, William (2003), *Scottish Gaelic*, Munich: Lincoln Europa.

MacAulay, Donald (1992), 'The Scottish Gaelic Language', in Donald MacAulay (ed.), *The Celtic Languages*, Cambridge: Cambridge University Press, pp. 137–248.

McCloskey, James (1983), 'A VP in a VSO Language?' in Gerald Gazdar, Ewan Klein and Geoff Pullum (eds), *Order Concord and Constituency*, Dordrecht: Foris, pp. 9–55.

McCloskey, James (1996), 'Subjects and Subject Positions in Irish', in Robert D. Borsley and Ian Roberts (eds), *The Syntax of the Celtic Languages: A Comparative Perspective*, Cambridge: Cambridge University Press, pp. 241–83.

McCloskey, James (2006), 'Resumption', in *The Blackwells Companion to Syntax*, Oxford: Blackwells, pp. 94–117.

Ramchand, Gillian (1996), 'Two Types of Predication in Scottish Gaelic', *Natural Language Semantics* 4, pp. 165–91.

Ramchand, Gillian (1997), *Aspect and Predication: the Semantics of Argument Structure*, Oxford: Oxford University Press.

NOTES

1 Many thanks to my consultants Murchadh MacLeòid, Marion NicAoidh, Beathag Mhoireasdan and especially Iseabail NicIlleathain, and to Jule Landgraf and Marc Wringe for much help along the way. Many thanks too to Will Lamb and to the editors for comments on an earlier draft. The work reported here was supported by a Leverhulme Major Research Fellowship.

2 Recall that (5) shows that the sequence [Aspectsimp VerbNonFin Obj] is a constituent, hence the bracketting.

3 The relative proclitic is often deleted after *cò*, 'who' and other question words that end in a vowel; hence it is represented here in brackets to mark its optionality.

Index